FACING EAST FROM INDIAN COUNTRY

FACING EAST FROM INDIAN COUNTRY

A Native History of Early America

DANIEL K. RICHTER

HARVARD UNIVERSITY PRESS

Cambridge, Massachusetts, and London, England • 2001

Library of Congress Cataloging-in-Publication Data

Richter, Daniel K.
    Facing East from Indian country : a Native history of early America / Daniel K. Richter.
        p. cm.
    Includes bibliographical references and index.
    ISBN 0-674-00638-0 (alk. paper)
    1. Indians of North America—First contact with Europeans.   2. Indians of North America—
    History—Colonial period, ca 1600-1775   3. Indians, Treatment of—United States—History.
    4. United States—Discovery and exploration.   5. United States—Politics and government—
    To 1775.   I. Title.

E98.F39 R53 2001
970'.00497—dc21
2001024997

To Tom and Mary

CONTENTS

Maps and Illustrations

FACING EAST FROM INDIAN COUNTRY

PROLOGUE:
EARLY AMERICA AS
INDIAN COUNTRY

NOT LONG AGO, I visited St. Louis. As I first entered my hotel room, its window framed an unremarkable nighttime urban vista. Nineteen stories below, two venerable bridges spanned the Mississippi. On the right, on the opposite bank, a modern-day grain elevator owned by an agribusiness conglomerate dominated a dreary postindustrial skyline. In the center, demanding all attention, were the gaudily flashing lights of two riverboat casinos. Yet as I walked closer to the window to draw the curtains against the casinos' glare, Eero Saarinen's Gateway Arch suddenly entered the picture from the right. To take in its vastness, I had to shift my line of vision in a way that made the bright lights and bridges disappear. From a perch about one-third as high as the arch, I gazed through it facing east, toward the country that early nineteenth-century folks who lit out for the territories thought they had left behind.

Saarinen intended his monument to be viewed from the opposite direction, facing west, from the Illinois side of the river. But unless they can walk on water, all who actually visit must approach it the way I looked through it, facing east. They find that the arch is rooted in an urban national park, the Thomas Jefferson National Expansion Memorial. If they descend into the earth beneath its base to board a tram to the top, they discover a Museum of Westward Expansion that movingly portrays the impact of Euro-American conquest on Native Americans. Aboveground, though, the museum is invisible. Nothing can be seen except the gleaming arch itself and, behind it, green terraces that rise from the riverbank to the dome of the old St. Louis Courthouse, which, viewed from Illinois, the arch was designed to frame. It is not just any courthouse. There, in

1847 and again in 1850, an enslaved African-American couple named Dred and Henrietta Scott sued for their freedom. Although the second trial's jury of local Whites decided in their favor, every higher level of a judicial system devoted to the protection of American liberties refused to agree. In 1858, speaking for a Supreme Court more deeply divided on why than on whether freedom must be denied, Chief Justice Roger Brooke Taney declared that people like the Scotts were "regarded as beings of an inferior order" who "had no rights the white man was bound to respect."[1]

Haunting courtroom; subterranean museum; triumphal arch dominating both. Perhaps no other plot of ground in the United States more eloquently symbolizes how freedom and unfreedom, expansion and dispossession, entwined to create the nation's story than does this park named for a president whose own life so profoundly wove together the same conflicting strands. Part of that national story is the persistent idea that the west was a land of new beginnings. Did not Jefferson famously declare "that the earth belongs in usufruct to the living; that the dead have neither powers nor rights over it"?[2] Yet those who poured through St. Louis in the early 1800s could not so easily abandon their past, and neither could Jefferson's nation. Trends that played themselves out west of the Mississippi grew from three hundred years' experience in the east. Between the early sixteenth century and the early nineteenth, ugly patterns of racial antagonism took root, but the course of their growth was not nearly so straightforward as might be suggested by the old saying about Pilgrims who fell first on their knees and next on the aborigines. Whites and Indians had to *learn* to hate each other—had even to learn that there were such clear-cut "racial" categories as "White" and "Indian"—before "westward expansion" across a steadily advancing "frontier" could become the trajectory for a nation that was itself a belated result of the same learning process. Perhaps the strangest lesson of all was that in the new nation Whites were the ones entitled to be called "Americans." Indians bizarrely became something else.

It was not always so. Throughout the period before the United States declared its independence, the vast majority of eastern North America was neither English nor French nor Spanish territory. It was, clearly, Indian country, and Europeans most often used the term *American* to describe descendants of the original inhabitants. Had I been in St. Louis a thousand years ago, I would have found myself in the cultural heartland of that eastern Indian country. I would not have been able to rise nineteen stories in the air to look across the Mississippi, but I could have climbed to a considerable height on a since-leveled earthwork that was the centerpiece of a ceremonial site or perhaps even a major town. Had my eyesight been particularly sharp and the day especially clear, I might have just been able to glimpse the far more impressive earthen mounds of what was probably the largest American city that existed north of Mexico before the late eighteenth century, the site near East St. Louis known today as Cahokia. In its heyday it was home to more than twenty thousand people. Towering a hundred feet above a fifty-acre artificial plaza, its main temple mound covered sixteen acres at its base and contained twenty-two million cubic feet of hand-deposited earth. Surrounding the temple and plaza, at least a hundred smaller mounds supported ceremonial structures or covered the accumulated burials of generations of the city's elite residents.[3]

Cahokia and such other major centers as those now known as Coosa and Etowah in Georgia, Moundville in Alabama, and Natchez in Mississippi were home to highly stratified societies, organized as chiefdoms and characterized by a sharp divide between elites and commoners, a specialized artisanry, widespread trading networks, and elaborate mortuary rituals, to which the burial mounds attest. Surrounding networks of agricultural hamlets provided food to support the urban centers, where priests and chiefs who probably called themselves "Great Suns" apparently conducted rituals centered on the solar cycle and the seasons to ensure the success of crops and the power of the community. At Cahokia, for example, a massive woodhenge, or circle of posts, served as an astronomical observatory, and the main plaza was oriented on a perfect north–south line to trace celestial movements. Chiefs displayed their power by dispensing to their followers and to visitors from far and wide ritual objects that symbolized the sun, the cardinal directions, and agricultural productivity.[4]

These societies, which scholars now call "Mississippian," flourished during the global climatic warming trend from approximately 900 to 1350 known as "the Medieval Optimum." This increase of a few degrees in average annual temperature was the same one that led Norse adventurers

Artist's reconstruction of the city of Cahokia, c. 1100 A.D.

Painting by Lloyd K. Townsend. Courtesy of Cahokia Mounds State Historic Site, Collinsville, Illinois.

to colonize a once-and-future frozen waste and accurately call it Greenland, while briefly finding the Newfoundland coast a welcoming locale. Throughout eastern North America, well beyond the Mississippian heartland, the warm period fostered a burst of agricultural creativity, focused on improved varieties of two old crops, squash and maize, and one new one, beans. As the agricultural revolution gradually spread, for the first time these "Three Sisters," rather than hunting and gathering, became the principal food source for Native people throughout the east, with the exception of far northern regions where the growing season was too short. In most societies, farming came to be women's work, and female kin groups controlled the fields, the food they produced, and the houses in which those who ate it lived. Men were responsible for the animal-protein side of the diet and, as a result, spent much of their time away from the female-dominated world of the village. Seasonal hunting, fishing, and fowling camps were where most male labor took place. The "forest," Native people taught, belonged to men; the "clearing," to women.[5]

In the middle of what Europeans reckoned as the fourteenth century, the warm period came to an end, replaced by a "Little Ice Age" that would continue into the 1800s. By 1492 many of the Mississippian cities were in decline, victims of decreased agricultural productivity resulting from climatic change, of the inherent instability of chiefdoms as long-term political systems, and perhaps of a loss of faith in religious leaders whose authority rested on their pretensions to control the forces that allowed crops to flourish. As populations dispersed and polities reinvented themselves, the southeastern heartland came to be dominated by speakers of Muskogean languages, whose descendants would come to be known in the eighteenth century as Creeks, Choctaws, and Chickasaws. Eastward and northward from the Muskogean area were speakers of languages of three other major linguistic stocks, all of them inhabiting a landscape of agricultural villages and dispersed fishing and hunting territories but none of them approaching the Mississippian level of population density, social stratification, or political centralization. Siouan speakers dominated the southern Piedmont. Iroquoian speakers, divided for many centuries between a southern group consisting of ancestors of the Cherokees and Tuscaroras in present-day Georgia, Tennessee, and North Carolina and a northern group including the Iroquois, Hurons, Susquehannocks, and others encircling Lakes Erie and Ontario, occupied most of the east's midsection. Surrounding them in a vast inverted U from the Ohio River through most of present-day Canada and down the coast to the Chesapeake were speakers of Algonquian languages. Each of these great linguistic groupings had even less in common than did the Germanic and Romance families of Europe, and each contained several related but mutually unintelligible languages further diversified into countless local dialects. Nearly everywhere, villages composed of 500 to 2,000 people were the norm; these might be linked in loose regional confederacies or short-lived more tightly centralized polities, but for the most part each community was independent of the others.[6]

Indian country was decentralized and diverse, but not disconnected. Routes of trade and communication, most of them millennia old and following the great river systems, crisscrossed the continent. The goods that moved along them were, for the most part, few and rare—rarer and perhaps more valuable than the gold and spices that western Europeans of the same era traveled the world to acquire. Some closely neighboring peoples might exchange crucial resources—corn, for instance, for meat or fish—and some at slightly greater distance may have controlled access to particularly valuable quarries that provided the raw material for stone tools or weapons. But long-distance exchange centered on exotic substances such as marine shells and beads made from them, chunks of rare minerals such as mica, and pieces of copper cold-worked into various forms. The presence of such items at archaeological sites deep in the continental interior—of shell beads from the mid-Atlantic and Gulf coasts, of copper from the Great Lakes region, of quartz from the Rocky Mountains—attests to the existence of such trade. The fact that exotic goods are most often found in cemeteries and burial mounds suggests that their primary value was believed to be spiritual rather than utilitarian, or rather that their utility rested on concerns deeper than mere food, drink, and shelter.[7]

Later Indian stories that describe such items as gifts from "underwater grandfathers" or spirit beings further suggest both their rarity and their great significance to those who acquired them. That they were described as gifts rather than as commodities also suggests something about how such goods moved along the ancient communication routes; they probably passed from hand to hand in small-scale reciprocal exchanges, rather than through the marketplace behavior that Europeans would recognize as trade. Nonetheless, reciprocity did not necessarily imply equality, and such exchanges often confirmed differential access to power, spiritual as well as political. Underwater grandfathers had more power than those on whom they bestowed their gifts, and so did the intermediary figures who in turn gave such gifts to others. Leaders enhanced, if they did not acquire, their status by access to tribute and control of exotic commodities. They displayed their lofty status by wearing rare, spiritually charged goods such as copper or shell on their bodies and by claiming titles such as *mamanatowick* (paramount chief), which shares Algonquian linguistic roots with *manitou* (spiritual power).[8]

Exact statistics will never be known, but in 1492 the diverse but interconnected area east of the Mississippi may have been home to more than 2 million Native people.[9] In subsequent decades those numbers shrank rapidly as European colonists unwittingly brought with them epidemic diseases to which Indians had no immunity. Still, as late as 1700, the Euro-American population barely exceeded 250,000, and the colonists were confined almost exclusively to coastal and riverine enclaves, most very near the Atlantic seaboard. By 1750 the population balance had shifted decisively, with Europeans and their enslaved African workforce exploding to nearly 1.25 million and the Native population probably shrinking to less than 250,000. Nonetheless, the vast area between the Appalachians and the scattered French outposts on the Mississippi remained almost entirely in Indian hands. It would take until the eve of U.S. independence for the number of Euro- and African Americans to exceed 2 million and return the population of the east to the level it probably sustained in 1492.[10] And it would take until nearly 1820 for the United States to gain hegemony between the mountains and the Mississippi. Only then could the kind of relentless westward expansion that the St. Louis arch symbolizes become possible.

The emergence of an aggressively expansionist Euro-American United States from what used to be the Indian country of eastern North

America is a problem to be explained, not an inevitable process to be traced from the first planting of English seeds on Atlantic shores to their flowering in the trans-Mississippi west. This book argues that the nature of that problem can fruitfully be explored through something like the visual reorientation I experienced when I faced east from my St. Louis hotel room. Like that of tourists contemplating Saarinen's Arch from the Illinois shore, our usual perspective on early American history faces west: the plot lines flow from Europe across the Atlantic and thence to the Mississippi. Words like "invasion" and "conquest" may now trip more easily from our tongues than quaint phrases like "the transit of civilization," yet the "master narrative" of early America remains essentially European-focused. While American Indians might make "contributions" to the dominant culture—corn, moccasins, snowshoes, or even, some wishfully tell us, constitutional democracy—Native people remain bit players in the great drama of a nation's being born and spreading, for better or worse, westward across the continent.[11]

Yet if we shift our perspective to try to view the past in a way that faces east from Indian country, history takes on a very different appearance. Native Americans appear in the foreground, and Europeans enter from distant shores. North America becomes the "old world" and Western Europe the "new," Cahokia becomes the center and Plymouth Rock the periphery, and themes rooted in Indian country rather than across the Atlantic begin to shape the larger story. The continent becomes a place where diverse peoples had long struggled against and sometimes worked with one another, where societies and political systems had long risen and fallen, and where these ancient trends continued right through the period of colonization. The process by which one particular group composed of newcomers from Europe and their descendants—themselves a diverse and contentious lot—came to dominate the others becomes a much more complicated, much more interesting, much more revealing, if no less tragic, tale.

But visualizing such a story in any detail is more complicated than looking through a different portion of a hotel window. In reexamining Plymouth Colony, for example, we might readily check the urge to look westward across the plow of a Pilgrim patriarch and instead try to peer eastward over the shoulder of a Wampanoag woman hoeing her corn.

Yet, as we try to imagine how that woman might have made sense of the newcomers, we come up against the hard realities that she left no direct record of her thoughts and that even her dialect of the Massachusett Algonquian language has long since ceased to be spoken. In these and other ways, the paucity of historical sources and the enormous distances in time and culture that yawn between the twenty-first and seventeenth centuries make it impossible to see the world through her eyes. We can only try to look over her shoulder—to appreciate the conditions in which she lived, to reconstruct something of the way in which her people might have understood the world, to try to hear Native voices when they emerge from the surviving documents, to capture something of how the past might have looked if we could observe it from Indian country. And still our vision remains clouded.

So the chapters that follow are as much about *how* we might develop eastward-facing stories of the past as about the stories themselves. As they proceed chronologically from the era of the Native discovery of Europe through the period when the United States became the continent's aggressively dominant power, they do not attempt an exhaustive treatment of the three centuries of eastern North American history they survey. Nor do they maintain a single point of view, a uniform mode of narration, or a consistent kind of evidence. Instead, they explore different *ways* of facing east appropriate for understanding something—though certainly never everything—about particular periods. Their aim is less to uncover new information than to turn familiar tales inside out, to show how old documents might be read in fresh ways, to reorient our perspectives on the continent's past, to alternate between the general and the personal, and to outline stories of North America during the period of European colonization rather than of the European colonization of North America.

"Any written history involves the selection of a topic and an arbitrary delimitation of its borders," the great American historian Charles A. Beard long ago observed. "This selection and organization—a single act— will be controlled by the historian's frame of reference composed of things deemed necessary and of things deemed desirable."[12] At this point in our fractious nation's experience, it seems more than necessary and desirable to find frames of reference capable of embracing the common, if often excruciating, origins of the continent's diverse peoples. A story line that follows only the exploits of the English-speaking few strips the past of much of its real drama, its explanatory power, and—increasingly in a century when people of European descent are again expected to become a minority in North America—its relevance for the present. Facing east on our past, seeing early America as Indian country, tracing histories truly native to the continent, we might find ways to focus more productively on our future. For better or worse, this native history belongs to us all.

Imagining a
Distant
New World

"History," said Beard's contemporary Carl Becker, is "an imaginative creation."[1] Perhaps no historical subject requires more imagination than the effort to reconstruct the period when Indian country first became aware of a new world across the ocean. All we have to go on are oral traditions of Indians who lived generations after the events described, written accounts by European explorers who misunderstood much of what happened in brief face-to-face meetings with Native people, and mute archaeological artifacts that raise more questions than they answer. Hard facts are very difficult to come by. Yet this very lack of information places us in much the same situation as most eastern North American Indians during the era of discovery. They probably heard mangled tales of strange newcomers long before they ever laid eyes on one in the flesh, and, when rare and novel items reached their villages through longstanding channels of trade and communication, they discovered European *things* long before they confronted European *people*. Rumors and objects, not men and arms, were the means of discovery, and we can only imagine how Native imaginations made sense of the skimpy evidence that reached them.

> *On the coast* of what will one day be called either Newfoundland or Labrador, Native hunters find that several of the traps they had set are missing, along with a needle they need to mend their fishing nets. In the place where these items had been is a smoothly polished upright timber crossed near the top by a second piece of wood, from which hangs the carved

effigy of a bleeding man. Flanking this remarkable construction are two other poles from which pieces of some woven substance flap in the breeze: one is white with two strips of red, mimicking the shape of the crossed timbers; the other bears an image of a four-footed, two-winged beast holding something in its paw. The hunters puzzle over two things left on the ground. One is clearly recognizable to them as a fishhook. The other has a sharp edge and a chunky shape. Both are made of a black substance covered with patches of reddish powder. The largest item is picked up by one of the hunters, who will, when he gets home, use stone tools to pound it into several small amulets, most of which he will give to his village headman. Over the next few years, the headman will redistribute them to honored visitors, who will carry them to their homes far in the continental interior.

Somewhere near the mid-Atlantic coast, an old woman hides in the woods with her daughter and several grandchildren. Both women scream as some twenty pale, bearded men, sweating in heavy armor and helmets, stumble upon them. The elder's suspicions abate a little when the men courteously offer her something to eat, but the younger disdainfully flings the food to the ground. As the women try to fathom the strange sounds issuing from what they consider to be incredibly ugly hairy faces, the men suddenly snatch one of the male children away from the grandmother and lunge for the young woman, who flees screaming into the forest, never to see her nephew again.

In an Indian dwelling, a woman tells her granddaughter about the first meeting between Native people and Europeans. One day, she says, a floating island appeared on the horizon. The beings who inhabited it offered the Indians blocks of wood to eat and cups of human blood to drink. The first gift the people found tasteless and useless; the second appallingly vile. Unable to figure out who the visitors were, the Native people called them *ouemichtigouchiou,* or woodworkers.

These three scenes are imagined, but they are rooted in verifiable historical events. The hunters' missing traps were purloined in 1497 by explorer John Cabot and his crew; the mid-Atlantic child was snatched from his kinswomen in 1524 by a detachment of Giovanni de Verrazano's mariners; and the tale of sailors who ate sea biscuits and drank wine was told to a French missionary in 1633 by a Montagnais who in turn had heard it from his grandmother years earlier.[2] This much we know from surviving documents, which also explain the nature of what the Europeans left behind and took with them. Cabot's crucifix and flags were sacred symbols that laid legal claim to the land for, respectively, his God (whose Son was portrayed dying on the wooden cross), his English sponsors (whose patron, Saint George, was evoked on the kingdom's white banner by a red cruciform), and his home republic of Venice (whose patron, Saint Mark, was represented on its flag by a winged lion bearing a book of the Gospel). To convince his royal sponsor, Henry VII of England, that a land in which "he did not see any person" was indeed populated, Cabot collected "certain snares which had been set to catch game," along with a large, red-painted wooden "needle for making nets."[3] Similarly, Verrazano justified taking "a child from the old woman to bring into France" in terms of his need to bring his sponsor, Francis I, living proof of his exploits and a potential interpreter to aid future travelers.[4]

Documentary evidence illuminates the European cast of characters, yet only imagination can put Indians in the foreground of these scenes. There is no proof that Cabot's men—largely fishermen from Bristol—dropped a fishhook or broke a rusty iron axe as they erected their crucifix and flags, or that the items they left behind were found and reprocessed in the way we have envisioned. Nonetheless, these things *might* have happened, because artifacts that archaeologists have unearthed from sites scattered across eastern North America attest to similar chains of events on subsequent occasions.[5] Similarly, there is no record of what happened to Cabot's crucifix and flags. Yet we know that if the Indians who owned the missing snares and needle had come upon them, they would not have found the idea of symbolic memorials to important events unfamiliar: northeastern Native people sketched elaborate pictographs in their houses or on the bark of living trees to record the success of war parties, hunting expeditions, and other exploits, and they carved images that they either raised on poles or affixed near the entrances to their houses.[6] Still, what might these particular oddly wrought symbols have meant to them? And on what rumors or personal experience did the young mid-Atlantic woman base her distrust of Verrazano's men, a distrust so richly confirmed by her narrow escape and the disappearance of what we presume was her nephew? And why, years later, did sea biscuits and wine, of all possible commodities, figure so prominently in a tale told not just in that one Montagnais house but widely among various peoples of eastern North America? Generations later, was the grandmother—who by then knew perfectly well what ships, biscuits, wine, and Holy Communion were—chuckling at the confused efforts of her ancestors to incorporate novel things into such familiar categories as islands, wood, and blood?

As we try to pierce the shadows for a clearer view of how Indian country made sense of the discovery of Europe, it helps to consider what written sources and oral traditions from later periods tell us about Native ways of conceptualizing relationships with outsiders. For eastern Indians, the world was a morally neutral universe of potentially hostile or potentially friendly spiritual forces—some human, most other-than-human—with whom one had to deal. People, animals, and spirit forces were all, in a sense, *persons* with whom one dealt in much the same way. No one could go it alone: human persons needed to band together in families, clans, and villages; they relied on animals and plants voluntarily to give themselves up to them as food; they hoped that more powerful beings such as the sun or the wind could be convinced to work on their behalf instead of against them. All of these relationships depended on reciprocal exchanges of goods and obligations, material or ceremonial. Especially when dealing with beings whose power was greater than one's own, it was important to fulfill ceremonial obligations that demonstrated not only reciprocity but respect.[7] A tale told among seventeenth-century Mohawks drives home the lesson. Natives canoeing on Lake George traditionally stopped to burn an offering of tobacco at a rock that housed the other-than-human person who controlled the winds. In 1667, when crossing the lake with some Indian companions, the prominent Dutch colonist Arent van Curler drowned in a storm. The story goes that the tempest came up in retaliation after the Dutchman had mocked the tobacco ritual "and in derision turned up his back-side towards the rock."[8]

In light of this emphasis on ceremonial reciprocity and respect, the exchange of goods—giftgiving—becomes a dominant motif in each of our three scenes. Yet the gifts are always unanticipated, if not disrespectful. To our conjectured hunters, the unseen Cabot apparently reciprocated for a red needle an incomprehensibly abstract red-and-white symbol, and for an animal trap an image of a strange beast. The crucifix he also left behind was carved with a degree of detail inconceivable to people unfamiliar with iron tools, but it clearly represented a man enduring torture. What kind of gift was this? And what kind of giftgivers were Verrazano's men, whose unexpected behavior lay not in the matter-of-fact arrogance with which they seized a child (Indian war parties routinely took captives of all ages), but in their offering of food, which deceived the grandmother into believing they were allies rather than enemies? And gifts of food also define the unanticipated in the story of the floating island: the wood was worthless, the blood inhumane.

The gifts defined the givers. Montagnais people, the grandmother said, called Europeans "woodworkers"; elsewhere in eastern North America, Indians commonly described them as "clothmakers," "metalworkers," or "axemakers."[9] The gift axe that Cabot's men may have left behind would have been recognized as a cutting implement, for in size and shape it resembled a stone celt. Yet the hunters who discovered it would have been far more impressed with its texture and colors: it was clearly a mineral, in its blackness something like the spiritually charged mica or coal they prized in long-distance trade, in its rusty patches resembling the red ocher that many Native cultures associated with death and burial and that the Beothuks of Newfoundland—to whom our hunters may have belonged —daubed liberally on their bodies and tools.[10] No doubt a gift from powerful spirit beings, the axehead was far too valuable to be used to chop trees. And so it slipped easily into ancient patterns of long-distance North American trade, steeped in spiritual significance and valued for its raw material rather than for its culturally irrelevant finished form. Whoever the bestowers of such things were, they seemed—initially at least—to come from a world quite unlike that in which ordinary human persons lived.

In the early decades of the sixteenth century, as fishers from Bristol, from Portugal, from France, and from the Basque country followed Cabot's route to the cod-rich waters off what they called Newfoundland,

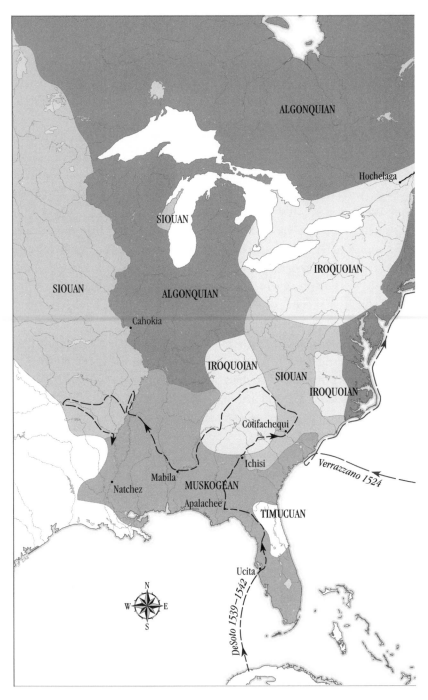

Eastern North America and the sixteenth-century discovery of Europe:
approximate distribution of major Native American linguistic families
and routes of principal European incursions.

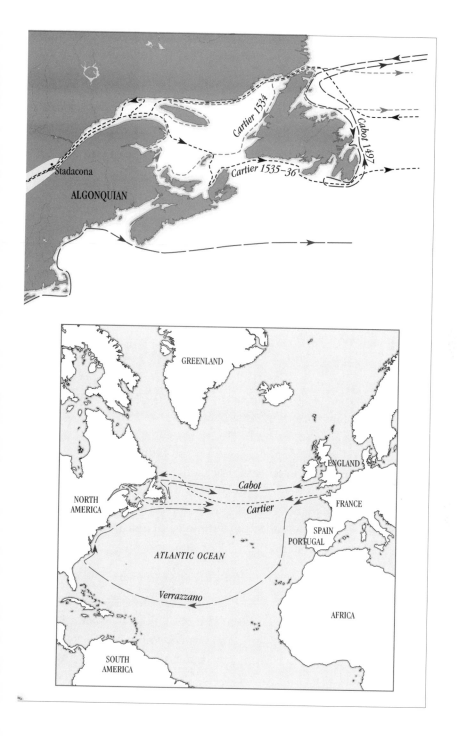

and as the Spanish developed their empire in the West Indies and Central America, European ships regularly converged on the Atlantic coast from two directions. Sometimes they stopped to trade with the Natives; when Verrazano in 1524 reached the shore of what later would be known as New England, he found Indian people ready and waiting with the furs they already knew that the newcomers coveted.[11] At other times, particularly on the vast coastline of the territory the Spanish called *la Florida,* which stretched from the peninsula northward to Chesapeake Bay, raiders such as Ponce de León in 1521, Lucas Vázquez de Ayllón in 1526, and Pánfilo de Narvàez in 1528 came ashore to seek gold or slaves to work in the mines of Cuba and elsewhere. Sometimes they met violent resistance from Native people. More often, starvation and ill health killed them off. An occasional castaway or newcomer taken in battle learned a Native language and provided the first firm clues about the customs and intentions of the invaders. Among such newcomers were probably Africans with firsthand knowledge of the Spanish slavery into which some captured Native Americans were being sold; one African woman may even have found her way as far inland as today's western New York, where she died and was buried at the end of the sixteenth century. Welcome or unwelcome, the travelers left behind weapons, tools, jewelry, and clothing that fell into the hands of Indian people. On other occasions storms drove ships ashore and littered the beach with gifts of iron, of silver, of brass much like native copper, and of glass that resembled quartz and seashells. These, too, entered ancient trade networks and spread throughout Indian country to substantiate wild stories about the existence of new lands across the sea.[12]

On two extended occasions during the 1530s, flesh and blood replaced rumors and things in the North American discovery of a new European world. Because the Europeans involved in these contacts wrote about their experiences, we have slender platforms from which to observe the events and—reading against the authors' grain—to imagine how the arrival of Europeans might have looked from a perspective in Indian country.[13] Transporting ourselves to the shores of Tampa Bay on the Gulf coast of Florida on Sunday, 25 May 1539, we barely see the sails of nine Spanish ships anchored three miles or so off the coast to avoid the treacherous shoals closer in. It is the Roman Catholic festival of Pentecost, commemorating the descent of the Holy Spirit on Christ's disciples. A party of ten Timucuan-speaking natives watching with us know nothing of that, but they are familiar enough with Spanish sails to know that these are no floating islands and that although their inhabitants may wield considerable spiritual power, their disembarkation is unlikely to be beneficial. As the first small boats set out for shore, they send word for those women and children not already dispersed to spring fishing or hunting camps to abandon their villages, and they set signal fires to warn others at a greater distance. The wisdom of those preparations becomes clear when the scouts encounter a Spanish advance party and find themselves in a skirmish. The Timucuas kill a pair of Spanish horses before being forced to retreat, but they leave two of their own people dying on the ground.

We are not sure if this is the first time these particular Florida natives have encountered horses, but we are certain they have never seen so many of the great beasts: more than two hundred land in the first boats. During the next week some six hundred men follow with a contingent of dogs trained for war and with at least thirteen pregnant sows. In command of this assemblage—which far outnumbers the force any village in the area can mount—is Hernando de Soto, the recently appointed governor of Cuba and *adelantado* of *la Florida.* As *adelantado,* de Soto bears royal authority to invest his considerable personal fortune (acquired when he accompanied Francisco Pizarro in the conquest of Peru and gained a reputation as a man "very given to hunting and killing Indians")[14] in an effort to conquer the people and presumed riches of southeastern North America. Within a week his army takes over an abandoned village named Ucita or Ozita and rechristens it *Spiritu Sancto,* "Holy Spirit." As the *adelantado* ensconces himself in the chief's residence, his men dismantle the remaining houses and destroy a temple topped by a carved wooden bird, salvaging the materials to build barracks for themselves. Meantime they brutally seize replacements for four previously captured Timucuan men brought with them to serve as interpreters and guides. When three of these in turn escape, a Native woman who supposedly helped them is thrown to the dogs. The same fate meets the remaining interpreter when he proves a less than cooperative guide.[15]

In a village a couple of days' journey inland are two people who regard the Spaniards' arrival more positively than do the kin of the Ucita victims. One used to call himself Juan Ortiz, although now he uses a Timucuan name, bears the tatoos of his adoptive clan and village on his legs and chest, and has nearly forgotten the language of his native Seville. A dozen years earlier he was captured on the coast by the people of Ucita, who nearly executed him and for three years barely tolerated his presence. Subsequently he escaped to the rival town of a headman named Mococo. There he abandoned any real hope of seeing Spaniards again, despite his host's repeated assurances "that, if at any time, Christians should come to that land, he would release him freely and give him permission to go to them."[16] The promises were neither empty nor disinterested. Mococo apparently hopes his guest will broker an alliance with the Spanish that will help him defeat his coastal enemies of Ucita and three other towns and, presumably, open a channel of trade with the newcomers previously blocked by his inland location.

When word of de Soto's landing reaches Mococo, therefore, he sends Ortiz along with a reception committee that, taking no chances in enemy territory, travels well armed. The Timucuans show themselves to the mounted Spanish, but before any pleasantries can be exchanged, the invaders' horses charge and send the Native people fleeing into the woods. Ortiz barely escapes death at the point of a Spanish lance by making the sign of the cross and shouting the name of the Virgin and a few other remembered Castilian words. This violent encounter exposes the futility of Mocoço's dreams of alliance with the powerful newcomers. A few days later de Soto will dismiss the headman with a suit of European clothes and a vague promise of protection.

To the *adelantado,* Ortiz, with his mastery of two Timucuan dialects and his knowledge of Indian culture and diplomacy, is a welcome discovery, yet little else seems promising. The small coastal villages of Tampa Bay hoard no gold or silver and, particularly in the spring well before harvest time, do not even contain enough stored maize to feed his troops. In what seems like a deliberate attempt to protect their immediate neighborhood, both Ortiz and Mocoço deny any knowledge of the wealth the Spanish desire, but they speak vaguely of a much larger town a hundred miles or so to the north, where a chief with the hereditary title of Paracoxi extracts tribute from all the villages in the region and where the land is "more fertile and abounding in maize."[17] So, taking Ortiz along as interpreter, the army vacates Tampa Bay, and a pattern is established: No, one set of Native leaders after another tells the invaders, there is no gold and little food here, but if you travel farther inland or over the mountains (into what just happens to be the country of my enemies), you might find what you seek. Thus, when de Soto is disappointed at the town of the Paracoxi, his destination becomes Anhaica Apalachee (modern-day Tallahassee). To that southernmost of the surviving Mississippian cities, his army fights its way by late October. There and in its satellite communities, de Soto finds sufficient food to support his men and settles in for the winter, apparently only slightly inconvenienced by Native raiding parties that attack work details or set fires in the town. The families of Apalachee's hereditary chiefs evidently abandoned their capital on the Spaniards' approach. We do not know if they will ever return.

By March, with messages dispatched to Cuba, with his troops somewhat refreshed, and with his herd of pigs increased to a self- propelled foodstore three hundred strong,

de Soto is ready to resume his quest. His entourage plods
northeastward through present-day Georgia, perfecting tactics
first used in the previous year's march through the Florida
peninsula. Occasionally, when traversing the wide forested regions separating heavily populated areas, the Spaniards capture a hunting party and, if the Indians fail to provide satisfactory information on what lies ahead in words Juan Ortiz can
fathom, throw a victim to the dogs or burn him alive to encourage others to talk. More often, when traversing settled
districts de Soto goes through the motions of Mississippian
diplomatic ritual; the *adelantado* even carries a chair in which
to seat himself during ceremonies with chiefs carried on their
retainers' shoulders. Invariably the formalities end when, one
way or another, leaders agree to provide several hundred men,
who are shackled together to haul the army's equipment. Also
likely to be requisitioned are several dozen women, who, after
a hasty baptism by one of de Soto's four priests, will satisfy
what one Spaniard describes as the soldiers' "lewdness and
lust."[18] To preclude trouble, the chief and his retinue are held
hostage until the army—pillaging corn supplies, burning the
occasional refractory village, and planting crosses on temple
mounds—reaches the territory of the next chiefdom, when
the cycle begins again.

"Who are you? What do you want? Where are you going?" a
chief from the town of Ichisi, in present-day northern Georgia, asks during one of these encounters. De Soto replies that
he is "a Captain of the great King of Spain; that in his name he
came to give them to understand the sacred faith of Christ,
and that they should know him and be saved, and give obedience to the apostolic church of Rome and to the Supreme
Pontiff and Vicar of God who resides there, and that in the
temporal world they should recognize as king and lord the
Emperor, king of Castile . . . and that they would treat them
all well, and with peace and justice, like his other Christian
vassals" if—but only if—they submit. This is an abbreviated
version of the *Requirimiento,* a document that Spanish bureau-

crats insist should be read to Indians about to be conquered. Like some sixteenth-century Miranda warning, it explains the Indians' limited rights and confirms the legality of their slaughter should they choose to resist.[19]

Whatever they make of such speeches, Native leaders repeatedly claim that the riches the Spanish seek lie farther on, in the chiefdom of Cofitachequi. In May 1540, near present-day Camden, South Carolina, de Soto's army finally reaches a spot directly across the Wateree River from its capital. The town's inhabitants are already familiar with Spanish goods, if not with Spanish people; they not only have carefully preserved glass beads and metal items but have fashioned leather helmets, armor, and footwear in styles that seem strikingly familiar to the Castilians. We watch as a young female leader—the Spanish call her "The Lady of Cofitachequi"—is ceremonially carried to the riverbank in a white-cloth-draped litter, from which she enters a canoe graced by a canopy of a similar material. When she reaches de Soto's side of the stream, she removes a string of freshwater pearls from her neck and places it over the *adelantado*'s head. Gifts of blankets and skins, turkeys and other foods, follow.

De Soto rends the ceremonial drama with a blunt inquiry about where more of the pearls might be found. The Lady directs him to one of several nearby towns abandoned two years earlier when "a plague in that land" forced the inhabitants to seek new homes.[20] There, he and his officers personally loot a mortuary temple of more than two hundred pounds of pearls preserved in the body cavities of the deceased; the desecration comes easily to de Soto, the bulk of whose Peruvian wealth was acquired in much the same way.[21] The corpses also yield European glass beads, rosaries and crucifixes, and "Biscayan axes of iron,"[22] which no longer seem to the Cofitachequis quite such mysterious gifts from another world. The pearls (de Soto finds their quality poor, but they are virtually the only valuables he has located in a journey now approaching a thousand miles in length) are loaded with other booty on the backs

Cofitachequi as it might have appeared to the de Soto expedition in 1540: conjec-
tural diorama of the Mulberry Site, Camden, South Carolina.
Courtesy of South Carolina State Museum.

of the inevitable requisition of Cofitachequi porters, and the
army sets off again holding the Lady hostage.

And so we follow de Soto's trek: across the Appalachian
Mountains into the modern states of North Carolina, Tennessee, Georgia again, and Alabama, always chasing reports of
wealth in the town over the next hill or down the next river.
Armed resistance builds steadily until, in October, the Spaniards' luck runs out in the Tascaloosa city of Mabila, in what
will later be called western Alabama. Despite a warning from
his spies that something is up, de Soto insists on entering the
town's heavily fortified walls to demand the right to spend the
night there, because he is "tired out with sleeping in the open
field."[23] Several thousand warriors hide inside Mabila's houses
as a ceremonial welcome for de Soto and his advance party
provides cover for Indians waiting in ambush. When the attack

comes, several Spaniards die before the remainder flee the
town and regroup for a daylong battle that culminates in ruth-
less slaughter. When it is over, Mabila lies in smoking ruins. Inside are the bodies of perhaps two thousand Tascaloosas,
along with the ruins of all the pearls and other treasure de
Soto has collected. Twenty or so Spaniards, including de Soto's
nephew, are dead. The wounds of some of the nearly two
hundred invaders who are seriously injured are treated with
the fat of their slaughtered enemies.

For nearly a month de Soto's now ragged army, reduced by
cumulative losses to closer to four hundred than six hundred
men, tries to recover strength. It sets off again and huddles for
a brutally cold winter in a small abandoned village in what will
be known as northeastern Mississippi. In March 1541 the
town's former inhabitants burn the Spanish camp, and with it
most of the invaders' remaining saddles and padded armor.
Still the Spanish plod on, in a journey as increasingly night-
marish for them as for the Indians whose countries they continue to pillage and whose people they continue to enslave
when they can. They move across the Mississippi River and
into the country of the Caddos in modern-day Arkansas, another winter comes and goes, and in March 1542 Juan Ortiz
dies after a brief illness. In May, in the Natchez country, when
disease also claims the *adelantado,* his men sink the corpse in
the Mississippi River to protect it from the indignities they are
sure Indians will perpetrate on it. At last, after the survivors
wander through much of what will later be Arkansas and east
Texas, they improvise a forge on the banks of the Mississippi
and pound the chains of their slaves into nails and hardware
for boats. In June 1542 they board the seven vessels they have
been building and float out of sight, down the river to the
Gulf and the Spanish settlements on the Mexican coast. As
they fade from view, a few of the pigs they leave behind—later
residents of the area will call their descendants "razorbacks"—
remain with us on the shore,

but surviving documents reveal nothing about how, if at all, Native people recovered from the devastation the conquistadores left behind or what stories they told themselves to make sense of invaders from another world.

As de Soto lay dying in the spring of 1542, far to the north, in what is now called St. John's Harbor, Newfoundland, Frenchman Jacques Cartier prepared to head home, convinced that he had found not only the gold the *adelantado* had been looking for, but diamonds too. This was Cartier's third voyage to a country he called "Canada," a word for which scholars have proposed at least two origins. The most likely supposes that, when the French used gestures and a few mutually intelligible words to ask the Natives what they called the place, the response in an Iroquoian language was something to the effect of "This is our village." To French ears it sounded like *Canada*, and the word for "a town" was so defined in a glossary attached to a printed account of Cartier's exploits.[24] The other explanation, which is almost certainly apocryphal, derives the term from the Spanish phrase *acá nada*, or "nothing is here."[25] This folk etymology nonetheless seems appropriate in light of the fact that, when Cartier returned to France, experts confirmed that his ship contained nothing but iron pyrite ("fool's gold") and commonplace quartz crystals.[26]

In search of how Cartier and his entourage may have looked to the people of Canada, we might travel backward in time to July 1534, when the Frenchman arrived on the first of his three voyages.[27] Standing on the southern coast of what is now called the Gaspé Peninsula,

> we see forty to fifty canoes full of Micmacs abandoning their fishing as two ships come into view. Hoisting the skins of furbearing animals aloft on pieces of wood, they try to lure the newcomers ashore to trade. Inexplicably to the Indians, Cartier's ships turn about and sail for the opposite shore. Micmac canoeists give chase and surround the ships, waving and shouting "We wish to have your friendship!"[28] but two panicky musket shots drive them off. Shortly, however, they re-

turn and get close enough to be struck by a pair of lances wielded from the decks before they have to retreat again. The next day, when the Europeans' nerves have calmed and they have found safe anchor for their ships, they send two men ashore with a load of knives, hatchets, and beads. Soon some 300 Micmac men and women are wading through the shallows dancing and singing and rubbing the arms of Cartier's crew as a sign of welcome. Trading proceeds until the Indians have "nothing but their naked bodies" left to exchange.[29]

That the Natives have clearly come to trade demonstrates that European ships are already familiar sights to the people of territories ringing what Cartier labels the Gulf of St. Lawrence—the Micmacs (whose villages extend from the Gaspé southward through present-day New Brunswick, Prince Edward Island, Nova Scotia, and Cape Breton), the Montagnais of Labrador, and the Beothuks of Newfoundland. Fifty miles or so to the northeast, on the Bay of Gaspé, however, a group of St. Lawrence Iroquoians from the interior is far less well acquainted with floating islands, although they almost certainly have heard of their existence. Later in the month, as the Iroquoians, fishing for mackerel, look up to see Cartier's vessels approach, they therefore hesitate before surrounding the ships with their canoes. The now more experienced Europeans almost immediately toss them iron knives, glass beads, and other small items, but the Iroquoians are prepared with nothing to exchange for these gifts.

As the French get ready to sail on, they erect a thirty-foot wooden cross, in the center of which they place a shield decorated with fleur-de-lis and letters spelling out *Vive le roi de France*. The Iroquoians' leader boards a canoe with his brother and three sons and follows the Europeans to their ships. Remaining a safe distance away, he makes a lengthy speech, during which he points to the cross, imitates its shape with his fingers, and gestures toward the surrounding land. The French, who understand none of his words, assume that he is asserting claims to the country and announcing that they "should not set up any cross without his leave."[30] We are less certain of what the words mean, but we can see what happens next. Luring the canoe closer with a gesture that promises an iron axe in exchange for the bearskin the headman wears, the Europeans drag the whole party on board. By gestures, Cartier assures the Indians that he means them no harm and offers them food and drink. The cross, he dissimulatingly explains, stakes no claim to their territory; it is merely a marker to allow the French to find the spot again when they return with a "good store of iron wares and other things"—along with two of the headman's sons, who will be taken home to be trained as interpreters.[31] How much of the message gets through clearly is uncertain, but, after an additional bestowal of iron gifts and brass necklaces, the headman, his brother, and one of the young men return to shore reasonably amicably. The others, named Taignoagny and Domagaia, remain on deck wearing ill-fitting French shirts, coats, and caps. The next day their kinsmen paddle out to say their farewells and to assure them they will not tear down the cross that promises their return.

Cartier and—perhaps more astonishingly to their kin—Taignoagny and Domagaia return to Canada within the year, this time with three ships and plans to stay the winter. We know almost nothing about the intervening experiences of the two Iroquoians in Cartier's home port of St.-Malo in Brittany or other European locales they may have visited. During those months, however, they apparently learned enough French, and their hosts enough St. Lawrence Iroquoian, to communicate some important pieces of information about their native land. Their home village (or at least the principal of the five communities that spoke their language) lies far inland along a broad river (the St. Lawrence), whose entrance Cartier had missed in his survey of the gulf. From that village of Stadacona (the word means "here is our big village"), on the site of present-day Quebec City, the river continues much farther to a large town called Hochelaga ("place at the mountain") at modern Montreal, and thence far onward, perhaps to-

ward a passage to Asia.[32] In answer to what must have been
endless questions about the location of rich cities and hoards
of gold, Taignoagny and Domagaia also speak vaguely about
what the French understood to be a fabulously wealthy "Kingdom of Saguenay," located far to the north and west along a
river flowing into the St. Lawrence. In part, the tale probably
reflects the Iroquoians' own hazy knowledge of the source of
the native copper that is among the riches their people most
prize. But doubtless it also includes wishful thinking on the
part of Cartier, a desire to please (or dupe) their hosts on the
parts of Taignoagny and Domagaia, and the same kind of rumor of riches over the next hill that de Soto chased through
the southeast.

As the fleet casts anchor near what the French would chris-
ten the Île d'Orléans, a few miles down the St. Lawrence from
Stadacona, Taignoagny and Domagaia struggle to make themselves recognized in their strange clothing and the long hair
that has replaced the partially shaved heads with which they
left home. When the confusion is cleared up, a group of
women dances, sings, and brings all the visitors fish, maize,
and melons. The next day Donaconna, the principal headman
of Stadacona, leads a fleet of canoes to conduct a welcoming
oration; Cartier reciprocates with the ubiquitous sea biscuits
and wine, carried to Donaconna's canoe. In light of the long
year the kin of Taignoagny and Domagaia have waited for
their return and of the importance Donaconna's people attach
to the arrival of men promising unprecedented riches from
another world, this should be only the beginning of the celebration. According to the region's diplomatic customs, the visitors should debark from their vessels for additional ceremonies outside the village gates and then enter the town to take
up lodging in the houses of its leaders. Days of feasting,
speeches in council, and exchanges of gifts should follow to
seal the alliance.[33]

None of this happens. Instead, Cartier finds a harbor for his
two larger ships at the Île d'Orléans, and, before even visiting

the village itself or distributing more than a few token metal items, he demands that Taignoagny and Domagaia guide his third craft on to Hochelaga. Not surprisingly, after an evening of consultations with Donaconna and other village leaders, the two weary Native travelers lose their enthusiasm for the voyage and offer excuses, warnings, and ruses designed to prevent the French and their precious cargo from going to a rival town. Donaconna, with the same purpose in mind, ceremoniously gives three children to the French for adoption; one is his own niece, another Taignoagny's brother. Cartier reciprocates with a gift of swords and brass bowls, but, despite a visit the next day from three masked shamans bringing warnings from the spirit world of dangers upriver (and a similar call from Taignoagny and Domagaia, who deliver messages allegedly from Jesus and Mary), he persists in his design. Without Native guides, Cartier and some of his men set off for a short visit to Hochelaga and several villages and fishing camps along the way, where, they tell us when they return in mid-October, they invariably received warm ceremonial receptions, were introduced to sacred shell beads, heard more stories of the origins of copper in Saguenay, and planted a cross.

Donaconna is less than enthusiastic in welcoming Cartier back. Before the Frenchman's rude departure, his peaceful intentions had already become suspect because he insisted on wearing a sword whenever he went out in public. While their leader was gone, the French had constructed a trench, palisade, and artillery emplacements to protect the ships on which they continued to sleep and eat. Two days after Cartier's return, tensions ease somewhat when he emerges from his amphibious fortress "with all his gentlemen and fifty mariners well appointed" at last to pay a proper ceremonial visit to Stadacona.[34] There will be *only* visits, however. Spurning their hosts' hospitality, the Europeans settle in for the winter behind their trench and palisade on the Île d'Orléans. While to all appearances most of the Stadaconans nonetheless interact with the French "with great familiarity and love," a minority, led by

Taignoagny, expresses considerably less pleasure with their ill-mannered guests.[35]

In December Cartier forbids all contact with Stadaconans of both factions, when he learns that disease has killed some fifty villagers. Despite the precautionary quarantine, the French are soon falling desperately ill as well. By March 1536, 25 of the 110-member crew have died, and only a handful can walk. We do not know what is killing the Stadaconans, but the French ailment is an uncontagious nutritional disorder, scurvy. Were Cartier not so intent on concealing from his Native hosts the extent of his men's weakness (on one occasion he has them throw stones at Stadaconans who get too near, and on another he orders the few who are able to lift tools to make a furious racket to suggest that the entire crew is busily preparing the ships for departure), he might learn far sooner from Domagaia that a concoction brewed from the vitamin-C-rich bark and leaves of the white cedar would restore his men to health.[36]

Good relations with the Stadaconans will not be revived as easily as the Frenchmen's strength. During the winter the French, shivering in their sickbeds, remain incommunicado for weeks on end, encouraging their hosts to suspect the worst of them. In April Donnacona and Taignoagny, having left to hunt deer with many of their villagers two months earlier, bring several hundred newcomers to Stadacona. Perhaps this is a normal seasonal migration of the sort typical among many of the Iroquoians' Algonquian-speaking neighbors, whose small winter communities commonly join much larger agglomerations for the spring and summer. Or the newcomers may be allies whom Taignoagny has convinced Donnacona to recruit for an assault on guests who have long overstayed their welcome. We will never be sure, because, under cover of a friendly council, Cartier takes Donnacona, Taignoagny, Domagaia, and two other leaders prisoner. In a replay of events in 1534, Cartier then assures his prisoners, and the women who bring strings of shell beads to redeem them, that he will restore them safely the next year. Donnacona publicly pledges to return in a few months, and the ships set off downriver.

Five years, not one, pass before we see Cartier's ships at Stadacona again. With him in 1541 are several hundred prospective French colonists but none of the Iroquoians who left Canada in 1536. When Donaconna's successor inquires after their fate, Cartier admits that the chief has long since died in France, but then claims that the others "stayed there as great lords, and were married, and would not return back into their country."[37] In fact all but Donaconna's niece have perished, and she has been prevented from returning to keep the distressing news secret. The Stadaconans, who remember Taignoagny's less-than-enthusiastic tales of Brittany, no doubt suspect as much, but their new headman welcomes Cartier nonetheless, by placing his headdress on the Frenchman's brow and wrapping shell beads around his arms. Cartier reciprocates with "certain small presents," promises more to come, and partakes of a feast.[38] Next day he heads upriver in search of a spot to settle his colonists and establish a base for further explorations of the countries of the Hochelagans and Saguenay. At a place he calls Charlebourg-Royal, some nine miles above Stadacona, at the mouth of the Cap Rouge River, the French build a fort, plant a crop of turnips, and find their worthless fool's gold and quartz crystals. As the colonists settle into Charlebourg-Royal for the winter,

our ability to imagine the scene suddenly ends. The published narrative left by a participant ends abruptly with the words "The rest is wanting."[39]

Yet other sources reveal that Cartier's people—or most of them—survived until spring, as increasingly unwelcome guests. Not only had they settled in the Stadaconans' territory without permission, but they had done so at an upstream location likely to cut the town off from any trade benefits the Hochelagans and other inland peoples might enjoy. Come spring, Cartier, having lost perhaps thirty-five men in skirmishes with his hosts, packed up his colonists and sailed for home. In the Newfoundland waters where we first imagined meeting him, he encountered a fleet bearing more colonists under the command of Jean François de la Roque, seigneur de Roberval, who replaced Cartier at Cap Rouge. We know few details of the reception this party encountered except that, after a punishing winter during which untreated scurvy killed at least fifty of their number, in 1543 they too abandoned Canada. As far as we know, no Europeans traveled up the St. Lawrence River for another forty years.[40]

For most of that time, our view facing east from the continental interior becomes almost entirely obscured by lack of documentary sources. Nonetheless, archaeological evidence demonstrates that dramatic events were occurring. In the southeast and the Mississippi Valley—the most densely peopled portion of the continent—nearly all the remaining great chiefdoms collapsed. Most of their mounded cities and ceremonial centers, from Cahokia to Apalachee, were abandoned in favor of smaller, more decentralized, and less hierarchically organized communities that were the ancestors of Cherokees, Creeks, Choctaws, and Chickasaws; in many cases, however, the precise ethnic links between older and newer configurations are unclear.[41] In the north, meanwhile, among the Iroquoian-speaking peoples of the interior, a contrary trend proceeded, as small groups coalesced into fewer and larger communities. North and south of Lake Ontario, two large leagues of Iroquoian-speaking nations formed, of the Hurons and of the Haudenosaunee, or Iroquois, respectively. Many of the St. Lawrence Iroquoians were evidently absorbed by components of these two groups. Other Iroquoian-speakers—the Susquehannocks—moved south, from scattered small villages in the present-day border region between New York and Pennsylvania to a few large towns in the lower Susquehanna and Potomac River watersheds, where they displaced an indigenous population known to us only as the Shenks Ferry people. These consolidations of Iroquoian-speaking peoples left vast swaths of territory, including much of the St. Lawrence Valley and what is today southern New York State and northern Pennsylvania, largely empty of permanent human inhabitants.[42]

The extent to which these widespread population movements resulted from the Indian discovery of Europe (much less from the particular phase in that discovery represented by de Soto and Cartier) is difficult to measure. Both the northern and southern settlement trends had been gradually under way for centuries. Since about A.D. 1000, when the agricultural revolution first reached the northeast, the tendency among Iroquoian-speakers had been toward ever larger and ever fewer communities. By contrast, many of the Mississippian chiefdoms had been in demographic decline since the Little Ice Age began in the mid-fourteenth century. Still, even after we make full allowance for these long-term trajectories, the accelerated pace of change in the decades after de Soto and Cartier remains striking. In a few cases the transformations can be linked directly to the European incursions. The Tascaloosa chiefdom, for instance, apparently never recovered from its army's defeat in the battle of Mabila and disappeared from the map as a recognizable entity. De Soto's enslavement of thousands of Native men and women—many of whom died under their burdens or were abandoned deep in enemy territory—must have had a deep effect on communities already in demographic and political flux. His confiscations of what may have been many towns' entire harvests perhaps added a season of famine to the effects. And it is likely that his looting of mortuary temples, his planting of crosses on sacred mounds, and his humiliation of chiefs whose claims to divine status were literally brought to ground when he displaced them from the shoulders of their retainers and made them walk powerlessly through their domains, all dealt severe blows to the religious beliefs that held together Mississippian cultures and chiefdoms.[43]

The "plague" in Cofitachequi, the feverish death of de Soto on the Mississippi, the scurvinous winters the French spent on the St. Lawrence, and the mysterious ailment that killed fifty Stadaconans during Cartier's winter sojourn might suggest that disease played a large role in the reorganization of sixteenth-century populations. For more than ten thousand years, North Americans had been isolated from the microbial environment common, and deadly, to the peoples of Europe, Asia, and Africa. In the Eastern Hemisphere those millennia had seen the development of a variety of viral "childhood" diseases, among them smallpox, measles, mumps, and chicken pox. Most European adults retained immunity from youthful bouts with the microbes, and dense urban populations provided sufficiently large pools of young victims to keep the viruses alive. Among

Western Hemisphere peoples with no immunities from prior exposure, viruses were likely to strike nearly everyone and to kill, directly or through secondary respiratory infections, as many as half. In the Caribbean, Mexico, and Central America, wherever the Spanish settled in large numbers, cumulative epidemics slashed Native populations by 75 to 95 percent during the sixteenth century.[44]

Yet for eastern North America, the evidence for early to mid-sixteenth-century catastrophic diseases is far from conclusive. Archaeologists have found in Florida at least one mass grave dating from the de Soto period, but the same site also preserves the bones of people who appear to have been slain by metal weapons, suggesting that disease was not the killer. For the more interior locale of Cofitachequi, the "plague" that de Soto's anonymous chronicler described was said to be "in that land," not necessarily among its people, who may have moved elsewhere because of crop failures rather than human illness. Moreover, the person who wrote the story down did so years after the event, elaborating—perhaps even fictionalizing—an original text of uncertain authorship. Even if authentic, the account of the plague would have had to rely on words that Juan Ortiz interpreted into Spanish from a Timucuan translation of a story related by someone whose first language was Siouan or Muskogean; so it is difficult to place much weight upon it.[45] Nor should the vaguely described "fevers" from which Ortiz, de Soto, and many of their compatriots died necessarily be taken as evidence of diseases previously unknown in North America. The ailments could have been caused by almost anything, but after several years trooping through the interior, the Spaniards almost certainly did not perish from viruses they brought from Europe.[46] Similar uncertainty exists for Canada. If the Stadaconans knew the cure for scurvy (caused by a vitamin deficiency, not a microbe), presumably their deaths in the winter of 1535–36 were from some other malady, but there is no positive archaeological or other evidence that viruses struck their region during this period. Without discounting the possibility of localized epidemics and while giving full weight to the possibility that crop failures and political disorganization provoked deadly (but indigenous) opportunistic infections, we must consider the role of disease problematic for most of sixteenth-century eastern North America.[47]

More likely factors in the population movements were rivalries over ac-

cess to the material objects by which the existence of Europe had first become known. For most of the century, such items remained exceedingly
rare, and thus had effects out of proportion to their scanty appearance in
the archaeological or documentary record. In this light, one of the greatest results of the de Soto and Cartier expeditions may have been the refuse they left behind. Like vast inland shipwrecks, they provided favored
inland peoples an unprecedented source of wealth, perhaps for years to
come. For other groups not so blessed by luck or geography, a relative
handful of scavenged iron nails or glass beads may well have been worth
fighting and dying over, particularly when access to them was controlled
by longtime enemies. Wars over access to European goods probably explain the southward migration of the Susquehannocks to locations nearer
the mouth of Chesapeake Bay in the period around 1580. In the southeastern interior as well, as the Mississippian chiefdoms collapsed, some
groups seem to have begun moving closer to the coastal sources of European goods. That the process was not entirely peaceful is suggested by a
simultaneous trend for communities to resettle in defensible inland locations. That something profound was happening to spiritual beliefs and
cultural identity is suggested by the fact that few of the societies that replaced the Mississippians had anything like their hierarchical social systems and elaborate burial rituals.[48]

All of these elements provide clues, but for the most part the middle
years of the sixteenth century remain a historical mystery. We just do not
know exactly how people redrew the map of eastern North America,
how they redefined their relationships with one another, and how they
fitted their discoveries of Europe into those processes—if at all. In the ab-
sence of hard evidence, we are thrown again upon our imaginations if we
are to make sense of what was happening in Indian country. If we could
transport ourselves back to 1570 and visit three places we have been before, might we overhear people telling stories such as these?

> *Stadacona:* Long before the woodworkers arrived, times had
> been very hard. Each year, it seemed, summers had turned
> cooler and shorter, and, often as not, corn, beans, and squash
> refused to support us. None of the shamans could find the

right ceremonies to encourage the Three Sisters to reciprocate by feeding us well. In fact the people who were sick when Cartier was here died either of hunger or because the Three Sisters were angry at them and struck them down in some other way. The shortage of food made some lineages give up and move to the countries of the Hurons and Mohawks, where people spoke something like the real language, where the land yielded better crops, and where villages grew stronger because they banded together into confederacies and practiced new rituals that brought them power. Our enemies took many other people away, either as captives or by killing them. Two hundred died at the hands of the Micmacs the same summer that Cartier first arrived. The Hurons and, especially, the Mohawks also started raiding us constantly, and the attacks only got worse after some of our people had joined them voluntarily. "We have told you three times about the Great Law of Peace," said the Mohawks, "and if you do not join our League we will have to knock you on the head."[49]

As all this was happening, our people ceased listening to the hereditary chiefs. Donnacona not only failed to return from France; he failed in his promise to make a firm alliance with the woodworkers that would give us access to their weapons and their many other gifts from the Underwater Grandfathers. These, he had said, would give us the power to triumph over our enemies. After Cartier went away for the last time, Donnacona's lineage never recovered from the embarrassment, and no one listened to the nephew and grandnephew who succeeded to his title. Instead, every young man who got his hands on a few of the glass beads and pieces of copper that come from France began to think he was a chief, and he could give enough of these things to his followers to make them go along with him. The quarrels among these so-called chiefs caused more and more people to leave our town for elsewhere, and we became defenseless against our enemies. Last week the Mohawks finally came as they said they would. They burned Stadacona to the ground and took nearly everyone they found alive captive. Most of our lineage escaped, but we cannot stay here any more. This is Mohawk country now.

Cofitachequi: The Great Sun (the woman the invader called "the Lady of Cofitachequi") returned home after she was captured by the Spanish, but the shamans told some of the young men that they must put her to death. For a woman to be the Great Sun, they argued, threw the world out of balance. True, in the past it had happened on rare occasions that a woman had become paramount chief when there were no men of the right age and talents in her lineage to inherit the title, but no Great Sun had ever brought such disaster on the people. *She* was the one who told us we must stop wearing the kind of headdress and moccasins that had always helped us know who the real people were. *She* was the one who insisted instead that we must restyle them to look like those worn by the Spaniards she once saw on the coast. *She* was the one who said we should hoard all those beads, "iron," "crucifixes," and other things she said were gifts from spirit beings who would make us powerful. The stranger with the dark skin and the curled hair tried to tell us that she was terribly wrong—that the Spaniards would take us from our land as they had done with him and make us work in their "sugar" fields—but she had him killed for his sacrilege. Soon thereafter the plague struck the land, the corn failed us, and hundreds of people died in that village nearby. Then the invader arrived, and we knew that what the stranger had told us was true.

No one lives here now. The land is dead, and the temple mound is defiled. Families went off in all directions to live with other people who spoke something like the real language. Many people say they will never again live under a paramount chief, never again live in a village where people who have reached a certain age and have some wisdom are not considered equals.

Cahokia: Has anyone ever lived here? Although there are stories that this is a spiritually powerful spot, and occasionally
bands from the north and west come to bury their dead or
burn tobacco to please the spirit beings who must have raised
these oddly shaped grass-covered hills above the floodplain, no
one has any memory of human persons who might have
called this place home. And no one has yet heard anything but
rumors about visitors from another world.

The last imagined tale—the least speculative of the three—reminds us that the great changes occurring in Native American life during
the sixteenth century were not all, or even primarily, set in motion by Europeans.[50] Indian country had its own historical dynamics, its own patterns of population movements, conquests, and political and cultural
change that had been going on for centuries. Cahokia disappeared from
the map sometime around 1400, long before even the first rumor of Europe arrived on Native shores, and it is quite possible that Stadacona and
even Cofitachequi would also have disappeared even if Cartier or de Soto
had never existed. Europeans, the things they brought with them, and the
rumors that spread about them in Native communities had important effects as they entered the existing framework of North American history.
Still, 1492 did not rend the fabric of the continent's time. The sixteenth
century remained rooted in all that had gone before, and it owed more to
the agricultural revolution and the Little Ice Age than to the bearers of
Christian flags.

If anything else emerges from the shadows of the sixteenth-century Indian discoveries of Europe, it is a persistent theme of conflict and distrust.
But the nature of that conflict bears close attention, for its most remarkable aspect is not the violence that erupted between Natives and newcomers. Cartier clearly wore out his welcome, and nothing can be said in defense of the vicious de Soto. Nonetheless, almost everywhere they went,
these Europeans found people trying to make some kind of alliance with
them, trying to gain access to the goods and power they might possess,

trying to make sense of their flags and their crucifixes, their *Requirimientos* and their sea biscuits. These efforts to reach out to people of alien and dangerous ways are more striking than the fact that, in the end, enmity won out over friendship. But most striking of all is the way in which the arrival of the newcomers exacerbated conflicts of one Native group with another: Mocoço versus Ucita, Micmacs versus Stadaconans, Stadaconans versus Hochelagans; everyone discouraging advantageous Europeans from traveling to the next town, but encouraging dangerous ones to pay their neighbors a visit. Both within and among Native communities, contact with the new world across the seas inspired bitter conflicts over access to what the aliens had to offer—conflicts that would spiral to unimaginably deadly levels in the decades ahead. Perhaps that Montagnais grandmother wasn't chuckling after all when she told the story of strangers who offered her people blocks of wood to eat and cups of blood to swallow.

CONFRONTING
A MATERIAL
NEW WORLD

AS THE SIXTEENTH CENTURY gave way to the seventeenth, rumors yielded to firsthand experience. When permanent colonies of newcomers began to dot the Atlantic coast and the banks of rivers flowing from the interior, their actions intensely affected local Native communities. But for most of Indian country, the still-distant Europeans' conscious activities were less significant than the powerful material forces that their arrival unleashed. Wherever Europeans settled, intercultural commerce flourished, and even in areas far from colonial centers, expanded trade not only reordered Native economies but dramatically reshaped Native cultures in ways beyond European control or comprehension. The arrival of substantial numbers of colonists also sparked complex changes in the natural environment, with serious implications for Indian farmers and hunters everywhere. Again, these changes occurred in ways no newcomer could have anticipated. Finally, Europeans unwittingly imported microbes that scythed through one Native community after another and reshaped the human landscape in the most potent way of all. Within a generation or so, this trio of economic, ecological, and epidemiological forces remade Indian country into "a world every bit as new as that confronting transplanted Africans or Europeans" in the same period. Native people, of course, did not literally travel to this "Indians' New World," but the changes forced upon them were just as profound as if they had resettled on unknown shores. Far into the continental interior, impersonal material forces remade Indian country long before any substantial numbers of Europeans left their coastal enclaves.[1]

In 1564 approximately three hundred Huguenots—French Protestants—built a colony they called Fort de la Caroline in Timucua country,
near present-day Jacksonville, Florida. This intrusion did not go unno-
ticed by the Spaniards who claimed *la Florida*. Within a year, *adelantado*
Pedro Menéndez de Avilés established a post at St. Augustine and
marched his troops forty miles to the north to slaughter the Frenchmen,
whom he regarded not only as trespassers but as vile heretics. Thus began
a Spanish occupation of strategic spots in the southeast that would last for
nearly two hundred years. Meanwhile, far to the north, from Newfoundland to the appropriately renamed Cape Cod, English, French, and
Basque fishing fleets became regular visitors. Some of the Europeans set
up semipermanent camps on the coast, where Native people increasingly
exchanged the pelts of beaver and other furbearing animals for manufactured goods. For a generation, these incursions on southern and northern
coasts—joined by occasional failed efforts such as the short-lived English
attempt to colonize Roanoke Island in the 1580s—remained the only permanent European presences on the continent. Then, in rapid succession,
in 1607 English adventurers moved into the Chesapeake Bay and established Jamestown, in 1608 French traders and missionaries built Québec
on the site of Stadacona, and in 1609 Henry Hudson sailed up the river
that came to bear his name. Within less than two decades, such well-
financed European trading companies as the Dutch West India Company
(chartered in 1621), the Company of New France (the Hundred Associ-
ates, 1627), and the Massachusetts Bay Company (1629) built upon these
efforts and shipped thousands of families not just to the Atlantic coast but
to spots well in the continental interior, such as present-day Albany, Montreal, and Springfield.[2]

When European people arrived in large numbers, so did European objects, and up and down the Atlantic seaboard Native Americans quickly
became enmeshed in a new system of intercultural commerce with profound effects on everyday life. At first the changes seemed natural and entirely positive; their cumulative impact on society as a whole became apparent only after they had become irreversible. The glass beads and bits of
metal that provided most Indian people their first evidence of Europe's
existence fitted seamlessly into existing patterns of small-scale exchanges
of rare items. As the pace of trade quickened and European goods be-

came more common, imports continued to be integrated into familiar cultural niches. Most often in the early years, European manufactures became raw materials to be processed by indigenous technologies for indigenous purposes. A copper kettle, for instance, was likely to be immediately cut up into small pieces by its original owners—or, more often, by people much farther along the redistribution chain—and turned into ritual items, jewelry, cutting implements, or weapons. Iron goods such as axeheads and knives were routinely reprocessed into needles, awls, and a variety of other sharp tools. As late as 1600, in most areas of eastern North America, the Native people valued material goods from Europe primarily as raw materials to be fashioned into familiar kinds of objects and as markers of the privileged status earned by those with access to them. Both uses derived their significance from Native contexts, rather than from the European economic and social environment for which the goods had originally been designed. A kettle was prized for its copper, not for its carrying capacity, and that copper was likely to be fashioned into an ornament hung conspicuously around a headman's neck to display his powerful connections to its source.[3]

Only after the establishment of large-scale European colonies—and the much bigger and more predictable patterns of trade they allowed—did Indians begin to use imported goods in ways that resembled the purposes for which they had been designed. Initially, permanent European settlements, whose officials almost invariably attempted to enforce government-sanctioned trade monopolies on competitors from their own or other nations, may in fact have narrowed the range of goods available to Indian customers. At Tadoussac, on the Gulf of St. Lawrence, for instance, the twenty or more vessels whose traders used to jostle one another annually had been reduced by 1620 to two French company ships. But what the new colonial order may have lacked in variety, it more than made up for in predictability and quantity of goods. "These two ships," a Jesuit missionary reported, "bring all the merchandise which these gentlemen use in trading with the savages; that is to say, the cloaks, blankets, nightcaps, hats, shirts, sheets, hatchets, iron arrowheads, bodkins, swords, picks to break the ice in winter, knives, kettles, prunes, raisins, Indian corn, peas, crackers or sea biscuits, and tobacco."[4] When brass kettles became available by the dozen, iron knives by the gross, and woolen cloth by the yard, they ceased to be treated as raw materials and instead became direct replacements for traditional Native items: brass kettles for ceramic pots, iron axes for stone celts, woolen blankets for animal skins. The new things were always in some practical way superior to the old—lighter, sharper, more durable—but they were used in very familiar contexts. Even the addition of maize and tobacco (grown elsewhere in the Americas and in the Caribbean) to the inventory of the Tadoussac traders probably had strong Native precedents among northern Algonquian hunter-gatherers who had long exchanged meat and skins for the produce of their Iroquoian agriculturalist neighbors.[5]

The seamless way in which the new trade goods slipped into familiar cultural patterns may at first have obscured the deep changes that they caused, but by no means were all those changes negative. One of the most important of the familiar uses to which the new items were put was as tools. For Indian men and women, any number of everyday tasks became much easier. Something as basic as firemaking was radically simplified not just by axes that made firewood more readily obtainable but by flint and steel "strike-a-lights," which made the cumbersome practice of carrying smoldering coals in specially treated tortoise shells obsolete outside the ceremonial realm, where it continued to be used to kindle ritual council fires. Similarly, more easily started blazes, along with metal ladles and kettles, transformed cooking technology. "Now they generally get kettles of brass, copper, or iron," New England Indian superintendent Daniel Gookin wrote of his mid-seventeenth-century Native neighbors. "These they find more lasting than those made of clay, which were subject to be broken; and the clay or earth they were made of, was very scarce and dear."[6] Brass kettles were not only stronger than earthenware (or the hollowed-out wooden troughs also previously used for cooking), but they could be easily transported almost anywhere and be placed directly over flames. It was no longer necessary to heat rocks on coals and then to place them carefully in a heavy, fragile pot to raise broth to a boiling point. At home, soup could simmer almost untended in a kettle hung directly over a fire all day and night. In a hunting camp, hot meals became regularly available for the first time once both kettles and fire became easily transportable.[7]

New tools and new materials made life not only easier but, in countless ways, aesthetically richer. Beadwork of all kinds flourished with the influx of glass baubles and the needles, thread, and cloth needed to mount them. Anything carved of wood, shell, antler, bone, or soft stone achieved hitherto unimagined realms of complexity once iron knives, chisels, and awls replaced their flint predecessors. Animal, human, and other-than-human forms could be rendered in unprecedented detail. The difference in effect upon even such a mundane item as a decorative hair comb was dramatic. Among Northern Iroquoians, combs that had had no more than five thick teeth and had been ornamented with simple abstract images blossomed into works of art with as many as twenty-five thin teeth and elaborate zoö- or anthropomorphic designs, some of which apparently memorialized a specific event in the owner's life. Much of the new artistic energy unleashed by imported tools went into artifacts associated with the spiritual realm: ritual masks, ceremonial pipes and staves, and, most notably of all, the entire complex of ritual and practice associated with sacred wampum beads.[8]

"With this wompompeage they pay tribute, redeem captives, satisfy for murders and other wrongs, [and] purchase peace with their potent neighbors, as occasion requires," said Gookin; "in a word, it answers all occasions with them, as gold and silver doth with us."[9] Archaeological evidence indicates that beads made from the shells of the whelk and the quahog clam, respectively white and "black" (actually purple) in color, were highly prized in much of eastern North America long before European contact. The relatively rare pre-European-contact beads came in many sizes and shapes, but "true wampum"—small tubular beads finely drilled for stringing—became possible only with the introduction of iron tools. In the 1620s, as Dutch traders established their trading settlements in the Hudson Valley region, they discovered a huge market for shell beads and introduced standardized techniques for wampum manufacture to Algonquian peoples of the southern New England coast, where whelk and quahog were abundant. By the late 1630s the tiny beads were being churned out by the tens of thousands, to be traded for European manufactures from the Dutch, who would in turn exchange the wampum for furs from peoples farther in the interior. Iroquoian-speakers, in particular, made wampum beads, strings, and belts integral to much of their religious and political life. At midcentury, as many as 3 million individual wampum beads were in circulation in the countries of the Five Nations Iroquois alone, nearly 300 for each man, woman, and child. The vastly increased supply did not so much devalue what was once rare as create an innovative cultural phenomenon rooted in unprecedented abundance.[10]

The direct and indirect impact of such simple implements as the iron awls that made wampum possible, then, could be profound. Trade with Europe produced a vast efflorescence of traditional forms that sometimes, as in the case of wampum, mutated into entirely new—but indigenously rooted—patterns. Thus the mortuary ceremonialism that had, for centuries, apparently been the driving force for cultural interaction and long-distance trade in eastern North America blossomed after the discovery of Europe. In countless local variants, the practice of interring artifacts with the dead expanded to unprecedented dimensions, even among peoples who had apparently not previously engaged in it. In the Huron country, the periodic Feast of the Dead, in which the bones of the recently deceased were reburied in a communal grave, became a massive ceremonial redistribution of trade goods. Among peoples who did not practice group burials, brass kettles, iron tools, strike-a-lights, and imported weapons routinely accompanied individuals to the villages of the dead, along with glass and shell beads and ritual items made with or by trade goods. One Seneca girl who died in the 1650s, for example, rested under belts and necklaces made of some 43,000 wampum and glass beads, most of them presumably contributed not by her own relatives but by the clan whose ceremonial obligation it was to conduct her funeral. In New England, meanwhile, headmen took with them to the grave the wampum, clothing, and jewelry that marked their rank. And aboveground in much of the northeast, cemeteries that may have been the first levels of incipient burial mounds briefly became elaborate shrines filled with images intricately carved with imported tools—until they became all-too-visible invitations for European grave robbers seeking the treasures buried beneath.[11]

Imported tools, then, had great and sometimes unanticipated impacts. This was also the case with weapons, which were, after all, only specialized kinds of tools, used for hunting as well as for war. As tools for hunting, firearms were hardly the most important new imports. Early seventeenth-century matchlock muskets were so heavy that they had to be propped on a forked support to be fired, and they were virtually useless in wet weather, which tended to extinguish the smoldering length of fuse used to ignite the gunpowder. That ignition produced a loud report prior to a still louder blast that expelled the ball from the barrel; swift prey such as deer or birds got a split second's warning to flee, and the hunter had no chance for a second shot, which could occur only after an awkward re-loading of the weapon through its muzzle. The fact that the animal was in flight before the gun finished firing may not have mattered, however; unrifled barrels and inconsistently sized shot made muskets so inaccurate that they could be aimed in only the general direction of a target anyway. Finally, if a ball did make contact, it was likely to do severe damage to a valuable pelt or hide. All told, for hunting, the bow and arrow remained more predictably accurate, stealthily quiet, quickly reloadable, and reliably lethal.[12]

But neither arrows nor guns were the favored weapon for hunting the furs most sought after by traders seeking to fill an insatiable European demand for broad-brimmed felt hats made from beaver pelts. "The castor or beaver is taken in several ways," an early French missionary reported. In springtime, "a trap baited with the wood it eats" caused "a heavy piece of wood" to crush the prey. Winter hunts involved varied assaults on the dams in which the creatures lived. "A net made of good, strong, double cord" might be submerged with bait into a hole cut in the ice nearby. Or, more frequently, hunters would use trade hatchets to break open the upper story of the beaver dam (no easy task, because "the materials of which it is composed are wood and mud, so well joined and bound together") and then bludgeon the animals as they escaped into the water from a lower exit and tried to surface in order to breathe. Hunters strode "over the pond or frozen river, carrying a long club in their hands, armed on one side with an iron blade made like a carpenter's chisel, and on the other with a whale's bone," the missionary explained. "They sound the ice with this bone, striking upon it and examining it to see if it is hollow; and if there is any indication of this, then they cut the ice with their iron blade," slaying the beaver "with their big club, which they call *ca ouikachit*." That specialized club (for which both the whalebone and the

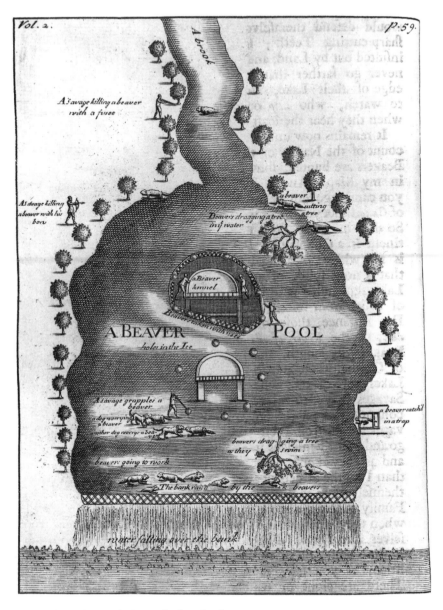

Native American techniques for hunting beaver.

From Louis Armand de Lom d'Arce, baron de Lahontan, *New Voyages to North-America* (London, 1703). Dechert Collection, Annenberg Rare Book and Manuscript Library, University of Pennsylvania.

iron cutting edge were acquired from European traders) provides a grue-some example of the role played by imported goods in technological in-novations that were rooted in Native traditions.[13]

Here, as with other sorts of weaponry, the fundamental innovation was not firearms, but the introduction of metal cutting edges. Hatchets and war clubs embedded with iron blades made hand-to-hand combat far deadlier than stone and wood alone. More importantly, arrows tipped with brass were significantly more lethal than those with flint heads. Their lighter weight allowed them to travel faster and truer, and their keener edge could pierce the wooden armor that protected warriors from most traditional arrows. The advantage for people equipped with even small supplies of brass was substantial. Not surprisingly, an arms race be-gan very early, in the years when iron axeheads and brass kettles were val-ued primarily as raw materials for Native manufactures. Many of the re-processed pieces of brass archaeologists have unearthed from late sixteenth-century sites are projectile points. And as late as 1610, northern Algonquian peoples who had a secure source of French trade goods had the upper hand over inland Iroquoian foes who still relied on arrows like the one "tipped with a very sharp bit of stone" that wounded Frenchman Samuel de Champlain in that year. The only iron axes the Iroquois pos-sessed, Chaplain reported, were those "which they sometimes win in war."[14]

Within two decades, however, the proliferation of European settle-ments had introduced enough metal into North America to promote a rough balance of power among the surviving participants in this first arms race. As intercultural trade in general moved into a phase when plentiful imported goods began to be used intact rather than as raw mate-rials, firearms became one of the most intensely sought after of those goods. By the 1620s one of the major drawbacks of early muskets was be-ing overcome, as "arquebuses" or "snaphaunces" with flintlock mecha-nisms began to replace cumbersome matchlocks. But for the most part it was precisely the same qualities that made muskets inferior hunting weapons that made them so desirable in human combat: their frightful noise and confusing smoke, their unpredictable inaccuracy, their awful ability to smash flesh and bone. As outnumbered early European colonists well understood, the psychological edge such firearms provided was enormous; the practical benefit of keeping bowmen pinned down and out of range was greater still.[15]

Despite official policies in all colonies designed to preserve a European monopoly of force, the incentives on both sides of the trading relationship were so great that well-placed Native people inevitably acquired firearms sooner rather than later: by the late 1610s in the Chesapeake region, by the early 1620s in southern New England, by the late 1630s in the Great Lakes area. Used in combination with brass-tipped arrows, iron hatchets, and modified clubs, firearms evened the odds against Europeans, as English forces who tried to storm a Virginia Algonquian village in 1622 learned from Native defenders who ambushed them with "some shot out of English pieces" while others "shot with Arrows manfully."[16] But the effect against Native opponents who owned no such weapons was even more dramatic. Near Montreal in June 1643, for example, a party of Huron canoeists floating down the St. Lawrence River was surprised by some forty Mohawk Iroquois, who sprang from behind trees to "fall upon them, frighten them with their arquebuses, put them to flight, and take twenty-three of them prisoners, with their canoes and the peltry."[17]

That episode—typical of countless raids that Iroquois war parties carried out on less well-armed Indian neighbors in the 1640s—illustrates a skillful integration of the shock value of firearms with other battlefield tactics and explains the tremendous Indian demand for the new weapons. The attack also suggests the economic importance that beaver pelts had come to have for Native Americans. For weapons, tools, and any number of basic commodities of everyday life, the fur trade had become absolutely crucial. "The Beaver does everything perfectly well," one headman joked to a French missionary in the early 1630s; "it makes kettles, hatchets, swords, knives, bread; and, in short, it makes everything."[18] Those marvelous qualities of the furry rodent gave it vast influence over seventeenth-century Native American life. The ease with which peltry could be exchanged for mundane commodities allowed a great efflorescence of Native artistic expression; energies and ingenuity that previously would have gone into such basics as making durable pots or chipping usable stone-cutting tools was now freed for finer work with imported tools and materials. Over time, disuse eroded more mundane craft skills. Among artifacts recovered from mid-seventeenth-century Iroquois sites, for instance, considerably less than half are of native manufacture, and flint projectile points, stone tools, and ceramic pots are virtually absent.[19] The inability to make a decent pot or airworthy flint arrowhead (even if one had wanted such things) meant that their replacements now *had* to be purchased. Ironically, to continue to live as "Indians," Native people needed to trade with Europeans. And to trade with Europeans, Native people needed beaver pelts or something equally valuable, such as the ability to make wampum.[20]

The social and cultural implications of the beaver pelt's economic importance were many and deep. Male work habits and migratory patterns transmuted in ways that oriented winter and spring hunts almost entirely to beaver; among the northern Algonquian hunter-gatherers in whose territories the thickest, most desirable pelts were found, commercial hunting was likely to crowd out almost all other economic pursuits, and to make communities almost entirely dependent on European trading partners for nearly all their supplies. Farther south, where women's agriculture remained the economic mainstay of villages that were, as a result, able to preserve much more of their traditional stability, winter hunts were nonetheless likely to take men farther from home for longer periods than previously. Quite likely, they would have to enter contested or enemy territory to get the prized pelts, as did that Mohawk war party in 1643.[21]

Wherever the beaver were found, and for hunter-gatherers and agricultural peoples alike, the vast explosion of material wealth profoundly reshaped patterns of social interaction and political authority. As with material transformations, the social impact seldom involved the direct mutation of Indian into European cultural patterns. There is little evidence from the early to mid-seventeenth century that anything resembling the acquisitive, individualistic, profit-seeking values of Western European capitalism became widely sanctioned in eastern Native America, where traditional economic patterns remained strong. Individuals who engaged in openly acquisitive behavior encountered social disapproval rooted in almost universal Native attitudes toward property rights, which emphasized need and use rather than possession and accumulation. Food, clothing, tools, houses, land, and other forms of property belonged to individuals and families, but only to the extent that they could make active use of them. Conversely, excess or abandoned property should be made available to those without. To hoard goods when others needed them was one of the most extreme forms of antisocial behavior.[22] In this context, status and authority went not to those who *had* the most, but to those in a position to *give* the most away. When headmen wore copper and wampum or otherwise exhibited markers of wealth and power, therefore, it was less to show what they possessed than what they were able to provide for their people. "The chiefs are generally the poorest among them," explained one Dutch colonist, "for instead of their receiving anything . . . these Indian chiefs are made to give to the populace."[23] But of course such chiefs *did* have to receive the goods they distributed from somewhere— from nearby communities that owed them tribute, from control of vital trading connections, from contributions members of their extended families made to the collective resources of their clans, and from villagers at large, who, at least in some Algonquian-speaking societies, owed a sort of tax in labor or food to replenish the stores from which chiefs demonstrated their largesse.[24]

There is little evidence that any of these basic values, with their emphasis on reciprocity and redistribution of goods, changed in most seventeenth-century Native communities. What did change in major ways, however, were the kinds of individuals and groups who controlled the redistribution of resources. Formerly weak villages that may have owed tribute to larger and more powerful neighbors could be transformed into dominant powers by their geographical proximity or political ties to European trading partners. Similarly, within communities, an age-graded and kin-based leadership structure in which headmen and clan mothers regulated the flow of goods and political allegiance faced disruption when skillful young hunters acquired wealth that they could redistribute independently of their elders and kinswomen—or even use to make those traditional leaders jump to their tune.[25] A group of Dutchmen traveling in the Mohawk Iroquois country in 1634 witnessed one such bid for status when "a good hunter named Sickaris" took advantage of the fact that the two principal headmen of the village were absent hunting and usurped their privilege of entertaining the visitors, making sure that they saw "in his house 120 pelts of marketable beaver that he had caught with his own hands" and no doubt intended to use to purchase European goods for re-distribution to his followers.[26] In such ways, traditional forms of economic and political behavior remained intact even as traditional patterns of status and authority eroded. The forces of economic change unleashed by European colonization interacted with Native American practices to produce a new world that neither colonists nor Indians could previously have imagined.

The arrival of large numbers of Europeans in the early seventeenth century also transformed the relationship between human beings and the environment in complicated and unpredictable ways. Nothing better illustrates the ecological forces at work than the results of the extensive beaver hunting that was so central to the economic transformation of Native life. Not surprisingly, the great economic demand for beaver pelts led to overhunting and, in turn, to temporary regional extinctions. The effect was exacerbated by wasteful destruction of beaver dams, and thus of the nesting places of young animals whose mothers were taken. Large areas of New England and present-day New York and Pennsylvania were probably empty of the creatures by the 1640s. The effect on the species as a whole was, in the long run, minor; populations of beaver can quickly rebound if left unhunted. But even the temporary removal of an organism from a regional ecosystem can have substantial effects. And, apart from human beings, few organisms more strikingly transform the shape of the ecosystem they inhabit than do beavers.[27]

The ponds that formed behind beaver dams did more than hold water; they trapped soil runoff and decaying organic material from surrounding areas, which might otherwise have washed away in spring floods. Water instead seeped gradually through what were, in effect, "irrigation works and reservoirs to preserve watersheds and equalize stream flows" throughout the year. The still pools and slow flow fostered an increase in water temperatures that encouraged the growth of plankton and insects, and thus of the fish and waterfowl that fed on them. Dead, fallen, and waterlogged trees provided habitat for still other insects, birds, and small mammals, while aquatic plants and the new growth that sprouted from the trunks of trees felled by beavers provided forage for deer, moose, and bear. Before the commercialization of hunting, beaver of course occasionally moved on and abandoned their dams, and when those structures collapsed, they exposed fecund sedimentary soils that soon became rich meadows. But when beaver went virtually extinct in an entire region, the results were far less benign. Fewer dams meant increased water flows and thus soil erosion, which destroyed complicated habitats and made scarce the deer, fish, and fowl that exploited them—and which had long been important food resources for Native people. Meantime, the expansive meadows left behind when dams disappeared became desirable haying and pasturage lands for the European families who arrived in such great numbers beginning in the 1630s. "Without these natural meadows," a New England colonist later concluded, "many settlements could not possibly have been made."[28]

And Europeans possessed and used meadows and the rest of the landscape in ways dramatically different from those of Native Americans. Those differences did not stem from the concept of ownership of private property per se. Native people certainly were familiar with the idea that the rights to farm, hunt, or fish on particular parts of the landscape could be owned, although those rights were usually vested in kin groups and villages, rather than in individuals as in England or France. Even that latter contrast was not so marked, for individual ownership was not absolute in early modern Europe either, where property was still encumbered by feudal obligations, where towns owned pastures and woodlands in common, and where patriarchs tended what were, after all, "family" farms. Not ownership itself, but the *meaning* of ownership was what set eastern Indians and western Europeans apart. Native communities treated land as a "resource," which could not in itself be owned any more than could the air or the sea. As with other forms of property, what people owned was the right to use the resource for a particular purpose—to farm, hunt, fish, gather wild plants, procure firewood, build a village— and these rights were not necessarily exclusive or permanent; once a resource was no longer being used, ownership rights faded. Europeans, by contrast, treated land as a "commodity" that was itself inherently and irrevocably owned, along with all its resources. Use had nothing to do with it; a vacant lot was still the exclusive property of its owner, a fixed feature of the landscape. When European "fixity sought to replace Indian mobility," an irreconcilable "conflict in the ways Indians and colonists interacted with their environments" came to the fore.[29]

The contrasting modes of interaction between humans and their environment are illustrated by the ways in which Native and European agriculturalists used the land. Perfected relatively recently during the Medieval Optimum and honed in the harsher conditions of the Little Ice Age, Indian agriculture was supremely adapted to the eastern North American environment. Its productivity put its European counterpart to shame. Annual eastern Indian corn yields may have been nearly nineteen bushels per acre. Although that return was roughly equal to what European cereals provided under similar environmental conditions in the same period, it was achieved with far fewer individual plants: one kernel of maize might return as many as two hundred kernels at harvest, yet contemporary wheat yielded only about fifteen grains for each seed. A western European acre thus had to be densely packed with a single crop, but a North American acre had plenty of room left for beans and squash as well as corn. All three were planted in the same hills, and as they grew together, bean vines climbed the natural support of the corn stalks while the nitrogen-fixing nodules in their roots returned the favor by fertilizing the soil. The squash plants, meanwhile, spread their leaves everywhere to provide natural weed control. Together, the Three Sisters thrived on an agricultural process of impressive simplicity. A digging stick to make a hole in which to plant the seeds and a hoe to build up a hill around the growing plants were the only tools necessary. Once the squash vines began to spread, almost no weeding or other tending was necessary until the crops matured. By sweat-of-the-brow European plow-and-sickle standards, remarkably little work was involved.[30]

Corn, beans, and squash reinforced one another in the cooking pot as well as in the field. Beans are an excellent source of the essential amino acids lysine and tryptophan, both of which are present in maize in such small quantities as to make that grain's nutritional value on its own very low. But lysine and tryptophan combine with the principal amino acid in maize, zein, to produce a highly nutritious protein, allowing the two foods together to accomplish what neither could do alone. Moreover, maize contains a higher proportion of carbohydrates and sugars than

Seventeenth-century Huron women grinding corn.

From François Du Creux, *Historiae Canadensis, seu Nouae-Franciae libri decem, ad annum usque Christi* (Paris, 1664). Dechert Collection, Annenberg Rare Book and Manuscript Library, University of Pennsylvania.

other cereal grains; when processed with lime or roasted over an open fire, it also releases substantial niacin. Squashes, baked or boiled, are an excellent source of C and other vitamins. Supplemented with game and fish and wild fruits and berries, the resulting diet was far superior to anything crooked-boned, bad-teethed Europeans—who worked so hard for their daily bread, and little else—could imagine.[31]

But all of this Indian abundance depended on a kind of mobility and flexible use of the landscape that would prove incompatible with the colonists' ways of interacting with the environment. The one thing the North American environment failed to provide was an animal species that could have been efficiently domesticated for food. Necessarily, then, hunting, fowling, and fishing continued to make crucial contributions to Native American diets long after the agricultural revolution had made corn, beans, and squash the major staples. Fishing, in particular, was vitally important. In inland areas it might contribute as much as 20 percent of an otherwise agricultural diet; in areas closer to the sea, entire villages relocated seasonally to take advantage of maritime abundance while their crops matured unattended some miles inland. Fishing and hunting required far more extensive territories than the area occupied by a village and its surrounding fields. These territories surrounding Indian towns thus were far from empty, and far from unused. Indeed, forests were frequently managed with deliberately set fires that cleared out the underbrush and encouraged the growth of young plants on which deer and other small game fed.[32]

Even the most settled and apparently fixed element in the Native landscape—the agricultural village—depended on an extensive and flexibly used territory. The same women who cultivated the fields also collected wild plants from far-flung locations. More importantly, despite the efficiency of Native agricultural practices and the fertilizing benefits of annual burnings of the previous season's stubble, soil gradually lost its productivity, and new fields regularly had to be opened ever farther from a village. Meantime, hundreds of people dependent on wood, bark, and vegetable fibers to make everything from houses to baskets had a voracious appetite for trees; together the two trends gradually leveled most nearby forests. In an Indian town itself, wood and bark construction materials steadily rotted, while houses and storage pits became infested with insects and other pests. After about two decades, a village site thus outlived its usefulness, and a community had to move on to start over in a different locale, usually a few miles away. These factors explain why permanent Mississippian cities had had to depend on a network of relocatable outlying agricultural villages to support them.[33]

Wherever large numbers of Europeans took up residence, new kinds of boundaries imposed themselves on the formerly flexible landscape. The ecological impact of European agricultural "fixity" went much further than the erection of fences around agricultural fields and pastures. Where Native women had cultivated their multiple crops in elegantly messy tracts that shifted in location over the years, Europeans plowed vast expanses clean, sowed a single crop per field, removed the stubble or allowed their grazing livestock to consume it, and planted repeatedly until the soil was exhausted. To make way for these fields, trees had to be cut down. The denuded soil that was left behind became far more subject to erosion, and the ecological uniformity of single-cropping had the paradoxical effect of encouraging specialized weed and insect pests that might otherwise never have gotten a foothold and might now just as well attack Native as European fields.[34]

Ironically, however, the most mobile aspect of European fixity—livestock—virtually ensured that the environment in which Native people had lived would lose its fluidity. Wherever horses, cattle, chickens, and pigs went, they took over ecological niches formerly occupied by wild game whose existence was already being threatened by clearings, plows, and fences. Particularly in the early years of European colonization, when land was plentiful and human labor scarce, most of these "domesticated" animals were left to forage for themselves for most of the year. Chickens roamed farmyards and village streets at will. Horses, cattle, and sheep grazed pastures and meadows clean, further depleting plant biodiversity and leaving little for wild competitors to eat.[35] Pigs, meanwhile, wandered everywhere and ate everything. Unlike horses, cattle, and chickens, they served no purpose except as food. With no daily need to be yoked, milked, or egged, their foraging grounds tended to be farther from European villages, and their owners—who branded them or notched their ears in distinctive patterns so they could recognize them—might not see them for weeks on end. Far from home, in the woods, they omnivorously gobbled everything that deer, elk, moose, or bear might have dined on; starved game simply disappeared. At the seashore, pigs were likely to dig up clams before Indian women could get to them. Worse still, the wayward porkers regularly emerged from the woods to wreak havoc among corn, beans, and squash in Native fields that, unlike those in European villages, were traditionally unfenced. Pits in which food was stored also proved irresistible to animals whose snouts were designed for rooting. No wonder, concluded English colonist Roger Williams, that "of all English cattle, the swine (as also because of their filthy dispositions) are most hateful to all Natives, and they call them filthy cut throats, etc."[36]

The arrival of European farmers—with their roaming livestock, their concepts of fixed property, and their single-crop plow agriculture—combined with the ecological impact of the fur trade to transform utterly the material environment of much of eastern North America and make traditional patterns of life impossible anywhere in the vicinity of European settlements. European and Indian ways of using the land could no more share the same ecosystem than could matter and antimatter share the same space. "Our fathers had plenty of deer and skins, our plains were full of deer, as also our woods, and of turkeys, and our coves full of fish and fowl," the Narragansett headman Miantonomo concluded in 1642. "But these English having gotten our land, they with scythes cut down the grass, and with axes fell the trees; their cows and horses eat the grass, and their hogs spoil our clam banks, and we shall all be starved."[37]

Starvation, however, was a mild fate compared with the third great material force that joined economic and ecological transformations to reshape Indian country: disease. Although the role of imported viral ailments in sixteenth-century North America in general remains a matter of controversy, it is clear that by the 1580s European microbes were levying a serious toll in some locales. The English party that attempted to establish a colony on Roanoke, off the coast of present-day North Carolina, in 1585 marveled that Native "people began to die very fast, and many in short space" after the newcomers visited their villages. "In some towns about twenty, in some forty, in some sixty, and in one six score" perished.[38] Roughly two hundred miles to the north and two decades later, the Virginia Algonquian leader Powhatan observed cryptically that he had "seen the death of all [his] people thrice, and not one living of those three generations, but" himself. It is unclear whether his reference was to epidemics spread from Roanoke or elsewhere or a metaphor for the painfully gained wisdom about "the difference of peace and war" that he had accumulated as a man who was "old, and ere long must die." In either case, death was a pervasive presence in Indian country.[39]

Diseases entered a fatal new phase after 1600, when for the first time substantial numbers of European families—including the youngsters most likely to carry viral "childhood diseases"—began to settle in eastern North America. The medical carnage was frightful—and made more so because it occurred at precisely the moment that Native people were also being forced to come to grips with the economic and ecological implications of the arrival of large numbers of Europeans. In 1617, what one English colonist described as "a great mortality" struck both Jamestown and its Native neighbors; its impact was "far greater among the Indians," who endured repeated bouts over a three-year period.[40] Almost simultaneously, from 1616 to 1618 along the southern New England coast, an epidemic or series of epidemics killed perhaps 75 percent of the coastal Algonquian population. Entire towns—including that of the later famous Squanto—disappeared, with no one remaining to bury the dead. A few years after, Englishman Thomas Morton found so many "bones and skulls" lying about that he could only compare the scene to "a new found Golgatha."[41] In the early 1630s, a smallpox epidemic—the first disease outbreak the sources allow us to identify positively by name—whipsawed through the Great Lakes region, cutting such populous peoples as the Iroquois and Huron confederacies in half. Yet the dying had just begun. Dutch colonist Adriean van der Donck was not exaggerating when he reported in the 1650s that "the Indians . . . affirm, that before the arrival of the Christians, and before the small pox broke out amongst them, they were ten times as numerous as they now are."[42]

It takes more than a little historical imagination for us to fathom what it must have meant to watch most of one's fellow villagers die or to be among the few to survive when everyone else succumbed. Modern studies of "virgin soil" epidemics not only confirm the likelihood of the appalling death rates, but also outline some particularly cruel patterns in the distribution of victims within a given community. Viral infections such as smallpox, measles, chicken pox, and mumps strike hardest not at the weakest but the strongest age groups—those between ages fifteen and forty, whose fully developed immune systems produce the most violent reactions in the form of the pustules, swellings, and fevers characteristic of these diseases. With literally everyone sick, and the able-bodied adults more incapacitated than the rest, the everyday work of raising crops, gathering wild plants, fetching water and firewood, hunting meat, and harvesting fish virtually ceased. Thus the old and the young ill received little fresh food and next to no nursing care, opening the door to opportunistic secondary infections that could kill just as surely as the principal viruses. So, many young and elderly victims who otherwise might have survived their relatively mild struggles with diseases also died because the young adult caregivers who might have nursed them to health were themselves so appallingly stricken. Moreover, any care that was given was likely to be counterproductive. Communal healing rituals in which villagers crowded around the victim provided opportunities for viruses to spread further, while the sweats and fasts that were central to those rituals in most Native cultures exacerbated conditions that are best treated by keeping the patient's skin dry and the body well nourished.[43]

Those who "fell sick of the small pox," wrote Plymouth Colony governor William Bradford,

> died most miserably; for a sorer disease cannot befall them, they fear it more than the plague. For usually they that have this disease have them [the pox] in abundance, and for want of bedding and linen and other helps they fall into a lamentable condition as they lie on their hard mats, the pox breaking and mattering and running one into another, their skin cleaving by reason thereof to the mats they lie on. When they turn them, a whole side will flay off at once as it were, and they will be all of a gore blood, most fearful to behold. And then being very sore, what with cold and other distempers, they die like rotten sheep. The condition of this people was so lamentable and they fell down so generally of this disease as they were in the end not able to help one another, no not to make a fire nor to fetch a little water to drink, nor any to bury the dead. But would strive as long as they could, and when they could procure no other means to make fire, they would burn the wooden trays and dishes they ate their meat in, and their very bows and arrows. And some would crawl out on all fours to get a little water, and sometimes die by the way and not be able to get in again.[44]

Despite such horrors, in any single epidemic, many survived; statistically, the odds were a little better than one in two. Those who caught and endured smallpox would be immune to it for the rest of their lives, although that said nothing about their chances against the battles with measles or influenza that probably lay in their future. Some communities were more fortunate than others: one village might remain a viable working unit; the next might be left with too small or demographically skewed a population to feed or defend itself. Refugees and remnants, families and fragments of families, individuals and ad hoc bands resettled and coalesced into new, polyglot communities that blended kinship structures, traditions, and dialects. In short, new peoples formed from pieces of the old. Most of the Native American nations that survive to our day were, to one degree or another, created in the melting pot set boiling by seventeenth-century epidemics.[45]

Clearly, the process was not random. Survivors apparently did not wander the landscape like either the walking dead or the violent renegades that populate our own day's cinematic visions of a future holocaust, but instead probably drew upon existing connections of real or fictive kinship, economic relationships, and linguistic affinities to recreate community life. But the process was far from peaceful and seldom pretty, particularly when combined with the economic stresses resulting from the simultaneous growth of dependence on European trade—stresses that could only be compounded as epidemics disrupted work patterns and erased craft skills that might otherwise have mitigated the demand for trade goods. The recoalescing population centers, then, were engaged in a desperate struggle against not just microbes but one another, as they scrambled for access to the resources necessary to survive: trade goods and the pelts to exchange for them, and—even more pressingly—the *human* assets needed to build and maintain a viable community. Indeed, it is probably not too much to say that people were the scarcest resource of all in the Indians' new world.[46]

So communities went to war with one another to obtain them. We will never know precisely how societies in the process of combining and redefining traditions, beliefs, and cultural practices first explained their demographic dilemmas to themselves and then took the decision to make war against one another to obtain human resources—or if, indeed, any conscious collective decision ever was taken. Archaeological, linguistic, and folkloric evidence indicates that almost everywhere in eastern North America and long before contact with Europeans, warfare had involved the taking of captives, at least some of whom were either adopted or enslaved by the victors. Specific practices varied widely, from the forced incorporation of women and children, to the ceremonial torture and execution of male prisoners (whose spiritual power if not physical strength would thus be incorporated into the victorious group), to the unquestionably indigenous practice of scalping as a symbolic substitute for taking an enemy alive. However distasteful such practices might appear, there was nothing particularly unique or cruel about them. We need only remind ourselves of the ingenuity of Europeans in an age of drawings, quarterings, and beheadings, of the almost universal practice of enslaving war prisoners in human history, or of the modern-day killing fields of central and eastern Europe. The point is, that to one degree or another eastern North American Indians were familiar with the idea that warfare could be used to acquire people.[47]

The linkage between deaths from epidemic disease and warfare to seek replacements for the dead was complex and often indirect. Hints in early written sources confirmed by folklore recorded much later suggest that Native people generally did not regard epidemics as random natural phenomena. Disease was always someone's fault, a form of malevolent attack. That "someone" might be a person's own soul, frustrated in its pursuit of some end and expressing its displeasure in an attack on the body. More frequently it was a human or other-than-human person using disease as a weapon. The Algonquians of Roanoke seem to have interpreted the epidemics that struck villages visited by the English in precisely these terms. According to colonist Thomas Hariot, "they were persuaded that it was the work of our God through our means, and that we by him might kill and slay whom we would without weapons and not come near them."[48] A similar belief about the cause of disease among the Mohawk Iroquois is suggested by a mid-1630s encounter between a group of Dutch travelers and a headman who was called Adriochten (meaning "he has caused others to die") "living one quarter mile from the [Native] fort in a small cabin because many Indians . . . had died of smallpox."[49]

Disease, then, was perceived as the result of a hostile act, what Western

culture would call a "crime." In most human societies that are not organized as states, the response to crime tends to stress restoration for the
victim rather than punishment of the offender; with punishment in the
hands of family groups rather than a coercive state, endless cycles of revenge would otherwise result.[50] This must have been particularly the case
when the alleged perpetrator wielded such a devastating and mysterious
power as the ability to make others sicken and die; better to compensate
the victim than to further enrage the perpetrator. According to Hariot,
the Roanoke Algonquians "could not tell whether to think" the English
who brought death with them were "gods or men." Similar fears of great
spiritual power (a more accurate term perhaps than Hariot's "gods")
might explain why the Mohawks banished the dangerous Adriochten
from their village but otherwise left him safely alone. Families and communities who could not do anything about the aggressor focused their energies on curing the one who was attacked. Healing rituals often involved
attempts to remove the disease weapon from the afflicted body, through
sweats, purges, vomiting, or a shaman's efforts to suck a spiritual projectile from a wound; shamans, Hariot superciliously observed, "earnestly
make the simple people believe, that the strings of blood that they sucked
out of the sick bodies were the strings wherewithal the invisible bullets
were tied and cast."[51]

When victims nonetheless died, the aggrieved parties were the families
to which they belonged, and compensation might well take the form of
filling the void that the departed's life and labor had left. In many areas of
eastern North America, a cultural pattern known as the "mourning war"
required young men to raid their enemies for war captives who would be
adopted, enslaved, or ritually killed to replace the loss and ease the grief
of those who mourned the death of loved ones. Mourning-war raids
were, on a fundamental level, an extension of the grieving process, an integral part of protracted funeral rites by which the loss of loved ones was
redressed and the balance of spiritual and material forces was symbolically restored. In keeping with a general principle of a justice that focused
on the aggrieved rather than on the perpetrator, the target of a raid need
not be directly to blame for the deaths that inspired a mourning war, although every people had traditional enemies who could be accused of almost any crime. What really mattered was the opportunity to take from

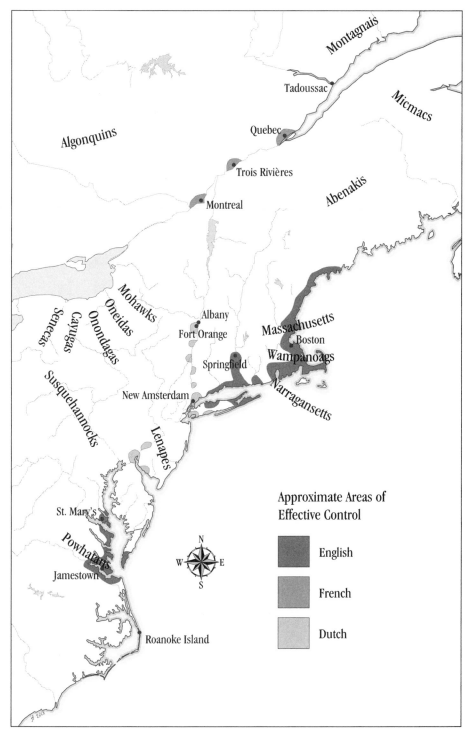

Eastern North America in the mid-seventeenth century: selected Indian nations and European outposts.

somewhere the prisoners who were the primary objective; booty, territorial gain, and other military benefits were distinctly secondary. The
mourning-war pattern seems unquestionably old in eastern North America, but it assumed explosive new forms and vastly expanded scope under
the demographic pressures of the seventeenth century. Particularly in a
context of violent grief in polyglot communities with conflicting traditions and few clear sources of traditional authority, nice distinctions between restoration for victims and bloodthirsty revenge must frequently
have blurred. In any case, only those communities fortunate enough to
retain a critical mass of warriors, kinship structures, and ceremonial specialists could mount any effective response at all. Less fortunate individuals and family fragments had to seek refuge in stronger communities
where they were welcomed as bodies to fill the void.[52]

For a quarter-century after the epidemics of the 1630s, no peoples were
more successful in the desperate race than the Five Nations Iroquois, who
raided far and wide to replenish their disease-ravaged population. A nineteenth-century descendent of the ethnic mixing that resulted recalled the
oral tradition of the wars this way:

> Their plan was to select for adoption from the prisoners, and cap-
> tives, and fragments of tribes whom they conquered. These captives
> were equally divided among each of the tribes, were adopted and in-
> corporated with them, and served to make good their losses. They
> used the term, *we-hait-wat-sha,* in relation to these captives. This
> term means a body cut into parts and scattered around. In this man-
> ner, they figuratively scattered their prisoners, and sunk and de-
> stroyed their nationality, and built up their own.[53]

The targets of such raids, quite naturally, viewed the situation in a less
favorable light. According to Gookin, reflecting the attitudes of southern
New England Algonquians with whom he worked, the Iroquois

> manner is, in the spring of the year, to march forth in parties several
> ways, under a captain, and not above fifty in a troop. And when they
> come near the place that they design to spoil, they take up some se-

cret place in the woods for their general rendezvous. Leaving some of their company there, they divide themselves into small parties, three, or four, or five in a company; and then go and seek for prey. These small parties repair near to the Indian habitations, and lie in ambushments by the path sides, in some secure places; and when they see passengers come, they fire upon them with guns; and such as they kill or wound, they seize on and pillage, and strip their bodies; and then with their knives, take off the skin and hair of the scalp of their head, as large as a satin or leather cap; and so leaving them for dead, they pursue the rest, and take such as they can prisoners.

For Gookin, the only "good effect the war had" on New England Algonquians driven from their homes was "to turn them from idleness; for now necessity forced them to labor with the English in hoeing, reaping, picking hops, cutting wood, making hay, and making stone fences, and like necessary employments, whereby they got victuals and clothes."[54]

These contrasting portraits of mid-seventeenth-century warfare powerfully convey the turmoil that the forces of economic change, ecological transformation, and epidemic diseases created—and the constraints those forces placed on Native Americans trying to come to terms with their new world. The range of choices, of course, was far greater than a plunge into the Iroquois melting pot on the one hand or manual labor for the English on the other. The demographic disaster of imported disease ensured that the Native communities that responded to ecological transformations and economic opportunities had to reinvent themselves, in countless ways large and small. The Indians' new world, then, was not merely the product of abstract material forces; it was also the creation of individuals and shattered families who recombined and reinvented themselves to survive in unprecedented circumstances. In all of this, eastern Native people were anything but passive victims unable to change. The profound economic, environmental, and epidemiological constraints they faced make their efforts to rebuild Indian country more, not less significant. As Nathan Huggins once said of African American history, "it is exactly this triumph of the human spirit over adversity that is the great story."[55] The same is true for Native American history from the early seventeenth century onward.

LIVING WITH EUROPEANS

IT IS MUCH EASIER to reconstruct the abstract forces that constrained the seventeenth-century Native world than it is to recover the personal experiences of the people who struggled to give that world human shape. Early colonists recorded countless Indian names (as best they could reproduce them in the Latin alphabet) and glimpsed the activities of Indian people who visited them or in whose villages they sojourned, but they seldom developed any real understanding of their subjects' motives or broader experiences—and so, in most cases, neither can we. Nonetheless, a handful of individuals do emerge strikingly from fragmentary references in documents preserved from the period. Among them are three whose stories have been told repeatedly since then: the Virginia Algonquian "princess" Pocahontas, the Mohawk Roman Catholic candidate for sainthood Kateri Tekakwitha, and the Wampanoag Metacom, or "King Philip," who inspired a bloody war against Puritan New England. Verifiable evidence about these figures is so scant that it may never be possible to determine the "truth" about their lives, but enough information is available to reveal how each confronted the forces of material change and tried to incorporate Europeans into an Indian world on indigenous terms. Their stories illuminate the dilemmas that all seventeenth-century Native people faced.

Every North American schoolchild knows—or thinks she knows—the story of Pocahontas:

*A beautiful Indian princess welcomed the English colonists to James-
town in 1607 and fell in love with the dashing young Captain John
Smith. When Smith was captured by her father, the great chief
Powhatan, she risked her life to save her lover from a brutal execution.
Thereafter a frequent visitor to the English settlement, she brought the
colonists food and thwarted her father's plans to do them in. When
Smith was injured in a gunpowder explosion and forced to return to
England, Pocahontas pined away, but ultimately fell in love with another colonist, John Rolfe. She was baptized a Christian, took the
name Rebecca (recalling the biblical matriarch who left her own people to marry Isaac and become the mother of a nation), and married
Rolfe, with whom she had a son named Thomas. On a visit to England in 1616, she tragically died and was buried in a village church at
Gravesend. But her legacy of love that triumphed over racial barriers
lived on in the numerous Virginian descendants of her son.*

Almost every particular of this familiar story—or, rather, the two distinct tales of Pocahontas and Smith and Pocahontas and Rolfe that anima-
tors from Disney Studios reconflated not long ago—is either incorrect or
misleading.[1] References to a girl or woman named Pocahontas appear in
the writings of at least four seventeenth-century English chroniclers: London courtier John Chamberlain, Virginia colonists William Strachey and
Ralph Hamor, and, most importantly, the colony's sometime president
and lifelong historian Smith.[2] Their works reveal that "Pocahontas" was a
nickname, or perhaps even just a descriptive term, meaning something to
the effect of "playful one" or "mischievous girl." It is possible, therefore,
that not every Pocahontas they mention was the one who later became
famous. That person's formal public name was Amonute; her personal,
secret name, known only to her kin until revealed to a literate English audience, was Matoaka.[3]

Little is known about her life prior to the establishment of Jamestown.
She was born in 1595 or 1596 as one of perhaps ten daughters and twenty
sons of Powhatan, the *mamanatowick,* or paramount chief, who presided
over the approximately thirty local communities and 15,000 people of
Tsenacommacah, the "densely inhabited land" later called the Virginia
Tidewater. Her mother was one of numerous wives of Powhatan, but the

older woman's identity is otherwise a mystery. The missing information is crucial for evaluating Pocahontas' status as a "princess," for among her people, as among most Native societies in eastern North America, political office descended in the female line. Thus neither Pocahontas nor her potential husband would have had any hereditary claim to Powhatan's chiefdom; as Smith observed, "her marriage could no way have entitled [her spouse] by any right to the kingdom," which would descend to the *mamanatowick*'s maternal nephews, not to his own children.[4] Whatever exalted social status she may have inherited through her mother's line, there is no particular reason to assume that she was her father's favorite. Indeed Strachey identified her youngest half-sister as the "great darling of the king's."[5]

There is no evidence that Pocahontas met Smith or any other English person before the end of 1607, when the captain's exploratory party was captured, he was brought to her father's village, and she supposedly rescued him from death. At the time, Pocahontas was a prepubescent girl of about twelve; Smith was a squat bearded man in his late twenties. Whether the Englishman's life was actually in danger on that occasion, whether Pocahontas acted on her own or on her father's or others' instructions, or even whether the girl intervened at all are matters of debate, in part because of the contradictory accounts Smith himself wrote. His early books give no hint that his life was in peril when he was held prisoner, but after Pocahontas became famous for her marriage to Rolfe he published increasingly elaborate stories of how "she hazarded the beating out of her own brains to save" his.[6] Still, the most likely interpretation of what happened is that the "execution" and "rescue" were part of an elaborately staged ceremony, designed to establish Powhatan's life-and-death authority over Smith, to incorporate the English as subordinate people within the *mamanatowick*'s realm, and to make Pocahontas an intermediary between the two leaders and their communities.[7]

Such a relationship is suggested by the fact that Pocahontas subsequently appeared in Jamestown several times accompanying parties bearing food and messages from Powhatan to his English tributaries. These trips were not all business, however; Jamestown residents told tales of how a youngster wearing the non-garb traditional for children in her society would "get the boys forth with her into the market place and make them wheel, falling on their hands turning their heels upwards, whom she would follow, and wheel her self naked as she was all the Fort over." *Au naturel* cartwheels notwithstanding, there was no romance between Smith and Pocahontas, who at best shared the fondness of an older man for a younger girl he later described as "the very nonpareil of [Powhatan's] kingdom."[8] After Smith's departure—more the result of a revolt against his leadership than of concern for his health, which could not have been improved by a long ocean voyage—she apparently went about her life much as she would have if the English had never arrived. In about 1610, at the age of fourteen or fifteen, she married a "private captain called Kocoum" and went to live with him in an outlying town in Powhatan's domain.[9]

Her relationship to John Rolfe began some three years later with another capture, this time of Pocahontas by the English. War between colonists and the Powhatans had broken out shortly after Smith's departure, largely because of incessant English demands for food tribute. Also in dispute were English claims to land in an area at the heart of Powhatan's chiefdom stretching fifty miles up the James River from Jamestown to the outpost of Henrico, which the colonists established in 1611. Following a policy of divide and rule, the English had made peace with one of the constituent elements of Powhatan's paramount chiefdom, the Patawomecks. In their country in April 1613, Englishman Samuel Argall convinced one of that nation's headmen to lure Pocahontas—who was on an extended visit to her father's erstwhile tributaries—on board his vessel.[10] The young captive spent most of the next year as a hostage at Jamestown, under the supervision of Deputy Governor Thomas Dale, and at Henrico, in the house of the Reverend Alexander Whitaker. During that period she received instruction—indoctrination might be a better word—in Christianity. Dale, promulgator of the colony's infamously draconian "Laws Divine, Moral and Martial," was hardly known for his light touch; during a previous term as governor he had sentenced some English wrongdoers "to be hanged, some burned, some to be broken upon wheels, others to be staked, and some to be shot to death."[11] Whitaker's approach may have been no more subtle. He wrote approvingly that "Sir Thomas Dale had labored a long time to ground in her" a rote knowledge

of the Apostles' Creed, the Lord's Prayer, and the Ten Commandments in English.[12]

During her captivity Pocahontas came to know John Rolfe, a twenty-eight-year-old bachelor who had recently shipped to England a trial sample of the tobacco he had been experimenting with since first importing seeds from the West Indies in 1611.[13] Rolfe became smitten with the then-eighteen-year-old woman, "to whom," he said, "my hearty and best thoughts are, and have for a long time been so entangled, and enthralled in so intricate a labyrinth, that I was even awearied to unwind myself thereout." Whether Pocahontas requited her suitor's love is unknown. Perhaps at first he simply represented a way out of the oppressive tutelage of Whitaker and Dale. In any event, what Rolfe feared might be only "the unbridled desire of carnal affection" was, he convinced himself, outweighed by the higher goals of the "good of this plantation for the honor of our country, for the glory of God for my own salvation and for the converting to the true knowledge of God and Jesus Christ, an unbelieving creature."[14]

In March 1614, as Rolfe sorted out his feelings, Dale took Pocahontas with him when he marched an army into the heart of Powhatan's domain, "burned . . . some forty houses, and . . . made freeboot and pillage" to demonstrate who was in charge. Despite this show of force, Powhatan balked at Dale's efforts to impose a peace treaty until, in the midst of negotiations, Rolfe wrote a letter to the governor confessing his attraction to Pocahontas and suggesting a diplomatic marriage to seal an alliance. Powhatan—who had several weeks earlier proposed "that his daughter should be [Dale's] child, and ever dwell with [him], desiring to be ever friends"—agreed to the match immediately. Pocahontas, having, according to Dale, "made some good progress" in her catechism, hastily received baptism, and within ten days the union was blessed with Anglican rites at Jamestown. No one seemed to worry about the bride's inconvenient previous marriage to Kocoum.[15]

Two years later, with Indians and English seemingly enjoying an age of peace and colonists madly planting Rolfe's tobacco everywhere, the couple and their infant son traveled to England. The family was accompanied by a man named Uttamatomakkin (whom English sources described as

Pocahontas during her visit to London, 1616.

Engraving by Simon van de Passe. National Portrait Gallery, Smithsonian Institution.

an adviser to her father) and perhaps ten other people from Tsena-commacah. Sometime after their arrival in June 1616, Smith (who Pocahontas had been told was dead) went to see her in her lodgings and wrote for her a letter of introduction to Queen Anne, in which he told the rescue story in public for the first time.[16] In January 1617 the Indians were ceremonially received at court, where they were "graciously used" by King James I. They also sat "well placed" at a performance of a theatrical work by Ben Jonson, amid grumbling by some courtiers that Pocahontas was "no fair lady," despite "her tricking up and high style and titles." Two months later she succumbed to an unidentified ailment at Gravesend, as she prepared to travel home on a ship commanded by the same Samuel Argall who had captured her.[17]

Hopes for the kind of peaceful ethnic relations the Rolfe-Pocahontas marriage symbolized expired with her. Powhatan died in early 1618, leaving his paramount chieftainship to a series of elderly relatives. Effective leadership, however, passed long before his death to the Pamunkey chief Opechancanough and a charismatic religious figure named Nemattanew, or "Jack of the Feather," who promised his followers that European musket shots would do them no harm. In November 1621, as the two were mobilizing forces to resist English expansionism, Nemattanew got into a scuffle with colonists who accused him of murdering an Englishman and took a fatal shot from one of the guns to which he claimed immunity. His movement lived on, however, and in March of the next year Opechancanough planned a series of carefully coordinated assaults that killed at least 330 English—perhaps one quarter of the colony's population—in a single day. A decade of brutal retaliatory warfare ensued, until the exhausted English imposed peace terms.[18]

The conceptual distance the victors had traveled since the days of the Rolfe-Pocahontas marriage is perhaps best measured by comments made during the war by Virginia governor Francis Wyatt. "Our first work is expulsion of the savages to gain the free range of the country for increase of Cattle, swine, etc.," he wrote. "It is infinitely better to have no heathen among us, who at best were but as thorns in our sides, than to be at peace and league with them."[19] So things stood until 1644, when Opechancanough—reputedly 100 years old and unable to walk unassisted—was carried into the field on a litter to lead his people in a final desperate campaign against the English. In March 1646 English forces captured him and displayed him in a cage at Jamestown. Despite his disabilities and "eye-lids . . . so heavy that he could not see," he defiantly protested the indignity until one of his guards shot him in the back.[20]

What might we make of these intertwined tales and their murderous end? Euro-Americans have usually faced west to focus on what the narratives mean for them and their own story. From this perspective, Pocahontas' main purpose was to make possible the survival of the Jamestown colony, and thus the future development of the United States. Her story conveys lessons about a road not taken, about an intercultural cooperation that should have been, about a Native American who not only welcomed colonizers with open arms but so thoroughly assimilated to their ways that she changed her name and her religion in order to become one with them. As a twentieth-century biographer put it, "Pocahontas did not share her people's hostility, and it is that fact that catapulted her into history . . . Encountering a new culture, she responded with curiosity and concern, and she accepted the potential for change and development within herself. She rose, surely and dramatically, above the ignorance and savagery of her people."[21] Opechancanough presumably did not.

An eastward-facing perspective on the limited documentary evidence about Pocahontas, however, suggests a very different meaning for her stories. What if we think of her not as the sexy savior of Jamestown but instead as "a young exile, who died at age twenty-two in a foreign country"?[22] Significantly, the only attempt to record Pocahontas' own words was made by that less-than-reliable source John Smith after his visit with her in England in 1616. When her old acquaintance first encountered her, "she turned about, obscured her face, as not seeming well contented." Hours later, after Smith had begun to doubt her ability even to speak English, Pocahontas finally

> began to talk, and remembered me well what courtesies she had done, saying, "You did promise Powhatan [that] what was yours should be his, and he the like to you; you called him father being in his land a stranger, and by the same reason so must I do you," which though I [Smith] would have excused, I durst not allow of that title, because she was a king's daughter. With a well set countenance she said, "Were you not afraid to come into my father's country, and caused fear in him and all his people (but me) and fear you here I should call you father? I tell you then I will, and you shall call me

child, and so I will be for ever and ever your countryman. They did tell us always you were dead, and I knew no other till I came to Plymouth [England]; yet Powhatan did command Uttamatomakkin to seek you, and know the truth, because your countrymen will lie much."[23]

If Smith's version of Pocahontas' words is accurate, at least three powerful messages emerge. First is a pervasive tone of profound sadness—if not embittered disillusionment. This is not the song of an enlightened savage happy to live in civilization at last, but rather the lament of a "stranger" trapped by duty far from home in a world of congenital liars. Yet duty strongly emerges as the second message conveyed by Pocahontas' words, if they are her words. She conveys a firm sense of her social role and how she must play it. She defines that role neither as the Christian convert Rebecca nor as the wife of John Rolfe; instead, she is the one obligated to call Smith "father" and "be for ever and ever" his "countryman." In Native eastern North America, obligations were always supposed to be reciprocal. The third message, therefore, is the failure of Smith and his mendacious countrymen to uphold the standard of reciprocity. He refuses to let her call him "father" and has apparently forgotten his pledge to "Powhatan [that] what was yours should be his, and he the like to you."

So it seems plausible that, far from being a youthful rebel who defied her father's will to join the English invaders, Pocahontas was a dutiful child who fulfilled a very traditional function in Native politics and diplomacy.[24] Her role in whatever happened during Smith's 1608 captivity defined him as her adoptive parent, and thus also established kinship relations between him and her biological father and, presumably, her mother's clan as well. (There would be nothing odd about having two or more "fathers." Virginia Algonquian children probably used the same term of respect—which only imperfectly translates into English—to address both a male parent and his brothers.) Pocahontas' later marriage to Rolfe—a match both sides understood as an act of diplomatic alliance—vastly strengthened already existing connections. Through her, the English and the Powhatans became fictive kin, and the ceremonial, political, and economic basis for peace, as people of Tsenacommacah understood that concept, became possible. Thus, a month after the marriage, Powhatan "inquire[d] how his brother Sir Thomas Dale fared, after that of his daughter's welfare, her marriage, his unknown son, and how they liked, lived, and loved together." When told all was well, "he laughed heartily, and said he was very glad of it."[25]

We need not idealize either the motives of Powhatan or the unanimity of his people to appreciate the genuine, if fragile, potential that Pocahontas' adoption and marriage represented or the ways in which that potential resonated with traditional Native practices. When Pocahontas took the name Rebecca and went to live among Europeans, she did so not to abandon her culture but to incorporate the English into her Native world, to make it possible for them to live in Indian country by Indian rules. In this light, it could not be more wrong to assert that she broke decisively with her people. To the contrary, Pocahontas played a familiar diplomatic role and may in fact have had very little choice in either her casting or her performance. Nor need we demonize the English to appreciate the tragedy that resulted from their failure to fulfill reciprocal obligations of kinship that they did not—or would not—understand. "Your king gave me nothing," Uttamatomakkin complained to Smith after an audience with James I that inexplicably included none of the gifts that any chief worthy of the name should have bestowed to display his power and largesse. Not surprisingly, when he returned to Tsenacommacah after Pocahontas' death, Powhatan's agent had little good to say about the English.[26] The story of Pocahontas, then, does represent a road of intercultural cooperation that tragically was not taken—but a road toward cooperation on Indian, rather than English, terms. To take that road, Smith and others in positions of authority over European colonists would have had to acknowledge that they were living in Indian country, that what they called "Virginia" was not theirs alone to govern. Whether that acknowledgment would have been enough—whether Powhatans and English could ever have found a way to share Tsenacommacah on mutually advantageous terms—will never be known. But Pocahontas' diplomatic marriage suggests that there was a genuine moment when an alternative history might have been made. Perhaps that is the deepest tragedy of her story.

Among North American Roman Catholics, a story of another young Native woman who converted to Christianity has long been nearly as familiar as that of Pocahontas:

> In 1660 a four-year-old Mohawk Iroquois named Tekakwitha was orphaned by a smallpox epidemic that killed her mother, father, and brother. The disease scarred her face and weakened her eyes. An uncle who was a prominent village chief adopted her, and as she grew in years she became noted for her solitary ways, her industrious work habits, and, especially, her repugnance toward sexual intercourse and proposals of marriage. These pure habits combined with her physical disabilities to alienate her from her family.
>
> One day in 1675 a Jesuit missionary visited her as she lay in her house with an injured foot. She responded immediately to his message and proved a remarkably apt pupil; surely God's grace had been preparing her for this moment all her life. At Easter in 1676 she was baptized with the name Kateri (Catherine, after St. Catherine of Siena) and quickly became the most pious of the small band of Christians in her mostly pagan village. Her refusal to work on the Sabbath and her continued rejection of marriage offers infuriated her family and fellow villagers, who physically assaulted her and spread rumors that not only was she not a virgin, but she had incestuously fornicated with her uncle. In 1677 she escaped her persecutors and fled to Kahnawake, a mission village, or reserve, the Jesuits had recently established on the St. Lawrence River near Montreal. There she inspired a religious revival among female converts, who joined her in taking vows of chastity and in practicing ever-more-rigorous physical penance for their former lives of sin. Fasting and self-flagellation took their toll until she died in 1680, at the age of twenty-four.
>
> Almost immediately, astonishing things began to happen. Some said the marks of her childhood bout with smallpox marvelously disappeared from her face within a few minutes of her death. Her priests—using medieval language reserved for saints whose bodies were believed immune to the stench of decay—claimed she "died with an odor of sanctity." Those who prayed at her grave professed to be

*healed, and in the nearly three centuries since, the faithful have attrib-
uted miracles to "the Lily of the Mohawks." In 1980 Pope John Paul II
beatified her, making her the first Native American candidate for
sainthood.*

Beneath the vocabulary of Roman Catholic piety, this story deeply par-
allels the westward-facing tale of Pocahontas. Despite the prevailing hostility of her people, a young woman welcomes a European visitor to her
country, willingly embraces Christianity, and goes off to live and die
young among her adoptive people, but not before she leaves behind a legacy of interracial harmony, this time through saintly miracles rather than
biological descendants.

Unlike the fragmentary and sometimes contradictory references to
Pocahontas contained in diverse seventeenth-century documents, the historical evidence on Tekakwitha seems at first glance remarkably consistent. Pierre Cholenec and Claude Chauchetière, two Jesuit priests who
worked with her at Kahnawake, each wrote biographies within a few
years of her death. They framed a religious, rather than historical, narrative—one designed to inspire the faithful with the example of a woman
they deeply believed to be a saint, rather than to present a flesh-and-blood
portrait. Modeling their work on the *Lives of the Saints* from which Roman Catholics had long sought inspiration, "the Jesuit missionaries who
knew Kateri Tekakwitha transformed her from a Mohawk girl to the
Blessed Catherine Tekakwitha, the savage saint, the first Iroquois virgin,
and protectress of all Canada." She was "born a Mohawk, but she died a
symbol."[27] So, even more clearly than the similar tale of Pocahontas, this
story of Kateri Tekakwitha lies in the realm of myth—if by "myth" we
mean something that may not meet "scientific" standards of factual proof
but that nonetheless conveys some broader truth, some deeper cultural
meaning. It is, of course, no more possible to prove that Kateri
Tekakwitha lived a life of virgin purity and continues to work miracles to
this day than to prove that the Jesus in whom she is said to have believed is
the Son of God. Yet people *have* believed in such things, and have believed
in them not as fictions but as meaningful, truthful ways of making sense
of their world. "A myth is a story . . . which *explains* a problem," one
scholar argues. "Very often, the problem being 'solved' by a myth is a con-

tradiction or a paradox, something which is beyond the power of reason or rational logic to resolve."[28]

What contradictions or paradoxes were the authors of the Kateri myth, like those North Americans who continue to embrace it, trying to resolve? On a personal scale, whatever private pains those who have prayed to Kateri down through the years have endured, her mythic story has provided meaning, hope, even healing. But on a broader, cultural level, the stories of Kateri and Pocahontas help to resolve the moral contradictions raised by the European colonization of North America and the dispossession of its Native inhabitants. They prove that at least some "good Indians" appreciated what the colonizers were trying to do for them and eagerly joined them in the cause. Seventeenth-century Europeans offered as their primary justification for the colonization of America their Christian obligation to spread the Gospel, to bring heathen lands and peoples under the dominion of Christ. In this light, the transformation of Tekakwitha into Catherine, like that of Pocahontas into Rebecca, proved that the higher aims of colonization were being achieved. Beyond such moral abstractions, there were practical concerns. Rebecca was brought to England to publicize the accomplishments of a Virginia that many in the British Isles considered to be a place from which, as Chamberlain scoffed, "there is no present profit to be expected."[29] Similarly, the Jesuit authors of Kateri's biography needed a success story. Many people in both France and New France resented the expense of the missions, questioned the political influence wielded by the missionary order, and doubted that their methods could ever turn Indians into good Christians. "The Lily of the Mohawks" refuted them all.

But such mythic truth flows from the spiritual, psychological, and political needs of Euro-Americans. What if we face east to try to fathom the mythic needs of the Native women who, according to Cholenec and Chauchetière, joined her in strenuous ascetic piety and of the later generations of Native American Catholics who have joined Euro-Americans in their belief in her powers? And what of Kateri herself? Can we search beneath the myth to recover any glimpses of *her* personality, of the contradictions or paradoxes she may have struggled with as she embraced an alien faith? Kateri left no written words of her own. It is likely that she never learned to read or write in either Mohawk or French, and the only

Catherine tekakoüita Jroquoise du Saut
S Louis de Montreal en Canada morte
en odeur de Sainteté.

Kateri Tekakwitha, "the Lily of the Mohawks."

From Claude-Charles Bacqueville de La Potherie, *Histoire de
l'Amerique septentrionale* (Paris, 1722). Dechert Collection,
Annenberg Rare Book and Manuscript Library, University of Pennsylvania.

statements Cholenec and Chauchetière attributed to her reflect such predictable pieties as her resolution to "have no other spouse but Jesus
Christ."[30] All written sources trace back to the hagiography of Cholenec
and Chauchetière. The same appears to be true of popular oral traditions

about Kateri, even those told today among contemporary Native people, who sometimes repeat the slanders—accurate or not—attributed to her opponents in the seventeenth-century missionary's story. To label her a "prostitute" or a "leaking pot" who traitorously revealed Iroquois secrets to the French may only invert the Euro-American myth in a way that gets us no closer to an understanding of the motives and circumstances of Tekakwitha and other Native people who embraced a Christian identity in the seventeenth century.[31] The truth about the historical individual behind the religious narrative is probably irrecoverable.

Yet one way of gaining some perspective is to examine more generally the responses of seventeenth-century eastern Indians to Christianity and its missionaries. The cultural gap between Native and Christian doctrine was enormous. Indeed, the very concept of "doctrine," as a set of specific concepts to which all believers were expected to agree, was as foreign to eastern North America as the literate culture in which its sacred texts were embedded. We know very little about the specifics of religious beliefs among Kateri's people and their neighbors, except that those beliefs were highly diverse and involved a wide array of spiritually powerful beings with which people dealt as they went about their lives. The nature of the spiritual power such beings wielded was mysterious. Iroquoian languages used variants of the word *orenda*, Algonquian languages *manitou*, to describe this "impersonal force that permeated the world, observable in anything marvelous, beautiful, or dangerous."[32] Deceased ancestors, animals, trees, winds, waters—all were other-than-human persons with whom it was important to maintain mutually beneficial relationships because they possessed or controlled this power. As a result, those relationships and their ceremonial maintenance, rather than any specific set of dogmas, doctrines, or beliefs about the characteristics of particular spiritual beings, were at the heart of religious life and provided a constant theme in the wide diversity of practices and concepts within and across the many cultures of eastern North America. Vision quests through fasts, sweats, self-induced pain, or mind-altering substances similarly can be understood as means of achieving altered states of consciousness in which more direct relationships with other-than-human persons and the *manitou* they could mobilize might be established.[33]

In a context in which the control of relationships rather than the mas-

tery of doctrine took precedence, religious specialists, or shamans, derived their status from their knowledge and effectiveness in the ceremonies necessary to maintain proper relationships with other-than-human
persons. Their ability to manipulate spiritual power earned them not just
respect but fear. The same shaman who could use his ceremonial skills to
heal the sick, make crops grow, or convince game animals to give themselves up to hunters could also use his influence with other-than-human
persons to inflict illness, wither crops, and drive away the deer. Shamans
and witches were two sides of the same coin, because spiritual power, like
the beings who wielded it, was morally neutral. As English traveler John
Josselyn put it, New England Native people "acknowledge[d] a god
who[m] they call *Squantam,* but worship him they do not, because (they
say) he will do them no harm." By contrast, a being Josselyn understood
to be called *"Abbamocho* or *Cheepie* many times smites them with incur-
able diseases, scares them with his apparitions and panic terrors, by reason whereof they live in a wretched consternation worshiping the Devil
for fear."[34]

Josselyn erred in calling Squantam (known more often by his
Narragansett name, Cautantowwit) a "god" and equating Abbamocho
(Hobbamock) with "the Devil." Other-than-human persons were no
more inherently "good" or "bad" than human ones. What mattered was
the character of interpersonal connections and the degree to which their
power could be mobilized beneficially or malevolently; other-than-
human persons bent on harm required much more ritual attention than
those more kindly disposed. Nor—unless relationships somehow turned
tyrannically dangerous—were any of these spirit beings, shamans, or ceremonies due exclusive human allegiance. Although basic moral principles
remained constant, the beings with whom one dealt, and the ways in
which one dealt with them, changed with time and situation in much the
same way that human ties evolved over a life course. So Native religions
were inclusivist, ready to incorporate new ideas and ceremonies, and generally tolerant of differences of opinion, as long as those differences did
not result in perceived harm to other people.[35]

All of this was profoundly alien to the worldview of seventeenth-
century European Christians. Whether Catholic or Protestant, all Christians were exclusivist—insistent on a single religious Truth as revealed in

the Bible and interpreted by educated, ordained priests or ministers. The Christian deity was, as the first of his Ten Commandments declared, "a jealous God" who demanded that his followers place "no other gods before him." Not only this general idea but many specific Christian doctrines must have seemed strange to seventeenth-century Native Americans. What, for example, was a "shepherd" and what did it mean for him to "care for his sheep"? What were people who knew nothing of state-organized governments to make of a concept such as the "kingdom of heaven"? How could Indians whose concepts of justice focused on restitution for the victim grasp the threat of eternal punishment for one's "sin," much less the notion of freely given divine "grace" that wiped those sins away with no compensation to the aggrieved? Some concepts were literally as well as figuratively untranslatable. Iroquoian grammar, for instance, made it impossible for priests to invoke their deity "in the name of the Father, and of the Son, and of the Holy Spirit." Instead (in a revealing glimpse of the ways in which relationships, rather than dogma, were woven into Indian spirituality), the terms had to be *"our* Father, *his* Son, and *their* Holy Spirit." But nothing could have been more alien than the insistence of those priests that Indians abandon the multitude of ritual practices by which they negotiated the web of relationships that determined the course of everyday life. "As they do not disturb our prayers, and as even the most superstitious attend them," one Jesuit missionary complained, "so they cannot suffer any opposition to their ceremonies."[36]

The chasm between European and Indian religions at first glance could not appear greater. But, as the missionary's comment indicates, the gap may not have yawned so wide as we might think. The same inclusiveness that was so alien to missionaries made it perfectly possible for Native Americans to incorporate elements of Christianity into their spiritual world. Our Father, his Son, and their Holy Spirit joined the diverse other-than-human persons who already populated the universe, and perhaps were even more powerful than any of them. Roman Catholic priests, with their celibacy and crossdressing in long black robes, their prayers and rituals, and their ability to manipulate potent forces, were shamans not to be taken lightly, lest they turn those forces against those who stood in their way. Prayers, hymns, veneration of artifacts (a crucifix or reliquary), ceremonial feasts (Holy Communion), symbolic baths (baptism), self-inflicted torments (physical penance), even such forms of ritual purity as a vow of sexual monogamy or complete celibacy had precedents in the spiritual life of Native Americans accustomed to the varied ways in which shamans taught people to deal with other-than-human beings.[37]

To the extent that their ceremonial practices resembled familiar Native patterns, French Roman Catholic priests initially had a distinct advantage over English and Dutch Protestant missionaries. Processions, chants, incense, bells, visual aids—all were integral to seventeenth-century Catholic piety and to the ceremonies surrounding the central mystery of the Mass, and all must have at least been recognizable to Native people as religious behavior. By contrast, Calvinist Protestants spurned all such rituals as idolatry, and focused instead on the austere preaching of the naked Word. As a Dutch Calvinist clergyman in New Netherland complained, Indians who wandered into his church on Sunday would "stand awhile and look, and afterwards ask me what I am doing and what I want, that I stand there alone and make so many words, while none of the rest may speak."[38]

On a practical level, too, Catholics had considerable advantages over Protestants, at least in the early seventeenth century. The great international religious monastic orders—the Dominicans, the Franciscans, the Jesuits—possessed the financing, the experience, and, most important, the full-time well-trained personnel to carry out sustained and effective missionary activities. Calvinists, whose doctrine of the priesthood of all believers held that ministers claimed professional status only in the context of their relationship with a particular congregation of church members, had no comparable means of deploying people whose sole occupation was to preach to Indians. "How can the Gospel be propagated without some special ministers, having the power Apostolical, to go forth to convert Indians or pagans?" asked a critic of New England Congregationalism.[39]

No Catholic religious order was better prepared for missionary work under the auspices of papal apostolic authority than the Society of Jesus, the Jesuits. Founded in 1540 for "the defense and propagation of the faith" and "the progress of souls in Christian life and doctrine," its priests were professional educators, forged in the struggle to save Europe from Protestant heresies. Many of those who served in the North American missions came with long prior teaching careers in schools and universities, and quite a few were accomplished linguists. Moreover, by the time Tekakwitha was baptized in 1675, over a generation of collective experience in North America had honed the linguistic, pedagogic, and political skills necessary to win a following in Native villages.[40]

Early on, the composition of that following could be explained in terms of Indian religious emphases on the control of relationships to mobilize spiritual power. Missionaries were entitled to respect not just because of the power they wielded as shamans but because they were representatives of a European community with which political ties, economic exchange, and military alliance were important. As one French Jesuit concluded, "the spiritual interests of these Missions depend largely on temporal affairs, and above all on the state of men's minds regarding the peace with the French." Indeed, given the fluid boundaries most Native people seem to have drawn between human and other-than-human persons, it would be misleading to try to distinguish among the political, material, and spiritual aims of those who dealt with European shaman-diplomats. The missionary who initially tutored Tekakwitha had arrived in her village under the terms of a 1667 treaty with the French in which Mohawk headmen "brought some of their families to serve as hostages, and be answerable for their countrymen's good faith" and "declared, among other things, that all their desires were to have some . . . Fathers with them, to cement the peace."[41]

Such diplomatic reciprocity was particularly important to Iroquois leaders in 1667 because the treaty of that year marked a brief moment of Iroquois weakness and French dominance in the Great Lakes region; it was not exactly an agreement among equals. The firearms advantage that since the 1630s had allowed Iroquois war parties in search of furs and captives to overrun such neighboring peoples as the Hurons, Eries, and Algonquins was being lost as enemies supplied from New France, New England, and the Delaware and Chesapeake Bays caught up in the Native American arms race. More dangerously, the economic links to New Netherland essential to that weapons advantage had collapsed in 1664, when the duke of York's English forces conquered the Dutch colony. And most significantly, Louis XIV had assumed direct control of New France in 1663 and had sent a thousand soldiers to North America with orders "totally to exterminate" the Iroquois, whose wars with the St. Lawrence

colony's Native trading partners had so often spilled over to involve
French colonists. In September 1666, those troops invaded the Mohawk
country and burned all its major villages. Early the next year, Mohawk
headmen had little choice but to agree to peace. Their counterparts in the
other four Iroquois nations had already done so two years earlier.[42]

As shamans and diplomats, then, missionaries entered Tekakwitha's
country from a position of great strength. In order to understand how she
and others may have come to see Jesuit power in positive terms and to
welcome an alliance with it, it helps to envision the deep divisions likely
to have prevailed in Native communities at such a particularly difficult
moment, when the social turmoil characteristic of mid-seventeenth-century eastern North America was compounded by the devastation left behind by the invasion of 1666. No doubt, many people reacted sullenly to
French shamans—sorcerers?—who preached the alien values of an enemy power. But others—clan chiefs, would-be headmen raised up by the
general ferment, military leaders more concerned with Indian than with
European foes—saw opportunities for new trading partners, new sources
of firearms, new alliances that might reinvigorate the community's spiritual and temporal power. Nor were the only, or even the most significant,
divisions among leaders who disagreed over political and diplomatic strategies. The cumulative result of the mid-seventeenth-century epidemics
that had struck all eastern Native groups and the successful military campaigns that the Iroquois had until recently waged against their neighbors
was that recently incorporated war captives made up an extraordinary
proportion of those who lived in their villages. Incredible as it may seem,
it is likely that as many as two thirds of the population traced their origins
to places elsewhere than Iroquoia.[43]

Among the throngs of captives was Tekakwitha's mother, an Algon-
quin prisoner who had been married to a native Mohawk. In a matrilineal
society, the girl's kinship ties therefore were already weak before smallpox
killed both of her parents and cast her adrift. The writings of Cholenec
and Chauchetière (whose understanding of matrilineal kinship may have
been only slightly better than that of the European audience for which
they wrote) are vague about the identity of the prominent "uncle" with
whom Tekakwitha went to live. Perhaps he was her father's brother;
more likely he was the headman of the lineage into which her mother

had been adopted. In either case, the young woman probably lacked the kind of kinship ties that might have rooted her in the community and have made up for the visual handicap that made her an economic liability to those with whom she lived. Factors such as these probably explain both the eagerness of her guardians to marry her off and their resentment when she refused the matches. It does not take much of a stretch of our imaginations to understand why a young woman trapped in such circumstances might find something attractive in the preaching of the French missionaries. Nor is it hard to imagine that, when the person now named Kateri left the Mohawk country to resettle at Kahnawake, she found there the kinship, the social acceptance, and the spiritual power she had never before had—under the tutelage of priests who supported her efforts and held her up as a model of piety, among the sisterhood of women who joined her in her chastity and penance, and within a broader community that identified itself as both Indian and Catholic.[44]

But these speculations about Kateri Tekakwitha's motives take us beyond the historical sources. What we can say is that such a story is consistent with general patterns in which hundreds of seventeenth-century Indians resettled in mission villages, both Catholic and Protestant. In an era when epidemics, war, and economic transformations were everywhere causing new communities to form from fragments of old ones, *reserves* and "praying towns" were among the many places in which Native Americans were reinventing themselves. Some, perhaps among them Kateri, relocated because their lives in former circumstances had been intolerable. Others, including many of Kateri's Mohawk contemporaries, did so in the midst of bitter political disputes. Others who migrated to mission villages did so because they were refugees whom epidemics and warfare had left with no other homes. Still others no doubt sought material benefits or simply followed kin who for whatever reason had previously determined to move. Most presumably found some sincere spiritual meaning in the beliefs they crafted from missionary teachings and their own religious traditions. In any number of ways, thousands of Native people thus found "a lifeboat to weather the storm" and "used Christianity to revitalize their lives in a world growing more and more unfriendly."[45]

Whatever factors may have been at work, there is no reason to doubt

that many—perhaps most—Indian converts to Christianity came deeply
to believe in the doctrines as well as the practices of the new belief system, without abandoning basic elements of the cultures in which they
had been born.[46] Oral tradition holds that the people of Kahnawake were
called *ongwe honwe tehatiisontha*, "real men who make the sign of the
cross."[47] They were neither the transculturated saints that European
mythmakers hoped they would be, nor the traitors to their people that
skeptics of our own time suspect them to have been. Who, after all, *were*
their people other than the members of the communities in which they
now found themselves? And what to them was Christianity but a way of
making sense of their condition and mobilizing the spiritual power the
missionaries inadequately described as "grace"? The inner life of Kateri
Tekakwitha may be beyond our capacity to recover, but the forces that
converged on her and on others who converted to Christianity in the seventeenth century are not. From an eastward-facing perspective, her story,
like that of Pocahontas, rises from deep roots in her own culture and her
own time. She symbolizes one of the many ways in which Native Americans tried to come to grips with the challenges of the seventeenth century
by incorporating people, things, and ideas from Europe into a world still
of their own making.

A third Native American biography is less well known today, for
neither a Disney film nor popular devotion keeps it alive. But in the eighteenth and early nineteenth centuries the mythic life of the New England
Algonquian leader "King Philip" was, if anything, more familiar to Anglo-
Americans than those of either Pocahontas or Tekakwitha. The story of
King Philip takes at least two distinct forms. Anglo-Americans in the colonial period told it something like this (the quotations come from a 1716
book titled *Entertaining Passages Relating to Philip's War*, written by the son
of Benjamin Church, military hero of the New England colonies' war
against Philip's Native forces in 1675–76):

> *The Pilgrim colony of Plymouth had lived in harmony with its Indian*
> *neighbors since the time of the First Thanksgiving in 1621. The wise*

policies of the Wampanoag chief Massasoit combined with the justice of the Puritan founders to preserve the peace. As was the practice among New England Indians, after Massasoit's death his office descended to his sons, first "King Alexander" (Wamsutta) and then "King Philip" (Metacom or Metacomet). Unlike his father, Philip inexplicably harbored deep resentments against the English. Almost immediately, he began "plotting a bloody design" and "sending his messengers to all the neighboring sachems, to engage them in a confederacy with him in the war." He bullied such peaceful Indians who tried to resist his recruiting efforts as the "squaw sachem" Awashonks by threatening to "send his men over privately, to kill the English cattle, and burn their houses . . . which would provoke the English to fall upon her, whom they would without doubt suppose the author of the mischief." Philip's minions soon "began their hostilities with plundering and destroying cattle," but "did not long content themselves with that game," because "they thirsted for English blood."[48] Between the summer of 1675 and the spring of 1676, a dozen or more English towns fell to his fury, forcing the colonists to abandon most of what is now western Massachusetts and northwestern Connecticut.

Finally, thanks to Benjamin Church's military genius and a few loyal Indian allies, in August 1676 Philip was cornered in a swamp and shot by a Christian Indian named Alderman. As the smoke of battle cleared, "Capt. Church ordered his body to be pulled out of the mire on to the upland, so some of Capt. Church's Indians took hold of him by his stockings, and some by his small breeches, (being otherwise naked) and drew him through the mud unto the upland, and a doleful, great, naked, dirty beast, he looked like. Capt. Church then said, 'That for as much as he had caused many an English man's body to lie unburied and rot above ground, that not one of his bones should be buried.' And calling his old Indian executioner, bid him behead and quarter him. Accordingly, he came with his hatchet and stood over him, but before he struck he made a small speech directing it to Philip; and said, 'He had been a very great man, and had made many a man afraid of him, but so big as he was he would now chop his ass for him'; and so went to work, and did as he was ordered. Philip having

one very remarkable hand being much scarred, occasioned by the split-
ting of a pistol in it formerly, Capt. Church gave the head and that
hand to Alderman, the Indian who shot him, to show to such gentle-
men as would bestow gratuities upon him; and accordingly he got
many a penny by it. This being on the last day of the week [before the
Puritan sabbath], the Captain with his company returned to the is-
land, tarried there until Tuesday; and then went off and ranged
through all the woods to Plymouth, and received their premium,
which was thirty shillings per head, for the enemies which they had
killed or taken, instead of all wages; and Philip's head went at the
same price."[49]

Church's book was repeatedly reissued, most notably in an 1825 edition reprinted at least ten times in the next two decades. In that later period, however, its gruesome portrait competed with a quite different Anglo-American image. One of the most popular dramatic productions of the pre–Civil War era was an 1829 play about King Philip by John Augustus Stone called *Metamora; or, The Last of the Wampanoags*.[50] The renowned Euro-American melodramatic actor Edwin Forrest played the title role hundreds of times in scores of theaters across the United States. He had chosen the script as the winner of a $500 prize he had offered for "the best tragedy, in five acts, of which the hero, or principal character, shall be an aboriginal of this country."[51] In the play,

When Benjamin Church meets the hero and calls him "Philip," the In-
dian leader rejects the name. "I am the Wampanoag chief,
Metamora," he proudly declares. Even the play's English colonists are
struck by "that lofty bearing—that majestic mien"—with which
earth's "proudest son" carries himself. "Is justice goodly? Metamora's
just. Is bravery virtue? Metamora's brave," an orphaned colonial boy
named Walter exclaims. "If love of country, child and wife and home,
be to deserve them all—he merits them," despite the fact that, as an-
other character points out, "he is a heathen." The English threat to
his country, his wife, and his home compels Metamora to take up a
cause to which the spirit of his father, Massasoit, calls him. "Chief of
the people, wake from thy dream of peace, and make sharp the point

of thy spear, for the destroyer's arm is made bare to smite," Massasoit
pleads in a vision. *"O son of my old age, arise like the tiger in great
wrath and snatch thy people from the devourer's jaws!"*[52] *Metamora's
crusade is, of course, doomed, but there is no sordid death in a swamp
for this hero. He prepares nobly for the end by first dispatching his beloved wife, Nahmeokee, with a merciful stab to save her from the
"white man's bondage."*[53] *As he falls to the bullets of Church's men,
Metamora pronounces "curses on you, white men! May the Great
Spirit curse you when he speaks in his war voice from the clouds! Murderers! The last of the Wampanoags' curse be on you! May your
graves and the graves of your children be in the path the red man shall
trace! And may the wolf and panther howl o'er your fleshless bones,
fit banquet for the destroyers!"*[54]

These apparently very different stories about King Philip might better
be understood as two aspects of a single mythic tale of the "savage" who
futilely resists the inevitable triumph of civilization. In Church's version,
Philip's savagery is complete and ignoble; the Indian leader is "a doleful,
great, naked, dirty beast" who deserves his fate. By contrast, Stone's
Metamora is what literary scholars recognize as a "noble savage" who
embodies all the virtues that "civilized" men lack. Both mythic Philips are
the antithesis of the civilized Christian European; positively or negatively
portrayed, Metacom's significance lies in his rejection of everything a
character like Church stands for. Facing westward, then, both of these
Philip stories are countermyths to the narratives of Pocahontas and
Kateri Tekakwitha. Philip irrationally (if perhaps nobly) scorns the conquerors with whom the young women more sensibly choose to assimi-
late. Indian to the core, he would rather fight than switch, although his efforts as the "last of the Wampanoags" are doomed. Despite its supposedly
ennobling vocabulary, such a "vision of Indian decline provided Euro-
Americans with ideological justification for forcibly removing Indians
from Native homelands." Narratives "about 'the last full-blooded Indian'
. . . betrayed their assumptions about racial purity, their wishful thinking
about Indian erasure, and their inability to grasp the complicated mosaic
of Indian survival."[55]

The lives of Pocahontas and Tekakwitha reflected patterns and choices far more deeply rooted in Indian culture than Euro-American myth-makers would have us believe. Might King Philip's story have been similarly complicated? Might his life too involve an effort to adapt to the new-comers' presence on Native terms? A few years before Metacom's War, at least one European colonist desperately hoped to place King Philip in exactly the same mythic category of Christian convert into which contemporaries were placing their idealized Pocahontas and Kateri. In 1671 Puritan missionary John Eliot published his *Indian Dialogues*, a collection of fictionalized typical conversations between Christian Indians and skeptical compatriots based on his nearly twenty years of experience in dealing with Native people. It is clear that the missionary and the Wampanoag leader had met, and it is likely that they discussed religion, but it would appear that Eliot engaged in more than a little wishful thinking in his discussion of Metacom's attitude toward Christianity.[56] Still, the missionary's portrait deserves attention, in the context of the other stories of Christian conversion we have been examining:

> "Old Mr. Eliot himself did come unto me," Philip said. "He was in this town, and did persuade me. But we were then in our sports, wherein I have much delighted, and in that temptation, I confess, I did neglect and despise the offer, and lost that opportunity. Since that time God hath afflicted and chastised me, and my heart doth begin to break. And I have some serious thoughts of accepting the offer, and turning to God, to become a praying Indian, I myself and all my people. But I have some great objections, which I cannot tell how to get over, which are still like great rocks in my way, over which I cannot climb." Philip's pride and his devotion to the worldly power and privileges of being a sachem prevented him from embracing the religion Pocahontas and Tekakwitha adopted. "In the way I am now," he said, "I am full and potent, but if I change my way and pray to God, I shall be empty and weak." Nonetheless, some glimmer of divine grace flickered in his heart. "Oh what mountains of sin have I heaped up in my wicked life!" he lamented. "My heart doth loathe myself to remember them. They make me abhorring to God."[57]

Fantastic as this version of Metacom's spiritual life may be, it points to a crucial factor in constructing an eastward-facing story of his life, for

Christianity was an inescapable force among Southern New England Algonquians in his day. If Pocahontas and Tekakwitha were unusual in their early embrace of European religion, Metacom might be forgiven for believing a day was at hand when non-Christian Indians would be in the minority. By 1650 English Calvinists had at least a handful of missionaries with time, linguistic talents, and political resources that approached those of French Jesuits. Eliot and his colleagues Thomas Mayhew Jr. and Richard Bourne, especially, had abilities similar to Kateri's confessors Cholenec and Chauchetière. Although these missionaries never enjoyed the funding or institutional support available to priests of the Society of Jesus, the New England Company for the Propagation of the Gospel, incorporated in 1649, provided them with funding from the British Isles in some ways similar to that enjoyed by the French fathers. And New England also found its parallel to the St. Lawrence *reserves* in what New Englanders called "praying towns." Pioneered by Eliot at Natick, Massachusetts, in 1651, these communities offered controlled environments in which residence was more tightly regulated and Christian morality as rigorously enforced as it was at Kateri's Kahnawake. In such environments, missionaries could appeal to the emotions of proselytes (some of whom were literate and many of whom knew some English) through word and prayer in a way that may in the long run have been even more effective than the nonverbal messages of Catholic ceremonies. Moreover, by cultivating a corps of literate Native teachers stationed in nearly every praying town, Puritans created an indigenous leadership that French Catholics, with their exclusively Euro-American clergy, could not match.[58]

In New England, the Protestant message assumed more power when, during a smallpox epidemic in 1650, it appeared that "the Indians who call[ed] upon God" were more likely to survive than, as Eliot put it, "their profane neighbors [who] were cut off."[59] As a result of these and other factors, by 1674, on the eve of the war that bears Metacom's English name, approximately 2,300 Native people lived in the praying towns of Massachusetts Bay, Plymouth, Martha's Vineyard, and Nantucket. Although for southern New England as a whole that figure represented only a little over 10 percent of a total Algonquian-speaking population of perhaps 20,000, in Plymouth and eastern Massachusetts the percentage was more like 25 percent. Among Metacom's Wampanoags, more than 600 out of 1,000 people had resettled in Christian communities. Of these varied souls, only about 350 throughout New England had met stringent Puritan standards for baptism; "all those we call praying Indians are not all visible church members, or baptized persons," Daniel Gookin explained.[60] Nonetheless, the trend toward Christian domination was clear.

Christian or not, New England Algonquians lived in a sea of some 60,000 English colonists. No place in that sea was more central than Wampanoag country, squeezed between the ill-defined boundaries of Rhode Island and Plymouth colonies. Metacom's home in the village of Sowams on Mount Hope Neck, near present-day Bristol, Rhode Island, was, moreover, less than thirty miles from territory claimed by Massachusetts to the north and Connecticut to the west. As this pinched geographical situation suggests, he had lived among and on intimate terms with the English all his life. Far from the stereotype of the untamed and implacable "savage" portrayed in the first two Philip narratives, Metacom knew and understood the English and their ways very well. Indeed, he not only regularly conversed with Eliot and his colleagues but also dealt frequently with colony and local officials. And—although he apparently never learned English and could not himself read and write—in the early 1670s he employed a literate, bilingual Christian Indian named John Sassamon as his secretary and aide. This relationship turned sour when Metacom, giving further evidence of both his wealth and his blending of cultural traditions, had Sassamon draw up a will for him. Sassamon supposedly "made the writing for a great part of the land to be his" own at the leader's death, but cleverly made the document "read as if it had been as Philip would."[61] Because of this deceit, and because Metacom had apparently more generally concluded that his aide was a spy, when Sassamon died mysteriously in early 1675, many Indians as well as English assumed Metacom had had him killed. Plymouth Colony's subsequent unilateral trial and execution of the presumed assassins was the spark that ignited the war of 1675–76.

If that war had not intervened to cloud our vision, Philip might have been remembered as a figure who every bit as thoroughly bridged the cultural divide as did Pocahontas and Tekakwitha. As one historian concludes, "Metacom's War was not a war between strangers but rather one between neighbors," who over the course of two generations "had learned much about each other in the course of trading, working, negotiating, socializing, suing, complaining to their leaders about one another, occasionally fighting, and—in a few cases—attending school and church and even living together."[62] Against this background of intense Indian-English interaction, a fourth portrait of Philip—this one from a present-day scholar—jars us thoroughly into an eastward-facing mode of making sense of Metacom's story:

> For three centuries historians have depicted Philip in many ways—as a savage chieftain, an implacable foe of innocent Christian settlers, and a doomed victim of European aggressors—but never as a keeper of swine.[63]

"Keeper of swine"? The language is inelegant, and certainly inadequate to characterize a complex personality. Nevertheless, at one point Metacom did keep a herd of pigs; in 1669 the clerk of Portsmouth, Rhode Island, threatened to take him to court unless he ceased ferrying them to "Hog Island" and turning them loose to forage on town lands. Perhaps nothing better symbolizes the economic and ecological incompatibility of European and Native American agriculture than swine. So perhaps nothing better symbolizes Metacom's efforts at cultural coexistence on his own terms than that he kept some of the very animals that most Native people found so odious. Just as effectively, the response of the Portsmouth town clerk—who had apparently never threatened any such legal action against an English hog owner—symbolizes the unwillingness of many colonists to accept those terms and their determination to use their court system to impose their will on Native people.[64]

It had not always been thus. The ability of Metacom and the Wampanoags to remain on their strategic piece of landscape was the product of a half-century-old policy of cooperation with English colonists in general, and of shrewd exploitation of ties with Plymouth Colony in particular. When the "Pilgrims" arrived at Plymouth in 1620, the people later known as Wampanoags were, along with their Massachusett neighbors to the north, almost unimaginably devastated by the epidemic that struck the New England coast from 1616 to 1618. Before the catastrophe, European visitors estimated that the several autonomous villages in the area around Cape Cod, Nantucket, and Martha's Vineyard could send

3,000 men into battle; if one of every five people was a warrior, that estimate would imply a total population of perhaps 15,000. By 1619, probably no more than 1,000 men, women, and children remained alive on the mainland. Compounding the disaster, the Massachusetts, the Wampanoags' traditional allies, had, if anything, been struck even harder, while the Narragansetts, their enemies to the west, apparently escaped almost unscathed and so were able to force the Wampanoags to cede territory to them.[65]

This weakened condition explains Massasoit's willingness to make a treaty with the Plymouth colonists in 1621. Its main points, as briefly summarized by Plymouth governor William Bradford, seem at first glance unexceptional. At second glance they appear remarkably one-sided. Massasoit agreed "that neither he nor any of his should injure" the English and that, if an injury did occur, "he should send the offender, that they might punish him." The English made no similar pledge to send lawbreakers to the Indians for punishment, but they did agree to a mutual return of any stolen property. More significantly, the two peoples became military allies: "If any did unjustly war against him, they would aid him; if any did war against them, he should aid them"—in the latter case, apparently, regardless of justice. Furthermore, Massasoit was to "send to his neighbors confederates to certify them of this, that they might not wrong them [the English], but might be likewise comprised in the conditions of peace."[66] This treaty—celebrated a year later in the First Thanksgiving—was less a reflection of godly Pilgrims making peace with the Indians than of a hardheaded divide-and-rule strategy. The Plymouth-Wampanoag alliance was to be the centerpiece of a broader network of diplomatic relationships and military intimidation of the Wampanoags' rivals designed to make Plymouth Colony the dominant political power in southern New England.[67]

Yet Massasoit and his people gained as much from the relationship as did the English. Reeling from disease and intimidated by the Narragansetts, the Wampanoags gained a powerful trading partner and ally. Their relationship with Plymouth allowed them not only to defend their own land base against colonial expansion, but to profit from the wampum trade and to extract tribute from their Indian neighbors, who had to deal with them before they could deal with the English. For both the

Wampanoags collectively and Massasoit personally, such benefits ran deep indeed. The extent to which, before the epidemics and the Pilgrims' arrival, there had been any centralized political leadership over the many local villages of today's southeastern Massachusetts is unclear. It is quite possible, however, that there had not, in fact, been anything like a Wampanoag or Pokanoket nation until Massasoit invented it from the surviving remnants who coalesced at Mount Hope Neck and a few other locations such as Mashpee on Cape Cod in the 1620s. Even if they did build upon already existing political affiliations, the unprecedented wealth, status, and influence of Massasoit and his descendants depended upon their successful manipulation of connections to the English. They were who they were, not because they were unspoiled noble or ignoble savages, but precisely because they adapted to and worked with European colonists.[68]

Like his older brother Wamsutta, Metacom, who was born in about 1640, was a product of the intercultural relationship and had never lived in a world without Europeans. If, as a genealogist has recently argued, they were grandsons rather than, as usually stated, sons of Massasoit, they would have been two generations removed from those who had. (Among Southern New England Algonquians, unlike most other eastern North American peoples, office descended primarily through the male line.) Members of "a confident and wealthy class of native American leaders" who thought themselves "surely the equal of any Englishman," they grew up in a "golden age" of material prosperity quite different from the era of disease and demoralization their grandparents faced in the 1610s.[69] "The roytelet now of the Pokanokets, that is the Plymouth-Indians, is Prince Philip alias Metacom, the grandson of Massasoit," Josselyn wrote, capturing something of the self-confident place that successful adaptation had carved out for such a leader. In the early 1660s, striding the streets of Boston with "a coat on and buckskins set thick with . . . [wampum] beads in pleasant wild works and a broad belt of the same," which Josselyn "valued at twenty pounds," life must have seemed good indeed. The trade goods that made up his conspicuous attire demonstrated both to his own people and to outsiders that Metacom had the political skill and personal connections necessary to survive in the bicultural world of mid-seventeenth-century New England.[70]

Speaking for his brother as well as for himself, Wamsutta acknowledged the extent to which their position depended on their relationship to
Plymouth in 1660, when he appeared before the colony's legislature to an-
nounce "that in regard his father is lately deceased" he was "desirous, according to the custom of the natives, to change his name" (that is, assume
a title appropriate to his new status), and that he hoped "the court would
confer an English name upon him."[71] The names the English chose for
Wamsutta and Metacom—Alexander and Philip, respectively—recalled
Alexander the Great and his half-brother and successor. For the Plymouth
colonists, the allusion to the ancient Macedonians evoked at least two
meanings. In the book of Acts, the Apostle Paul had a vision of Macedonians crying out to him, "Come over . . . and help us." Anyone familiar
with the official seal of the neighboring Massachusetts Bay colony would
have seen an image of a Gospel-starved Indian with the same words flowing from his mouth.[72] Yet these Puritan dreams of the Indians, which reso-
nate so well with Eliot's dreams of Metacom's redemption, must be
placed against the culture's popular interpretation of who the ancient
Philip was and what he had done: supposedly a bumbling halfwit, he had
presided over the collapse of his brother's great empire.[73] Pious hopes or
smirking insults—either way the names suggest the ideological domination English colonists wished to exert over their Native neighbors.

   From the 1660s through the early 1670s, that domination became more
than ideological, as the material conditions that had allowed the
Wampanoags and Metacom to flourish withered. A key factor was the im-
plosion of the wampum trade, on which much of southern New England
Native prosperity had been built. Previously, the shell beads had circulated
as currency within the New England colonies; this entirely Euro-American practice is the origin of the erroneous idea that wampum was "Indian
money." By the 1660s, however, the flourishing foreign commerce of the
colonies had brought sufficient silver coinage into the region to render
wampum superfluous. As colonists ceased to accept it in payment, traders
dumped their supplies on the already depressed markets of neighboring
New York colony, where the beads' value against specie fell over 200 percent within the decade. With wampum suddenly almost worthless to Europeans, the Wampanoags and their southern New England neighbors

Seal of the Massachusetts Bay Company: an Indian pleads:
"Come Over and Help Us."

From Increase Mather, *A Brief History of the War with the Indians in New-England*
(London, 1676). The Library Company of Philadelphia.

who had little direct access to furs found themselves with only one commodity that was in demand: land.[74]

For two generations, the Wampanoags' diplomacy had placed them in
alliance with the English against other Southern New England Algonquians whose real estate the colonists coveted. This strategy was most notable in the Pequot War of 1636–37, which opened up territory for the new
colonies of New Haven and Connecticut, and in 1645, when an English
threat of war forced the Wampanoags' old enemies the Narragansetts to

cede claims to most of the rest of the present-day Connecticut. In their willing participation in the game of divide and rule, the Wampanoags were hardly alone; the Mohegan leader Uncas, for instance, was the English point man in the Narragansett business and equally owed his position to cooperation with the colonists.[75] But by the 1660s the game was up for the Wampanoags. With no resources but land that the colonists wanted and few Native neighbors left toward which to channel European expansionism, their turn was next. They were now "dependents on, rather than partners in, New England's business," one historian concludes. "And that business . . . was strictly land development."[76]

If Metacom harbored any doubts about how seriously the balance of power had shifted away from the Wampanoags—and about how much English courts, churches, and praying towns were the wave of the future—those doubts must have been resolved by the episode that placed him in office in 1662. Wamsutta, having refused a demand that he appear in Plymouth to explain rumors of an Indian conspiracy against the English, was seized at gunpoint and hauled off for interrogation. Suffering from a fever and hardly able to stand, he barely survived a humiliating dressing down by Governor Thomas Prince. On the way back to Sowams, he died. Whether or not the English were directly responsible for Alexander's death, the naked display of power could not be ignored.[77] In 1671 the message of domination was reinforced. Metacom, having already been compelled to surrender a sizable cache of guns, but having resisted English demands for complete disarmament, was summoned to Plymouth to explain himself. Facing the governors of the Old Colony, Massachusetts Bay, and Connecticut in a meeting "conducted almost as though it were a criminal trial, with Philip at the bar of justice," he had to sign a treaty acknowledging "that he and his people were subject both to the royal government and to the colony government, and bound by their laws."[78]

That the colonists meant what they said about the authority of their legal regime was demonstrated in June 1675 when Plymouth executed those who allegedly killed John Sassamon for informing Plymouth governor Josiah Winslow that Metacom "was endeavoring to engage all the sachems round about in a war."[79] But the significance of the executions went still further. Governor Winslow had not even given any credit to Sassamon's report of military preparations, such was his contempt for

Metacom's power. Sassamon, moreover, was a "praying Indian," and his death—whether by accident or by foul play—seems to have been an occasion for Native Christian political opponents of Metacom to move against him. All the accused—Mattashunannamo, Tobias, and Wampapaquan— were close advisers of the Wampanoag leader; the accusers included a Christian named William Nahauton and an alleged eyewitness to the crime named Patuckson, who was apparently deeply in debt to Tobias. The influence of Native Christians also became evident in the composition of the trial jury, which featured six praying Indians sitting with the twelve English colonists who made the real decisions. It could not be more clear that the kind of mutually beneficial coexistence based on political and religious independence on which Metacom's predecessors had thrived was dead. If there was any future for Indians in New England, it lay in religious conversion and political capitulation.[80]

Or in preparations for violent revolt, which may have been only a rumor when Sassamon reported them in 1674 but in 1675 became a reality. As each side readied for battle, Rhode Island lieutenant governor John Easton (who was as worried about Plymouth Colony's intentions as he was about those of the Wampanoags) invited Metacom to explore ways in which affairs might still be reconciled. Metacom, or a spokesman for him, summarized his people's exasperation with their treatment by Plymouth, and in particular with the ways in which colonists had used their legal system to turn what had been a mutually profitable relationship into a relentless exercise of raw political power. The Wampanoags

said they had been the first in doing good to the English, and the English the first in doing wrong, [and they] said, when the English first came, their king's father was a great man and the English as a little child. He constrained other Indians from wronging the English and gave them corn and showed them how to plant and was free to do them any good and had let them have a 100 times more land, than now the king had for his own people, but their king's brother [Wamsutta], when he was king, came miserably to die by being forced to Court as they judged poisoned, and another grievance was [that] if 20 of their honest Indians testified that a[n] Englishman had done them wrong, it was as nothing, and if but one of their worst

Indians testified against any Indian or their king when it pleased the English that was sufficient. Another grievance was that when their kings sold land the English would say it was more than they agreed to and a writing must be proof against all them, and some of their kings had done wrong to sell so much [that] he left his people none and some being given to drunkenness the English made them drunk and then cheated them in bargains, but now their kings were forewarned not for to part with land for nothing in comparison to the value thereof. Now [those] whom the English had owned for king or queen [of Indian nations] they would disinherit, and make another king that would give or sell them their land, that now they had no hopes left to keep any land.[81]

Within days of this speech, apparently before Metacom himself had completed his military and diplomatic preparations, Wampanoags began attacking Plymouth towns. As their successes mounted, nearly all Southern New England Algonquian peoples (including many who used to pray to the Protestant God) joined the war. The only major exceptions were some Mohegans, Pequots, and Niantics who allied themselves with Connecticut. For a few months the Algonquian coalition seemed capable of pushing all the region's colonists back into the sea. Of some ninety English towns, more than fifty were attacked and at least twelve destroyed. The tide began to turn, however, during the winter of 1675–76. English forces, unable to engage their enemies in set battles, waged war against Native corn supplies instead, inducing severe food shortages and keeping the Indians on the run in the most difficult part of the year. Together, the two forms of hardship opened the way to a third, epidemic disease. Metacom and a substantial portion of his forces retreated to a winter encampment north of Albany, where they hoped to recover their health, replenish their weapons, and enlist additional allies. Instead they were attacked by Mohawks, who had long been at war with many elements of the southern New England Algonquian coalition and had been encouraged in their efforts by New York governor Edmund Andros. In the summer of 1676, victorious English forces—with the significant help of their remaining praying-town allies and other Indians—hunted down their enemies, including, as Church gleefully reported, Metacom himself.[82]

As with Pocahontas and Tekakwitha, most of what made Metacom tick remains beyond our reach. But we do know that, like Rebecca and Catherine, Philip willingly assumed a European name. Like theirs, his story—however mangled by later Euro-American myth-makers—would not even be remembered had he not attempted the kind of cultural adaptation that such a name implied. So, whatever else he may have been, Metacom was not a rebel against cultural change or against the English presence per se. It would be far more accurate to say he re-belled on behalf of *cooperation*—on behalf of the system of relatively equal intercultural relations under which he and his people had previ-ously prospered, but that the mid-seventeenth-century English were de-termined to destroy. On the eve of the outbreak of hostilities, in disillu-sioned words eerily reminiscent of those attributed to Pocahontas shortly before her death, Metacom told Easton that he "had a great fear to have any of their Indians . . . called or forced to be Christian Indians." Perhaps recalling his betrayal by the Christian John Sassamon, he said "that such were in everything more mischievous, only dissemblers, and then the English made them not subject to their kings, and by their lying to wrong their kings."[83]

At the very moment Metacom perished horrifically in a New Eng-land swamp, hundreds of miles to the south Virginians were waging their own brutal war against the heirs of Pocahontas. The conjunction of late-summer events in 1676 was more than a coincidence. For thirty years, In-dian-English relations had proceeded in remarkably similar ways in the two regions—with the notable exception of the Chesapeake colonists' lack of the Puritans' missionary zeal. In 1646, after Opechancanough had been captured and shot, Virginia governor Sir William Berkeley had made a peace treaty with the surviving fragments of the Powhatan chiefdom.

Under its terms, Chickahominies, Pamunkeys, Mataponis, and others became tributaries of the English government, and in theory the York River became the boundary between Indian and English territories. Colonists establishing new plantations quickly spread across the river, however, leaving the Indians confined to small patches of territory analogous to the praying towns of New England. Like the New England Algonquians, the 4,000 or so Indians who lived among some 40,000 Chesapeake colonists faced increasing subordination to English law, government, and culture. They lacked, however, a Metacom—and the betrayed tradition of successful cooperation with the English that he represented—to focus their grievances.[84]

The colonists, though, had a young English aristocrat named Nathaniel Bacon to focus *theirs*. In a society in which even Governor Berkeley admitted that "six parts in seven at least are poor, indebted, discontented, and armed," the prospects for coexistence with Native people were bleak; impoverished, propertyless Euro-Virginians who resented the dominance of the colony by a tiny elite pinned their grim hopes for the future on aggressive expansion into Indian country, where they might acquire tobacco land for themselves.[85] In their eyes, Berkeley's efforts to keep the peace by building defensive forts and enforcing boundaries between Native and English territories were among the many ways in which he betrayed the colonists' true interests. Levying new taxes to pay for these and doing so in a way that seemed to fall most heavily on the landless poor—who, because of their lack of property, had no right to vote—only increased the rage of what the elite referred to as "the giddy multitude." When Bacon, an ambitious recent arrival whose social status and kinship ties to the governor had earned him a seat on the colony's council, had a personal falling-out with Berkeley, he found a ready pool of political allies, although there is no evidence that he had any genuine concern for the mass of Virginia's poor. As unsympathetic royal investigators later put it, "he pretended and boasted what great service he would do for the country, in destroying the common enemy, securing their lives and estates, liberties, and such like fair frauds . . . which he seduced the vulgar and most ignorant people to believe . . . so that their whole hearts and hopes were set now upon Bacon."[86]

The tensions Bacon would exploit exploded in July 1675, when a group of Doeg Indians tried to take an English planter's hogs in retaliation for his failure to pay for goods he had purchased from them; their contemporary Metacom might have appreciated the symbolism of that blow against the most hated of all livestock. The Doegs were killed in the effort, however, and several months of raids and counterraids ensued, drawing into the conflict both English colonists from neighboring Maryland and a powerful Native ally of the Doegs, the Susquehannocks. Longtime customers of traders from Virginia and, especially, Maryland, the Susquehannocks had only recently accepted an invitation from the latter colony's government to abandon the Susquehanna Valley of present-day Pennsylvania for new homes on the Potomac River—closer to markets and farther from the Five Nations Iroquois enemies they had been fighting for decades. In December, after Berkeley's government had proven unable to control the escalating feud between colonists and Indians, some 1,000 Virginians and Marylanders took matters into their own hands and surrounded a Susquehannock fort. Under the cover of peace negotiations, the freelancers (led by, among others, John Washington, great-grandfather of George) assassinated several Susquehannock headmen.

That treachery brought down a full-scale war on both Chesapeake colonies every bit as deadly as the struggle going on in New England at the same time. Without authorization from Berkeley's government, Bacon assumed control of volunteers who indiscriminately killed Indians, including people from such previously uninvolved communities as the Pamunkeys and Appomatoxes, easy targets whose treaty-guaranteed lands were closest to the plantations. Declared rebels for their exploits, Bacon and his followers turned their fury on Berkeley's government and were joined by countless others—disfranchised poor and disgruntled rich, black and white, bound and free—who saw the chance to express their rage if not better their lot. The chaotic civil war known as Bacon's Rebellion collapsed shortly after its putative leader died of dysentery in October 1676. Rightly or wrongly, royal commissioners sent to investigate placed much of the blame on Berkeley, who was sent back to England and replaced by one of their number, Herbert Jeffreys. A few legal reforms were passed, but for the "giddy multitude" little else changed.[87]

Although the commissioners acknowledged that "violent intrusions of

divers English into their lands" had caused the war, Bacon's Rebellion was
an unmitigated disaster for the Native population of the Chesapeake region.[88] The Susquehannocks drifted back north in small bands. Powerless
against their Iroquois foes, most resettled under duress in Iroquoia, as had
thousands of others vanquished during the midcentury wars among the
region's Native peoples. Meanwhile, peace treaties with Virginia's tribu-
tary Indians in 1677 and 1680 effectively confined the Pamunkeys and their
allies to territories within a three-mile radius of their existing towns.[89]
Even those meager boundaries held no better than had earlier ones. After
Berkeley's experience, the colony's rulers discovered the political wisdom
of a relentlessly expansionist policy. "A governor of Virginia has to steer
between Scylla and Charybdis, either an Indian or a civil war," concluded
Alexander Spotswood, who held that post from 1710 to 1722; "Bacon's Rebellion was occasioned purely by the governor and council refusing to let
the people go out against the Indians who at that time annoyed the frontiers."[90]

"Indians who . . . annoyed the frontiers." That short descriptive
term embeds two powerful assumptions that, by the late seventeenth century, had become as common among New England colonists as among
Virginians: Native people were irrevocably opposed to English interests,
and they belonged, if anywhere, out on "the frontiers," far away from the
colonists they "annoyed." The English-speaking cultural descendants of
New Englanders and Virginians who have written most histories of the
North American continent have tended to make those assumptions seem
natural, and therefore to make clashes like Metacom's War and Bacon's
Rebellion appear inevitable. If the life stories of Rebecca, Kateri, and
Philip had any meaning for them, it was to drive the message of cultural
incompatibility home: Indians must either surrender gracefully to a superior Christian civilization or die in a futile attempt to resist.

Facing east from Indian country, however, the stories of Pocahontas,
Tekakwitha, and Metacom suggest a different set of possibilities. Each of
them sought cooperation rather than conflict, coexistence on shared regional patches of ground rather than arm's-length contact across distant

frontiers. By adoption and marriage, Pocahontas fulfilled her duty to Smith and Rolfe, made them kin, and so incorporated the Jamestown colony into the Powhatan political universe. By migration to Kahnawake, Tekakwitha joined hundreds of other Native people who embraced the Christian religion and recreated Native ties of kin and community in the shadow of French Montreal. In a comparable way, by shrewd exploitation of economic and political relationships that Massasoit had cultivated with the English, the young Metacom assumed he could advance the Wampanoags' unprecedented wealth and status to new heights. His community—like the Kahnawake Mohawks and indeed briefly Powhatan's chiefdom—had at one time flourished because of its proximity to Europeans, not despite it. If a mutually beneficial partnership collapsed, Indian inflexibility was not to blame.

Pocahontas and Metacom perished embittered and disillusioned, surrounded by their enemies; Tekakwitha passed with "an odor of sanctity" among people she loved. None of these three early deaths is understandable apart from the material forces that reshaped the lives of all Native Americans in the seventeenth century. But the contrasts among the three life stories demonstrate that there was nothing inevitable about the ways in which human beings—European and Indian—shaped their responses and in which Native people continued to adapt their traditions creatively to new conditions. Not all the North American world was New England and Virginia, and not all colonial history was the story told by the English-speaking victors.

NATIVE VOICES IN
A COLONIAL WORLD

THE COLONIAL HISTORIES told by English-speaking victors shout across the centuries, but stories told in Native voices are far more difficult to hear. Through the era of Tekakwitha and Metacom, literate Indians remained exceedingly rare, and surviving documents they penned in either Native or European languages are rarer still. Records composed by Europeans for Europeans provide virtually our only sources of written information about how Native people may have seen the world and understood relationships between their communities and the colonizers, and, for the most part, these records tell us much more about their authors than about the Indians whose lives they purport to describe.[1]

Nonetheless, two substantial bodies of documents created by late seventeenth-century colonists do record—in English translation—Native Americans telling stories about their own situations. In the praying towns of Massachusetts before Metacom's War, Puritan missionaries transcribed the conversion narratives, or spiritual autobiographies, of their Indian converts. In Albany and other strategic colonial towns, government scribes meticulously recorded the speeches of Native diplomats negotiating with representatives of imperial governments. These two kinds of documents differ dramatically in their nature and purposes, and, as translations made by Europeans with biased motives and limited linguistic talents, they present multitudinous problems to their readers. Still, they share two great strengths: they preserve something of what Indian people said at important personal and political moments in their lives, and they originated as largely self-contained oral texts, whose structure was largely

under the Native speaker's, not the European scribe's, control. Read carefully, each in its very different way reveals Indian people trying to adapt
traditional ideals of human relationships based on reciprocity and mutual
respect to a situation in which Europeans were becoming a dominant
force in eastern North America.

On 13 October 1652, missionary John Eliot convened a group of
Massachusetts Bay clergy and political leaders at Natick—the praying
town he had established a little over a year earlier—to hear a group of his
proselytes make public professions of their faith. If the assembled wor-
thies found the speeches convincing, the Native Christians would be permitted to establish what Puritans called a "gathered church" of "visible
saints." For a variety of reasons, things did not go as planned. Only five
speakers were able to tell their stories before daylight waned, and the audience, clearly impatient with the whole business, determined that "the
place being remote in the woods, the nights long and cold and people not
fitted to lie abroad, and no competent lodgings in the place for such persons, and the work of such moment as would not admit an huddling up in
haste," it was time to close up shop. An Indian church would not be gathered at Natick until 1663.[2]

In the meantime, however, to solicit financial and spiritual support for
his work, in 1653 Eliot and Thomas Mayhew, his missionary colleague on
Martha's Vineyard, published in London *Tears of Repentance,* a collection
of twenty-six conversion narratives by fifteen Natick people.[3] The most
extensive narratives in the collection were two by a literate man named
Monequassun, who assisted Eliot as a schoolmaster. English Puritans on
both sides of the Atlantic read his October speech this way:

Monequassun,
   *The confession which he made on the fast day before the great assembly
   was as followeth*
   I confess my sins before the Lord, and before men this day. A little
while since I did commit many sins, both in my hands and heart;
lusts, thefts, and many other sins, and that every day. And after I

heard of praying to God, and that others prayed to God, my heart did not like it, but hated it, yea and mocked at it; and after they prayed at Cohannet I still hated it, and when I heard the Word I did not like of it but thought of running away, because I loved sin. But I loved the place of my dwelling, and therefore I thought I will rather pray to God, and began to do it; a little I desired to learn the Ten Commandments of God, and other points of catechism; and then a little I repented, but I was quickly weary of repentance, and fell again to sin, and full of evil thoughts was my heart. And then I played the hypocrite, and my heart was full of sin. I learned some things, but did not do what God commanded, but I sinned and played the hypocrite; some things I did before man but not before God.

But afterward I feared because of my sins, and feared punishment for my sins, therefore I thought again I would run away; yet again, I loving the place, would not run away, but would pray to God; and I asked a question at the [missionary's] lecture, which was this, "How I should get wisdom?" The answer made me a little to understand. But afterward I heard the Word, "If any man lack wisdom, let him ask it of God, who giveth liberally to all that ask, and upbraideth none." But then I did fear God's anger, because of all my sins, because they were great. Afterward hearing that Word, that Christ is named Jesus, because he redeemeth us from all our sins, I thought Christ would not save me, because I repent not, for he saveth only penitent believers; but I am not such an one, but still a daily sinner. Afterward hearing that Word, "Blessed are they that hunger and thirst after righteousness for they shall be filled," then I thought I am a poor sinner and poor is my heart. Then I prayed to God to teach me to do that which he requireth, and to pray aright. Afterward hearing that Word, "Who ever looks upon a woman to lust after her, hath already committed adultery with her in his heart," then I thought I had done all manner of sins in the sight of God, because he seeth lust in the heart, and knoweth all the evil thoughts of my heart; and then I did pray unto God, "Oh! give me repentance and pardon."

Afterwards when I did teach among the Indians, I was much humbled because I could not read right, and that I sinned in it; for I saw that when I thought to do a good work, I sinned in doing it, for I knew not what was right nor how to do it. In the night I was considering of my sins and could not find what to do. Three nights I considered what to do, and at last God showed me mercy, and showed me what I should do. And then I desired to learn to read God's Word, and hearing that if we ask wisdom of God, he will give it, then I did much pray to God, that he would teach me to read.

After a year's time, I thought I did not rightly seek, and I thought I sinned, because I did not rightly desire to read God's Word, and I thought my praying was sinful, and I feared, how should I, my wife, and child be clothed, if I spend my time in learning to read; but then God was merciful to me, and showed me that Word, "Say not, what shall I eat, or drink, or wherewith shall I be clothed. Wicked men seek after these; but first seek the Kingdom of Heaven, and these things shall be added to you"; then I prayed God to teach me this Word, and that I might do it. And then I desired to read God's Word, whatever I wanted.

Afterward hearing that we must make a town, and gather a church at Natick, my heart disliked that place; but hearing that Word, "That Christ met two fishers, and said, 'Follow me, and I will make you fishers of men,' and presently they left all and followed him"; hearing this I was much troubled, because I had not believed Christ, for I would not follow him to make a church, nor had I done what he commanded me, and then I was troubled for all my sins. Again hearing that Word "That the blind man called after Christ, saying, 'Thou Son of David have mercy on me'; Christ asked him what he would have him do; he said, 'Lord open my eyes'"; and presently Christ gave him sight, and he followed Christ: then again my heart was troubled, for I thought I still believe not, because I do not follow Christ, nor hath he yet opened mine eyes. Then I prayed to Christ to open my eyes, that I might see what to do, because I am blind and cannot see how to follow Christ, and do what he commandeth, and I prayed to Christ, "Teach me Lord what to do, and to do what thou sayest"; and I prayed that I might follow Christ: and then I thought, "I will follow Christ to make a church." All this trouble I had to be brought to be willing to make a church.

And quickly after, God laid upon me more trouble, by sickness

and death; and then I much prayed to God for life, for we were all
sick, and then God would not hear me, to give us life; but first one of
my children died, and after that my wife; then I was in great sorrow,
because I thought God would not hear me, and I thought it was because I would not follow him, therefore he hears not me. Then I
found this sin in my heart, that I was angry at the punishment of
God. But afterward I considered, I was a poor sinner, I have nothing,
nor child, nor wife; I deserve that God should take away all mercies
from me; and then I repented of my sins, and did much pray, and I
remembered the promise to follow Christ, and my heart said, I had
in this sinned, that [I] followed not Christ, and therefore I cried for
pardon of this sin. And then hearing of this Word, "Who ever believeth in Christ, his sins are pardoned, he believing that Christ died for
us"; and I believed.

Again hearing that Word, "If ye be not converted, and become as
a little child you cannot go to heaven"; then my heart thought, "I do
not this, but I deserve hell fire forever"; and then I prayed Christ,
"Oh! turn me from my sin, and teach me to hear thy Word"; and I
prayed to my Father in heaven. And after this, I believed in Christ for
pardon.

Afterward I heard that Word, that it is a shame for a man to wear
long hair, and that there was no such custom in the churches. At first
I thought I loved not long hair, but I did and found it very hard to cut
it off; and then I prayed to God to pardon that sin also: Afterward I
thought my heart cared not for the Word of God. But then I thought
I would give myself up unto the Lord, to do all his Word. Afterward
I heard that Word, "If thy right foot offend thee, cut it off, or thy
right hand, or thy right eye; it's better to go to heaven with one foot,
or hand, or eye, than having both to go to hell"; then I thought my
hair had been a stumbling to me, therefore I cut it off, and grieved
for this sin, and prayed for pardon. After hearing that Word, "Come
unto me all ye that are weary and heavy laden with your sins, and I
will give rest to your souls"; then my heart thought that I do daily
hate my sins, Oh! that I could go to Christ! And Christ looketh I
should come unto him, and therefore then I prayed, "Oh! Christ help
me to come unto thee." And I prayed because of all my sins that
they may be pardoned.

For the first man was made like God in holiness, and righteousness, and God gave him his covenant; but Adam sinned, believing
the Devil, therefore God was angry, and therefore all we children of
Adam are like the Devil, and daily sin, and break every law of God,
full of evil thoughts, words, and works, and only Christ can deliver
us from our sins. He that believeth in Christ is pardoned; but my
heart of myself cannot believe. Satan hath power in me, but I cry to
God, "Oh! give me faith, and pardon my sin, because Christ alone
can deliver me from hell"; therefore I pray, "Oh! Jesus Christ deliver
me." Christ hath provided the new covenant to save believers in
Christ, therefore I desire to give my soul to Christ, for pardon of all
my sins. The first covenant is broke by sin, and we deserve hell; but
Christ keepeth for us the new covenant, and therefore I betrust my
soul with Christ. Again, I desire to believe in Christ, because Christ
will come to judgment, and all shall rise again, and all believers in
this life shall then be saved; therefore I desire to believe Christ, and
mortify sin as long as I live; and I pray Christ to help me to believe.
And I thank God for all his mercies every day: and now I confess before God that I loath myself for my sins and beg pardon.

Thus far he went in his confession; but they being slow of
speech, time was far spent, and a great assembly of English understanding nothing he said, only waiting for my [Eliot's] interpretation, many of them went forth, others whispered, and a
great confusion was in the house and abroad. And I perceived
that the graver sort thought the time long, therefore knowing
he had spoken enough unto satisfaction (at least as I judged) I
here took him off. Then one of the elders asked if I took him
off, or whether had he finished? I answered that I took him off.
So after my reading what he had said, we called another.[4]

At first glance, a Native voice seems nowhere to be heard in this document. Monequassun's interminable expressions of self-flagellating piety
are off-putting to modern readers, who are likely to squirm in their seats
far more quickly than did his original audience. And, when we can manage to follow it, the rhetoric strikes us as hardly "Indian" at all—whatever
that vague adjective might mean. Although the tormented Monequassun

Tears of Repentance:
Or, A further
Narrative of the Progress of the *Gospel*
Amongst the

INDIANS
IN
NEW-ENGLAND:

Setting forth, not only their present state and condition, but sundry Confessions of sin by divers of the said *Indians*, wrought upon by the saving Power of the Gospel; Together with the manifestation of their *Faith* and *Hope* in *Jesus Christ*, and the Work of Grace upon their Hearts.

Related by Mr. *Eliot* and Mr. *Mayhew*, two Faithful Laborers in that Work of the Lord.

Published by the Corporation for propagating the Gospel there, for the Satisfaction and Comfort of such as wish well thereunto.

Isay. 42. 3. *A bruised Reed shall he not break; and the smoaking Flax, shall he not quench.*

London: Printed by *Peter Cole* in *Leaden-Hall*, and are to Sold at his Shop, at the Sign of the Printing-Press in Cornhill, near the Royal Exchange. 1653.

MAMUSSE
WUNNEETUPANATAMWE
UP-BIBLUM GOD
NANEESWE
NUKKONE TESTAMENT
KAH WONK
WUSKU TESTAMENT.

Ne quoshkinnumuk nashpe Wuttinneumoh *CHRIST* noh asoowesit

JOHN ELIOT.

CAMBRIDGE:
Printeuoop nashpe *Samuel Green* kah *Marmaduke Johnson.*
1663.

John Eliot's Indian Bible and collection of Native American conversion narratives.
Annenberg Rare Book and Manuscript Library, University of Pennsylvania; The Library Company of Philadelphia.

used his native Massachusett tongue, even in this English translation he appears to be speaking a foreign language. In part, that was because many Christian terms—especially those dealing with the concepts of sin and redemption central to a spiritual autobiography—had no direct equivalents in Algonquian vocabulary. A glance at the title of Eliot's Massachusett-language "Indian Bible" illustrates the problem: the four most important of the eleven words in *Mamusse Wunneetupanatamwe Up-Biblum God Naneeswe Nukkone Testament Kah Wonk Wusku Testament* are European imports.[5]

Monequassun, of course, learned his Christian vocabulary from Eliot, who recorded his words. The possibility arises, then, that—as happened a few years later in Eliot's frankly fictionalized *Indian Dialogues*—the missionary, not the Indian, composed the speech. There are strong indications, however, that the phrases in *Tears of Repentance* are indeed those of Natick people, heavily influenced but not dictated by their teacher. One clue is that Eliot recorded multiple versions of the stories of Monequassun and eight other converts. Though similar in the general outlines, the renditions vary markedly in detail and emphasis, suggesting considerable spontaneity in the speakers' performances. That Eliot tells us the assembled Anglo-American elders were restless is another important clue that Monequassun was speaking in his own voice, as is the more general impression Eliot conveys that the entire October performance was something of a disaster. Would the missionary have fabricated such an imperfect and inconsistent record of his big day, especially with a well-connected skeptical audience present to contradict him? Questions remain, but it seems likely that the narratives recorded in *Tears of Repentance* are a reasonably authentic record of the converts' speeches.[6]

That said, however, the accuracy of any record of an Indian-language oral performance that comes down to us only in European words written by European hands remains problematic. Even under the best of circumstances, translation is a tricky art, dependent not only on the linguistic aptitude of the translator but on an ability to make subtle cultural references comprehensible in foreign contexts. In 1652 Eliot had been studying Massachusett under the tutelage of John Sassamon and a Montauk Indian named Cockenoe for the better part of a decade, had been preaching in the language for six years, and was at work on a translation of the cate-

chism that would be published two years later.[7] Yet "the Apostle to the Indians" was apparently far from completely fluent; in recording the confessions, he admitted, "Oft I was forced to inquire of my interpreter (who sat
by me) because I did not perfectly understand some sentences." At best,
he said, his transcripts had "rather rendered them weaker (for the most
part) than they delivered them; partly by missing some words of weight
in some sentences, partly by my short and curt touches of what they
more fully spake, and partly by reason of the different idioms of their language and ours."[8] Those "different idioms" were no minor issue. The
complex discursive universe of symbols and associations in which words
are embedded ensures that translation from any language into another—
even by the most skilled interpreter—can never be straightforward.[9]

More than limited linguistic skills and the need to summarize got in the
way of clear translation from the Massachusett tongue to English and ob-
scures our ability to hear the converts tell their stories in their own way.
On that long October day, Eliot apparently acted as both translator and
scribe, although he had some assistance from bilingual Indians. He had to
ask converts to speak unnaturally slowly in order to give him time to
write; how much that may have disrupted their trains of thought cannot
be easily estimated. Moreover, any attempt to summarize a complicated
Massachusett performance in simple English must have stripped away
much of what actually transpired. On at least one occasion, for example,
Eliot was so caught up in scribbling that he failed to notice that the leader
Waban—his first important proselyte, whose influence the missionary
had carefully cultivated if not created, and perhaps the most important
man in Natick—"spake . . . with tears." That Boston minister John Wilson
did notice in a way that got recorded for us to read is the exception rather
than the rule.[10] Oral narratives reduced to written texts lose not only tears
and laughter but the verbal emphases and body language that convey
much of the emotional content of the speakers' messages.

Further complications derive from Puritan theological assumptions
and rhetorical conventions. Even if Monequassun had been born and
raised in London rather than in Massachusett country, these conventions
would have made his speech seem quite foreign to us, for the structure of
any conversion narrative was rooted in Calvinist teachings about how
God's grace worked in people's lives. To Puritans, one of the remarkable

aspects of divine mercy was that God voluntarily placed limits on his omnipotence. Through the "covenants" he made with humankind, he agreed to operate by rational procedures that mere mortals could understand. In keeping with this fundamental belief, English Puritan theologians identified a "morphology of conversion"—a predictable set of stages through which God made a person aware that he or she was predestined for salvation. To modern, secular ears this morphology may sound like a dry doctrinal checklist. To seventeenth-century Puritans, however, it described a profound personal spiritual experience, a psychological transformation, an emotional rather than intellectual phenomenon. Not doctrine, but "prayer, meditation, and the almost sensual joy of intimate communion with a living God were for Eliot, as for other Puritans, at the heart of true religion."[11]

Among the most elaborate and widely known attempts to delineate the morphology of conversion was that of clergyman William Perkins, who identified ten stages. First was attention to God's word as articulated by scripture or preaching, perhaps with the assistance of a particular stroke of misfortune "to break and subdue the stubbornness of our nature." With the sinner's attention thus focused, the next stage brought a genuine understanding of divine law and of the nature of good and evil. This produced, third, an awareness of one's own specific sins and, fourth, what Perkins labeled "legal fear" and others called "conviction" or "humiliation"—a profound awareness of how innately sinful one was, of how utterly helpless one was to measure up to God's standards. In the depth of this despair, so crucial to the psychology of Puritan religious experience, God gave his predestined saints, fifth, an ability to consider seriously the Gospel's promise of salvation and, sixth, the gift of the first glimmer of faith, of "a will and desire to believe." Both of these, Puritans argued, were entirely God's doing. Humans were deluding themselves if they thought they could achieve them by their own efforts. Nonetheless, the sixth stage almost immediately gave way to a seventh, marked by desperate combat between faith on the one hand and despair and doubt on the other. This struggle—which would not cease until the "glorification" that most believed came only after mortal life had ended—was also central to the Puritan experience. Indeed, the surest sign of false, hypocritical belief was a prideful certainty that one was well and truly "saved." Still, eighth, God did give his saints in this world some "assurance" of his mercy. That enabled, ninth, a new kind of "evangelical sorrow" that transcended mere legalism to produce "a grief for sin, because it is sin," disruptive of one's relationship to God. Finally, Perkins argued, in the midst of struggle and continued human imperfection, God gave his saints sufficient grace to begin, however imperfectly, to obey his commandments and to perform the truly good works that were the product, not the cause, of salvation.[12]

Others condensed Perkins' list to as few as five stages, and one widely held view was that a conversion narrative really only had to testify to the movement from legal fear to reliance on divine grace. "I knew no more of that work of conversion," a preacher concluded, "than these two general heads, that a man was troubled in conscience for his sins, and afterwards was comforted by the favor of God manifested to him."[13] But, long or short, to one degree or another, Puritan ministers taught their flocks to tell stories about themselves that in some way conformed to the morphology. As Eliot put it, Christians should "try their hearts by the Word of God, to find out what change the Lord hath wrought."[14] The result was a highly constrained literary form, the product of intensive training in how the conversion process was supposed to work. These formal constraints, however, no more prevented personal imaginative expression for conversion narrators than they did for contemporary European composers of sonnets or fugues. Measuring themselves against the morphology of conversion, English-speaking Puritans charted distinctive accounts of their individual spiritual lives; each produced a unique, emotional, turn on standard themes.[15] Variations within the common framework existed for groups as well as individuals. Conversion narratives written by first-generation New England colonists, for example, differed in important ways from those written by their English Puritan contemporaries and by their second-generation colonial successors.[16]

This tendency for different groups to approach the common themes of the conversion narrative in distinctive ways provides our best opportunity to locate a distinctively Native voice amid the cacophony of interfering noises heard in the conversion narratives.[17] A content analysis of the speeches published in *Tears of Repentance* shows that all the Natick converts described their progress at least through the first four morphological stages of hearing the Word, understanding the law, recognizing their personal sinfulness, and despairing in "legal fear." Like Monequassun, upon whom God "laid . . . trouble, by sickness and death," six narrators associated their harkening to the Word with their own or family members' illnesses. One of them, Antony, further had his attention focused while he and a partner were operating a pit saw: a piece of wood got loose, struck his head, and nearly killed him.[18] Having heard the Word and recognized their sins, all but one narrator described how, in the midst of despair, God had given them an awareness of his promise of salvation. "Hearing of this Word, 'Whoever believeth in Christ, his sins are pardoned,'" Monequassun recalled, "I believed." The exception was a "poor publican" named Ephraim, whose Massachusett name Eliot said he had "forgotten." "I think that God will not forgive me my sins: every day my heart sinneth, and how will Christ forgive such an one?" he lamented. "I pray but outwardly with my mouth, not with my heart; I cannot of myself obtain pardon of my sins."[19] No Puritan would have been surprised at this. Any human being could reach "legal fear" by his or her own efforts, but only God's mysterious predestined grace, apparently not revealed to poor Ephraim, could take one further.[20]

On those further stages, the conformance of the Natick narratives to the standard morphology of conversion is less clear. Only five of the narrators explicitly referred to the divine gift of faith or the will to believe. These, along with three others, also described, often in considerable detail, the seventh stage of combat between faith and doubt that consumes so much of Monequassun's tale. Thus eight narrators at least implicitly told stories that conformed to Puritan expectations of the workings of grace through faith.[21] Significantly, however, seven did not do so, and even those who did diverged from their Anglo-American counterparts in the vagueness with which they described the arrival of faith in their lives. English colonial saints almost invariably recalled a specific occasion on which they first perceived God's grace at work.[22] None of the Natick converts did so. Moreover, they rarely discussed the final three steps in the standard morphology: "assurance," "evangelical sorrow," and the grace-inspired ability to do truly good works.[23] These elements, particularly "assurance," occur infrequently in Anglo-American narratives as well. It was, after all, difficult to speak of one's assurance of salvation without lapsing into the kind of prideful certainty that labeled one a hypocrite on the way to hell. "As for assurance of faith I can't or dare not say but I hope I have closed with the Lord Jesus as mine," said one Cambridge Puritan who got the tone right; "therefore . . . in some poor measure I can see and do truth after that he hath broke the reigning power and dominions of my sins."[24]

Notably, what Puritans called the "evidences" of graceful good works are mentioned in only one Natick account, and then in a particularly revealing way. "I thought God would not pardon me and yet I would cast away my sins," said John Speen when he told his story. "I did greatly love hunting, and hated labor: but now I believe that word of God, which saith, 'Six days thou shalt labor,' and God doth make my body strong to labor"—presumably for the greater glory of the Creator and the benefit of the community. Although Speen gave God credit for his newfound ability to work hard, perhaps because he emphasized his own, rather than God's, determination to "cast away" sin, Eliot considered "this confession . . . short in some main points." Having gotten the Calvinist message about the futility of human effort, Speen told his story again at a later date, this time stopping safely at a stage-six account of his faith: "I deserve not one mercy of God, but Christ hath merited all mercies for us."[25] So much for good works as evidence of grace. Indeed, it is hard to escape the conclusion that the Natick converts found it appropriate to tell stories focused far more on "that a man was troubled in conscience for his sins" than on that he "afterwards was comforted by the favor of God manifested to him."

The Natick converts described the sins for which atonement and comfort remained elusive in distinctive ways. Monequassun began his narrative with the words "I confess my sins before the Lord, and before men," and, like most of the fifteen converts, he went on to discuss various categories of transgressions. Few narrators went into specific salacious detail, but the vast majority of offenses they chose to emphasize involved what Puritans called the "Second Table" of the Ten Commandments, sins against people rather than against God alone.[26] Each of the thirteen narrators who mentioned particular sins referred to infractions of the Second Table; only six also mentioned the First Table.[27] By far the commandment most honored in the breach was the Seventh, "Thou shalt not commit adultery," noted in twelve of the confessions. Only four narrators specifically charged themselves with breaking their marriage vows, but eleven (including three of the confessed adulterers) spoke, as did Monequassun, more vaguely of their "lust" or "lusts." By this they probably meant any number of ways in which they succumbed to bodily desires. Puritan theologians used the Seventh Commandment to cover a multitude of sins, including fornication, drunkenness (interestingly not mentioned specifically in any of the Eliot narratives), and associating with loose characters.[28] The Eighth Commandment—"Thou shalt not steal"— figured in five of the narratives; three mentioned theft and two the ill-gotten gains of gambling. Three narrators charged themselves with lying (breaking the Ninth Commandment), two with covetousness (the Tenth), and one with killing (the Sixth). What is sometimes referred to as the Eleventh Commandment, Christ's injunction to "love thy neighbor as thyself," was violated by four narrators, who mentioned their hatred of others.[29]

Of the more rarely mentioned First Table commandments, only the First ("Thou shalt have no other Gods before me") and the Fourth ("Remember the Sabbath Day to keep it holy") appeared in the narratives. Perhaps because it was so self-evident a sin among people who must have grown up paying ceremonial respect to a multitude of other-than-human persons, only five of the fifteen found it necessary to mention, as Nataôus ("William of Sudbury") did, that they "loved to pray to many gods."[30] Similarly, sabbath-breaking as such was mentioned by only three converts, among them a man named Magus, who joined John Speen in evoking the Fourth Commandment to put his difficulties with European work habits in the context of rebelling against God's plan for six days of labor and one of rest.[31] Finally, one more sin mentioned specifically by at least six narrators needs to join the list of First Table offenses: pride, which Puritan diarist Michael Wigglesworth labeled "the vilest idolatry that can be imagined." To break the Second Commandment by "adoring some self-excellency," he explained, was "to adore a sinner, an enemy to god."[32]

The selective emphasis on sins against people sets the Indian narratives apart from their English and New English counterparts, in which sins against God alone overwhelmingly predominate. One study of a group of colonists' confessions recorded by three Massachusetts Bay clergymen, for instance, concludes that First Commandment transgressions alone accounted for about 40 percent of the sins mentioned in narratives, a figure greater than all references to Second Table sins combined.[33] The English colonial emphasis on First Table sins in turn reflects a stress more on be-lief—on conditions of the heart—than on behavior in religious experi-ence. Christian behavior and Christlike virtues were, of course, vitally im-portant, but for the English saint these took on merit only when they flowed from the God-given grace within. Even the grammar that English Puritans chose reflected this primacy of belief over behavior. In the later stages of the widely read conversion narrative of Elizabeth White, for in-stance, "almost all the verbs have to do with perceptions, rather than ac-tions: 'heard,' 'hearing,' 'saw,' 'seeing,' 'thought,' 'found Christ to me.'" By contrast, in the early sections describing her life before her experience of grace, "even negative verbs are active: 'I questioned,' 'I doubted,' 'I fell.'" Such a tale of progress "from a condition of doing to a condition of being or abiding" is notably absent from the Natick narratives.[34] Even as Monequassun in a quite orthodox way described his own combat be-tween faith and doubt, his verbs remained active: "I betrust my soul with Christ"; "I desire to believe"; "I pray Christ to help me to believe"; "I thank God for all his mercies every day: and now I confess before God that I loath my self for my sins and beg pardon." Others took a similarly strenuous approach to their spirit-led repentance. "I desire pardon in Christ; I betrust my soul with Christ, that he may do it for me," exclaimed Ponampam.[35] Active behavior rather than perceptive belief seems to have been paramount to the Natick converts.

To some degree, this emphasis on action must have arisen because sev-enteenth-century Protestant missionaries relentlessly hammered home the sinfulness of basic patterns of behavior rooted in Native culture. In his first recorded sermon, for example, Eliot began "with a repetition of the Ten Commandments, and a brief explication of them, then showing the curse and dreadful wrath of God against all those who break them, or any one of them, or the least title of them, and so applied it to the condi-tion of the Indians present, with much sweet affection."[36] Native kinship patterns, work habits, housing styles, sartorial preferences all seemed pro-foundly ungodly to missionaries unable to separate Christianity from Eu-ropean culture; thus what they called "civility" became a prerequisite to "sanctity." In his introduction to *Tears of Repentance,* Eliot explained that

until Indians "were come up unto civil cohabitation, government, and Labor, which a fixed condition of life will put them upon, they were not so
capable to be betrusted with that treasure of Christ, lest they should scan-
dalize the same." There was, in his mind, no sense in attempting to judge
the state of Indians' souls until their behavior measured up, as shown in
their "being come under civil order, and fixing themselves in habitations,
and bending themselves to labor, as doth appear by their works of
fencings, buildings, etc., and especially in building, without any English
workman's help or direction, a very sufficient meeting-house."[37] New
England cleric Cotton Mather later put it more bluntly. Eliot's task, he
said, "was to make men of them, ere he could hope to see them saints;
they must be civilized, ere they could be Christianized."[38]

With such messages—on their surface entirely inconsistent with Calvinist critiques of "works righteousness"—constantly thrown at them, it
is no wonder that the Native converts stressed the sinfulness of their behavior, even when, as in most cases, they seemed vague or even confused
about the specifics of their transgressions; "I cannot tell all my sins, all my
great sins, I do not see them," Ephraim confessed. But when we examine
what is *missing* from these discussions it becomes clear that the Natick
Christians were not simply parroting back the judgments of their English
missionaries. With one important category of exceptions, none of the
fifteen converts explicitly criticized basic elements of Southern New England Algonquian culture. That exception—worshiping a pantheon of pretended deities—proves the rule, for only four of the fifteen even bothered
to mention something so basic. Moreover, they blamed themselves
alone—not their communities, upbringing, or kin—for their idolatries. "*I
confess that before I prayed, I committed all manner of sins, and served
many gods,*" said Nataôus. "*I did commit all filthiness, I prayed to many
gods,*" echoed Nishohkou, joined by Poquanum, who "prayed to many
gods, and used Panwaning [powwowing]," as did Robin Speen, who himself once "was a Panwan."[39]

The same stress on individual rather than collective sin appears in the
confessions of two other converts whose initial scoffing at Christianity
might legitimately have been attributed to their religious upbringing, the
influence of those around them, and the inherent sinfulness of Indian society. "*I believed not, that God made the world, but I thought the world*

was of itself, and all people grew up in the world of themselves," confessed Magus. Similarly, said Poquanum, "*I* did not think there was a God, or that the Bible was God's book, but that wise men made it." Totherswamp atypically laid some of the blame on "having many friends who loved me, and I loved them, and they cared not for praying to God, and therefore I did not."[40] Yet neither his nor any of the other narratives suggests that Natick Christians took to heart Eliot's oft-repeated message that the "Indians' forefathers were stubborn and rebellious children . . . and hence Indians that now are, do not know God at all."[41] In their refusal to condemn their own cultural background, the Natick Christians laid claim to their Native identity. But in a profound way they also proved themselves better Calvinists than their missionaries as they emphasized the solitary confrontation between the individual and his God and, finding assurance elusive, shuddered at their own sinfulness.[42]

But as people both Indian and Christian, they nonetheless emphasized relationships among human persons. When their narratives mentioned kin and community, it was usually in the context of ties that kept souls in Natick or other villages where Christians lived and forced them to hear the Gospel even when they didn't want to listen. As Ephraim put it, "ever I thought I would forsake the place because of praying to God," but thinking about flight was easier than action. "When I heard the Word I did not like of it but thought of running away, because I loved sin," Monequassun said, "but I loved the place of my dwelling, and therefore I thought I will rather pray to God, and began to do it." John Speen similarly recounted: "When I first prayed to God, I did not pray for my soul, but only I did as my friends did, because I loved them." Magus, though admitting that "none of our rulers believe[d] or pray[ed] to God," professed similar bonds to people in Natick who were Christians. Others dreaded what might happen should they leave their Natick kin behind. "I feared if I did run away some wicked men would kill me," said Antony. "When some of my neighbors began to pray, I went away into the Country," seconded Owussumag, "but I could find no place where I was beloved."[43]

None of the Natick narratives discusses migration to the praying town in terms of a desire to flee the heathen ways of more traditional villagers. Indeed, surprisingly, only two mention the decision to move to Natick at all. In a preliminary confession Monequassun gave before making the speech reprinted here, he said that, "being called to confess, to prepare to make a Church at Natick," he was reluctant to move because he "loved Cohannet" rather than hated it, in large part, no doubt, because that town was already home to a substantial population of Eliot's converts who were reluctant to resettle outside their home territory. Peter similarly "believe[d] that God calleth us to Natick, that here we may be ruled by God, and gather a Church," but he too omitted any criticism of his former, unnamed, abode.[44] Like Monequassun and Peter, the other thirteen narrators had moved to Natick only within two years of telling their stories, a relocation that must have been a significant event in their lives. Yet they apparently accorded it little spiritual significance.

Indeed, those who, like Ephraim, John Speen, Antony, and Owussumag, spent their first weeks in town scoffing at Christianity and thinking about fleeing must have relocated for reasons that were anything but religious. For a generation, New England Native refugees from disease and English expansion had been settling and resettling in new communities. Natick may have thus appeared to be only one such place, albeit with a particularly Protestant bent. Moreover, in the 1650s—twenty years before Metacom's War—the choice of a location protected by politically powerful English colonists may have seemed exactly the kind of fruitful adaptation symbolized by Metacom's brief career as a pig farmer.[45] Others, among them no doubt the newly influential leader Waban, may have seen the move as a way to escape the influence of sachems, who, as Eliot put it, "plainly see that religion will make a great change among them, and cut them off from their former tyranny" and so "openly contested . . . against our proceeding to make a town."[46] In any event, the relative lack of a religious magnet at Natick contrasts strongly with the story of Kateri Tekakwitha and other migrants to Roman Catholic *reserves* in New France and, for that matter, with those of first-generation New England colonists, who frequently made their voyage to North America a central act in their salvation dramas.[47]

As they told their stories, the Natick converts used two concepts over and over; in English these translated as *pardon* and *anger*. "Pardon," not surprisingly in narratives focused on sin, occurs in each of the fifteen narratives, and indeed on every page of Eliot's compilation. "I loath my self for my sins and beg pardon," Monequassun concluded, using the word for the eleventh time. Almost as common is the word "anger," which figures prominently in the stories of twelve narrators. "God was angry" and "I was angry at the punishment of God," Monequassun said. Rage, both divine and human, takes many forms and has many targets in the Natick narratives. "I was angry, because I was proud," "I was angry with my self," "I would be very angry, and would lie unto men," confessed Nataôus; "Christ would have me to forsake my anger."[48] The wife of convert Totherswamp confirmed that, until her "husband did pray he was much angry and froward, but since he hath begun to pray he was not angry so much."[49] As any reader of Jonathan Edwards' famous eighteenth-century sermon *Sinners in the Hands of an Angry God* knows, wrath was a commonplace in Puritan rhetoric. Still, the prevalence of "anger" and "pardon" in the Natick narratives is striking.

Words such as these emphasize interpersonal relationships, among people and between people and their God, rather than creedal belief or abstract faith. The essence of eastern North American Native spirituality was the maintenance of respectful reciprocity in a complicated world of human and other-than-human persons. That essence permeates each of the characteristics that set the Natick narratives apart from their Anglo-American counterparts and from the messages Eliot thought he was conveying to his proselytes. Harmonious relationships, and the need to restore them when disrupted, came to the fore. Behavior counted more than belief, works more than faith, ceremony more than orthodoxy. Anger was the greatest transgression; the Natick community was treasured for its web of relationships rather than for its piety; and sins against the Second Table outranked those against the First. Among the rarely mentioned First Table sins, deeds such as sabbath-breaking, praying to (as opposed to believing in) multiple gods, and ritual powwowing took precedence over states of mind. Similarly, the early stages of the morphology of conversion, which centered on human actions, dominated the narratives, while the latter phases, focused on psychological states and the free gifts of God, became truncated. And those gifts, like many others bestowed in a European cultural framework, apparently seemed hard to comprehend. Native concepts of justice—rooted in concepts of reciprocity and balanced relationships—stressed compensation for the victim rather than punishment of the perpetrator. Protestant Christianity utterly inverted these values, less in its emphasis on punishment for sins (that, at least, involves the divine victim extracting something to restore balance to the relationship) than in its incomprehensible mystery of divine grace, in which the aggrieved party—God—is the one who gives the gift of eternal life to the sinner.

Yet that promised gift of life must have meant something, particularly to Native people who witnessed repeated deadly epidemics. "I much prayed to God for life, for we were all sick, and then God would not hear me, to give us life," Monequassun said, "but first one of my children died, and after that my wife; then I was in great sorrow, because I thought God would not hear me, and I thought it was because I would not follow him." So real comfort apparently remained out of reach. "Come unto me all ye that are weary and heavy laden with your sins, and I will give rest to your souls," Monequassun heard his new lord proclaim, but the convert could only pray desperately, "Oh! that I could go to Christ! . . . Oh! Christ help me to come unto thee." The other Natick Christians whose stories survive in *Tears of Repentance* found assurance similarly elusive. None was convincingly able to say that, having been "troubled in conscience for his sins," he was now "comforted by the favor of God." What they perhaps did find, however, was the kind of human relationships and the kind of human community so insistently prized in their conversion narratives. To Monequassun's compatriot Owussumag, Natick was a "place where I was beloved," if not by an angry God at least by Native men and women who found there a place to rebuild their lives in ways that adapted Algonquian traditions to the realities of English colonial power.[50] If we face eastward and listen hard enough to the way the Natick converts told their stories, we might understand a little more fully how those traditions interacted with Protestant Christianity to help these people make sense of their material and spiritual conditions.

On 25 September 1679, twenty-six years after Monequassun and the other Natick converts told their stories and three years after Metacom's death, a Mohawk Iroquois orator—his name is not recorded—gave a vastly different sort of speech at Albany, New York. The diplomatic dele-

gation for which he spoke had been invited to the Hudson River town by
the same Governor Edmund Andros who had encouraged Mohawk
forces to intervene in King Philip's War. But the business at hand concerned the aftermath of that other great Anglo-Indian war of the mid-
1670s, Bacon's Rebellion. Iroquois warriors traveling southward to coerce
remnant bands of Susquehannocks and others who had fought the Virginians under the protection of the Five Nations and New York were getting into skirmishes with Chesapeake colonists caught in the crossfire—
or, more often, whose cattle made tempting targets for Indian raiders in
search of food. In an attempt to halt the violence, in 1677 Andros had
hosted a council between Iroquois headmen and Henry Coursey, a repre-
sentative of the government of Maryland who was also authorized to
speak on behalf of Virginia. Mutual pledges were exchanged, but the
clashes continued, in part, Iroquois leaders said, because there had never
been any face-to-face contact between official delegates from the Old Dominion and the Five Nations.[51]

So on that early autumn day at Albany in 1679, a Virginian named William Kendall prepared awkwardly to read a message from his colony's
government to the "Maquas," as the people of Albany called the Mohawks. That nation, everyone was satisfied, had not participated directly
in the southern campaigns, but presumably its spokesmen wielded
influence over their confederates who had. Besides, they were the only Iroquois who had thus far responded to Andros' invitation to meet the Virginians; no Cayugas or Senecas ever did show up, although spokesmen for
the Oneidas and Onondagas would arrive a few days later. Worse still for
Kendall, his colleague Southy Littleton, who had traveled with him from
Jamestown, had fallen ill (fatally, it would soon turn out) and could not
join him in his public duties. New York Indian affairs secretary Robert
Livingston carefully recorded what happened next:

*Propositions made by Col. William Kendall, Agent
for the Country of Virginia, to the Maquas in the
Court House of Albany the 25th of September 1679*

I am come from Virginia upon occasion of some of your neighbors
doing of mischief or harm in our country which upon the interposi-

tion and persuasion of the governor here, we have wholly passed by and forgive, and being informed you're not concerned therein, but disowning such action, we did desire to see you, and to let you know, that continuing the like good peaceable neighborhood, you shall find us the same, and willing to do you friendship at all times, but [we] must acquaint you, that we have a law in our country, that all friendly Indians coming there near any Christians must stand still, and lay down their arms in token of friendship, and there [be] received and treated accordingly, otherwise [they] may be destroyed as our enemies, which we desire you to take notice of, there being many of our people abroad and in the woods, was given

/S/ William Kendall	f. 150: zewant [wampum]
	11 ells duffels
	3 vats rum
	3 rolls tobacco
	25 wheat loaves
	10 ditto brown

Maquas Answer upon the Propositions made by Col. William Kendall, authorized by the Governor and Council and burghers of Virginia, at the Court House of Albany the 26 September 1679.

After that the presents were given, said we are glad to see and speak with you here whom we have never seen here before and have well understood your proposition, thanking you for your presents and shall give you an answer in the afternoon.

Post meridiem

Brethren

1. You have had no small trouble to come here from Virginia being so long a journey and having sent for us; we are upon your desire and our Governor General's consent come here in this appointed house to hear you speak and to give answer.

We do not answer yet upon your proposition but do make the prefixed house clean and in order to come to our proposition, meaning by cleaning of the house, that they will answer uniformally [*sic*] and with an upright heart; do give a fathom of zewant.

2ly. We spake just now of your long journey which undoubtedly hath not been without a great deal of trouble, especially ye being an old man as I am; do give a fathom of zewant to mitigate your hard journey.

3ly. It is told us in the preface and we do very well remember the covenant made with Col. Coursey in presence of his honor [Gov. Andros], which covenant we have kept hitherto and shall continue therein inviolably, and are very glad to see you here to renew the covenant. Therein you do exceed them of the east, meaning them of New England, who did likewise make a covenant with us but have not seen them here yet to renew the same. Do give a fathom of zewant.

4ly. We have now spoke of the covenant made with Col. Coursey and likewise now understood that we must continue the like good peaceable neighborhoods which we shall not only perform, but keep the inviolable chain clear and clean, meaning the Covenant Chain and therefore desire that you may do the same. Do give a belt [of] zewant 12 deep.

5ly. We have understood that the mischief and harm our [neighbors] have done to you in your country as upon the interposition and persuasion of our Governor wholly passed by and forgiven by you, for which we are very glad. Let it be buried in oblivion, for if any mischief should befall them we should not be free of it, seeing we are one body. We approve of that law which you have in your country concerning laying down of our arms as a token of friendship which we do undertake to perform; do give a belt 14 [rows] high [of] zewant.

6ly. It is made known to us before the propositions that the other authorized from Virginia (meaning Col. Littleton) is dead, for which we are very sorry and do lament and bewail his death, but do admire that upon the making known of the death of such a person nothing

is laid down, according to our custom, meaning [a] present. Do give
a black belt of zewant 13 [rows] deep to wipe off your tears.
   This is a true copy translated
     Compared and revised per me
      R. Livingston, Secretary[52]

This account of the first two days of negotiations that would stretch
well over a month fills only a few of the thousands of manuscript pages of
"treaty minutes" in which English (and Spanish and French) government
officials recorded Indian words in translation. As with the texts in *Tears of
Repentance,* myriad linguistic, cultural, and historical problems compli-
cate our interpretation of such a document. The Mohawk speechmaker
would have been neither a civil chief nor a warrior, but an orator—a
highly trained ritual specialist who on such formal diplomatic occasions
spoke for the councils of his nation's villages and phrased their arguments
in a ceremonial vocabulary that differed nearly as much from everyday
Mohawk speech as did the King James Bible from the ordinary discourse
of New England farmers raised in East Anglia. Livingston, whose translation was presumably based on hastily scrawled notes, may have spoken
some Mohawk but certainly was unable to comprehend much of what
the orator said. For that, he relied on the far more expert work of Arnout
Cornelisz Vielé, who interpreted for most of the important Euro-Indian
conferences that took place at Albany in the late seventeenth century.
Vielé's father was an Albany Dutch trader. His mother's identity is uncertain, but she was probably a Mohawk woman, and so he would have been
thoroughly bilingual from a very young age. But not trilingual. Like most
residents of a colony only recently conquered from the Netherlands, he
spoke no English, so Livingston had to retranslate Vielé's words to create
the English document reproduced here. Moreover, like Eliot before them,
Vielé and Livingston summarized much, elided details, and omitted sub-
tleties of body language and emotion. By the time they reached the written page, Indian "speeches simply could not retain any lyricism after being put through the wringer of three languages by interpreters more
concerned with meaning than style."[53]
   Lyrical or not, in however attenuated a form, the style nonetheless
survives. Diplomatic council speeches were as rhetorically formulaic as

were conversion narratives. But that formula was more bicultural in origin than was the clearly European Calvinist discourse the Natick converts
manipulated. On the one hand, Livingston's document, *as* a document,
conforms to the conventions of English legalism. It begins with a precise
record of date and venue and the credentials of "Col. William Kendall,
Agent for the Country of Virginia," as "authorized by the Governor and
Council and burghers" (that is, the House of Burgesses). It ends with the
legal notice that it is "a true copy translated compared and revised" by the
duly appointed "Secretary." In between, the carefully worded message
Kendall was deputed to read is recorded verbatim, along with a list of the
goods he delivered, attested with his signature for superiors in New York,
Williamsburg, and London to verify and for posterity to consult in the archives. From the perspective of Kendall and Livingston, the production of
this official record—this paper trail leading to a signed document con-
firming a message delivered and agreed to, of an arrangement established
under the terms of European international law—was the main point of a
diplomatic council.[54] In this period, however, the English almost never
used the word "treaty" to apply to such a final, Indian-signed document,
reserving that term instead for written agreements among European sov-
ereigns. Instead, in the North American context, "treaty" referred to the
entire process of meeting, or "treating," with Indian leaders; "treaty minutes" were the record of that process.[55]

Within the legal forms of a European understanding of the treaty process, another set of purposes and stylistic conventions is encoded. Just as
religion scholars have identified a morphology that structured Puritan
conversion narratives, so students of Indian diplomacy have identified a
"treaty protocol" that shaped the speeches of Native leaders when they
negotiated with Europeans. Originating in the internal political practices
of the Iroquois League, the protocol spread in the mid-seventeenth to
early eighteenth century to other Native groups and to French, English,
and Spanish officials throughout the northeast, the Great Lakes, and the
southeast, accreting along the way a variety of non-Iroquois Indian and
European customs. By the early eighteenth century, treaty conferences
throughout eastern North America conformed to very similar ceremonial
patterns. The minutes from Albany in 1679 document an early stage in
their evolution.

At the height of its development, the treaty protocol ideally consisted of nine stages. First came a formal invitation to attend a meeting at a recognized or "prefixed" place or "council fire." This invitation, accompanied by strings or belts of wampum (Dutch colonists called the beads *zewant*), established a right for the hosts to set the agenda and speak first; it also obliged them to provide ritual and material hospitality for the visitors. Second was a ceremonial procession, by foot or canoe, by which the visitors arrived at the site of the council. Third was the "At the Wood's Edge" rite, in which the hosts offered rest and comfort to visitors presumed to be tired from a long journey. Each side offered the other the "Three Bare Words" of condolence, to clear their eyes, ears, and throats of the grief-inspired rage that prevented clear communication—the rage that, if unchecked, provoked mourning wars and spiraled into endless retaliatory feuds. After at least one night's rest, the council itself began with, fourth, the seating of the delegations and, fifth, an extensive Condolence ceremony, in which tearful eyes were again ritually dried, minds and hearts cleansed of the "bile of revenge," blood wiped "from the defiled house," graves of the dead "covered" to keep grief and revenge out of sight, clouds dispelled to allow the sun to shine, and fire kindled to further illuminate the proceedings. Sixth came a "recitation of the law ways," a rehearsal of the history of two peoples' relationships with each other, the basis of their peaceful interactions, and the way in which their forebears had taught them to behave. Almost universally, the connection was described in terms of fictive kinship; two peoples were "Uncle" and "Nephew," or "Father" and "Child," or "Brother" and "Brother," and addressed each other with the authority or deference appropriate to the power relationship inherent in such terms. The recitation of the law ways articulated ideals rather than grubby realities. Kinship terms and other names by which relationships were described served an educative function to remind participants of what their attitudes toward each other *ought* to be.[56]

Only in the seventh stage, after the ritual requirements for establishing a peaceful environment had been fulfilled, could what Europeans considered the business of a treaty council—the offering of specific "propositions"—take place. To be considered valid, each "word" had to be accompanied by an appropriate gift, usually of wampum strings ("fathoms") or

Native orator reading a Wampum belt.

From [William Smith,] *An Historical Account of the Expedition Against the Ohio Indians, in the Year MDCCLXIV* (Philadelphia, 1766). Dechert Collection, Annenberg Rare Book and Manuscript Library, University of Pennsylvania.

belts prepared specially for the occasion. "Presents among these peoples despatch all the affairs of the country," explained a French missionary who understood the process much better than Livingston. "They dry up tears; they appease anger; they open the doors of foreign countries; they deliver prisoners; they bring the dead back to life; one hardly ever speaks or answers, except by presents."[57] Wampum gifts in particular confirmed the validity of a speaker's words in several interrelated ways. As a sacred substance, wampum underscored the importance of what was being said. As a valuable commodity, it demonstrated that the speaker was not talking only for himself or on the spur of the moment, but that he had the considered support of the kin and followers who had banded together to collect the treasured shells and have them strung. And, as carefully woven patterns of white and black beads, wampum also became a mnemonic device, allowing belts or strings to be "read" accurately both by a speaker delivering a message as instructed and by a recipient recalling promises made years before.[58]

While propositions and wampum were offered by the hosts, visitors were to listen politely but not respond substantively until at least the next day. Hasty replies were not only disrespectful but indicated that the negotiator had not conferred with his colleagues and therefore could not be speaking with their approbation or with properly prepared wampum. Only when each of the hosts' propositions had been answered could the visitors introduce new points. The same expectations of polite listening and postponed responses applied throughout a treaty conference. Thus, as at Albany in 1679, the whole affair could last for weeks. Once the substantive dialogue finally ended, the eighth step was the affixing of marks to any documents Europeans might insist upon. The ninth step consisted of a feast and the presentation of final gifts from the hosts. Unlike symbolic wampum, these tended to be of more material value: food, cloth, tools, weapons, and, too often, liquor—all of which leaders would redistribute to their followers.[59]

The broad outlines of this treaty protocol are clearly evident in the Mohawk speeches Livingston recorded. Most of the major divergences are explained by a single factor: in 1679 English officials, and certainly Virginia's delegates, had not yet learned the rules. As a result, the Mohawk speaker had both to educate his rude interlocutors and do much of their ritual work for them. After Kendall's unceremonious reading of his message and dumping of trade goods, the Mohawk orator waited until the next morning to respond with noncommittal politeness, and then called the proceedings to a halt so he could begin them over properly in the afternoon. His ritual began, in Livingston's English translation, with a single word: "Brethren." This kinship term, which Mohawk and other Iroquois almost universally insisted on using when dealing with representatives of English colonies, established firm expectations for the relationship. Brethren might be older and younger, temporarily stronger or weaker, than each other. They might often be rivals and sometimes come to blows. But, in a way no imperious English governor liked to acknowledge, they were fundamentally equals; none of the obedience fathers and uncles could expect of children and nephews applied. Just as important, as Brethren, the two parties were supposed to be inescapably bound to one another despite short-term quarrels.[60]

With the ideal nature of the relationship established, the Mohawk speaker offered comfort to a weary visitor that should have been offered earlier at the wood's edge, he cleaned the "prefixed" council house, he proffered condolence for the "great deal of trouble" the "old man" Kendall must have put himself through, and he presented gifts "to mitigate" the Virginian's "hard journey"—thus fulfilling the ceremonial requirements of the first five stages of the treaty protocol. Next, his recitation of the law recalled "the covenant made with Col. Coursey," which the Mohawks had "kept hitherto and shall continue therein inviolably." That covenant, the speaker reminded the Virginians, needed to be renewed regularly, something he claimed the New Englanders had failed to do. The Mohawk's fourth and fifth propositions, corresponding to the seventh stage of the treaty paradigm, responded specifically and affirmatively to Kendall's message and verified the words with wampum belts. The substantial width of these was particularly noteworthy in contrast to the less impressive "fathoms" that ratified earlier propositions.

Because the business of the treaty would not be completed for several more weeks, the final stages of the protocol are absent from the document reproduced here, but the scandalized tone of the Mohawk orator's final proposition reveals the very different priorities of Native and European diplomats. The speaker "admire[d]"—a better modern translation might be "was astonished"—that Littleton's death was allowed to pass with only a simple announcement and no opportunity for mourning and exchanges of condolence gifts. Continuing his lesson in appropriate treaty behavior, the orator proclaimed that the Mohawks were "very sorry and do lament and bewail his death," presenting "a black belt of zewant 13 [rows] deep to wipe off your tears."

Drying tears, setting minds straight, establishing clear channels of communication, reciprocal exchanges of friendly words and symbolic gifts—these, not mundane details of whether Mohawks would agree to stand still and lay down their arms when they ran into a Virginian in the woods, were the essence of eastern North American Indian diplomacy. In societies in which no leaders held a monopoly of force and in which a single grieving family could start a mourning war and provoke a devastating cycle of revenge raids and counterraids, detailed agreements thrashed out by a few leaders in a smoke-filled longhouse had little hope of keeping peace between peoples. It was far more important to address the root causes of violence between people and groups and to create a climate in which peaceful rather than murderous thoughts prevailed and people saw the concrete benefits of their relationships to each other.

To create such a climate, treaty councils had to be ceremonially structured public, participatory events. One of the many details that Livingston failed to record—ill-informed or unconcerned as he was about Native expectations—was how many Indian people were present. But typically, such conferences attracted dozens if not hundreds of men, women, and children. Their presence, like their gifts of wampum, gave visible evidence that their spokesmen had broad political support. Yet what the audience took home from the treaty was even more significant. All those in attendance needed to hear and see the rituals of condolence if they were to set aside rage and be convinced that harm done the other side was, as the Mohawk speaker said, "wholly passed by and forgiven" and "buried in oblivion." They needed to hear the ritual recitation of the history of their relationship with the other side in order to "remember the covenant" and "continue the like good peaceable neighborhoods." And they needed to see that the relationship brought them concrete benefits; Kendall's fairly meager gift of 150 florins in wampum (perhaps worth £3 sterling), 3 ells (a little less than 4 yards) of the sturdy duffel cloth

that Native people used for outer garments, 3 vats of rum, 3 rolls of tobacco, and 35 loaves of bread was probably not very convincing.[61]

Whatever the case, if the lessons and benefits of treaties were to remain relevant, the relationship had to be regularly reconfirmed, its rituals
continually reenacted to "keep the inviolable chain clear and clean" of
rust and other forms of decay.[62] In this context, the Mohawk orator's
claim that Massachusetts had failed to renew its treaties bears closer scru-
tiny. The sources of tension between the Five Nations and the New Englanders paralleled those that plagued the Chesapeake. Iroquois war parties—continuing the struggle against Metacom's allies that they had only
recently been encouraged to wage—were attacking the New England colonists' Indian allies and sometimes colonists themselves who got in the
way. The most troublesome episode was the Mohawk capture of some
two dozen Indians at Mogoncog, near Natick, in June 1678, most of
whom were taken back to Iroquoia and apparently executed. Although
there had been plenty of diplomatic contact over these issues, Massachusetts officials violated the protocol of Native diplomacy at every turn. In
1677, before the Mogoncog affair exacerbated tensions, Governor John
Leverett sent the Mohawks a letter warning them against "neglect of attending what was concluded at Albany, namely to be friends to all our
friend Indians which was one of the great things we aimed at": no personal contact; no formalities; no gifts to verify the words.[63] Similarly, after
the captures, although Sylvester Salisbury, the officer in charge of the Albany fort, was convinced the prisoners could have been ransomed for perhaps 200 florins, there was no attempt to follow protocol. "My thoughts
is," Salisbury wrote to his superiors in New York City, "that if the New
England people had any kindness for them, they would have sent a man,
[in] time [e]nough to have been at Albany, to have spoken with Tayadory
[the leader of the Mohawk war party], for he was long enough on his
way." Instead, Salisbury complained, Leverett waited two weeks to write
him and ask him "to threaten the Maquas for them."[64]

When a delegation from New England finally did arrive in person,
again they refused to follow procedures. Instead of inviting the Iroquois
to the "prefixed" meeting place at Albany, they had orders to barge right
into the Mohawk country, demand the release of the prisoners, and invite

"some of their sachems or chief men to treat and conclude with our commissioners and those of the other colonies who are also herein concerned at Hartford about the middle of September next, or at Hadley if they like that place better, or rather than fail at Boston, if they choose it."[65] When they heard this, the Mohawks evidently insisted that everyone go back to Albany for a proper council. Livingston's minutes of what then transpired explain why the Mohawk orator told the Virginians that the covenant with New England had never been properly renewed:

> *The Maquas Answer to the Propositions Propounded to Them*
> *this Day by Mr Samuel Ely and Ben Waite Messengers Sent*
> *by the Governor and Council of Boston and in the*
> *Court House of Albany this 1st Day of August.*
> *Anno Dom. 1678.*

The Names of the Sachems:
Conachkoo, Soriwezee, Karahize, Kaewannere, Auworongee, Turie, Interpreted by Arnout Cornelisz Vielé.

1. They do say, that the English of New England and they have always been good friends, and are so still, and must acknowledge to have been always welcome and well received by the English in their plantations, but nevertheless that this is the ordained place to hear propositions in, let them come from what part they will, to speak with them, and were spoke to here last year by Major [John] Pynchon etc. in the presence of the governor general.

2. You say there is a fault committed in taking away of those Indians at Mogoncog. 'Tis true we acknowledge it, but in who lies the fault? It may be in our young Indians who are like wolves, when they are abroad; possibly in the North Indians that live among us, and the Indians of Magoncog are not the less to blame, they not dwelling as friend Indians in the woods, having a castle so well fortified with stockadoes, which friend Indians need not have, therefore [we] did imagine them to be enemies, for these Indians that live in or about the English plantations, without fortifications, we did never any harm to.

You have spoken to us by way of discourse without giving of any presents (though usual upon business of consequence) and we shall answer you the same way that never by us is practiced.

3. That which is now done by our young Indians or soldiers, viz. the taking of those Indians at Magoncog, we give them no thanks for, neither was it by your order, but it is as we have said, when they are abroad are like wolves in the wood.

4. Brethren you had wars with the Indian enemies before we [did], for when divers of your towns were burnt down, then our governor general [Andros] did encourage us, and told how his friends in New England were involved in a great war with Indians and that some of your enemies were fled to Hoosic, encouraging us to go out against them, and we and our governor general being as it were one body, went out, upon his desire against them, and killed some and put the rest to the flight, and so have continued the war ever since, and if we came to night to your praying Indians, why were not we warned and bid hold up, and go no further? Therefore the Brethren may be assured of our good heart and the continuation of peace and friendship on our sides.

5. The Brethren desire that we should restore all the captives that we have of your friend Indians taken by our folks, which we do not refuse to do. You desire likewise that we may come to Hartford, Hadley, or Boston, to treat with your commissioners there, to that end there might be a right understanding of all affaires betwixt us etc., which we cannot resolve upon to come and treat in your government, this place being thereunto ordained, but let Major Pynchon (or any other whom the Brethren please to send) come here as he did last year. We shall then in his honor the governor-general's presence deliver up the demanded for prisoners and treat of all affairs, seeing this is the house to hear propositions in, as Major Pynchon well knows. This governor general and you of New England and we are one in one triple alliance with another.

Upon this following proposition we cannot forbear (according to our custom) but give a small present though of little value being a fathom of zewant.

6. Brethren, the covenant that was made here last year betwixt

Major Pynchon and us in the presence of the governor general is as fast firm and inviolable as ever it was, and if our warring against the Indians of the north in general doth not please you, pray acquaint us here therewith.

7. They do repeat again that the covenant made with the Brethren is as firm as ever it hath been, and do present some zewant made round as a circle which they compare to the sun, saying that their alliance is as firm and inviolable as the sun, and shall have such a splendor as the beams thereof, and say furthermore that if any will speak with them, that this is the appointed place, as they of Maryland have done, and that in the governor-general's presence.

8. Brethren, there is a troop or 2 of our Indians out, against your and our enemies, who know nothing of this, and if they should come to your habitations, let not them be kept fast, or any harm done to them and if they should ignorantly take any of your friend Indians then shall be no harm done to them but restored again to any whom you shall commissionate to receive the same, with the rest provided our governor general be present.

This is a true copy translated, compared and revised per me

Albany   ROBERT LIVINGSTON SECRETARY.

datum up supra[66]

This speech was certainly not lacking in what any European diplomat would have called substantive (or rather ingeniously unsubstantive) content. The orator made excuses worthy of the slyest European politician, spread the blame for the unpleasantness on everyone but the Mohawk village councils, and dodged the inconvenient fact that most of the prisoners were dead by postponing repatriation to a future date. All of these were secondary to his main purposes, however. As with the 1679 address to the Virginians, the formalities of treaty protocol—and the New Englanders' failure to follow them—were far more important: Albany, not the Mohawk country, Hartford, or Boston, was the established council fire; Governor Andros was the person who kindled it; words, if they were to be believed, had to be accompanied by gifts. It becomes particularly significant, then, that, despite a pledge to imitate the English in talking without giftgiving, the sixth and seventh propositions were too important to be made without wampum. Both propositions stressed not an agreement but a *relationship*, "as fast, firm, and inviolable as ever it was." New Englanders must have found these statements meaningless, empty rhetoric, however dressed up they might be in metaphors of solar splendor. Native people, however, considered them to be what mattered most.

The ceremonial language of personal relationships focuses attention on what the Mohawk orator had to say about the role of New York governor Andros. Several times he emphasized that treaties must take place not just at the Albany council fire but under Andros' auspices. "If any will speak with them," he reminded them "that this is the appointed place . . . and that in the governor general's presence." In 1677, when Maryland's representatives came to the appropriate treaty location, another Iroquois orator, speaking for the Cayugas and Senecas, explained that "We have always had a firm covenant with this government which hath been faithfully kept by this governor general (for which we do give him hearty thanks, whom we have taken to be our greatest lord), for he hath put aside all mistakes which hath happened."[67]

Two puzzling words leap out from Livingston's record of this 1677 Iroquois speech: "always" and "lord." In literal terms, "always" seems to make little sense at all, for it referred to a relationship not yet three years old. After a brief reoccupation during a recent Anglo-Dutch war, New York had returned to English control by treaty only when Andros became its governor in the fall of 1674. The previous English regime, from 1664 to 1673, had shown less interest in an alliance with the Iroquois than in maintaining cordial relations with the Five Nations' New England Algonquian and French enemies.[68] Nor had all been sweetness and light when the Dutch West India Company had controlled the Hudson River colony. Before the English conquest of 1664, the small European population of New Netherland (well under 10,000 people) was a remarkably multicultural mix, not only from the United Provinces of the Netherlands but also from Sweden, Finland, the German principalities, and elsewhere. This motley lot had built its economy on peaceful commerce with Native Americans—but only those who had something worth trading for, as demonstrated by the colony's brutal wars against less fortunate Native people of the Lower Hudson Valley and Long Island in the 1640s and 1650s.[69] "The Dutch say we are brothers and that we are joined together with chains, but that lasts only as long as we have beavers," an Iroquois spokesman explained concisely in 1659. "After that we are no longer thought of."[70]

If, less than two decades later, another Iroquois used a word that meant "always," he must have been voicing a hope for the future rather than an account of the past. In terms of the diplomatic protocol, "always" set "law ways," educating English people about the ideals on which relations with the Iroquois should be based. The need for such education—and the gulf between the ideal of "always" and the more complicated reality of past experience—would have been apparent to any Native person who considered the violent and untrustworthy reputation that English colonists had earned everywhere in North America, particularly in the 1670s and especially in the Chesapeake region from which Coursey hailed. The general outlines of the havoc English people had wreaked on the Susquehannocks and the Native peoples of the Chesapeake must have been familiar to the Iroquois orator who tried to teach Maryland's governor about the "firm covenant" that bound Iroquois to New York's Governor Andros. Similarly, the intimate involvement of Mohawks in Metacom's War suggests that the speaker understood well the ferocity with which New Englanders had turned on their Algonquian neighbors. It is likely, too, that he understood the dangers of following the footsteps of Wamsutta and Metacom toward a meeting—or rather inquisition—in a New England capital. Those examples clarify the Mohawks' insistence that all negotiations with the English take place through a single royal governor, at a single authorized location, rather than through a host of competing voices at locations under no central supervision. What better way to counter the dangers of divide-and-rule than to minimize the possibilities for division?

Still, given recent history, how could any Native leader pin much hope on the English, much less call one of their governors his "greatest lord"? At first glance, it might seem highly unlikely that the orator said anything of the sort, and that Livingston was wishfully putting words in his mouth. "Lord," with its connotations of nobility and feudal obligations, seems to be a European concept if ever there was one. Nonetheless—although we have no way of knowing with certainty what Mohawk term the orator used in 1677—there is good reason to believe that the orator said something for which "greatest lord" is a reasonably accurate translation. When

seventeenth-century Jesuit missionaries described the lineages in which
Iroquoian hereditary chieftainships descended, they sometimes called
them, collectively, "nobles." More to the point, two hundred years later,
when native Mohawk-speakers set down in English the sacred story of
their founding of the Iroquois League, they regularly used the word
"lord" as a translation for *rotiyanehr*, a term more often glossed by outsiders as "hereditary chief" or "sachem" (a word of New England Algonquian origin). "Lord," "noble," and "sachem" may well, then, have
been equivalents, all struggling toward a meaning that in Mohawk combined the concepts of "great" or "honored one" with "one who keeps the
peace," for the Mohawk root -*yanehr*- refers to peace as well as to law.[71] If
so, the law ways evoked by the term that Vielé and Livingston translated
as "lord" called upon Andros—and by extension the English imperial government—to fulfill the main functions of a civil chief: to establish relationships of balance and reciprocity both inside and outside the community, to make and keep the peace, to "put aside all mistakes which hath
happened."

But it was not just a hope, because, from a very different cultural background, Sir Edmund Andros had set out to play just that role. A military
man with a lifetime of loyal service to the Stuart royal family, he had been
sent by his own "greatest lord," the king's brother and closest adviser,
James, duke of York, to impose imperial authority not only on recently re-
acquired New York but on the North American continent as a whole. As
Andros came to see it, the chaos that had ripped New England during
Metacom's War and the Chesapeake during Bacon's Rebellion—and that
continued to threaten both regions in their controversies with the Iroquois during the late 1670s—was a symptom of the more general lack of
central authority in English North America. Perpetual conflict, he concluded, was what the English "must expect and be liable to, so long as
each petty colony hath or assumes absolute power of peace and war."[72]
Andros was improvising as he went along, but all his initiatives in Indian
diplomacy were guided by the principle that he, as the agent of royal authority, should supervise relations between all the English colonies and
their Native neighbors. The careful records of Indian treaties that
Livingston kept for him built legal precedents to guide future governors.[73]

Andros' encouragement of Mohawk intervention in Metacom's War

was thus aimed not just at bringing that conflict to an end, but also at extending the reach of his government eastward and northward into New
England. After Metacom's death, at the same time Andros sponsored treaties between the Iroquois and New Englanders, he also brokered an end
to a long-running war between the Five Nations and the Mahicans, who
had sheltered Metacom's retreat toward the Hudson and who had suffered a severe defeat in the Mohawk assault. Moreover, he invited both
Mahicans and Algonquian refugees from New England to resettle under
joint New York and Iroquois protection at Schaghticoke, some twenty
miles northeast of Albany—a strategic spot that expanded New York's
territorial claims toward New France and Massachusetts simultaneously.
The governor similarly offered his own protection to the Susquehannock
refugees who were resettling (sometimes under duress, as the troubles
with Virginians and Marylanders demonstrated) in the Iroquois and Delaware countries during the same period. They would soon be followed
northward by other refugees from the fighting in the Chesapeake, most
of whom would settle in the former territories of the Susquehannocks in
present-day Pennsylvania—again, among other things, providing the
New York governor a means to extend the geographic reach of his authority.[74]

The product of that effort was a set of English-Indian alliances that
came to be known in treaty speeches as "the Covenant Chain." From the
perspective of the duke's governor, the Chain expanded the boundaries of
his political authority, resettled Indian refugees in strategic buffer zones,
and vastly simplified matters by asserting the fiction that New York spoke
for all the English, and the Iroquois for all the Indians presumed to be
their clients. From an Iroquois perspective, meanwhile, the Covenant
Chain made Andros the kind of peacemaking civil chief worthy of being
called "our greatest lord." It is worth recalling that in 1674, when Andros
arrived in New York, the Iroquois had long been engaged in brutal wars
with their Indian neighbors—wars that, since the fall of New Netherland
in 1664, had turned against them. Many Iroquois also chafed under the
peace treaty imposed on them by the French in 1667, which, far from
strengthening Iroquois communities through reciprocity and balance, divided them deeply over the preaching of Jesuit missionaries and their increasingly successful campaign to encourage converts to follow Kateri

Tekakwitha to Christian *reserves* in Canada.[75] Andros' Covenant Chain did not just bring peace with the Mahicans, New England Algonquians, and Susquehannocks. In resettling surviving remnants of those nations on the margins of Iroquois country, Andros' arrangements conformed to long-standing Native cultural patterns in which defeated rivals were incorporated into the victor's society. No wonder the Iroquois spokesman at Albany in 1677 placed such a high value on the personal relationship between the Five Nations and their "greatest lord."[76]

Yet that term implied only a limited sort of authority in Native cultures. An Iroquois "lord" or sachem was entitled to enormous respect, but, in a society lacking the coercive mechanisms of a state or even of a chiefdom such as Powhatan's, he could not tell anyone what to do. "Each nation is an absolute republic by itself, governed in all public affairs of war and peace by the sachems or old men, whose authority and power is gained by and consists wholly in the opinion the rest of the nation have of their wisdom and integrity," early eighteenth-century New Yorker Cadwallader Colden explained. "They never execute their resolutions by compulsion or force upon any of their people." A Mohawk once put it even more concisely: "Brethren you know that we have no forcing rules or laws amongst us."[77]

This noncoercive tradition lends added significance to the kinship term "Brethren." As "greatest lord" Andros may have been due special respect, but as a brother he was no more than first among nonauthoritarian Iroquois equals also entitled to be called "lords." Realizing this, both Andros' successor Thomas Dongan and Andros himself when he became governor again in 1688 tried to rephrase the relationship in terms of an English Father and his Indian Children. "Let the old covenant that was made with our ancestors be kept firm," a Mohawk orator replied. "Then we were called Brethren, and that was also well kept; therefore let that of Brethren continue without any alteration."[78] In a matrilineal society such as theirs, a Father would not have been due the kind of obedience patrilineal Europeans attached to that term, but the metaphorical difference in generations would still have made the Iroquois unacceptably inferior partners in the relationship. Moreover, recent experiences with a French governor who insisted that his Indian allies call him "Father" would have made these Mohawk lords intimately familiar with the domination implied by that term. United as relative equals, "the governor-general and we are one, and one heart and one head," a Mohawk spokesman explained to Coursey in 1677. "The covenant that is betwixt the governor-general and us is inviolable, yea so strong that if the very thunder should break upon the Covenant Chain it would not break it in sunder."[79]

Just as the marriage of Pocahontas had tried to incorporate English Virginia into a Powhatan political and cultural landscape, these speeches attempted to integrate the English empire into a Native world—but now in ways that explicitly acknowledged that the balance of power had shifted toward the colonizers. The term frequently used to describe a strategy based on this recognition of unequal power is "accommodation." Yet, in keeping with fundamental Native religious and social values, the accommodationist strategy enacted during treaty ceremonies envisioned less a *submission* to a greater power than a *mobilization* of it. In what Europeans would call the spiritual realm, Native people believed that other-than-human persons such as the sun, the rain, or the Three Sisters of corn, beans, and squash possessed powers that less potent human persons could, through ceremonies and acts of reciprocity, turn to their benefit. In what Europeans distinguished as a more temporal domain, sachems and shamans similarly controlled forces that could be mobilized for the benefit of their people, or turned against them if the demands of reciprocity were not fulfilled. The Andros envisioned by Mohawk orators was a very human person—a "lord" but not a "god" or spirit being—but nonetheless he controlled preponderant resources of economic, military, and political power. In the continent they knew they had to share with Europeans, accommodationist Iroquois diplomats hoped to mobilize that power for themselves in an alliance "so strong that . . . the very thunder . . . would not break it in sunder."[80]

The Mohawk orator, speaking confidently for thousands of people who, despite European influence, controlled their own lands and governed their own villages, was far more able to shape the style and content of his message than was Monequassun, a lone sinner trying to convince English preachers and officials at whose sufferance the town of Natick existed that he had been granted grace sufficient to help establish a church. The contrasting extent to which Native rhetorical forms influenced the European documents in which these voices come down to us reflects the varying degrees of English colonial influence over two very different parts of seventeenth-century Indian country. From a position of relative equality, the treaty speeches of accommodationist orators attempted to mobilize European political might—particularly in its newly centralized imperial form—to protect the independence and enhance the strength of the Mohawks and their fellow Iroquois. From a position of relative weakness, Natick Indians used their conversion narratives to carve out a distinct cultural space within a Puritan structure of political and ideological domination.

Thus both the orator and the convert articulated visions of intercultural adaptation, of how Native and European people might share eastern North America given the reality of European power. And, whether employing the Native metaphor of an inviolable Covenant Chain that nonetheless needed periodic "brightening" or the European vocabulary of sins against the Second Table, they described relationships of reciprocity, kinship, and respect. English auditors, hurriedly seeking a peace agreement at Albany or squirming in their seats at Natick, had quite different agendas. Still, the cases discussed here reveal notable congruences between the aims of at least some Europeans and some Indians: Eliot needed his converts to demonstrate the success of his missionary efforts, and Andros needed his Iroquois allies to achieve his imperial ends. Read carefully, the written records that these Europeans used to document their efforts can reveal Native people using the power of the spoken word to articulate a distinctive vision of cultural coexistence on Indian terms.

NATIVE PEOPLES IN
AN IMPERIAL WORLD

AS THE SEVENTEENTH CENTURY gave way to the eighteenth, the struggle to define terms for coexistence with powerful European colonial neighbors preoccupied Indian people everywhere. Eastern North America was no longer a "new world" for anyone; Natives and Europeans shared histories on the land that, in some places, stretched back two hundred years. As we look backward from today, patterns might appear already well set, all part of a dreary, inexorable tale of European advance and Indian retreat. If we try to see the early eighteenth century on its own terms, however, things take on a very different aspect. It is true that a generation of brutal warfare ushered in the century and that most Indians and most colonists would never learn to share the continent. Nonetheless, between about 1720 and 1750, a stable, begrudging, mostly peaceful coexistence prevailed. Indian accommodationism played a part, but on the whole coexistence owed less to the conscious efforts of leaders on any side than to the ways in which both Native and immigrant peoples came to relate to the great European empires of the era. Facing eastward, the most remarkable characteristic of the early eighteenth century becomes neither conflict nor amity but instead the degree to which Indian and Euro-American—and particularly British-American—histories moved along parallel paths in a single, ever more consolidated, transatlantic imperial world.[1]

If the notion that Native and European colonial histories moved in parallel, rather than opposing, directions seems odd, it may be because the trajectory of *British-American* history during the early eighteenth century

is so unfamiliar to many of us. For Britain's colonists, the era took its initial shape during two great military conflicts in which European empires
contested the lands, trade, and riches of eastern North America—the War
of the League of Augsburg (known to colonists as "King William's War"
of 1689–1697) and the War of the Spanish Succession ("Queen Anne's
War" of 1702–1713). When these struggles came to an end with the Treaty
of Utrecht in 1713, a balance of diplomatic, political, and economic forces
had been painfully achieved, ushering in thirty-odd years of what has
been called "the Long Peace."[2]

In that period, British America achieved a remarkable degree of political stability. The contrast with the brittle power arrangements that had
prevailed in Puritan New England and Berkeley's Virginia could not have
been more striking. In every colony, self-assured American-born political
elites came to base their authority on the tripod of English common law,
British parliamentary forms of governance, and widespread voting rights
among property-owning adult males.[3] Early eighteenth-century British
North America was also notable for its economic prosperity. Britain's was
"An Empire of Goods," in which far-flung trading connections produced a
"consumer revolution." Even modest North American households came
to enjoy imported tea, coffee, sugar, and rum; cups, dishes, and flatware
with which to consume them; and countless other marvels previously
confined to the aristocracy, if available at all. Though uneven, cyclical,
and unequally distributed, the prosperity derived from North America's
integration into the transatlantic system was very real.[4]

The stability and prosperity of the empire also bequeathed British
America a rapidly growing, mobile, and ethnically and religiously diverse
population, to which immigrants from the German principalities and the
borderlands of northern Britain and Ireland made steadily increasing contributions.[5] Successive waves of transatlantic religious enthusiasm, later
called the "Great Awakening," increased the diversity by splitting
churches into ever more denominational variety.[6] Meantime, a growing
reliance on African-American slavery (despite its seventeenth-century
roots really an eighteenth-century phenomenon in most of North America) entrenched the hard racial underside of the American mosaic.[7] These
trends proceeded with only the slightest interruption when the Long
Peace gave way to renewed imperial warfare in the War of the Austrian

Succession ("King George's War" of 1744–1748). Everything changed, however, after the stunning British victory in the Seven Years' War (1754–1761 in North America, 1756–1763 in Europe) virtually expelled the French and Spanish from the eastern half of the continent. In Britain's vastly expanded imperial domains, the relationship between the metropole and North America assumed a new and, to many colonists, suddenly oppressive character.[8]

To later citizens of the United States, which was born in the colonial revolt that resulted from the new imperial relationship, the early eighteenth century has since been foreign historical terrain. The tourist mecca of Colonial Williamsburg exemplifies the nation's difficulty in comprehending the period on its own terms. People go there in search of such revolutionary heroes as Washington, Jefferson, and Henry. Yet the place actually symbolizes everything the Founding Fathers set out to replace. Williamsburg was designed to be an *imperial* capital. Constructed in the 1690s to supplant ill-starred Jamestown as the governmental center, it was the glory of the prosperous new British Virginia that arose from the ashes of Bacon's Rebellion—and that would be destroyed again by the American Revolution. In its architecture and ethos, it was far more attuned to such royal governors as Edmund Andros (the last of whose many imperial appointments ended in the Old Dominion just as the administration prepared to move to Williamsburg) than to Jefferson. Its Governor's Palace embodied royal majesty; its Capitol, with twin wings housing Burgesses and Royal Council, symbolized the balance of aristocratic and democratic, imperial and provincial, power under the British constitution. These and other imperial associations were one reason the republican revolutionaries moved their government to Richmond and left Williamsburg a virtual ghost town until its twentieth-century tourist rebirth.[9]

In its heyday, Williamsburg had frequently been the scene of treaty conferences, a powerful reminder of Indian and Euro-American coexistence in the colonial world that the American Revolution erased from historical memory. Also erased are the ways in which the same trends we have just traced for British America applied with equal force for Native America. In Indian country, too, the turn-of-the-century imperial wars set the terms for a Long Peace marked by political stability within an imperial

Minerva (4), representing Britain, commiserates with an Indian man (5), symbolizing
British America: a transatlantic empire in which Native Americans were integral parts.
From *The State of the Nation An: Dom: 1765 &c.* (London, 1765). The Library Company of Philadelphia.

framework, a consumer revolution within a transatlantic economy, and
an ethnically and religiously diversifying population within a steadily
hardening definition of racial categories. And in Indian country, too, the
British victory in the Seven Years' War changed everything by demolish-
ing the transatlantic structural framework that had allowed Native people
and European to coexist. British and Indian stories were parallel chapters
in a single eighteenth-century eastern North American tale.

Indian country's eighteenth-century peace and stability emerged
from seventeenth-century war and chaos. The complicated significance
of the wars that ushered in the Long Peace is suggested by the difficulty
people at the time, and ever since, have had in giving them simple names.

In histories of the United States, they are often lumped together as the "French and Indian wars." Yet, far from simply pitting the English against those two powers, these conflicts involved grand alliances of the various British colonies with their diverse Indian allies against the French of both New France and Louisiana with their multitudinous Native supporters, and the Spanish of Florida with their assorted Indian partners.[10] Complicating the picture still further is the reality that the mosaic of North American conflicts was integral to a global struggle among three empires for control, not just of North America, but of the European continent, the West Indies, and the entire Atlantic world. British colonists acknowledged this external dimension when they used designations like "King William's" and "Queen Anne's" to describe the wars. Similarly, the European names for these conflicts—the War of the League of Augsburg and the War of the Spanish Succession—place them in a broader imperial framework.

But that language won't entirely do, either. As we examine the reasons for Native American involvement as allies on all sides in imperial struggles for control of the continent, the European nature of the wars shrinks in significance. These were not just European but also indigenously *North American* wars that grew from longstanding, home-grown conflicts. Inter-Indian and Indian-colonial rivalries made them every bit as much a matter of Native Americans involving European allies in their battles as they were of Europeans involving Native Americans in theirs. Conflicts between and among dozens of Native peoples and nearly a score of European colonies intersected with the rivalries of European monarchs, merchants, and armies.[11] Such complicated struggles can be viewed from many fruitful vantage points, but three spots we have visited before—the Iroquoia of the English Covenant Chain, the St. Lawrence *reserves* of Kateri's French-allied descendants, and the southeastern interior of de Soto's rampage—reveal something of their texture for Native people. Details and casts of characters varied, but in each region Indians learned painful lessons about the limits of accommodation and about how to survive in the emerging transatlantic imperial world.

No one learned the lessons more painfully than the Iroquois leaders who had hoped to rely on Edmund Andros as their "greatest lord." The economic reforms and the diplomatic configurations that the New York governor arranged in the 1670s provided the Five Nations a secure source of trade goods and weapons, peace on their eastern flanks, and potential military reinforcements among their new Mahican, Susquehannock, and other Native allies in the Covenant Chain. Those people who had never accepted the peace terms that New France imposed on the Iroquois in the 1660s were now free to make their move. In the late 1670s and early 1680s, Five Nations war parties waged massive campaigns to seize furs and, especially, captives among French-allied Indians of the Great Lakes region. By 1684 the impact of those raids on the fur trade of New France brought the Iroquois and that colony again to open war. If the Iroquois thought their English allies would come to their aid, however, they were sadly mistaken; a secret treaty between England's Charles II and France's Louis XIV prevented Andros and his successors from lending them any open support. Thus the Five Nations had a particular interest in the outcome of England's "Glorious Revolution," which removed Andros' master James II from the throne in 1688. The new king, William III, was already fighting France in the War of the League of Augsburg and brought England into that conflict as a condition of his acceptance of the throne. To anti-French Iroquois, this was welcome news. Rejoicing to "hear there is war betwixt France and England," in June 1689 a Mohawk proclaimed that, "as they are one hand and soul with the English, they will take up the ax with pleasure against the French."[12]

But New York's divisive internal politics and empty coffers ensured that the Iroquois did nearly all the North American fighting and dying in the first imperial war. When the European crowns made peace at Ryswick in 1697, conflict between the Five Nations and French-allied Indians only intensified, and the outnumbered Iroquois faced military disaster. Diplomatically, meanwhile, their position became untenable. In European international law, the crown that could claim an exclusive alliance with the Iroquois could also declare suzerainty over their territories south of Lake Ontario. Thus, the government of New France insisted that its Native allies continue their war until the Five Nations made a separate peace that would place them under French jurisdiction. New York just as vociferously argued that the Iroquois nations were English subjects and therefore automatically covered by the Ryswick treaty. Each European power retained enough political influence in Native villages to prolong the stalemate for more than three years, during which Indian allies of the French relentlessly pounded their Iroquois foes. If accommodation with the English governor as "greatest lord" had been intended to keep the peace and mobilize power on behalf of the Iroquois, the accommodationists' strategy had failed utterly.[13]

In 1700 a faction of Iroquois leaders broke the diplomatic logjam by overpowering their New York–allied domestic opponents and engineering a surrender to New France. The breathing space this created allowed other leaders to turn capitulation into partial victory by reinventing Iroquois relationships with both imperial powers. At a massively attended council at Montreal in the summer of 1701, more than a dozen Indian nations allied to the French made peace with the Five Nations. In exchange for a pledge of Iroquois neutrality in future wars between European empires, Governor Louis-Hector de Callière promised to enforce the peace and to guarantee the right of Iroquois to hunt north of the Great Lakes and to trade at the French post of Detroit. But unbeknownst to the French governor, other Iroquois leaders were almost simultaneously participating in a conference at Albany, where they surprised their hosts with a deed conveying ownership of the same Great Lakes lands to the English. The document, the Iroquois diplomats insisted, should be sent to "the great King of England to acquaint how that the French of Canada encroach upon our territories . . . and to pray that our great King may use all means to prevent it." In giving each imperial power an equivalent paper claim to the same territory (territory that the Iroquois themselves did not control), this "Grand Settlement of 1701" promised to counter power with power and to preserve Iroquois independence through a new, far more subtle form of accommodation. In theory, each empire now had a stake in preserving Iroquois economic interests as well as peace between the Five Nations and its erstwhile Indian enemies.[14]

Yet the balance-of-power diplomacy harbingered in 1701 remained elusive for the better part of a generation. During the second imperial war, French diplomats, traders, and missionaries used increasingly heavy-handed means to force the Iroquois to remain neutral, if not submit to French hegemony. Meantime, the peace that New France pledged to guarantee in the Great Lakes region proved elusive. As a result, in 1709 and 1711, when New Yorkers and New Englanders planned elaborate invasions of New France, hundreds of Iroquois enlisted in the efforts. Neither expedition ever left its staging area, however, and the debacles helped ensure that, as the Long Peace began, most Iroquois placed no more trust in the English than they did in the French. Experience had proven that acknowledging any governor exclusively as "greatest lord" was suicidal— particularly if that meant getting involved in imperial warfare. "If we should take up the hatchet . . . the governor of Canada would look down upon us with indignation, and set the people round about, who are his children, upon us, and that would set all the world on fire," one Iroquois orator explained.[15]

The dangers of too-thorough accommodation with a single European empire also became clear to one particular group of those many "Children" of the Canadian governor. As the turn-of-the-century imperial wars began, the situation of the *reserves* along the St. Lawrence River resembled that of the New England praying towns before Metacom's War. Although in comparison to English Puritans, French Jesuit missionaries tended to be far more open to traditional Native patterns of agriculture, housing, clothing, and even seasonal migration by male hunters, people who followed Kateri Tekakwitha's example and chose to live at the *reserves* had clearly thrown in their lot religiously, politically, and economically with the French. On the surface, at least, their accommodation with European imperial power appeared far more thoroughgoing than anything advocated by English-allied League Iroquois leaders.[16] Not surprisingly, when New France and the Iroquois went to war, the men of the *reserves* came under enormous pressure to enter the fray on behalf of their French Father. That for the most part they resisted the pressure suggests that they early recognized the dangers of dependence on a single European power. The *way* in which they resisted suggests both their determination to pursue an independent course and the constraints under which they operated.

The most populous and most militarily significant of the *reserves* were Kahnawake, another predominantly Mohawk community near Montreal that came to be known as Kanesatake, and a predominantly Western Abenaki village approximately fifty miles upriver from Montreal called Odanak or St. François.[17] Among the Mohawks of Kahnawake and Kanesatake (both communities actually derived from multiple Iroquoian and Algonquian-speaking roots), memories of the struggles between Catholics and traditionalists in the Iroquois homeland during Tekakwitha's generation remained fresh, and enmities ran deep. Nonetheless, communication and kinship ties with League Iroquois communities never entirely ceased, and, when war broke out, they provided a powerful check on internecine bloodshed. Although there were some deaths on both sides from the 1680s to the 1710s, to a striking degree Kahnawake and Kanesatake Iroquois went out of their way to avoid direct military engagement with the League Iroquois or with New York. In 1698—at the height of the crisis between the Five Nations and their western Indian foes—a French chronicler noted that when League Mohawks came to the *reserves* they were "left at perfect liberty, and walk[ed] daily in the streets of Montreal with as much confidence as if peace were perfectly ratified."[18]

Unwilling to engage in the fratricidal war that would result from war with New York but also in no position to betray their military obligations to the French, fighters from Kahnawake and Kanesatake demonstrated their loyalty by attacking New England instead. But in doing so, they fought a war that was more Indian than French in its origins, and their alliance was as much with the people of Odanak as with New France. Odanak, like Kahnawake and Kanesatake, was a community with diverse roots; Indians from at least twenty nations had settled there since its founding in the 1660s. The vast majority, however, traced their origins to present-day Vermont, New Hampshire, and northwestern Massachusetts, among such Western Abenaki–speaking groups as the Sokokis and Penacooks and such Southern New England Algonquian-speakers as the Pocumtucks. Nearly all had come to Odanak as refugees from Metacom's War and thus had every reason to welcome the chance to strike back against their old Massachusetts enemies under the guise of loyal service to the French.[19]

Yet even such a dramatic conjunction of Indian and French military interests occurred amidst crosscutting economic and cultural relationships that led the people of Odanak—like their Kahnawake and Kanesatake allies—to recognize the dangers of military engagement with, and the virtues of neutrality between, the European empires. Odanak people had many kin, and close economic and political connections, with Western

Abenakis who lived in several villages that continued to dot the upper
Merrimack, Connecticut, and Lake Champlain watersheds, including
some who had accepted Andros' offer to resettle at Schaghticoke under
the protection of the Anglo-Iroquois Covenant Chain. These relationships put the Odanak people in much the same position with respect to
New York as were the Kahnawake and Kanesatake Mohawks; they, too,
had powerful incentives to shy away from attacks on the Hudson River
colony that might engage them in battles with their own kin. Throughout
the turn-of-the-century wars, the Odanak people temporized, fighting
alongside the French only when their own interests, and their own local
controversies with English colonists, led them to do so. Like the League
Iroquois, then, the St. Lawrence *reserve* communities learned to tread a
careful independent course between the imperial powers.[20]

From a vantage point far to the south, a story of the first and second
imperial wars different in particulars but similar in outline comes into
view. Since the founding of St. Augustine in 1565, Spanish colonists—
never more than about 1,500 in the seventeenth century—had steadily expanded their influence over many of the Native peoples of southeastern
North America. By 1635, on the eve of the Pequot War far to the north,
Spanish officials in Florida had claimed that 30,000 Indians were associated with over forty Franciscan mission towns, or *reducciones*—so called
because Spanish clergy, like their English and French counterparts, believed that Indians must be "reduced to civility" before they could become
Christians. By 1675, on the eve of Metacom's War and Bacon's Rebellion,
epidemics and other factors had shrunk the nominally Christian population to slightly over 13,000. Approximately thirty-five *reducciones* stretched
from St. Catherine's Island, off the coast of present-day Georgia, through
the neighborhood of St. Augustine 150 miles to the south, to the
Apalachicola River nearly 300 miles to the west, on the present-day border
between Florida and Alabama. Spanish friars divided these towns into
four linguistic groups, or "provinces," from Guale in the east through
Timucua and Apalachee, to Apalachicola in the west. Most residents
spoke languages of the Muskogean family, but like countless people elsewhere in North America, they were of diverse backgrounds. The slightly
over 1,300 Indians of the Timucua province in 1675, for example, traced

their origins to what had been at least fifteen separate nations a century and a half earlier when Juan Ortiz had lived among one of them.[21]

There were many cultural and local differences, but the Florida *reducciones* were a phenomenon broadly similar to the praying towns of New England and the *reserves* of New France: religious and cultural conversion went hand in hand, and people settled there for a variety of spiritual, economic, and political reasons. Organized into a "Republic of Indians" rigidly segregated from the "Republic of Spaniards" centered at St. Augustine, the towns were ruled by accommodationist hereditary chiefs who had converted to Christianity. For these chiefs, or *caciques,* the benefits of the Spanish regime were substantial. Treated in Spanish law as a hereditary nobility, the *señores naturales,* or "natural lords," whose vassalage legitimated the king's right to Florida were entitled not only to diplomatic gifts but, more importantly, to enjoy the same rights of labor service from Indian commoners as were priests, churches, and the royal government. While abuses of the forced labor system in Florida seldom approached those in other parts of New Spain, and nothing on the scale of the Great Pueblo Revolt, which drove Spaniards from New Mexico in 1680, occurred in this part of the world, there were constant tensions and numerous small acts of armed resistance against Spanish authority. Just as often, however, the tensions pitted commoners against their own *caciques.*[22]

Nonmission Indians to the north of Florida resisted further expansion of the Republic of Indians, reportedly protesting "that, on their becoming Christians the Spaniards treat them as slaves, that they no longer have liberty, nor are they masters of their possession."[23] And, as was the case with Iroquois who had similar grievances against the French in this period, at least some of these Indians pinned their hopes on alliance with a newly expansionist English colonial government. The Carolinas, chartered by Charles II in 1663 as part of the same wave of imperial centralization that led to the conquest of New Netherland, were specifically designed to intrude on the purported boundaries of Spanish Florida. And, like initial European colonists everywhere, the English who established Charleston in 1670 were eager to profit from trade with the Native neighbors. They found ready partners in Indians trying to escape Spanish hegemony.[24]

But Carolina's early experience was very different from that of Virginia or New England a generation or two earlier, if only because many of the settlers—far from being bumbling newcomers from England—had emigrated from the thriving slave-based economy of Barbados. In stark opposition to the idealistic dreams of the colony's proprietors in England, some of the Carolina colonists almost immediately began encouraging Indian trading partners to raid their Native neighbors for slaves, who could be shipped to the West Indies far more profitably than crops could be marketed in the British Isles. As elsewhere in North America, in the southeast the taking of war captives had deep indigenous roots, and prisoners who were spared from death were adopted into families in a subordinate status that at least temporarily resembled slavery; many of the retainers of de Soto's "Lady of Cofitachequi," for example, apparently held this status. But the commercial value of enslaved captives, in tandem with the economic and demographic stresses that everywhere on the continent spurred war on a previously unimagined scale, made this region's inter-Indian wars perhaps the most violent of all.[25]

Thus, "what began as a trade for the skins of deer was transformed almost immediately into a trade for the skins of Indians," and one year's raiders became the next year's victims. First inland Westos captured Cusabos and others nearer the coast. In the early 1680s Savannahs (Shawnees) from farther in the interior seized formerly dominant Westos. Next, Siouan-speaking peoples of the Piedmont made slaves of Savannahs. While all this was going on north and west of Charleston, raids into Florida were being carried out by two Muskogean-speaking groups: the Yamasees, who had emigrated northward to escape Spanish domination and had apparently been joined by commoners from various *reducciones* who were equally determined to escape the oppression of their own *caciques;* and the clusters of towns the English lumped together as "Creeks," among whom were the people of what Spaniards called the province of Apalachiola. Beginning in 1702, the second imperial war provided a justification for Carolina troops to join the Yamasees and Creeks wholeheartedly in slave raids against the Republic of Indians. By the end of that conflict in 1713, none of the Florida *reducciones* survived, and thousands of their Timucua, Apalachee, and Guale residents had been killed or enslaved. Most of the captives were sold to the British Caribbean, but a substantial number labored alongside Africans in the newly expanding rice fields of the Carolina Low Country.[26]

The Long Peace would not come to the southeast until the region had endured its bloody equivalent of Metacom's War and Bacon's Rebellion, in the linked conflicts known as the Tuscarora War of 1711–12 and the Yamasee War of 1715–16. The Tuscaroras, whose homelands included much of present-day North Carolina, lived too far from Charleston to profit easily from trade with the Carolinians, yet too near to avoid the raids of Indians more strategically placed for the traffic in slaves. By 1711 their problems were exacerbated by Swiss and German immigrants to Carolina who began settling on their lands without permission. Tuscaroras captured the intruders' leader, Christoph von Graffenried, along with Carolina's provincial surveyor-general, John Lawson. At a council of headmen, Graffenried talked his way to freedom, but Lawson was condemned to death. Shortly thereafter, Tuscaroras attacked and killed more than a hundred Europeans. South Carolina coordinated joint retaliatory expeditions in which it enlisted the Yamasees and other Indian rivals of the Tuscaroras. By 1713 most of the nation's villages had been burned; perhaps 1,000 men, women, and children had been killed; and some 700 others had been enslaved. The 2,500 Tuscaroras who escaped became refugees.[27]

The Yamasees who helped to send them into exile were themselves in desperate straits. Under terms of Carolina legislation passed in 1707 they were confined to a fragment of their former lands on the Savannah River, and even this territory was being overrun by planters and their grazing cattle. Many were deeply in debt to Carolina traders who routinely enslaved Indians who defaulted. If Yamasee leaders hoped that their service on behalf of the Carolinians in the Tuscarora War would win them some relief, they soon learned otherwise and began building an alliance with similarly oppressed Creeks and others. In April 1715 members of the alliance attacked, destroying Carolina plantations and killing English traders wherever they could find them in Indian country. Even those operating as far away as the lower Mississippi Valley were not safe.[28]

During the winter of 1715–16, armed parties of Creeks and Carolinians each entered the country of the previously neutral Cherokees to pressure that populous nation to take sides. Although the Cherokees were deeply divided politically, they were as dependent on trade with the English as were their Native neighbors, and the same logic that earlier drove the Yamasees to side with the Carolinians led the dominant Cherokee faction to assassinate a Creek delegation that had come to their country to enlist the nation in their cause. Subsequently, Cherokees "fell upon the Creeks and Yamasees who were in their towns and killed every man of them." The united front of Cherokees and English dramatically tipped the military balance, and the Euro-Indian war quickly wound down, although the conflict between Cherokees and Creeks did not. Those Yamasees who avoided death or enslavement relocated to Florida, and many Creeks moved their villages farther west from Carolina, in hopes of establishing trade with the French of Louisiana. When the fighting subsided, vast areas of the Indian southeast were depopulated, some 7 percent of British Carolinians had perished, and the regional economy—including its brutal Native American slave trade—was shattered.[29]

Everywhere, then, the lessons Native people drew from the carnage of the period between Metacom's War and the Yamasee War were the same. Direct military confrontation with European powers was suicidal; some kind of diplomatic accommodation was the only route to survival. But an accommodation that relied solely on a single European power was an almost equally certain path to extinction. Whether in the form of the "greatest lord" Andros, the spiritual lord of the Christian God, the material lord of a briefly profitable intercultural trade, or the indigenous lords created by the Republic of Indians, accommodations that relied solely on Albany, or Quebec, or Charleston, or St. Augustine led to disaster. The Native peoples who survived and even prospered into the eighteenth century capitalized on their geographic position, their economic and military value to European governors, and their decentralized political systems to keep their options open, to maintain connections with more than one imperial power, and thus to maintain their cultural and political autonomy. As a frustrated New York Indian affairs secretary Peter Wraxall put it, "to preserve the balance between us and the French is the great ruling principle of the modern Indian politics."[30]

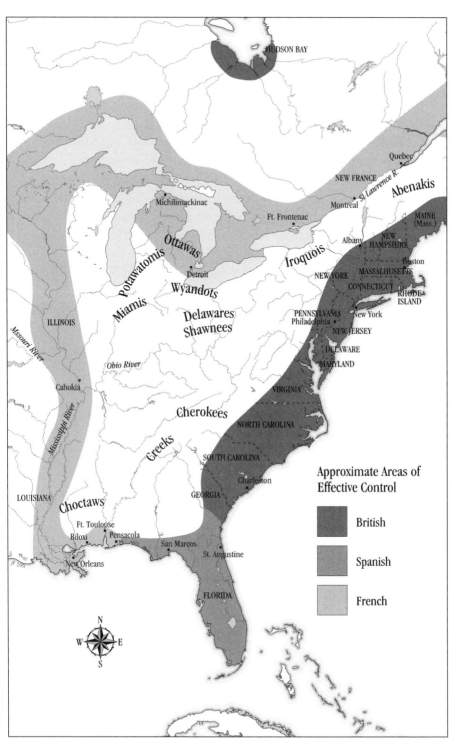

Eastern North America in the eighteenth-century imperial world: major Native powers and areas of European control.

A look at the map of eastern North America reveals the geographic factors that shaped "the modern Indian politics" during the Long Peace. Indian country remained vast, but it was entirely surrounded by a segmented ring of competing European imperial entities. From the new colony of Georgia (established in 1733) northeastward through the Carolinas to Nova Scotia, the Atlantic coast harbored an unbroken succession of populous, but often rivalrous, British provinces. An arc sweeping from Cape Breton Island through the St. Lawrence Valley contained the smaller but more politically unified *habitants* of New France. The French arc continued westward through the portages of the Great Lakes, then southward along the Mississippi River through *le pays des Illinois* and its semi-independent cluster of French villages—one of them on the ancient site of Cahokia. At New Orleans, the arc turned eastward across the Gulf coast to Biloxi and Mobile. Throughout this huge territory—considered part of New France in the north, called Louisiana from Illinois southward—a sprinkling of strategic forts, trading stations, and missions anchored Gallic claims. Closing the imperial circle were the surviving military outposts of Spanish Florida, which traced a thin line from Pensacola, through San Marcos, to St. Augustine and the contested boundary with Georgia.[31] Within this imperial circle, Indian country was dominated by six clusters of peoples whose welfare depended on their ability to exploit relationships with two or more of the surrounding European colonies.

In the northeastern quadrant were the paradigmatic modern Indians, the League Iroquois. The Treaty of Utrecht, which ended the second imperial war in Europe, declared them to be "subject to the dominion of Great Britain," yet guaranteed equal access to the Five Nations and "other Natives of America, who are friends to the same" for traders from New France. The same reciprocity applied with respect to Indians with ties to the French. The question of who, exactly, "ought to be accounted as subjects or friends of Britain or of France" remained disputed, and officials on both sides competed vigorously to confirm their diplomatic position.[32] In this competitive postwar situation, an important minority of Iroquois continued to consider their Covenant Chain relationship with New York to be strong and valuable. British officials and New York leaders meanwhile carefully cultivated an illusion of the kind of imperial suzerainty Andros had dreamed about in 1677. In 1710 four supposed Mohawk Iroquois "kings" were brought to London to publicize the connection. Despite the facts that none was a hereditary chief and that one was actually a Mahican rather than a Mohawk, the visit was a rousing public-relations success, and the League Iroquois became the best-known Native Americans in British circles. The publication of Cadwallader Colden's significantly titled *History of the Five Indian Nations Depending on the Province of New-York in America* in New York in 1727 and in an expanded London edition in 1747 reinforced a transatlantic image of strategically vital Indians loyally subordinated to the empire.[33]

But for most Iroquois leaders, the relationship with their British Brethren was a carefully cultivated mystique that overlooked the confederacy's countervailing economic and diplomatic ties to New France. Neutralists dominated Iroquois councils, while members of other factions did the important work of maintaining the close economic and diplomatic accommodations with both Albany and Montreal that ensured neither empire would write them off.[34] Contributing mightily to the wariness with which the Iroquois threaded their way between empires were the viewpoints of an array of refugees from wars with other English colonies who continued to be welcomed to Iroquoia and to points adjacent in present-day central Pennsylvania throughout the early eighteenth century. Most notable among these were between 1,500 and 2,000 Tuscaroras who, after their nation's defeat, migrated northward and were adopted as the Sixth Nation of the League. What one Anglican missionary described as the Tuscaroras' "implacable hatred against Christians at Carolina" lent political support to those among their new confederates who viewed all Europeans with suspicion.[35]

Much of the balance-of-power politicking among the Six Nations, the French, and the British centered on access to the Indian trade of the Great Lakes region that Iroquois diplomats had deeded to the English crown in 1701. The area the French called the *pays d'en haut*—the present states of Michigan and Wisconsin and adjacent northern Indiana, Illinois, and Ontario—was "a world made of fragments." A variety of survivors from the seventeenth-century Iroquois wars and from the great early-contact-era epidemics had coalesced into a loose network of refugee villages. Hurons mixed with other Iroquoian-speakers to become the people known as Wyandots. Ottawas, Miamis, Illinois, Ojibwas, Potawatomis, Foxes, and

others who spoke Algonquian languages lived interspersed with one another, sometimes in the same villages, more often in separate towns clus-
tered near French posts such as Michilimackinac or Detroit. At the turn
of the century, they had been held together by their common animosity
to the Iroquois and by their common status as Children of their French
Father. By the 1720s, however, the people of *pays d'en haut* were united
more by their own shared history in the region and by arrangements with
their former Iroquois enemies that allowed them to counterbalance
French influence with trade at the New York outpost of Oswego, and so
to practice their own version of the modern Indian politics. Just as Iroquois publicly proclaimed their fealty to the British Covenant Chain while
trading and negotiating with New France, Great Lakes Indians touted
their love of the French Father while selling their furs to New Yorkers.[36]

Another world made of fragments took shape in the area known as
"the Ohio Country," stretching from modern-day Pittsburgh through
West Virginia, Kentucky, and eastern Ohio. Like the *pays d'en haut,* in the
seventeenth century this region was depopulated by wars, epidemics,
and, apparently, outmigrations of people seeking closer access to sources
of European trade goods. In the early eighteenth century, it was re-
occupied by bands of Shawnees (who may have had ancestral claims to
the lands), "Delawares" (a polyglot group of Munsees, Lenapes, and others forced from homes in the mid-Atlantic region), and "Mingoes" (Iroquois from various nations who joined the westward migration). This diverse lot often settled in multiethnic and multilingual villages where they
discovered that they had much in common with each other. Many were
refugees twice-removed, having left homes in the Susquehanna watershed to which they or their parents had earlier migrated from elsewhere.
Determined not to move again, they shared a vigorous distrust of Europeans, particularly the Pennsylvanians, whom they blamed for their most
recent dispersal. Yet they were almost equally leery of the League Iroquois, whose protection under the Covenant Chain had proved illusory
and whose pretensions to diplomatic hegemony they increasingly resented. Able to trade with the French on the Mississippi and the Great
Lakes as well as with the British of Virginia, Pennsylvania, and New York,
the Ohio Country villages were strategically positioned to assert their independence of Europeans and Six Nations Iroquois alike.[37]

Southward from the Ohio Country lay the area that had become its own kind of fragmented refugee zone after the Yamasee and Tuscarora wars. Three dominant entities emerged from the carnage, and from the repeated political and demographic upheavals that had struck the descendants of the great Mississippian chiefdoms in the two centuries since de Soto's rampage: the Cherokees, the Creeks, and the Choctaws. Each was a complicated multiethnic mixture and each really coalesced as a political and cultural entity only in the early eighteenth century. Most Cherokees, having endured a deeply divisive decision to side with the Carolinians against the Yamasees and Creeks, almost immediately retreated from the grip of Charleston to make Virginians their primary, but not exclusive, trading partners. This British-versus-British balancing act intersected in complex ways with regional and factional divisions among "Overhill," "Valley," and "Lower" towns, with a potential alliance with French Louisiana, and with the emergence of what were sometimes described as "renegade" communities affiliated with Ohio Country villages. As did their counterparts among the Iroquois, Cherokee factional leaders and their colonial allies did their best to obscure all these complexities for a transatlantic British audience. In 1730 an eccentric Scottish baronet named Sir Alexander Cuming traveled from Charleston through Cherokee country to recruit six alleged chiefs for a highly publicized London interview with the Board of Trade. As had been the case with the visit of the "Iroquois kings" twenty years earlier, the embassy cultivated a mystique of exclusive loyalty that was one of the hallmarks of the modern Indian politics.[38]

While various Cherokee factions preserved their nation's independence through such diplomatic maneuvers, farther southward the Creeks, or Muscogulges, rapidly recovered from the Yamasee War to become, in many respects, the region's dominant economic and military power. Especially as their towns became magnets for survivors of slave raids and wars with Carolinians, the Creeks became an extraordinarily diverse lot, even by the melting-pot standards of eighteenth-century Native America. Only about half, including the Yamasees whom they incorporated, spoke Muskogean languages. As the century progressed, the remainder came to include Alabamas, Natchez, Shawnees, and countless others—including the extremely mixed Florida people later known as Seminoles, of whom a substantial proportion were escaped African-American slaves. Drawing on this diversity, Creeks pursued a complicated three-way balance-of-power diplomacy. In the Lower Creek towns along tributaries of the Apalachicola River, pro-Spanish leaders drew upon their Yamasee connections to cultivate ties to Florida and to welcome the establishment of Fort San Marcos on Apalachee Bay in 1718. Similarly, factions in the Upper Creek towns along tributaries of the Alabama River had encouraged the French to station a garrison at Fort Toulouse along that stream in 1716. These connections mitigated a heavy economic dependence upon Carolina traders that quickly reemerged after the Yamasee War, and helped to prevent such a war from happening again.[39]

Farther westward, in a zone where, as in the *pays d'en haut,* the French were the dominant imperial force, a final cluster centered on the Choctaws of the east-central portion of today's state of Mississippi. These people, too, comprised a diverse collection of migrants from elsewhere. Although they were, on the whole, firm allies and trading partners of their Louisiana French Father, diverse political and economic allegiances cut across regional divisions among "Eastern" and "Western" villages in the north and "Sixtowns" villages in the south. A bloody assault by pro-British Choctaws on Natchez, Mobile, and other French posts in 1747 demonstrated that at least some of these groups were linked to more than one imperial power. Louisiana, unable to compete with Carolina traders in either price or quantity of goods, tried to discourage Choctaws from joining the British commercial network by encouraging their rivalry with the much smaller Chickasaw population to their north, which did trade with Charleston. But, as was the case in the *pays d'en haut* and elsewhere, the French governor's insistence on being termed "Father" rather than "Uncle" only encouraged their allies' independence. The Choctaws treated Louisianans in the way "their matrilineal society taught them they should: as kind, indulgent nonrelatives who had no authority over them." And "the governors, well aware that the Choctaws could represent a formidable enemy at their gates, were forced to play this role."[40]

Wherever they were located, Indian communities of the continental interior depended on sophisticated leadership able to secure negotiating room for their people through nuanced accommodation with European empires. Yet the extent to which balance-of-power diplomacy was a coherent strategy pursued by farseeing Native leaders should not be overstated. Instead, it grew in ingeniously improvised ways from complicated patterns of factionalism and decentralized leadership. In a paradoxical way, it was precisely the *lack* of centralized political unity that made the modern Indian politics work: factional leaders independently cultivated ties to particular European colonies, cumulatively maintaining the multiple connections that warded off political dependence on powerful European neighbors.[41]

Helping to keep the centripetal forces from spinning out of control, while providing a general cross-cultural framework within which the intricate balances of power in eastern North America could be mediated, meanwhile, was the nearly universal ritualized system of intercultural diplomacy that Indians and Europeans had first taught each other at Albany in the late seventeenth century. As basic diplomatic forms spread throughout the continent, royal governors and Native leaders everywhere participated in similar grand public treaty conferences, addressed each other by similar kinship terms and inherited titles, spoke in similar metaphorical vocabularies, exchanged similar wampum belts, and recorded their transactions in similar written minutes. This culture of diplomacy increasingly drew diverse Indian communities into a single political world in which colonial governors appointed by distant crowns were focal points and could proclaim, as Virginia's Francis Fauquier did to a Cherokee delegation on George II's birthday in 1758, that "the King [was] the common father of all his people, White and Red."[42] Just as eighteenth-century British Americans found political stability in a transatlantic imperial framework, so too, in a parallel way, did Native Americans.[43]

While large nations and confederacies used diplomacy to survive in the continental interior, smaller clusters of survivors regrouped nearer the imperial ring, where opportunities to balance power against power were scarcer and integration into the transatlantic imperial world was an unavoidable fact of life. Perhaps the most successful of such peoples were the various Siouan-speaking communities of the Carolina Piedmont that became the Catawba Nation. Although their lands were steadily encroached upon by Anglo-Carolinians, they relied on Charleston's need for

a military buffer on the province's borders to preserve their cultural autonomy and, in the words of one early nineteenth-century observer, "be
Indians still."[44] On Virginia's frontiers, such survivors of Bacon's Rebellion as the Tutelos and Saponis exploited a similar function until the 1740s,
when they relocated under Iroquois protection to the Susquehanna River
watershed. There they joined diverse refugees from New England as well
as from points south who, as many Shawnees and Delawares migrated to
the Ohio Country, remained in territories those peoples had occupied
amidst powerful British and Iroquois neighbors.[45]

To the east and north of these, a handful of similarly mixed communities focused their accommodation, and their survival as distinctly Indian
groups, on conversion to Christianity, just as Natick people had done a
century earlier. Most notable among these were the Stockbridge community, founded by Congregationalists in western Massachusetts in 1734 and
relocated to New York State in 1785; the Moravian missions established at
several sites in Pennsylvania beginning in 1746; and Brothertown in New
York, founded by the Mohegan minister Samson Occum in 1775. The possession of some military strength and the threat, if not the realistic op-
tion, of moving westward out of the British orbit ensured that these communities would be allies rather than subjects of Euro-Americans,
although they lacked the real freedom of diplomatic movement that geography, economics, and sheer numbers gave to such peoples as the Iroquois or Creeks.[46] The Mohawks of Kahnawake and Kanesatake, meanwhile, found a similar spot between the two great empires, based on their
continued familial ties with Iroquoia and, in particular, their role as couri-
ers in an illegal trade between Albany and Montreal merchants exchang-
ing Canadian furs for New York woolens and wampum. Thus like various
small communities allied to the British, the *reserves* also kept their options
open.[47]

Slightly more maneuvering room was available to a loose confederacy
whose territories spread across present-day New Hampshire, Maine, and
New Brunswick. Composed primarily of family bands of Penobscots and
Kennebecs who spoke the Eastern Abenaki language, their villages relocated often, and families did so still more frequently. In peacetime many
of these groups welcomed French Jesuit missionaries while trading with
New Englanders, who tended to lump them together with the linguisti-

NATIVE PEOPLES IN AN IMPERIAL WORLD   173

cally distinct Western Abenakis of Vermont and Odanak as "Eastern Indians." Disputes over commerce and land combined with hatreds stretching
back to Metacom's War to produce frequent Anglo-Abenaki violence,
most notably during the conflict in the 1720s known variously as
"Dummer's," "Rale's," or "Gray Lock's War." During the Long Peace, the
government of New France held back from direct involvement in the
Eastern Abenakis' wars with the British—even in 1724, when New England forces burned the village of Norrigewock and killed and scalped its
resident priest, Sébastien Rale. French restraint thus reinforced the Eastern Abenakis' independent position between the two empires.[48]

Far less independence could be enjoyed by Indians who lived within the
borders and under the direct political authority of the British colonies.
Despite the wars of the seventeenth century, small Native American enclaves still dotted southern New England, Long Island, and the tidewater
Chesapeake. These retained considerable control over their lands, their
everyday political affairs, and even their Christian churches. Some were
blessed with out-of-the-way or agriculturally unpromising locales, such as
Martha's Vineyard, eastern Long Island, or the Pamunkey and Mattaponi
reservations in Tidewater Virginia. Others found a specialized niche in
the Euro-American economy, such as the whaling ships that sailed from
Nantucket with Native people among their crews. Others were less isolated from Euro-American land-hunger. The surviving praying town of
Natick and the "Indian district" of Mashpee in Massachusetts, the
Narragansett reservation in Rhode Island, the Pequot and Mohegan reservations of Connecticut, the Piscataway tributaries of Maryland, and the
"Settlement Indians" of South Carolina gradually lost their lands entirely
or clung to small holdings interspersed with those of Euro-Americans.
Still other Native people melted into a larger racially mixed population of
servants, day laborers, and freed slaves. Some—most notably the Lum-
bees of the Carolinas—lacked any communal land base, formal status in
Anglo-American law, or common ethnic and racial roots, and yet still
maintained a sense of collective identity—kept alive, as much as anything
else, by the prejudices of their Euro-American neighbors.[49]

The legal and institutional relationship, if any, of these encapsulated
communities to provincial governments varied widely. In many cases,
government-appointed Anglo-American trustees in theory guarded their

economic, educational, and religious interests, while in practice showing little real concern for the conditions under which they lived. Whether or not such arrangements existed, and whether or not Indians dwelled on legally recognized reservation lands, Native Americans who lived within colonial boundaries were subject to provincial criminal law, and their civil rights tended to be subject to many of the same formal and informal restrictions as those of free African- and Euro-American servants, with whom they often socialized and intermarried. By midcentury many such Indians spoke English as their first and perhaps only language and were at least nominally Christian in religion. Although many self-consciously embraced an Indian identity, that identity tended to be woven of folk tales from a variety of regional cultural sources, of a well-developed sense of oppression by the dominant culture, and of a sense of history influenced as much by the Anglo-American written record as by indigenous oral tradition. Like eighteenth-century Native people everywhere, their lives were profoundly shaped by colonial experience in the transatlantic world.[50]

For Indians, as for Euro-Americans, that world was knit together as an "Empire of Goods." Indeed, in many respects Native Americans experienced the full effects of the eighteenth-century consumer revolution even before most British Americans did.[51] "A modern Indian cannot subsist without Europeans and would handle a flint ax or any other rude utensil used by his ancestors very awkwardly," colonial official John Stuart explained in 1761; "what was only conveniency at first is now become necessity."[52] The list of conveniencies and necessities that tied Native Americans to transatlantic commerce was extensive. Indian country relied on trade with Europe and Europeans for items as diverse as weapons and ammunition, woolen textiles used for men's cloaks, women's skirts, and leggings for both sexes, ready-made linen shirts for men and shifts for women, vermilion and verdigris for body and face painting, tools of every kind from knives and hatchets to needles and scissors, brass kettles and pewter spoons, muskets and gun flints, jewelry, liquor, tobacco, and wampum (which in the eighteenth century was mostly turned out in Albany workshops). Apart from food and shelter, virtually every aspect of Indian material life depended upon economic ties with Europe. Given the role that imported tools and weapons also played in agriculture, hunting, and building construction, Stuart's conclusion that "a modern Indian cannot subsist without Europeans" becomes all the more apt. That fact, of course, reinforced the life-and-death importance of keeping open ties to more than one colonial power, and thus more than one colonial market.[53]

As consumers, however, modern Indians used imported goods in ways rooted in their own rather than European cultures; they were no more deculturated by trade than were twentieth-century North Americans who purchased Japanese televisions. Indeed, it is more accurate, and more revealing of the parallel rather than intersecting courses of Native and Euro-American histories, to describe eighteenth-century imports not as European goods but as "Indian goods" made in Europe to suit Native tastes. Commodities designed specifically for North American markets included the varieties of heavy woolen cloth known as "duffels," made in present-day Belgium, and "strouds" or "strowdwaters," manufactured in Gloucestershire. Inexperienced Euro-American traders soon learned that if duffels or strouds were not cut to precisely the right size and dyed in the appropriate shades of deep blue, dark red, or steel gray, the items were virtually unsalable. Similarly precise specifications applied to glass beads (for which fashions in size, shape, and color changed so precisely with the times that archaeologists find them the most reliable date markers for Native American sites), to brass kettles and iron axes (each of which was made to lighter and simpler specifications for Indian customers), and to muskets (which at Indian insistence were extremely lightweight and equipped with advanced flintlock mechanisms). When "trade axes" broke the first time they were used or "trade muskets" blew up in their Native owners' faces, the problem was not necessarily that unscrupulous merchants were pawning off cheap junk. In both cases, Indian customers' demand for inexpensive, lightweight, easily portable items stretched European technological capabilities to their limits. There was a good reason why, to be reliable, the thick-barreled standard-issue British army "Brown Bess" musket had to weigh more than twice as much as a thin-barreled trade gun.[54]

If the specifications of such artifacts—along with the cumulative effect

Creek leaders in London, 1730: transatlantic political and economic connections displayed.
From William Verelst, *Trustees of Georgia* (1734–35). Courtesy, Winterthur Museum.

seen in any number of surviving portraits and engravings depicting eighteenth-century Native people wearing and using them—reveal the complex ways in which Indians integrated themselves into the transatlantic
Empire of Goods without losing their distinct cultural identity, so too
does the way the acquisition and use of those goods fit into traditional
patterns of reciprocity and exchange. Traders traveling in Indian country
had to pay as much attention to Native customs as did diplomats at treaty
councils; moreover, they were likely to traverse routes that had been in
use centuries before the Indian discovery of Europe. In form if not in
function, exchanges continued to embody personal relationships, rather
than impersonal buying and selling. Convivial rituals—a shared smoke, or

drink, or meal—surrounded transactions, and gift exchange, rather than haggling, remained the convention even when all parties knew that everything had its price.[55]

The limited degree to which capitalist assumptions about property and accumulation penetrated early eighteenth-century Native societies is suggested by the comments of a group of Iroquois headmen on their way to a council in Philadelphia in 1736. According to Pennsylvania interpreter Conrad Weiser, the Native leaders were worried that their people, still imbued with the idea that excess goods were for the use of anyone who needed them, would simply walk off with the unattended possessions of merchants in the big city. "Those that have been in Philadelphia tell us [that] your goods lie alone . . . upon the street about the shops," one of them said. "We desire that it may be kept in house while we are there [so that] it may be seen for all when the shop is open. We will be very careful."[56] Expectations of reciprocity also remained strong. During the Philadelphia treaty council, an orator explained "that amongst them there is never any victuals sold, the Indians give to each other freely what they can spare." When Pennsylvanians charged them for food, the Iroquois were deeply offended that hosts "should take money of [sic] this score."[57]

Such traditional economic patterns came under tremendous stress in the mid-eighteenth century. There is considerable evidence that, in many parts of Indian North America, class lines were emerging between those with greater access to consumer goods (many of whom tended to be métis, or "mixed bloods," who imbibed the capitalist ethos of their Euro-American trader fathers) and those less well supplied.[58] These and other cultural implications of Native dependence on European trade, however, only entrenched Indian people more firmly in a broader narrative of eighteenth-century North American history in which British Americans also were plagued by increasing disparities of wealth and troubled by the apparent contradictions between republican virtue and capitalist acquisition. Socially and culturally, Indian and European histories lived parallel lives in the colonial world.[59]

And in that transatlantic world, Indians were producers as well as consumers. In its mature phase, what we often call the "fur trade" was a complex system in which Native peoples functioned as a labor force producing a variety of commodities for European markets. Just how complex

and historically dynamic the Indian side of the trade could be is illustrated
by the way in which the Creeks shrewdly exploited the changing demands
of the eighteenth-century transatlantic economy. Just as the chaos of the
Yamasee War threw southeastern trade networks into disarray, a series of
fatal bovine epidemics struck continental Europe, creating a huge market
among leather workers for North American deerskins to replace now-
scarce cattle hides. The Creeks—controlling territories that, largely as a
result of their own previous slave-raiding expeditions, were devoid of humans but thronging with white-tailed deer—were ideally placed to profit
from that demand. And so were the South Carolina merchants who, in
the mid-1730s, helped to make the new town of Augusta, Georgia, "the
heart of a vast trading system that stretched from the manufacturing and
commercial centers of the British Isles" to the Muscogulge country and
beyond. By midcentury as many as a million deerskins a year—half of
them harvested by Creeks—moved through the system.[60]

Whether Native peoples provided deerskins, beaver pelts, or slaves for
European markets, the changing role of Indian producers in the eighteenth-century Empire of Goods is perhaps more important than their
role as consumers in helping us to appreciate the complexities of Indian
economic dependence upon the transatlantic economy. Furs and hides
were raw materials; their processing into more valuable finished products
such as felt hats or leather goods took place in Europe. There, and in the
countinghouses of a string of merchant middlemen, profits and capital
accumulated while Indians merely consumed and produced. The lopsided
economic relationship was captured well by an Iroquois spokesman
whose commitment to traditional reciprocity did not preclude a shrewd
understanding of European capitalism. The New York trading post at Oswego was "a vast advantage . . . because we can get there what we want or
desire," he told provincial governor George Clarke in 1740. "But we think,
Brother, that your people who trade there have the most advantage by it,
and that it is as good for them as a silver mine."[61]

Silver mine or no, however, posts such as Oswego and Augusta—and
the intercultural trade that they represented and that was so vital to Native Americans—were of steadily declining economic significance to
Euro-Americans in the mid-eighteenth century. In the 1730s, while the
deerskin trade boomed, prices of furs plummeted in oversupplied Euro-

pean markets, with devastating impacts on the northern Native peoples who relied on the trade. Even after the market for furs revived somewhat in the 1740s, the Indian trade became less important every year for the increasingly diversified economies of the British North American colonies. Although absolute exports of furs and hides from New York and Pennsylvania fluctuated around a steady average, their relative significance in the rapidly expanding economies of those two breadbasket colonies declined steadily from the 1720s to the 1740s. Furs and hides accounted for approximately 40 percent of New York's total exports to London in the 1720s, but for less than 25 percent in the 1740s; the corresponding figures for Pennsylvania are 50 and 44 percent. Both sets of statistics ignore the rapid growth in the two provinces' grain trade with the West Indies and other ports to which no Indian commodities were exported.[62]

By the 1750s even the formerly booming Carolina deerskin trade was falling into a deep depression, with traders' warehouses overflowing with hides for which there was no longer a profitable European outlet.[63] New France defied the pattern. Its fur shipments grew in relative importance as those of the British provinces declined, but only because diplomatic and strategic rather than economic considerations primarily motivated its largely government-controlled Indian trade, the main purpose of which was to maintain alliances with the French Father's Native Children. In this case too, Indians were losing the political clout that comes from economic power, even as they became ever more thoroughly enmeshed in the transatlantic imperial world.[64]

The incompatible economic aims of Native and Euro-Americans—like the hearty distrust of Europeans that characterized Indian balance-of-power politics—show that parallel historical developments on a shared continent did not give birth to common interests. Quite the opposite; precisely because they were on similar courses, colonists and Indians were bound to collide should their trajectories ever intersect. Whatever diplomats may have proclaimed about the love between Fathers and Children or the unbreakable brotherly bonds of the Covenant Chain, the mutual benefits of trade, peace, and stability in eighteenth-century North America rested on anything but sweetness and harmony. A final category of parallel experiences drives the point home. The ethnic diversity and religious fervor that did so much to give the British provinces their distinctive "American" shape were equally important forces in Native life. Yet in neither case was the result tolerance or understanding. Instead, diversity wrought an increasingly pervasive view that "Indians" and "Whites" were utterly different, and utterly incompatible, kinds of people who could never peacefully share the continent.

Indian country had always been diverse, but in the eighteenth century multiplicity became an everyday fact of life. All the groups we know by such names as "Creek," or "Cherokee," or "Iroquois" were relatively new social forms produced by decades of disease, warfare, migration, and resettlement. And, nearly everywhere, people moved frequently, to the extent that "names of communities should often be regarded as 'addresses' rather than tribal designations."[65] Particularly in the Ohio Country and *pays d'en haut*—where peoples mixed most freely and where no preexisting overarching ethnic identity prevailed—this fluid situation inspired religious visionaries to seek new forms of unity that might reinvigorate the lives of refugees cut adrift from ancient traditions. Like the almost simultaneous outbreak of Protestant fervor in British America, this "Indians' Great Awakening" was at heart a religious phenomenon, but it had profound implications for polyglot peoples living in an imperial world.[66]

Among the Indian visionaries, the best known to Euro-Americans was "the Delaware Prophet" Neolin, who gained a wide following in the early 1760s. Yet he was only one of many who preached similar messages from the 1730s onward. Prophets called for the revival or invention of ceremonies that would restore the balance of forces between human and other-than-human persons and symbolically purge Indian communities of European corruption. Converts ritually ingested the "black drink," an herbal emetic that caused them to vomit out foreign contamination. They threw away their alcohol as the most vile contaminant, but also their fiddles, their fondness for gender-mixed dancing in the European style, and anything else that assaulted the newly clarified Native social and spiritual order. They pledged to wean themselves from trade goods, and they made a point of training their children in the use of old-fashioned bows and arrows. In this "nativist" rejection of European ways, followers of Indian prophets "did not retreat wildly into a pristine tradition that never was, hopelessly attempting to escape a world changed by colonial powers." To the contrary, "they self-consciously proclaimed that selected traditions and new (sometimes even imported) modes of behavior held keys to earthly and spiritual salvation, and they rejected the increasing colonial influence in native government, culture, and economy in favor of native independence."[67]

They also learned that, despite ancient rivalries among nations and speakers of different languages, they were all Indians. Central to nativist belief was the idea of separate creations—that the Master of Life had made Europeans, Africans, and Americans distinct from one another and purposely placed them on distinct continents. From this core teaching flowed several important implications: that Europeans had no right to consider themselves superior to Indians; that the Bible with its accounts of creation and salvation were "true," but only for the Europeans for whom it was intended; that Native creation stories and modes of spirituality were equally true and revealed what the Master of Life expected of them; that the mixing of European and Indian ways was the source of Native peoples' current problems; and—the key insight above all—that Indians were a single people with common interests that transcended national rivalries. Thus, in the same period that diverse colonists of varied European backgrounds were discovering in North America their first glimmerings of a "White" racial identity, nativist Indians perhaps even more compellingly discovered that they were "Red." Indeed Indians appear to have used that color term earlier and more consistently than did Euro-Americans, who continued to describe Native Americans' complexion as being only slightly more "tawny" than their own.[68]

When Presbyterian missionary John Brainerd visited a mixed council of Indians who had gathered at Wyoming on the Susquehanna River in 1751 to discuss a revelation lately received by a young woman in a trance, he got a lesson in the doctrine of separate creations and the hardening racial lines that the nativists perceived. "They told me that the great God first made three men and three women," Brainerd wrote. The nativists further explained that these three pairs were

the Indian, the Negro, and the White Man. That the White Man was the youngest brother, and therefore the White people ought not to think themselves better than the Indians. That God gave the White

Man a book, and told him that he must worship him by that; but gave none either to the Indian or Negro, and therefore it could not be right for them to have a book, or be any way concerned with that way of worship. And, furthermore, they understood that the White people were contriving a method to deprive them of their country in those parts, as they had done by the sea-side, and to make slaves of them and their children as they did of the Negroes; that I [Brainerd] was sent on purpose to accomplish that design, and, if I succeeded and managed my business well, I was to be chief ruler in those parts, or, as they termed it, king of all their country, etc. They made all the objections they could, and raked up all the ill treatment they could think of that ever their brethren had received from the White peo- ple; and two or three of them seemed to have resentment enough to have slain me on the spot.

I answered all their objections against Christianity, and likewise the many grievances laid to my charge, and whatever was spoken by any of them. But, when I had done, they told me that I had been learning a great while, and 'twas no wonder if I could out-talk them; but this did not at all convince them that I was not upon a bad de- sign, and therefore they would give me no liberty to preach to their people, but charged me not to come any more upon such an errand.[69]

Despite those who preached racial difference and hostility, coexistence in the imperial world remained possible because the interests of at least some groups in the British, French, and Spanish colonies coincided with those of at least some Indians some of the time. Missionaries were one such group (or at least Brainerd would have said so); traders were an- other. Whatever controversies they might inspire, and whatever long- term threats they might, in retrospect, present to Native cultures, neither group could exist without Indian constituents. Royal officials also found common ground with Indians, if only because they appreciated the stra- tegic value of intercultural alliances. Perennially short of resources, gov- ernors in wartime relied (or, rather, hoped to rely) on Native American al- lies to do most of the fighting against imperial rivals; at the least, it was crucial to keep neutral powerful nations that might go over to another

European side. And wartime alliances also had to be based on peacetime relationships—preferably ones that brought economic benefits to one's own colony rather than to its rivals and created a paper trail of treaties by which territorial claims could be traced in European international law. Military officers similarly ignored the customs of Native people at their peril, as any number of commanders learned when disgruntled Indian troops either failed to show up or turned around and went home. Finally, members of the small corps of interpreters and professional Indian agents who served every colony often genuinely transcended their political and military superiors' scorn for Native people and their customs. Yet there is little reason to believe that either they or the royal and military officials they served would have continued the forms of mutually respectful intercultural diplomacy a minute longer than instrumental military and strategic considerations dictated.[70]

Still, missionaries, traders, governors, warriors, interpreters, and the individual Indian people with whom they worked maintained some ties between the parallel worlds of Native and European North Americans. Occasionally the connections became thoroughly human, as sexual alliances between Euro-American traders and Native women produced *métis* offspring. In the early to mid-eighteenth century, however, the vast majority of these children grew up to live Indian lives in Indian communities. The few who tried to build identities that genuinely blended cultures found themselves deeply distrusted by all sides.[71] Those—White, Indian, or *métis*—who did build bridges based them more often on hardheaded practicality than on genuine affection. Just as significant, any common interests that did exist between peoples tended to derive more from joint participation in the transatlantic world than from shared experience in North America. Missionaries found far more financial support and moral commitment among philanthropists and government officials in Europe than among colonial parishioners. Traders, whatever their personal relationships with Native women, ultimately served the Empire of Goods. Governors, generals, and interpreters more often worked for their distant crowns than for closer-to-home provincial legislators, planters, *habitants*, or *criollos*. In this regard, the human ties functioned much like the rungs of a ladder. They both connected two parallel worlds and kept them from crashing together in a catastrophic collapse.

In New France, French Louisiana, and Spanish Florida, missionaries, traders, royal officials, military men, and interpreters accounted for a substantial share of the population and almost entirely determined government policy. Few others lived in Louisiana and Florida, and New France's relatively small population of farmers coexisted fairly easily with the few *reserves* scattered among them. In British North America, by contrast, the five interest groups constituted a tiny and relatively powerless minority among the colonists. Indeed, the economic goals of most British Americans were almost entirely antithetical to European-Indian accommodation. Not intercultural trade but capitalist agriculture, whether on family farms or on plantations worked by enslaved African laborers, was primary, and persistent immigration of agricultural labor was essential to economic prosperity. The result was an inexorable demand for new agricultural land—land that in one way or another had to be expropriated from its aboriginal owners. As the fur and hide trades declined in relative significance, the demand for agricultural land increased, and immigrants poured into Indian country under only the loosest of supervision by overwhelmed provincial governments. In the southeast the situation was compounded by the establishment of Georgia in 1733, which upset the fragile equipoise of Carolinian, Spanish, French, Creek, and Choctaw forces. Despite guarantees of Muscogulge lands that Georgia's James Oglethorpe promised in the 1739 Treaty of Coweta, Creeks quickly took to calling Georgians *Ecunnaunuxulgee*, or "People greedily grasping after the lands of the Red people."[72]

At midcentury the balance of forces and the fragile linking rungs that allowed parallel Native and European worlds to coexist collapsed most dramatically in the Ohio Country, where Indian animosities toward inhabitants of the British colonies were perhaps already higher than anywhere else in North America and were fueled by nativist fervor. The rapidly expanding populations of Virginia and especially Pennsylvania were repeating the kinds of land pressures that had earlier helped to produce Metacom's War and Bacon's Rebellion. As ever more Delawares and Shawnees were pushed westward into the Ohio Country, they also moved beyond the capacity of the Pennsylvania and New York governments and the councils of the Iroquois Confederacy to manage events through the increasingly tattered mechanisms of the Covenant Chain. At the same time, the French found their geographic claims to the region threatened and their Indian trade engrossed by peripatetic traders from Virginia and Pennsylvania. In 1749 New France responded with an expedition commanded by Pierre-Joseph Céloron de Blainville, who planted lead plates bearing the fleur-de-lis at strategic spots in the region. A chain of forts followed to enforce the claims, culminating in the establishment of Fort Duquesne, at the site of modern Pittsburgh, in 1754. Virginia militia under George Washington in 1754 and British regulars under Edward Braddock in 1755 failed miserably in their efforts to dislodge the French. Their defeats were the first battles in the global conflict that Europeans would call the Seven Years' War and British Americans would remember as *the* French and Indian War.[73]

There was little doubt which side most Ohio Country Indians would choose when the imperial wars resumed. Supplied with French arms from Fort Duquesne, Shawnees and Delawares struck back at those who had forced them out of homes farther east, and squatters' cabins burned all along the Pennsylvania and Virginia frontiers. Pennsylvania in particular, with its Quaker tradition of pacifism and almost complete lack of formal military institutions, was woefully unprepared to resist. Non-Quakers' plans to raise troops and build forts were further hampered by the longstanding refusal of William Penn's sons (who had converted to Anglicanism and were no pacifists) to allow taxation of their proprietary lands to pay for them. In 1756 the withdrawal of several prominent Quakers from the assembly and a compromise over taxation brokered by Benjamin Franklin loosed the impasse, but by that time undisciplined volunteer militias—vigilantes might be a better term—had already made brutal vengeance the basic mode of response to Indian attacks. That the province's new militancy included a bounty of $130 for the scalp of any Indian male over ten years of age encouraged reciprocal bloodshed of the most personal yet indiscriminate kind. Within a remarkably short time, "Penn's Woods became an abattoir."[74]

As Indians and Whites murdered each other in the Susquehanna and Ohio countries, more traditional European armies elsewhere began to turn the military tide, particularly after William Pitt took control of the British ministry in 1757 and plowed vast financial and military resources into North America. In August 1758 Anglo-American forces took Fort

Frontenac, on Lake Ontario, thus disrupting the French supply lines that supported Fort Duquesne and, through it, the Ohio Country Indians. At the same time, several thousand troops under the command of John Forbes methodically proceeded toward Duquesne. In October, after life-threatening efforts by brokers from each side to bring people together across the killing fields, British provincials, Ohio Country Indians, and Six Nations Iroquois convened in a treaty council at Easton, Pennsylvania. The Ohio Country Indians who were present made peace, but only after Pennsylvania renounced its claims to lands west of the Appalachian Mountains. Abandoned by its Indian allies and cut off from reinforcements, the French garrison at Duquesne withdrew. In November, without firing a shot, Forbes assumed control of what he renamed "Fort Pitt." Within a year the army of John Wolfe won its legendary victory over the marquis de Montcalm on Quebec's Plains of Abraham, and the capital of New France fell to the British. Montreal succumbed in 1760, and for all intents and purposes the French regime in North America came to an end.[75]

While all this was transpiring between the Ohio Country and the St. Lawrence, Carolina and Virginia officials had begun the Seven Years' War by courting Creek and Cherokee allies, or at least hoping to keep them out of the war. As in Pennsylvania, however, both frontier Whites and anti-English Indian factions were spoiling for a fight. Despite internal quarrels, the Creeks as a whole maintained their neutrality. The Cherokees were also polarized but were far less able to pursue a middle course. In 1756 some 600 people from the Overhills towns traveled to Fort Toulouse to participate in a council of alliance with the French. A minority of other Cherokees, however, succumbed to Carolina political pressure and participated in British expeditions. But on the whole, decades of colonial expansion and accumulated grievances poisoned the Cherokee-British relationship. In late 1759, convinced that a full-scale attack on Carolina was imminent, Governor William Henry Lyttelton launched an inconclusive expedition into Cherokee country. In subsequent months Cherokees inflicted major defeats on a second invading force and struck major blows on the frontiers of both the Carolinas and Virginia. By 1761, though, military developments in the north had disrupted the sources of arms and trade goods on which Cherokee success had depended, while freeing an army of over 2,500 British regulars and provincials to invade

Cherokee country a third time and burn some fifteen of the nation's villages. At the end of the year, the Cherokee leader Attakullaculla (Little Carpenter) accepted peace terms that ceded a large tract of land and acknowledged British sovereignty.[76]

The impact of British victory in the Seven Years' War went far beyond such particular defeats. When the Peace of Paris and related agreements transferred Florida, New France, and Louisiana east of the Mississippi and north of New Orleans to Great Britain in 1763, the structural framework upon which the modern Indian politics had depended for two generations imploded with a few strokes of European pens. The French Father was entirely gone from the continent, retaining only two tiny islands off the coast of Newfoundland. New Orleans and trans-Mississippi Louisiana passed into Spanish hands, but elsewhere the British in theory reigned supreme. Thus the ring of competing imperial powers that had provided an odd security to the Indian country it surrounded suddenly collapsed, replaced by a novel advancing frontier line—Reds defending the west, Whites pushing relentlessly across it from the east—that later generations of Americans would incorrectly define as the historic norm. A generation earlier, when Virginia governor Alexander Spotswood had complained of a colonial population eager to attack "Indians who . . . annoyed the frontiers," those frontiers had been plural, and Native and European peoples, however separate their day-to-day lives may have been, had shared a complicated landscape in which royal governors had "to steer between Scylla and Charybdis, either an Indian or a civil war."[77] Suddenly, in 1763, a far simpler, racially defined frontier line popped into view.

In what seemed a newly clarified situation complicated only by the feeble Spanish presence at New Orleans, many British government and military officials saw no need to maintain the former system of intercultural diplomacy. Freed at last from the worry that Indians might take their business and their arms elsewhere, commander-in-chief Sir Jeffrey Amherst sought to confine the Great Lakes and Ohio Country fur trades to army posts, to ban the sale of weapons, ammunition, and rum to Indians, and to halt the expensive custom of diplomatic giftgiving everywhere.[78] "It is not my intention . . . ever to attempt to gain the friendship of Indians by presents," he crowed.[79] A more detached commentator in Great Britain lamented that "our superiority in this war rendered our regard to this people still less, which had always been too little." As a result, "decorums, which are as necessary at least in dealing with barbarous as with civilized nations, were neglected."[80] The success of those "decorums"—of the treaty rituals through which a Mohawk orator nearly ninety years earlier had articulated his accommodationist vision of Native-European coexistence—depended on the balances of power at the heart of the modern Indian politics. In 1763 the shared Euro-Indian transatlantic imperial world in which that politics could be practiced and in which Natives and colonists could live parallel lives disappeared forever. In coming years, Euro-Americans would deliberately erase that past from their memories as they constructed a new future in which Indian nations—and the empires that made room for them—had no place.

SEPARATE
CREATIONS

THE END OF THE IMPERIAL WORLD that had made the coexistence
of Indians and European colonials possible ushered in the beginning of a
revolutionary era. Facing westward, an oft-told story centers on the challenges that the acquisition of a vastly expanded North American empire
raised for the British government in 1763. Addressing those challenges, the
ministry of George Grenville launched an ambitious program of imperial
reform, which sparked violent protests in the colonies and, ultimately, a
war for independence. For Euro-Americans, the revolutionary forces unleashed in 1763 would continue to evolve until the War of 1812, and the
British threat to U.S. independence, finally came to an end. In the new nation thus created, this half-century witnessed not a single revolution but
many: by provincial elites seeking to establish a virtuous classical republic, by artisans and farmers seeking economic and political freedoms at
odds with the dreams of their "betters," by women seeking vindication of
their intellectual and social equality, by African Americans seeking freedom in "the largest slave uprising in our history."[1] In the process, the minority who were White, male, and free wove these diverse strands together to invent a novel, polyglot, national identity. "What then is the
American, this new man?" J. Hector St. John de Crèvecoeur famously
asked as the first war for independence came to a close. "He is either an
European, or the descendant of an European, hence that strange mixture
of blood, which you will find in no other country."[2]

ʽ Notably, no Indian blood flowed in those idealized veins. As if in per-
verse confirmation of their prophets' nativist doctrine of separate cre-

ations, the first inhabitants of the continent were excluded from the process that created Crèvecoeur's new "American." A century after the event, Theodore Roosevelt, in his history, *The Winning of the West,* noted that "the revolutionary contest" had a "twofold character." In the east it was "a struggle for independence" but "in the west a war of conquest" against the Indian peoples of the trans-Appalachian interior, a region that might otherwise have become more logically "part of Canada" rather than the United States. Steeped as Roosevelt was in the "scientific" racism of his day, he believed it to be "of incalculable importance that America, Australia, and Siberia should pass out of the hands of the red, black, and yellow aboriginal owners, and become the heritage of the dominant world races," and the Revolutionary conquest of Indian country was crucial to that larger development. Anyone who thought otherwise, he scoffed, was "too selfish and indolent, too lacking in imagination, to understand the race-importance of the work." Indeed, "the rude, fierce settler who drives the savage from the land lays all civilized mankind under a debt to him."[3]

Today, recoiling from the Rough Rider's language, we might call such a campaign a war of "ethnic cleansing," and, if the century between Roosevelt's day and ours has taught us anything about the phenomenon in places like Rwanda or the former Yugoslavia, it is that although one party may be clearly more villainous than the other, the rage to destroy the hated other runs deep on all sides. If, in the 1990s, many Kosovars hoped to annihilate the Serbs who had first tried to cleanse the land of them, it should not be surprising that in the 1760s many Indians yearned to destroy the Euro-Americans and drive them from the continent. After nearly three centuries of colonial expansion, it would be surprising if they had not. During the Revolutionary era, ethnic cleansing was a powerful urge on both sides of a newly deepening racial divide. For many Indians as well as many Euro-Americans, purging the other from the land—and, just as important, cleansing one's own community of those who still believed in accommodation with the hated other—was integral to the creation of national independence and racial identity.

There were, then, at least two wars for independence—one Indian and one White. And both traced their origins to 1763. Not coincidentally, the same year saw two parallel campaigns of ethnic cleansing, one proclaimed by the Ottawa war chief Pontiac, the other by the Pennsylvania vigilantes known as "the Paxton Boys." A few months after the paroxysms of violence began, each sputtered to an inconclusive end as the institutions of British imperial government gained fragile control over the continent. Although neither movement was able to claim universal adherence on the side of the racial divide it sought to clarify, each in its extremism defined fundamental patterns that would shape the experiences of all eastern North Americans straight through from 1763 to the War of 1812. It would take more than fifty years for White Americans to win, and Indian Americans to lose, their respective wars for independence, for events on the battlefield, in the conference hall, and on the treaty ground to recast eastern North America conclusively as a White rather than Indian country. But the increasingly powerful idea that the continent must become one or the other—and nevermore both—was the cultural legacy of 1763.

As the formative year of 1763 began, no one yet knew with certainty that the long Anglo-French struggle for control of North America was over. The last French "Father," Governor Pierre de Rigaud, marquis de Vaudreuil-Cavagnal, had surrendered and sailed for Europe more than two years earlier, but the war continued elsewhere in the world. Everyone—French colonists certainly, but also Indians allied to the French and British officers in newly occupied posts surrounded by restive enemies—knew that European peace treaties often reversed battlefield gains and that the decision of a colonial governor to abandon his post could be overruled by higher-ups. British Indian agent George Croghan reported as late as April 1763 that western Native people "always expected Canada would be given back to the French on a peace" and insisted that "the French had no right to give up their country to the English."[4] Throughout Indian country, unsubstantiated rumors circulated among French and Natives alike that a Gallic fleet was on its way to the rescue. Meanwhile, people dreamed—desperately but not irrationally—that if only *habitants* or Indians would take matters into their own hands, Louis XV and his ministers would welcome the reconquest of lost territories and send the troops necessary to defend them.[5]

Such dreams gained added appeal from the behavior of the conquering

British military, which, despite a peace treaty held at Detroit in September 1761, gave almost no indication that life would be tolerable for former French allies under the new regime, that accommodation could mean anything other than abject surrender. Far from giving presents to cover the Indian dead, British officers insisted on the unconditional, unceremonial, and uncompensated return of Euro-American war captives, who in most cases had been traditionally adopted to replace Indian losses. Moreover, in 1762 crop failures and smallpox epidemics had swept through the *pays d'en haut* and the Ohio Country, and British commanders at Michilimackinac, Detroit, Fort Pitt, and elsewhere—hamstrung by Amherst's ban on diplomatic presents and a general lack of imported goods—had provided little or no assistance to Indian leaders who sought their aid. British traders, meanwhile, ignored Amherst's orders restricting intercultural commerce to military posts and flocked into Indian villages to sell their wares (at unprecedentedly high prices), while hunters and squatters encroached on trans-Appalachian lands that the 1758 Treaty of Easton had declared off limits. In these contexts, Amherst's policy of limiting Indian access to gunpowder and ammunition—vital commodities if Native people were to be able to get deerskins to trade—seemed not just mean-spirited but an act of aggression. If generosity and reciprocity defined alliance, none existed with the continent's new overlords. "The Indians, I see, continue their *old* way of reasoning," Amherst wrote in the spring of 1763. Such antiquated notions were "by no means satisfactory," and while he had "the honor to command" he was determined they should "not avail." He could not "see any reason for supplying the Indians with provisions."[6]

Yet there was a still deeper issue. At least since the Treaty of Easton, British officials had pledged that colonists would be barred from Indian lands west of the Appalachians and had denied any plan to establish military posts at strategic spots formerly held by the French. At Philadelphia in 1762, a spokesman for General John Forbes had bluntly assured one group of Delawares that "the English have no intention to make settlements in your hunting country beyond the Allegheny hills, unless they shall be desired for your conveniency to erect some store houses in order to establish and carry on a trade." Yet squatters crossed the mountains at the first opportunity, and the British army dug into a string of posts from

Fort Pitt to Detroit to Michilimackinac.[7] All of this was as troubling to longstanding Covenant Chain allies of the British as it was to abandoned Children of the French Father. As a Six Nations Iroquois spokesman who had long benefited from accommodationist policies put it in a message intended for Amherst in 1763,

> at the commencement of the war between you and the French, we were applied to by you, for our assistance, and told then, and often since, that if we took up the hatchet against the French, you would remove them off our lands, and restore them to us. It was also promised to us that if you should conquer the French, your hands would ever be open to us, and, that as the English were a wealthy and trading people, we should be supplied with goods at a very reasonable rate; all these promises we expected (after assisting you) would be fulfilled. But alas we find it quite otherwise; for instead of restoring to us our lands, we see you in possession of them, and building more forts in many parts of our country, notwithstanding the French are dead. This, together with the dearness of goods which are so high that all our hunting cannot supply our wants, gives our warriors and women the greatest uneasiness, and makes us apt to believe every bad report we hear of your intentions towards us.[8]

To followers of the Delaware prophet Neolin there was no question about the intentions of the English, or about the need for violent action to purge them from the country that the doctrine of separate creations set aside for Indians. The prophet lived at Tuscarawas Town, in present-day Ohio, and no direct report of his preaching in the immediate postwar period survives. There are, however, several accounts of disciples who elsewhere spread his word. By far the most detailed was recorded by Robert Navarre, a French resident of Detroit who claimed to have heard a speech by one of the most fervent of Neolin's disciples, the Ottawa leader Pontiac. Addressing a council of Ottawas, Potawatomis, and Wyandots in 1763, Pontiac explained that a Delaware man (Navarre did not name him as Neolin and described him only as of "la nation Loup," or the Wolf clan) was "eager to make the acquaintance of the Master of Life" and so had "resolved to undertake the journey to paradise, where he knew he re-

sided." Pontiac's speech deserves close attention. Like the conversion narratives of Natick people a hundred years earlier, it uses a religious vocabulary to make sense of the relationship between Indians and Europeans, it
describes a God who is angry with his Indian children because of the nature of their relationships to him and to each other, and it combines elements of Christian and Native beliefs in a new synthesis. The moral of
the story, however, could not be more fundamentally different.

As Pontiac told it, the Delaware prophet entered a trance and "in his
dream imagined that he had only to set out and by dint of traveling would
arrive at the celestial dwelling." The next day he embarked on his odyssey,
"not forgetting to take provisions and ammunition, and a big kettle,"
trade goods that had become essential to the Indian way of life. After
eight days of uneventful traveling, "three roads, wide and plainly
marked," opened before him. Trying the widest path, "he continued in it
for half a day without seeing anything to stop him, but, pausing a little to
take breath, he saw suddenly a great fire coming out of the earth," an in-
ferno that increased in intensity the closer he approached. Reversing
course, he next tried a narrower path, which finally led to "the same spec-
tacle."

He was once more obliged to turn about and take the third road
which he followed for a day without discovering anything. Suddenly
he saw before him what appeared to be a mountain of marvelous
whiteness and he stopped, overcome with astonishment . . . When
he arrived at the foot of it he no longer saw any road and was sad. At
this juncture, not knowing what to do to continue his way, he looked
around in all directions and finally saw a woman of this mountain,
of radiant beauty, whose garments dimmed the whiteness of the
snow. And she was seated.

This woman addressed him in his own tongue: "Thou appearest
to me surprised not to find any road to lead thee where thou wishest
to go. I know that for a long while thou hast been desirous of seeing
the Master of Life and of speaking with him . . . The road which
leads to his abode is over the mountain, and to ascend it thou must
forsake all that thou hast with thee, and disrobe completely, and
leave all thy trappings and clothing at the foot of the mountain. No

one shall harm thee; go and bathe thyself in a river which I shall show thee, and then thou shalt ascend."

The Wolf was careful to obey the words of the woman, but one difficulty yet confronted him, namely, to know how to reach the top of the mountain which was perpendicular, pathless, and smooth as ice. He questioned this woman how one should go about climbing up, and she replied that if he was really anxious to see the Master of Life he would have to ascend, helping himself only with his hand and his left foot. This appeared to him impossible, but encouraged by the woman he set about it and succeeded by dint of effort.

When the Delaware reached the top, the woman who had guided him was gone, and he was again at a loss how to proceed, especially after he remembered that he was naked and defenseless. Yet then "he heard a voice telling him to continue and that he ought not to fear, because, having bathed as he had, he could go on in assurance" toward the gate of a beautiful village. There "a handsome man, clothed all in white," escorted him to the presence of the Master of Life, "who took him by the hand and gave him a hat all bordered with gold to sit down upon." The traveler "hesitated to do this for fear of spoiling the hat," but did as he was told.

After the Indian was seated the Lord said to him: "I am the Master of Life, and since I know what thou desirest to know, and to whom thou wishest to speak, listen well to what I am going to say to thee and to all the Indians:

"I am He who hath created the heavens and the earth, the trees, lakes, rivers, all men, and all that thou seest and hast seen upon the earth. Because I love you, ye must do what I say and love, and not do what I hate. I do not love that ye should drink to the point of madness, as ye do; and I do not like that ye should fight one another. Ye take two wives, or run after the wives of others; ye do not well, and I hate that. Ye ought to have but one wife, and keep her till death. When ye wish to go to war, ye conjure and resort to the medicine dance, believing that ye speak to me; ye are mistaken—it is to Manitou that ye speak, an evil spirit who prompts you to nothing but wrong, and who listens to you out of ignorance of me.

"This land where ye dwell I have made for you and not for others.
Whence comes it that ye permit the Whites upon your lands? Can ye
not live without them? I know that those whom ye call the children
of your Great Father supply your needs, but if ye were not evil, as ye
are, ye could surely do without them. Ye could live as ye did live before knowing them—before those whom ye call your brothers had
come upon your lands. Did ye not live by the bow and arrow? Ye had
no need of gun or powder, or anything else, and nevertheless ye
caught animals to live upon and to dress yourselves with their skins.
But when I saw that ye were given up to evil, I led the wild animals
to the depths of the forest so that ye had to depend upon your brothers to feed and shelter you. Ye have only to become good again and
do what I wish, and I will send back the animals for your food. I do
not forbid you to permit among you the children of your [French]
Father; I love them. They know me and pray to me, and I supply
their wants and all they give you. But as to those who come to trouble your lands—drive them out, make war upon them. I do not love
them at all; they know me not, and are my enemies, and the enemies
of your brothers. Send them back to the lands which I have created
for them and let them stay there. Here is a prayer which I give thee
in writing to learn by heart and to teach to the Indians and their
children."[9]

There is little question about the meaning of the vision Pontiac described. What appeared to be the widest two of three possible paths—
accommodationist alliances with the French on the one hand and the British on the other?—led to the flames of what Christians called hell. The
one that seemed impassable—up a slope "perpendicular, pathless, and
smooth as ice"—turned out to be relatively easily climbed, if the traveler
followed the directions of a spirit guide "whose garments dimmed the
whiteness of the snow." She told him to use ceremony—ritual motions of
one hand and one foot—and, above all, to cleanse himself of his "trappings and clothing," especially the European trade goods with which he
had so carefully, but mistakenly, equipped himself for the journey. As if to
drive home the worthlessness of such imported things, when the traveler
reached the top, the Master of Life made him sit upon, and thus spoil, "a
hat all bordered with gold."

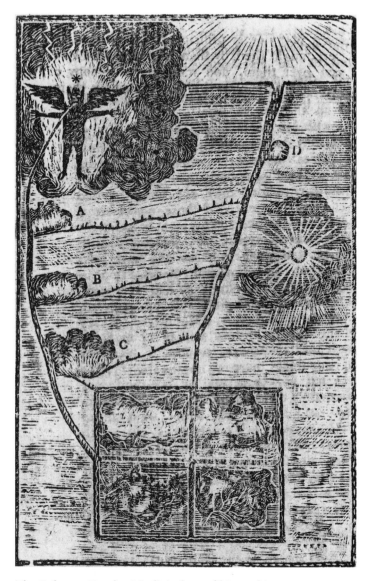

The Delaware Prophet Neolin's chart of his teachings, as reproduced from memory by Pennsylvanian John M'Cullough after his
captivity during Pontiac's War: the path that Native people could
formerly follow to the Master of Life is blocked by the corruptions
introduced by Europeans.

From Archibald Loudon, *A Selection of Some of the Most Interesting Narratives of the
Outrages Committed by the Indians in Their Wars with the White People* (Carlisle, Pa.,
1808–1811). The Library Company of Philadelphia.

The written prayer that the Master of Life gave the traveler, other sources tell us, was recorded not in European letters but in the pictographs Native people had used for centuries to record exploits in hunting and warfare. Neolin's disciples recited the prayer twice a day and taught the prophet's message with the aid of a chart—as Moravian missionary John Heckewelder described it, "a kind of map on a piece of deer skin." This "great book or writing" was used "to show to the Indians . . . the misery which they had brought upon themselves by neglecting their duty, and the only way that was now left them to regain what they had lost."[10] The map, another White observer explained, portrayed "the earth at the bottom and heaven at the top, having a straight line from one to the other, by which their forefathers used to ascend to happiness." That way, however, was now blocked by "a long square . . . representing the White people." One path led directly to the fires of hell, "the White people's place." Along this main way, however, a series of parallel paths denoting "all the sins and vices which the Indians have learned from the White people" led through fires of varying intensity back toward the otherwise obstructed route to happiness. Through these, Indians now must go, "the good road being stopped."[11]

Who was to blame for this situation and for the anger of the Master of Life? Not the British or the French, said Pontiac, but the Indians themselves. "If ye were not evil, as ye are, ye could surely do without them," said his Master of Life. "Ye have only to become good again and do what I wish, and I will send back the animals for your food." Becoming good entailed moral reform—temperance, familial stability, proper ritual—and unity among all Indians. It also involved the abandonment of some long-standing Native cultural practices. Most notably, the Master of Life insisted that he alone be the focus of ceremony and prayer, and not the lesser spirit beings and the evil Manitou "who prompts you to nothing but wrong." This monotheism, with its accompanying emphasis on eternal rewards and punishment and on sin that provoked a deity to anger, was borrowed from Christianity and from the missionaries whom Indians in the Ohio Country and the *pays d'en haut* had heard preach for generations. The story of a spirit journey, the metaphor of paths, and the emphasis on ceremony as right behavior, however, cast all in a framework of Indian cultural traditions that profoundly rejected the missionaries' teachings. And, most important, in Pontiac's telling the prophetic message called all Indians to a cleansing war against "the Whites"—a category that for Pontiac (yet perhaps not for Neolin himself) excluded the French but most assuredly included the British "dogs clothed in red" and all those associated with them.[12]

"Drive them out, make war upon them," the prophet said to Indians who in 1763 still desperately wanted to believe that the military tide could be turned and Britain's global victories be reversed. In May, under the guidance of this powerful vision, Pontiac inspired a regional coalition of several hundred Natives to lay siege to Detroit, a siege that lasted until November while he patiently awaited the arrival of a French army to take the fort and restore the old imperial order, perhaps as the first step toward the true Indian independence the prophetic vision called for. Elsewhere in the *pays d'en haut,* other Native groups only loosely if at all affiliated with Pontiac, but equally inspired by Neolin and other prophets, took full control of every British post, using varying approaches and tactics. The Chippewas who seized Michilimackinac lured the garrison into complacency by playing lacrosse outside the fort for several days and then used a well-placed stray ball as a ruse to storm through the gates. Trading their sticks for hatchets previously smuggled in by women who waited for them inside, they killed sixteen men and captured the rest. The Indians who took Fort Ouiatinon, near present-day Lafayette, Indiana, meanwhile, were almost polite in their conquest. As they bound the post's commander and threatened him and his men with death, they said they were "very sorry, but that they were obliged to do it by the other nations."[13]

Things were much uglier in the Ohio Country, where Senecas, Shawnees, and Delawares independent of Pontiac besieged Fort Pitt and destroyed every other western British post except Niagara. Inspired by Neolin's preaching, radical nativists such as these pursued a cleansing vision that was both purer in its hatred of *all* Europeans and more bloodily immediate in its provocations. In April 1763 in the Wyoming Valley (present-day Wilkes-Barre), persons unknown had set fire to the house of the Delaware leader Teedyuscung, built by the Pennsylvania government. Teedyuscung died in the blaze. Most of the rest of the residents of some twenty surrounding houses escaped with their lives, but the entire village burned to the ground. Circumstantial evidence suggests that the murderous arsonists worked for the Connecticut-based Susquehanna Company, whose claims to land in the area neither Indians nor the Pennsylvania provincial government recognized. Within two weeks of Teedyuscung's murder, the company's settlers occupied the ground on which his town had stood.[14]

These events combined with a host of more general grievances against the British and news of Pontiac's siege of Detroit to inspire warriors all over the Ohio Country to renew the war they had suspended after the Easton Treaty of 1758. Within two months, across a vast stretch of trans-Appalachian territory from Virginia northward through Pennsylvania, White colonists who had similarly squatted in Indian country were slaughtered or sent fleeing to the east, while—revealing the racial dimensions of the movement—enslaved African Americans were often spared. Hundreds of Whites were slain or captured, including, by October, the nine men and one woman foolhardy enough to remain at the Susquehanna Company's Wyoming settlement. In gruesome symbolism of what Neolin's followers thought of European goods—especially those used to build houses and farms on Indian lands—the Wyoming intruders were, a contemporary newspaper said, "most cruelly butchered; the woman was roasted, and had two hinges in her hands, supposed to be put in red hot; and several of the men had awls thrust in their eyes, and spears, arrows, pitchforks, etc., sticking in their bodies."[15] Through all of this, a few Ohio Country Indian groups tried to remain aloof from the violence and to find some basis on which to reach an accommodation with the British. Others struck hard against intruders on Indian land but professed no desire to take their cleansing campaign farther eastward than the mountains, and even offered the Fort Pitt garrison safe passage if the post were surrendered. Still others, however, insisted "that all the country was theirs—that they had been cheated out of it"—and pledged "that they would carry on the war 'till they had burnt Philadelphia."[16]

Yet by autumn the great Indian campaigns were faltering. Amherst, having shifted the bulk of his forces to the West Indies, had few resources with which to respond to the nativist war—much less to make good his threats to "extirpate or remove that vermin" by means ranging from the use of hunting dogs to the distribution of smallpox-infected blankets (a tactic actually implemented by Fort Pitt's commander in June 1763). Still, the commander-in-chief managed to mobilize enough troops to turn back the tide. In August a malaria-weakened force of Scots Highlanders, Redcoats, and Pennsylvania militia under the command of Henry Bouquet survived a march across the mountains and an attack at what became known as the Battle of Bushy Run to resupply Fort Pitt and, for the most part, lift its siege.[17] A few weeks earlier, another British force under James Dalyell had pushed through to Detroit but failed to dislodge Pontiac, whose men killed Dalyell and many of his troops on their one foray out of the fort. At the end of October, however, conclusive news of the Treaty of Paris reached Pontiac from trusted sources, dashing his hopes that French forces would arrive to take the post he had besieged. "The word which my [French] Father has sent me to make peace I have accepted," he wrote to the post's commandant, Henry Gladwin; "all my young men have buried their hatchets." When Gladwin, pleading lack of authority, refused to go through the ceremonies of making peace and distributing presents, Pontiac and a dwindling band of followers withdrew to the Maumee River, in present-day Ohio, to consider their next move.[18] As winter settled in, Amherst made plans to raise new troops in the colonies in preparation for a two-pronged assault the following year: Bouquet was to march into the Ohio Country from Fort Pitt, while other troops commanded by John Bradstreet were to push westward from Albany to Niagara and Detroit. Meanwhile smallpox—whether or not exacerbated by the biological warfare at Fort Pitt—combined with continued shortages of arms and ammunition to undermine the ability of Neolin's disciples to wage new offensives. At the end of the year, the war reached a stalemate.[19]

While Pontiac regrouped on the Maumee, just east of the Susquehanna River at a place called Paxton a group of Scots-Irish Presbyterians nursed their own vision of racial exclusivity on a continent purged of their enemies. According to a horrified Heckewelder, these Pennsylvanians had believed throughout the region's bloody reciprocal massacres of the Seven Years' War "that the Indians were the Canaanites,

who by God's commandment were to be destroyed; and that this not having been done by them at that time, the present war might be considered
as a just punishment from God for their disobedience."[20] Although such
religious doctrines were frequently attributed to them by their Pennsylvania opponents, in their later public statements the Paxtonians offered a
more secular, political, and strategic explanation of why Indians must not
be permitted to share the land with Whites:

> We have long been convinced from sufficient evidence that the Indi-
> ans that lived as independent commonwealths among us or near our
> borders were our most dangerous enemies, both in the last and pres-
> ent war, although they still pretended to be our friends . . . as they
> murdered our inhabitants, led them into captivity, were guides to
> other Indians, reported our weak and defenseless state to the French
> together with all our motions and dispositions against them; and at
> the same time wearing the cloak of friendship, they could readily ob-
> tain provisions, ammunition, and warlike implements to convey to
> our enemies. Their well known claim to freedom and independency
> put it in their power to harbor spies and give intelligence. They have
> ever asserted and exercised the right of making war and peace as in-
> dependent nations, never came under our laws, nor acknowledged
> subjection to our king and government; but they always governed
> themselves by their own customs, and exercised the power of life
> and death over their own people . . . Mournful experience has con-
> vinced us that no nation could be safe especially in a time of war, if
> another state or part of a state be allowed to live among them, free
> and independent, claiming and exercising within themselves all the
> powers of government, the powers of making war and peace, har-
> boring and corresponding with the enemies of the state wherein
> they live, received their spies, given them intelligence, and furnish-
> ing them with the means of support and implements of war. No
> such privilege has been granted to any commonwealth in any civi-
> lized nation in the world. But this had been allowed to Indians
> amongst us, and we justly complain of it as the source of many of
> our calamities; as they have all proved perfidious.[21]

Just as Neolin and Pontiac envisioned an Indian country purged of the British, these "Paxton Boys" (or, as they referred to themselves, "Hickory Boys") envisioned a Euro-American country purged of Indians, who, as a race were by definition their enemies. But like the Delawares and Shawnees, who often directed their bloody campaign against specific, personal targets, the Paxton Boys had their reasons for choosing particular victims on which to vent their generalized racial hatreds. Some of the Paxton militia had been the ones who discovered the tortured bodies of the Susquehanna Company squatters at Wyoming, and they were out for revenge. Much of their rage focused on a man known variously as Toshetaquah, Will Sock, or Bill Soc, a onetime Native diplomatic envoy for the British who, the Paxtonians were convinced, not only duplicitously consorted with enemy Indians but had himself killed and captured Pennsylvanians, if not at Wyoming then elsewhere. Whether any of this was true is doubtful; Toshetaquah may have been guilty of nothing more than holding his head high, speaking disrespectfully to his Euro-American neighbors, and maintaining communications with kin who lived in Indian country during what was, after all, a decade-long period of vengeance killings on both sides.[22]

Whatever the case, Will Sock lived near Lancaster at Conestoga Manor, in a village whose twenty or so inhabitants of mixed Indian ancestry—most of them had Christian names—carefully preserved a document and wampum belts recording a treaty with William Penn in 1701. One of them, an elderly Seneca named Sheehays, may even have been present himself on that long-ago occasion. As the Paxtonians saw it, however, such pretensions to ancient amity were only cause for further suspicion. "Knowing that the little commonwealth of Indians at Conestoga that pretended to be our friends, had done us much mischief, and were in reality our most dangerous enemies," they explained, "a number of persons living amongst us, who had seen their houses in flames, their parents and relatives butchered in the most inhuman manner determined to root out this nest of perfidious enemies; and accordingly cut them off." In mid-December 1763 Matthew Smith and several other men from Paxton reported that they had seen dozens of armed Indians at Conestoga. Before dawn on the fourteenth the Paxtonians, their numbers reinforced to about fifty, burned the town to the ground and killed all six people they found sleeping there. Sheehays was among them, but not Toshetaquah, who, with his wife Kanianquas, two other adult couples, and eight children, had been away from home during the attack. To protect these fourteen survivors, local officials rounded them up and lodged them in the Lancaster workhouse. On the twenty-seventh a well-organized lynch mob from Paxton broke in—no Lancastrian offered much resistance or claimed to know who they were—and slaughtered them all, hacking off hands and feet, smashing skulls, lifting scalps.[23]

Next the Paxtonians set their sights on Philadelphia and another group of Indians who had supposedly consorted with the province's enemies. These were some 127 Delaware and other Indians who had formerly resided in the Moravian mission communities of Nain and Wequetank; they had been moved to the city either for their own protection or because they were under suspicion for harboring the province's enemies— it depended on whom one asked. Most were Delawares, and so, like Tosehtaquah, no doubt communicated with kin who had participated in raids against Pennsylvanians, but their main crimes seem to have been simply that they were Indians and that they lived prosperously within the province's boundaries. When word arrived of the events at Lancaster, the Moravian Indians proposed that they be sent from the City of Brotherly Love to perhaps the only safe haven they could imagine—the British Isles. Shipped off toward New York instead, they were turned back by authorities of both that province and New Jersey, and wound up back in Philadelphia in late January 1764. Several hundred men subsequently marched from Paxton to deal with them, gathering additional recruits along the way. Benjamin Franklin and Governor John Penn (normally political foes) hastily mobilized a thousand Philadelphia residents, many of them Quakers, to oppose the marchers. Many thousands more—perhaps three-quarters of the city's population—probably sympathized with the westerners, however. Amid these tensions, Franklin and several other prominent Philadelphians negotiated with the Paxton leaders at Germantown, a few miles outside the capital, and got them to turn back in exchange for an agreement to publish their grievances and place them before the provincial assembly.[24]

"A Declaration and Remonstrance of the Distressed and Bleeding Frontier Inhabitants," which Smith and his associate James Gibson drafted, stands both as a mirror image of Pontiac's vision of racial separatism and as a stinging critique of people like Franklin and Penn who believed that there was such a thing as a friendly Indian with whom a mutually beneficial accommodation could be reached. The Moravian refugees were "known to be firmly connected in friendship with our openly avowed embittered enemies; and some . . . have, by several oaths, been proved to be murderers," the "Declaration" alleged. "We saw [them] with indignation cherished and caressed as dearest friends—but this, alas! is but a part, a small part, of that excessive regard manifested to Indians, beyond his majesty's loyal subjects, whereof we complain." Provincial officials had acted "as tributaries to savages," lavishing gifts on these and other Indians, lending them every benefit of the doubt, "while, at the same time, hundreds of poor distressed families of his majesty's subjects, obliged to abandon their possessions, and flee for their lives at least, are left, except a small relief at first, in the most distressing circumstances, to starve neglected, save what the friendly hand of private donations has contributed to their support." The Pennsylvania assembly, dominated by Quakers who were not only pacifists but had "a most violent attachment to Indians," had done nothing to support Bouquet's campaign against Fort Pitt or any other military expeditions, and even refused to pay a bounty for Indian scalps as "encouragement to excite volunteers to go forth against them." In stark contrast, the Paxtonians charged, when the Conestogas had been righteously "struck by a distressed, bereft, injured frontier," the government had inexplicably offered "a liberal reward . . . for apprehending the perpetrators of that horrible crime of killing his majesty's cloaked enemies."[25]

Was it any wonder "that a scene of such treatment as this, and the now adding, in this critical juncture to all our former distresses, that disagreeable burden of supporting, in the very heart of the province, at so great an expense, between one and two hundred savages, to the great disquietude of the majority of the good inhabitants of this province, should awaken the resentment of a people grossly abused, unrighteously burdened, and made dupes and slaves to Indians"? Smith and Gibson closed their declaration with a ritualistic "God save the King," but it was clear that neither monarch nor subjects who favored Indians were worthy of divine protection. Just as implacably as Pontiac imagined his Master of Life to pronounce that "this land where ye dwell I have made for you and not for others," the Paxtonians imagined their Presbyterian God to declare that only "dupes and slaves to Indians" could tolerate a savage presence "in the very heart of the province."[26]

Be that as it may, the Paxton Boys' crusade, like that of Pontiac and his various counterparts, soon sputtered to an end. The Moravian Indians— or those who had survived an epidemic that killed more than fifty during their Philadelphia confinement—escaped the cleansers' fury and, in 1765, left the city for new homes in the same Susquehanna valley the Paxtonians sought to purge. Meantime, despite the pledges made at Germantown, the provincial assembly never really considered the demands made in the "Declaration" and a more detailed "Remonstrance" that Smith and Gibson subsequently drafted. Some funds were appropriated for frontier defense, and in the summer of 1764 legislation funding a scalp bounty passed. In defiance of Paxton racial principles and in contrast to the payments offered for all adult male Indian scalps during the Seven Years' War, however, the law specifically protected allied Indians, in particular the Moravians and the Six Nations Iroquois. After a long Philadelphia pamphlet war between defenders and opponents of the Paxton Boys, assembly elections in the fall of 1764 united a "New Ticket" of eastern and western Presbyterians, Lutheran and Reformed "church" Germans, and Anglicans in support of Governor Penn and stronger anti-Indian policies, in opposition to the Quaker Party (led by the distinctly un-Quaker Franklin) and its allies among German pacifist "sects." Because of electoral rules that favored eastern elites, however, Franklin's group retained control of the legislature, and thus were able to deflect any remaining challenge from the Paxton Boys' supporters. Devoting ever more of its energies to a campaign to replace the proprietorship of the Penn family with royal government, the Quaker Party tried to change the terms of the debate. Silenced but by no means satisfied, the Paxton Boys' crusade reached the same kind of stalemate at the ballot box as Pontiac's had reached on the battlefield.[27]

Although neither succeeded in achieving its bloody goals, the crusades of 1763 crystallized long-simmering hatreds into explicit new doctrines of racial unity and racial antagonism. In parallel ways, Pontiac and

Cartoon supporting the Paxton Boys: Quaker merchant Abel James (left) dispenses tomahawks from a barrel belonging to "I. P.," prominent Quaker Party figure Israel Pemberton, who makes love to an Indian woman (right); meanwhile Benjamin Franklin offers a sack of "Pensilvania money," and seated Quakers heed the urgings of a devilish figure.

From James Claypoole Jr., *Franklin and the Quakers* (Philadelphia, 1764). The Library Company of Philadelphia.

the Paxton Boys preached the novel idea that all Native people were "Indians," that all Euro-Americans were "Whites," and that all on one side
must unite to destroy the other. Thus the formerly parallel worlds of
eighteenth-century North America crashed together. Still, mutual destruction was postponed—in part because the prophets of racial extremism failed to convert everyone on their putative sides to their dichoto-
mous views of the world. Cooler heads began to prevail in Indian country
after Pontiac withdrew from Detroit with nothing to show for it, just
as they did in Pennsylvania after the Paxton Boys retreated from Philadelphia.[28]

But a more important factor was the emergence of the British imperial
government as a third power between the two American extremes, forcing Indian and White worlds apart again in a fragile new simulacrum of
the transatlantic imperial world that the Seven Years' War had obliterated.
When word of the Indian crusades reached London, the ministry and the
Board of Trade concluded that Amherst's policies were "the causes of this
unhappy defection of the Indians" and that "nothing but the speedy establishment of some well digested and general plan for the regulation of our
commercial and political concerns with them can effectually reconcile
their esteem and affections."[29]

The centerpiece of the new "general plan" was the Royal Proclamation
of October 1763, news of which would not reach North America until
Pontiac had already lifted his siege of Detroit. While in form the Proclamation was an imperial fiat, in content the boundary it drew between Natives and Europeans at the crest of the Appalachian Mountains conformed to the principles negotiated at the Treaty of Easton and to
longstanding aims of Ottawa, Iroquois, Delaware, Shawnee, Cherokee,
and countless other Native American leaders seeking recognition of territorial integrity. The Proclamation declared "that the several nations or
tribes of Indians, with whom we are connected, and who live under our
protection, should not be molested or disturbed in the possession of such
parts of our dominions and territories as, not having been ceded to, or
purchased by us, are reserved to them."[30]

In conforming to previously negotiated agreements and extending
royal protection to Indians, the Proclamation utterly repudiated Amherst,
whose longstanding request for reposting was speedily approved, with

Thomas Gage named to succeed him as North American commander-in-chief. Continuing its rethinking of imperial-Indian relations, in July 1764 the Board of Trade considered an ambitious plan to centralize administration in the hands of two regional superintendents of Indian affairs responsible directly to Whitehall, fulfilling, at least on paper, a dream first articulated nearly a century earlier by Edmund Andros. The superintendencies themselves had been created in 1754; William Johnson of New York had held the northern post since 1756 and John Stuart of South Carolina the southern since 1762, and, during the Seven Years' War, the superintendents had been almost solely responsible for maintaining Britain's few Indian allies. Hitherto, however, their efforts had been crippled by the independent diplomacy of the provincial governors and especially by the military's control of their budgets; thus Amherst had been able to override Johnson's objections to the policies that provoked the carnage of 1763. Athough the British ministry never implemented the Board of Trade's "Plan of 1764," Gage, Johnson, and Stuart nonetheless tried to put its basic basic administrative principles into practice.[31]

The effectiveness of this limited new centralization remained to be tested (and would in the end be found wanting), but nonetheless the emphasis had clearly shifted from the military to Johnson and Stuart, from brute force to diplomacy, from imperial arrogance to something like "the *old* way of reasoning" that had provided transatlantic stability in previous decades. After long negotiations, in September 1763 Johnson had already secured a peace treaty with the Senecas and refurbished the Covenant Chain alliance with the entire Six Nations. By the summer of 1764, as Gage implemented the two-pronged pacification strategy that Amherst had designed in a very different context, diplomacy similarly prevailed. At Presque Isle in August, Bradstreet, his army en route from Niagara to Detroit, made peace with Shawnees, Delawares, and Wyandots from the Sandusky area; a few weeks later he offered similar terms to the Indians who had remained near Detroit after Pontiac's departure. In both instances, Bradstreet exceeded his authority by offering a final settlement rather than a mere truce, but the example led most Ohio Country Delawares, Shawnees, and Mingos similarly to negotiate with, rather than resist, Bouquet's forces as they marched westward from Fort Pitt. In the spring of 1765 at Johnson's Mohawk Valley home, a formal treaty council ratified a general peace with all the traditional protocol of condolences, speeches, and presents. A year later, Pontiac himself participated in a treaty with Johnson at Oswego and subsequently pronounced himself a great friend of the British.[32]

On a trip to the Illinois country in 1768, Pontiac got into a violent quarrel—with whom, and whether the dispute was political or personal, is unclear. Whatever the case, his actions led a local band council to approve his execution. As he left a trader's store within sight of the long-forgotten mounds of Cahokia in April 1769, a young man carried out the sentence, clubbing him from behind and then fatally stabbing him.[33]

By the time Pontiac died in the ancient heart of Indian country, the political and economic conditions that had originally thrust him into prominence had changed remarkably. The French Father never returned, but in many respects the British took on his former role north of the St. Lawrence and throughout the Great Lakes region. At Montreal, immigrant Scottish merchants used their transatlantic connections to drive French competitors from the market, but for the retail end of their commerce they relied on the same Franco-American *voyageurs* as had their predecessors. In the garrisons reestablished in the *pays d'en haut* after Pontiac's War, red coats replaced the former white, but officers played the same diplomatic roles as their French predecessors. Over time, necessity produced within the British army a group of interpreters and agents increasingly skilled in the Native American protocols that Amherst had so recently scorned. The old balance-of-power diplomacy was perhaps gone forever, but Native people in the continental interior were once again finding productive means of accommodation with the transatlantic European imperial world.[34]

Meantime, by the year of Pontiac's death superintendents Johnson and Stuart had gone far toward turning the Anglo-Indian boundary line unilaterally dictated by the Proclamation of 1763 into an agreement satisfactory to at least some Indian leaders, raising hopes that a semblance of the Native political autonomy that had prevailed in the pre-1760 imperial world might again be realized. The protracted negotiation of the southern segment of the Indian-White boundary began with the 1763 Treaty of Augusta, attended by Stuart, the governors of Georgia, South and North Carolina, and Virginia, and leaders of the Choctaws, Chickasaws, Cataw-

bas, Creeks, and Cherokees. The most difficult portions of the line concerned the Cherokees, not so much because of their defeat by British
forces in 1761 but because of the intense interest of real estate speculators
from Pennsylvania, Virginia, and the Carolinas in lands in Kentucky and
the Ohio Country, where Anglo-American squatters were already building homes. In 1768 Stuart and Cherokee leaders finally came to terms in
the aptly named Treaty of Hard Labor, which ceded lands east of a line
that terminated at the intersection of the Kanawha and Ohio Rivers. Almost simultaneously, at the Treaty of Fort Stanwix, Johnson and Iroquois
leaders negotiated a "Line of Property" that bisected present-day New
York and Pennsylvania from northeast to southwest and then followed
the Ohio River almost to its junction with the Mississippi River. Together,
the 1768 treaty lines opened a substantial chunk of land to British settlers—stretching the controversial Appalachian Mountain boundary set
by the Proclamation of 1763 to include much of present-day West Virginia
and Kentucky. The Treaties of Hard Labor and Fort Stanwix thus represented a seemingly rational compromise, a blueprint for peace that allowed an outlet for westward expansion by Anglo-Americans, yet guaranteed Native American rights to the land that undergirded their political
independence.[35]

Or so it might appear from the treaty ground at Fort Stanwix, or from
Whitehall. Facing eastward from Indian country, several major flaws appeared in this happy picture. First were the inconvenient facts that most
of the lands that the Six Nations ceded south of the Fort Stanwix Line of
Property did not really belong to them and that the Indian owners the Iroquois claimed to speak for had not empowered them to handle their affairs. A few Delawares and Shawnees from the Ohio Country were present at Fort Stanwix but were not included in the formal treaty, which the
Iroquois signed on their behalf. No spokesmen for the Cherokees—owners of most of present-day Kentucky and so the most relevant party—attended at all. Moreover, even if these Native proprietors had recognized
the Line of Property, the Stanwix and Hard Labor treaties did nothing to
address the thorny difficulty of precisely *which* colonists, from which colony, would claim rights to the newly ceded lands east of the boundary.[36]

This problem took on added significance because, although the Paxton
Boys' crusade had ended inconclusively in 1764, Indian-hating continued

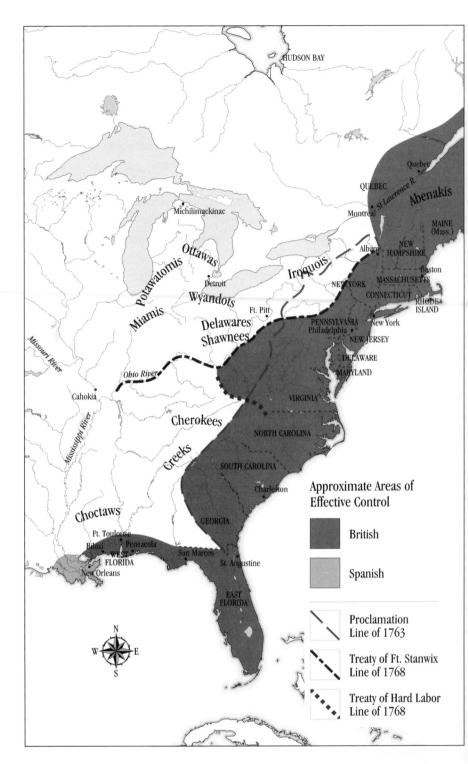

Eastern North America and the emergence of a racial frontier, 1763–1768: with the Proclamation Line and negotiated treaty boundaries, the British crown attempted to separate the territories of Native people and Euro-Americans.

to thrive among Pennsylvanians, particularly in areas from Lancaster westward. The most noteworthy of several murders occurred in 1768, when a German colonist named Frederick Stump was arrested for massacring ten Natives, and then was sprung from the Carlisle jail by a Paxton-like mob of sympathizers; he was never heard from again, and no one was brought to trial. Among other things, the participation of German Americans in this affair suggests that Indian-hating was hardly limited to the Scots-Irish and that animosity toward the other was helping to consolidate a new racial identity for Whites, just as it was among the diverse Delawares, Shawnees, and others who had rallied to Neolin's pan-Indianism.[37] Nor was White unity through Indian-hating a localized phenomenon. Near Saunton, Virginia, vigilantes who killed a group of Cherokees called themselves "Augusta Boys," in conscious imitation of their northern counterparts, whose views toward a government soft on Indians they shared. And, according to Gage, "all the people of the frontiers, from Pennsylvania to Virginia inclusive, openly avow[ed], that they [would] never find a man guilty of murder, for killing an Indian."[38]

With Whites literally getting away with murder, the stage was set for various speculators and squatters from Pennsylvania and Virginia to compete viciously for control of Kentucky. Matters came to a head in 1774, when agents of Virginia governor Lord Dunmore provoked a war between Virginians settled at Pittsburgh and the Shawnees in order to preempt the competing claims of Pennsylvanians and the promoters of a proposed new "Vandalia" colony. A brief but brutal conflict counted among its victims the family of the Mingo Tachnedorus, or John Logan, whose subsequent speech—later made famous by Thomas Jefferson—epitomized the plight of all who sought to remain aloof from the tides of mutual racial destruction:

I appeal to any White man to say, if ever he entered Logan's cabin hungry, and he gave him not meat; if ever he came cold and naked, and he clothed him not. During the course of the last long and bloody war Logan remained idle in his cabin, an advocate for peace. Such was my love for the Whites, that my countrymen pointed as they passed, and said, "Logan is the friend of White men." I had even thought to have lived with you, but for the injuries of one man.

Colonel [Michael] Cresap, the last spring, in cold blood, and unpro-
voked, murdered all the relations of Logan, not even sparing my
women and children. There runs not a drop of my blood in the veins
of any living creature. This called on me for revenge. I have sought
it: I have killed many: I have fully glutted my vengeance: for my
country I rejoice at the beams of peace. But do not harbor a thought
that mine is the joy of fear. Logan never felt fear. He will not turn on
his heel to save his life. Who is there to mourn for Logan? Not one.[39]

Later generations of Whites had many reasons to follow Jefferson in me-
morializing Logan's Lament—not least of which was the ability of the
speech to evoke genuine sympathy for Indians while also assuring White
audiences that Indians were, however tragically, disappearing from the
North American landscape.[40] For our purposes, however, the meaning of
the oration is more direct: on both sides, those who continued to believe
that Indians and Whites could reach an accommodation—and perhaps
even be friends—were increasingly being forced by the Michael Cresaps
of their respective worlds to choose sides.

So the British imperial government attempted to keep its two sets of
subjects apart and at peace. Officials at Whitehall took Indian complaints
about colonists seriously and, if they did not exactly take the Native side,
at least tried to be evenhanded. This approach ensured that Dunmore's
War would end in the same kind of imperially sanctioned stalemate as
had the violence of 1763. On the ground, the fighting stopped in October
1774 with the Treaty of Camp Charlotte, which forced a Shawnee faction
to acknowledge the Old Dominion's ownership of Kentucky, although
the signers by no means spoke for all Shawnees—much less all Cherokees
or Ohio Country Indians. But the previous June Parliament had already
discounted the Virginians' victory by designating the territory north and
west of the Ohio as part of the province of Quebec. To distrustful Anglo-
Americans, the crown seemed determined to deny trans-Appalachian
lands to Virginians and Pennsylvanians, promoters and squatters, alike.[41]

Thus the Quebec Act of 1774 became one of the "Intolerable Acts" that
would provoke British-American provincials to declare independence two
years later. Ever since 1763, conflict had been developing between Whites
who supported principles articulated by the Paxton Boys and those who

exercised institutional authority on behalf of the crown. At first the conflict had nothing to do with fealty to Britain itself; the authors of the Paxton "Declaration" had, after all, called themselves "loyal Subjects to the best of Kings, our rightful Sovereign George the Third."[42] Instead the controversy centered on the policies that specific officials carried out in the sovereign's name or on efforts to go over the head of elected legislature and compliant governors in defense of Indian interests—as opponents of the Paxton Boys did when they sought to revoke the Penn family's proprietary right to name Pennsylvania's governor and instead to make that office appointive by the crown.

The political dynamics of the contest are revealed by the fact that the entire system of treaties and boundaries negotiated with Native leaders in the years after Pontiac's War had been the work of imperial appointees such as Johnson and Stuart, rather than of provincial officials more in touch with the opinions of the White colonial population, among whom the program had precious little support. Although the Fort Stanwix Treaty conference was attended and the document signed by two members of the provincial council of Pennsylvania, the governor and chief justice of New Jersey, a commissioner from Virginia, and "sundry gents from different colonies," it was clearly negotiated by Johnson in his capacity as His Majesty's superintendent of Indian affairs in the north. Similarly, the Hard Labor Treaty was almost solely the work of Stuart. No Virginians even witnessed the negotiations; that province's royal governor, Francis Fauquier, refused to recognize the superintendent's authority at all. Almost universally, White Virginians objected to the treaty's terms, which guaranteed to the Cherokees thousands of acres for which provincials such as Thomas Jefferson and George Washington had already received patents from the Old Dominion's government. Also provoked were countless veterans of the Seven Years' War, who had been promised western lands as rewards for their service.[43]

These policies so deeply antithetical to the interests of real estate speculators, war veterans, and other Whites eager to acquire Indian lands were implemented during precisely the period when provincials were rebelling violently against parliamentary taxes and countless other perceived grievances with the efforts of British policymakers, who were trying to impose order on the expanded empire they had inherited from the

Seven Years' War. In this political climate, provincials who detested imperial centralization in the form of the Stamp Act of 1765 and the
Townshend Duties of 1767 (against which street protests still raged as the
negotiators met at Fort Stanwix and Hard Labor) were no more likely to
obey what they saw as an arbitrary Line of Property than what they considered to be unjust parliamentary taxation.[44]

And so, from the Proclamation of 1763 through the Quebec Act of 1774,
the British policies that held out the slimmest of hopes that Indians and
colonists might coexist through peaceful diplomacy assumed a central
place among the grievances that alienated most Euro-Americans from the
British crown—and from internal political forces such as Pennsylvania's
Quaker Party (now minus a sadder but wiser Franklin), with its triple errors of support for royal government, opposition to the Paxton Boys, and
advocacy of the accommodationist "old way of reasoning." In July 1774
William Johnson, who epitomized the approach to Indian relations that
was so deeply unpopular among most British Americans, died in the middle of a treaty conference he had called to try to halt the spreading violence of Dunmore's War.[45] At the moment of his passing, the entire system of centralized administration he symbolized was collapsing. The
First Continental Congress met in September. In subsequent months, effective political control of nearly every province fell into the hands of ex-
tralegal congresses and locally elected committees. In April 1775 at
Lexington and Concord, the crown's troops and its rebellious subjects
went to war.

As those subjects formally declared their independence a little over
a year after Lexington and Concord, many of them made clear that their
ideal world—unlike that of Johnson and the crown he served—had no
place in it for Indians. The Second Continental Congress' Declaration of
July 1776 vividly projected a universal vision of human liberty, evoking the
"self-evident" truths "that all men are created equal; that they are en-
dowed by their Creator with certain unalienable rights; that among these
are life, liberty, and the pursuit of happiness." But at the time, such noble
words were probably less significant than the specific list of grievances

against the British king that the Declaration "submitted to a candid world." Among these were the charge that the monarch had "endeavored to prevent the population of these states; for that purpose obstructing the laws of naturalization of foreigners; refusing to pass others to encourage their migration hither, and raising the conditions of new appropriation of lands." The lands in question were those denied to White Americans by the Proclamation of 1763 and the Quebec Act, both of which the constitution of the newly independent state of Virginia took pains explicitly to proclaim null and void.[46]

But the king was, according to the Declaration, guilty of far more than an unpopular program of keeping Native American lands out of the hands of colonists. He also had "endeavored to bring on the inhabitants of our frontiers the merciless Indian savages, whose known rule of warfare is an undistinguished destruction of all ages, sexes, and conditions."[47] The legitimate "inhabitants of our frontiers" clearly did not include those "Indian savages." In this sentiment, and in this presumption of an unholy alliance between crown and Natives, the Declaration of Independence was hardly alone. In 1775 Congress' "declaration . . . setting forth the causes and necessity of their taking up arms" had cited "certain intelligence, that . . . the Governor of Canada, is instigating the people of that province and the Indians to fall upon us."[48] The intelligence seemed so persuasive that in January 1776 Thomas Paine's *Common Sense* asserted that there were "thousands, and tens of thousands, who would think it glorious to expel from the continent that barbarous and hellish power, which hath stirred up the Indians and Negroes to destroy us."[49]

Yet, when those words were written, there was no firm military arrangement between the crown and the Indians, much less a concerted plot to mobilize Native forces against the rebels. The statements in *Common Sense* and the declarations of 1775 and 1776 were based on little more than vague rumors, fragmentary intelligence about contingency plans to mobilize loyalist support among Euro-Americans as well as African and Native Americans, and—mostly—conspiratorial fears rooted in the assumption that the crown and the Indians were natural allies. William Johnson's successor as northern Indian superintendent, his son-in-law Guy Johnson, did, it is true, draw on his powers as a common pleas court judge in Tryon County, New York, to condemn the Continental Congress and to raise a largely Mohawk loyalist militia that briefly, and bloodlessly, seized control of the county. In July 1775 rebels forced him to flee his home for Fort Oswego and then Montreal, where he redoubled his efforts to organize Mohawks and other Iroquois to fight for the crown. Still, nothing but Iroquois promises had come of those efforts before he left for England to seek clarification of his powers in November, and his superiors actually forbade him to deploy Indian troops against the rebel forces that invaded Canada in 1775.[50]

Meanwhile Guy Johnson's southern counterpart, John Stuart, had also been forced to flee his home, in the face of wild allegations—lent widespread credence by anonymous letters from his foes published in the *Virginia Gazette*—that he planned "to set the Indians upon" the colonists. Gage would in fact send Stuart orders to recruit Indian loyalists, but not until months after the charges were made, and even then the superintendent interpreted the orders as anything but a license to unleash widespread carnage. To the contrary, throughout early 1776 Stuart did everything he could to restrain Indians from raiding the Carolinas, because he knew such attacks would only drive wavering colonists over to the rebel side. On the Appalachian and Ohio Country frontiers, where violence was almost constant, it must have been hard to tell, but no Indians took up arms against the rebels in an organized way until a few weeks before the Declaration of Independence—its accusations already composed— was adopted. The raiders were Cherokees long angered by the group of Virginians who had established a colony they called "Watauga" beyond the Hard Labor Line in present-day Tennessee. But the immediate spark was the Cherokees' willingness to believe a rumor just as unsubstantiated as those circulating among Whites: Superintendent Johnson, some Native visitors from the north had mistakenly told them, had been tarred and feathered by the rebels.[51]

Such rumors demonstrate that many Indians as well as many Whites took it as an article of faith that the crown's policies toward Native Americans were a major source of revolutionary rage. During a Long Island celebration of the Declaration of Independence, a crowd demonstrated the reality of that rage by dressing an effigy of King George III in the feathered headdress of *"Johnson's* savages," wrapping it in the Union Jack, and then hanging and burning it.[52] No one would argue that the supporters of independence defined their cause *primarily* in opposition to that of Indians (indeed, those who had dumped the tea in Boston Harbor had dressed as faux Mohawks), but nonetheless racial themes persisted throughout the imperial crisis.[53] One of the earliest protest pamphlets, drafted long before anyone blamed the king rather than his ministers for their problems, was James Otis' *The Rights of the British Colonies Asserted and Proved* (1764). The Massachusetts pamphleteer evoked a "whole continent, of near three thousand miles in length, and in which, and his other American dominions, His Majesty has or very soon will have some millions of . . . good, loyal and useful subjects, White and Black." This American color chart, like Crèvecoeur's even more monochromatic later version, did not include Red. Otis went on to argue that Massachusetts alone had "expended more men and money in war since the year 1620, when a few families first landed at Plymouth, in proportion to their ability, than the three Kingdoms [of England, Scotland, and Ireland] together." He did not name names, but clearly the enemies in those wars were the same people he excluded from the category of "good, loyal and useful subjects." His American history was built on an irreconcilable conflict with the Native population.[54]

A little over a decade later, as attitudes toward the crown changed and the 1775 congressional declaration similarly recalled that the first English colonists "at the expense of their blood effected settlements in the distant and inhospitable wilds of America, then filled with numerous warlike nations of barbarians," there must have seemed few things more pernicious than the king's unholy alliance with the Indian enemy.[55] According to David Ramsay, who published a *History of the Revolution of South Carolina* in 1785, the Cherokee attacks that Whites wrongly accused Stuart of fomenting on the eve of the Declaration were enough to push many waverers into the revolutionaries' camp. "Several who called themselves Tories in 1775 became active Whigs in 1776, and cheerfully took arms in the first instance against Indians, and in the second against Great Britain," Ramsay concluded. "Before this event some well-meaning people could not see the justice or propriety of contending with their formerly protecting parent-state; but Indian cruelties, excited by royal artifices, soon extinguished all their predilection for the country of their forefathers."[56]

Nonetheless, there was nothing automatic about a military partnership between Native Americans and the crown during the U.S. War of Independence. Despite the racial hatreds cultivated in the previous decade, for most Native people the choices in 1776 were not nearly as clear-cut as we might expect. One of the great ironies of the Declaration of Independence is that it briefly reintroduced the conditions for "the modern Indian politics," with, on the one hand, its opportunities to steer an accommodationist middle course between competing imperial powers—now Britain and the United States—and, on the other, its potential for bitter internal conflict between Indian factions with connections to either pole. Within this strange-yet-familiar diplomatic framework, most Indian leaders initially attempted to remain neutral, while various factions kept open lines of communication to British and "Americans" alike. Militants—many of them nativists—sought to seize the opportunity to ally with the British and regain lost territories; others argued caution on the basis of the untrustworthiness of all Whites, the folly of what might prove a self-destructive war, the imperative to keep trading connections intact, or the need to accommodate whoever the eventual victor might be.

Accordingly, along the St. Lawrence, the various *reserve* communities, now called by the British "the Seven Nations of Canada"—resumed their not-to-be-taken-for-granted role as military buffers between colonizing powers. Meantime the Iroquois were triply divided among a faction led by the Mohawk Joseph Brant, who sought to fight for the British crown as he had done late in the Seven Years' War; a group led by Oneida and Tuscarora Protestants allied to New England missionary Samuel Kirkland; and a majority who hoped to remain aloof from the conflict. The last position became increasingly untenable, and by 1777 most Senecas and Cayugas had joined Brant's Mohawks as British allies. Many Oneidas and Tuscaroras, by contrast, enlisted with the rebels. In 1779 U.S. armies conducted a scorched-earth campaign through the countries of the Senecas, Cayugas, and the hitherto-neutral Onondagas, creating thousands of refugees who would spend the rest of the war encamped at British Niagara. In 1776, 1780, and 1781 similar U.S. expeditions ravaged the Cherokee country, oblivious to that nation's internal controversies over the decision of some of its warriors to enlist in the British cause. Creeks and Choctaws avoided the destruction suffered by Iroquois and Cherokees, but they too saw their neutrality erode under the twin pressures of U.S. arrogance and British incentives.[57]

As the war proceeded, almost no Native groups managed to preserve perfect neutrality, but few unanimously allied with the British and still fewer, unsurprisingly, with the United States. Even in the Ohio Country—with its tradition of pan-Indian nativism and its bitter memories of the Paxton Boys, the Fort Stanwix Treaty, and Dunmore's War—there were deep divisions within Indian communities. Although anti-U.S. militants prevailed in most villages, a major exception was the group of Ohio Country Delawares whose spokesman was a headman named Koguetagechton, or White Eyes. Having kept his faction out of Dunmore's War, after 1776 he similarly tried to remain neutral even after most Shawnees and Mingos had joined the British alliance. As elsewhere in Indian country, however, in the Ohio Country neutrality ultimately became impossible. Unwilling to cast his fate with the British-allied Iroquois, who had sold out his people at Fort Stanwix, White Eyes was driven into an alliance with the United States, sealed at the Treaty of Pittsburgh, which he and others signed in September 1778. In exchange for what the Delaware signatories understood merely as free passage to troops who would build a fort to defend their villages, U.S. negotiators cynically proposed that the Delawares might ultimately join the Union as a fourteenth state. As recorded on paper, however, the treaty went far beyond a right of free passage, committing the Delawares to take up arms against their Native American neighbors. More important, U.S. general Lachlan McIntosh clearly intended to use the new fort as a base for offensive operations. Commissioned a colonel, White Eyes accompanied McIntosh's army into Indian country in early November 1778 and failed to return alive. Although officials claimed he was a victim of smallpox, he was almost certainly shot by a trigger-happy Virginia militiaman. The Pittsburgh treaty—and the accommodation White Eyes had pursued with the United States—did not long outlive him. By 1780 nearly all Delawares had joined the British.[58]

And the region again became a killing ground for both sides. The fall and winter of 1781–82 saw a macabre replay of the massacre perpetrated by the Paxton Boys in 1763. Through years of bloodshed, three small

Moravian Indian communities—descended from those that two decades earlier had barely escaped slaughter in Philadelphia and had long since been forced to leave the Susquehanna—clung to their lands and neutrality in the Muskingum valley of today's eastern Ohio: Salem ("Peace"), Schönbrunn ("Beautiful Spring"), and Gnadenhütten ("Huts of Grace"). In August British agent Matthew Elliot showed up with a party of Wyandot warriors to convince the Moravians that they should move, for their own protection, to the British-allied Indian population centers on the Sandusky River. When they refused, the Wyandots treated their missionaries, Heckewelder and David Zeisberger, as captives and forced everyone to relocate to the Sandusky. After a half-starved winter, the Moravian Indians received permission to return to the Muskingum and harvest the corn they had left standing in their fields the previous autumn. As they settled into their houses at Salem and Gnadenhütten, a Washington County, Pennsylvania, militia under the command of David Williamson appeared and convinced some forty-two men, twenty women, and thirty-four children to gather at Gnadenhütten, from which he promised to escort them to Fort Pitt for their protection.[59]

At least some members of Williamson's militia were said to be former Paxton Boys; nearly all shared that group's attitudes toward Indians who claimed to be the friends of Whites. Once the militiamen had collected the Moravian Indians at Gnadenhütten and convinced them to give up anything resembling a weapon, they announced that the Indians would all be killed. Surely, the Pennsylvanians claimed, the Gnadenhütten people had harbored—if they were not themselves—murderers of Whites. Moreover, the "clothes, children's caps, tea-kettles, pots, cups and saucers, etc., saws, axes, chisels, pewter basins, porringers, etc.," found in the homes of these hard working Indian disciples of their missionary teachers could not possibly have belonged to them. In the racially bifurcated vision of the militiamen, these "were only made use of by White people and not by Indians," and so must have been plundered from frontier victims.[60] Thus condemned, the Indians spent the night praying and singing hymns. In the morning, Williamson's men marched over ninety people in pairs into two houses and methodically slaughtered them. One of the latter-day Paxton Boys bragged that he personally bludgeoned fourteen victims with a cooper's mallet, which he then handed to an accomplice. "My arm fails me," he was said to have announced. "Go on with the work. I have done pretty well."[61]

"I admit that there are good White men," the Delaware leader Buckongeahelas had conceded in a speech to the Gnadenhütten Indians the previous year. Yet, conveying attitudes now common on both sides of the racial divide, he went on to explain that the good ones

> bear no proportion to the bad; the bad must be the strongest, for they rule. They do what they please. They enslave those who are not of their color, although created by the same Great Spirit who created us. They would make slaves of us if they could, but as they cannot do it, they kill us. There is no faith to be placed in their words. They are not like the Indians, who are only enemies while at war, and are friends in peace. They will say to an Indian: "My friend, my brother." They will take him by the hand, and at the same moment destroy him. And so you (addressing himself to the Christian Indians) will also be treated by them before long. Remember that this day I have warned you to beware of such friends as these. I know the long knives; they are not to be trusted.[62]

In high diplomacy as well as in their massacres, the closing years of the U.S. War of Independence seemed to repeat the events of 1763. When Britain acknowledged the independence of the United States of America in another Treaty of Paris in 1783, the crown's negotiators ignored the network of Indian alliances built up in the previous two decades. The treaty made no mention whatever of Native Americans and simply transferred to the new nation ownership of all territory south of the Great Lakes, east of the Mississippi, and north of the Floridas, which, in related negotiations, were returned to Spain. As France's Native American allies had done earlier, Britain's Indian friends now also reacted with disbelief at their betrayal. From the Cherokee country southward, the British abandonment was virtually complete, and only slightly tempered by the reintroduction of a counterbalance to U.S. power in Spanish Florida.[63] As the Creek leader Alexander McGillivray understated, "to find ourselves and country betrayed to our enemies and divided between the Spaniards and Americans is cruel and ungenerous."[64]

Farther northward, however, the Treaty of Paris had far less impact. On the Appalachian frontiers and in the Ohio Country, raids and counterraids continued without reference to European diplomacy. In violation of the Paris treaty (and partly in retaliation for the failure of the United States to fulfill its financial obligations under that pact), British forces continued to occupy Detroit and other Great Lakes posts, thus providing supply bases for Native forces throughout the region. Moreover, British North American officials from Quebec's governor Frederick Haldimand down through the ranks of agents stationed in Indian country shared their Native allies' sense of betrayal by the crown's diplomats, and they worked as actively as they could—short of open war with the United States—to support them. In 1784 the governor granted a substantial tract of land on the Grand River in present-day Ontario to the Six Nations Iroquois who had fought the revolutionaries and spent much of the war as refugees at Niagara; ultimately roughly half of the Iroquois population relocated there. From that base, Joseph Brant worked with Native leaders from throughout the Ohio Country and *pays d'en haut* to create a Western Confederacy to coordinate the struggle against the United States and insist that the Ohio River become the border between Indian country and the new republic.[65]

In dealing with the Western Confederacy, the triumphant revolutionaries of the United States were determined, just as Amherst had been in 1763, to discard the niceties of diplomacy and to impose their will on Indians who had no place in their emergent republic. As John Dickinson, president of the Supreme Executive Council of Pennsylvania, put it, Indians should simply be notified "that peace has been made with Great Britain . . . that the back country with all the forts is thereby ceded to us; that they must now depend upon us for their preservation and, that unless they immediately cease from their outrages . . . we will instantly turn upon them our armies that have conquered the king of Great Britain . . . and extirpate them from the land where they were born and now live." Under this "conquest theory," if Indians were to be allowed to retain any lands east of the Mississippi, they would do so only through the benevolence of the conquerors. In a series of treaties extracted at Fort Stanwix in 1784, Fort

McIntosh on the Ohio in 1785, and Fort Finney at the mouth of the Great Miami River in 1786, U.S. commissioners grabbed nearly all of present-day western New York and Pennsylvania and eastern Ohio, where surveyors envisioned neat rows of townships in the newly created Northwest Territory. If the crown's protection of Indian land had been a major grievance before the Revolution, the victims now redressed that grievance with a vengeance.[66]

"We have full power to maintain our title by force of arms," Dickinson had crowed on the eve of the first of the postwar treaties.[67] The Western Confederacy proved otherwise when it utterly routed invading U.S. armies led by Josiah Harmar in 1790 and Arthur St. Clair in 1791; of St. Clair's 1,400 troops, 630 were killed or unaccounted for and nearly 300 more injured, proportionally one of the worst defeats federal troops would ever endure against any foe. Through the period of these Indian triumphs, the British government of Quebec remained officially neutral, but arms and other trade goods flowed from Detroit and other posts, and British agents who participated in the Confederacy's councils gave every impression that troops would support the Indians in a crisis. In August 1794 the western war reached its climax as Anthony Wayne's "Legion of the United States," retracing routes attempted by Harmar and St. Clair, marched methodically toward the Confederacy's population centers on the Maumee River. At the Battle of Fallen Timbers, Indian forces that initially failed to turn back Wayne's army sought refuge at a British post on the Maumee. Its commander, fearing he could not resist an assault by Wayne, closed the gates against his Native allies. Left stranded, the Western Confederacy's forces abandoned the field and turned Wayne's relatively minor victory into a major triumph. Over the winter, as word arrived of Jay's Treaty—the 1794 accord that required British withdrawal from the western posts—the various nations and factions of the Confederacy had to make the best deal with the United States that they could. In the summer of 1795 at the Treaty of Greenville, Indian leaders gave up their demand for an Ohio River boundary between Indian country and the United States and yielded most of the present state of Ohio to the victors.[68]

Still, the Greenville Treaty became possible because the new republic, as the old empire had done after 1763, had rediscovered the superiority of diplomacy, treaties, and ceremonial protocol to brute force. In the months after Fallen Timbers, Wayne relied far less on military intimidation by troops spread thinly in a chain of forts from modern Cincinnati to Fort Wayne than he did on tireless political skills in bringing various leaders and factions to peace. In ceremony and numbers of participants, the Treaty of Greenville resembled nothing seen on the continent since the days of the Seven Years' War. Thereafter, resurrecting an old vocabulary, the presidency of the United States settled into the ceremonial role of "Great Father" to the Indian "Children" with whom the government made treaties.[69]

Yet, for all the efforts made to restore the old diplomatic forms, the new Father had even less ability to mediate successfully between his Indian Children and the White population than had his British predecessor. As a result, the 1795 Greenville Treaty line had no more hope of holding than had the 1768 Line of Property. At best, the federal government settled for an effort to regulate and mitigate, rather than restrict or prohibit, the White expropriation of Indian country that had always been a goal of many rank-and-file revolutionaries. The basic federal strategy was crafted by President Washington's secretary of war, Henry Knox. His "civilization" program—elaborated after 1800 by the Jefferson, Madison, and Monroe administrations—sought to teach Indian peoples to abandon their traditional gendered economy of male hunting, female agriculture, and communal landholding in favor of male plow agriculture and animal husbandry, female domesticity, and, especially, private property. This shift toward a Euro-American way of life, the theory went, would allow Indians to prosper on a much smaller land base, opening up the vast remainder to White yeoman farmers. Of course it also envisioned the end of Indian culture and Indian political autonomy.[70]

In their ceremonial speeches to Native leaders, federal officials wrapped the civilization program in humanitarian rhetoric and promises of concrete aid in the form of plows and tools. But in practice they engaged in relentless efforts to relieve Indians of the "excess" land that made their extravagant hunting lifestyle possible. "To promote this disposition to exchange lands" President Jefferson went so far as to suggest to Indiana territorial governor William Henry Harrison in 1803 that he would "be glad to see the good and influential individuals among them run into debt, because we observe that when these debts get beyond what the individual can pay, they become willing to lop them off by a cession of lands."[71] Following the president's advice and pledging his "humble exertions to place upon a better footing the affairs of the wretched Indians," Harrison staged a series of treaties with Indians supposedly representing the Delawares, Miamis, Shawnees, Potawatomis, and other nations. By 1809 he had gained paper title to what is now southern Indiana, most of Illinois, and parts of Wisconsin and Missouri for an average price of less than two cents per acre.[72]

South of the Ohio River, the story was much the same. In the first decade of the new century, federal agent Benjamin Hawkins relentlessly pushed the civilization program among the Cherokees and especially the Creeks with whom he lived. Here, too, debt provided a powerful incentive for some leaders to sign a series of land-cession treaties; Creeks alone owed traders some $113,000 in 1803. But in the south matters were vastly complicated by the same kinds of overlapping Euro-American jurisdictional and real-estate claims that had earlier created such chaos in the Ohio Country during the period leading up to Dunmore's War. In 1805 the U.S. Senate refused to ratify a land-cession treaty Hawkins had brokered with the Creeks because the price paid (which would have gone to trader-creditors, not to Indians) was too high. This was only a minor complication when set against the fact that three treaties the state of Georgia had extracted under the conquest theory from purported Creek leaders in the 1780s had never been recognized as valid by either the federal government or the Creek National Council, but had nonetheless been the basis for a number of substantial land grants to Whites.[73] Additional confusion resulted from what was known as the Yazoo Land Fraud. Perpetrated by bribed Georgia legislators in 1795, this complicated affair, involving illegitimate grants of some 35 million acres of Choctaw and Chickasaw land in present-day Mississippi and Alabama, would tie up the U.S. Congress and courts for the better part of twenty years. Meanwhile, quite apart from the competing internal claims of private, state, and federal interests in the United States, the entire Gulf Coast remained an international zone of contention. East and West Florida had in theory been reunited as a single Spanish colony in 1783, but British traders continued to dominate the region's Indian trade from posts in Pensacola and else-

where. Meanwhile, from Pensacola to Mobile, much of western Florida
was claimed by the United States as being within the boundaries of the
Louisiana Purchase of 1803. Sometimes with Spanish permission but
more often without it, "Americans" moved into the area in droves, spilling
over into Creek territory in what is today Alabama.[74]

On multiple fronts, the contested territories of the southeastern interior were the targets of aggressive White squatters looking for the slightest excuse to expel Native inhabitants. In 1808 the major general of the
west Tennessee militia, whose name was Andrew Jackson, summarized
their position when he received what later turned out to be a false report
that a party of Creeks had killed some Whites settled on contested
ground. Dashing off a letter to President Jefferson, he evoked the same
specter of an unholy alliance between British imperial officials and Indians that had surfaced so frequently in previous decades. "These horrid
scenes bring fresh to our recollection, the influence, during the revolutionary war, that raised the scalping knife and tomahawk, against our defenseless women and children," Jackson wrote. "The blood of our inno-
cent citizens must not flow with impunity—justice forbids it, and the
present relative situation of our country with foreign nations require[s]
speedy redress, and a final check to these hostile murdering Creeks."[75]

In the face of such U.S. aggression and of myriad controversial land-
cession treaties, a new wave of nativist religious prophecies spread
throughout the trans-Appalachian west, preached in the north by the
Shawnee prophet Tenskwatawa and his brother Tecumseh and in the
south most notably by the Creek prophet Hillis Hadjo (Josiah Francis).
Tecumseh personally linked the two movements, both through kinship
(his mother was Creek) and through his travels with Hillis Hadjo in the
Creek and Cherokee country from 1809 through 1811. Tenskwatawa's
message—revealed to him in a trance by the Master of Life—was much
the same as that of Neolin half a century earlier: "Spirituous liquor was
not to be tasted by any Indians on any account whatever," reported a
White American who claimed to know the prophet's message well; "no
Indian was to take more than one wife"; "all medicine bags, and all kinds
of medicine dances and songs were to exist no more"; "no Indian was to
eat any victuals that was cooked by a White person, or to eat any provisions raised by White people, as bread, beef, pork, fowls, etc." Hillis

Tenskwatawa, "the Shawnee Prophet," late in his life.

From George Catlin, *The Open Door, Known as the Prophet, Brother of Tecumseh* (1830).
Smithsonian American Art Museum.

Hadjo called for a less thoroughgoing purge of imported goods and food-
stuffs, but his Creek followers shunned glass beads and agricultural tools,
refused to eat salted meat—a European innovation—and ritually destroyed hogs and cattle. In their revitalized ceremonial dances, they carried wands painted in the traditional southeastern color denoting war,
and so came to be known as Red Sticks. And, just as Pontiac a half-century
earlier had dreamed of the return of the French Father, the Red Sticks

spread rumors of an imminent restoration of British power in Florida and the revival of the old alliance. Perhaps enough time had passed since the British betrayal of 1783—and enough desperation had accumulated among nativists—to lead some to believe it might actually happen.[76]

Whatever may have been their attitudes toward the British, nativists among both Creeks and Shawnees had no doubts about who their real enemies were. Tenskwatawa insisted that Indians "were not to know the Americans on any account, but to keep them at a distance." Red Sticks called for the obliteration of "everything received from the Americans, [and] all the Chiefs and their adherents . . . friendly to the customs and ways of the White people."[77] As had been the case in the era of Neolin and Pontiac, then, hatred of the racial other translated into particular rage against any of their own people naive enough to think that Whites could be trusted. Contemptuous of accommodationist chiefs who signed land-cession treaties and cooperated with the civilization program, Tenskwatawa gathered his followers in new towns on symbolic spots—first at Greenville and then at the junction of the Tippecanoe and Wabash Rivers—in open defiance of the accommodationist Miami leader Little Turtle, who threatened to have him killed if he did so. Hillis Hadjo and his followers similarly renewed old rivalries; most of the Red Sticks apparently were non-Muskogee speakers, in contrast to the chiefs, many of them *métis*, who had cooperated with Hawkins, had signed land-cession treaties, and, in many respects, were the primary focus of their cleansing wrath. Both Tenskwatawa and Hillis Hadjo waged witch-hunts against their Indian opponents.[78]

Such internal battles between nativists and accommodationists gave Harrison and Jackson the openings they were looking for. In September 1811, while Tecumseh was traveling with Hillis Hadjo in the Creek country, Harrison staged a preemptive march toward Tenskwatawa's town, which President James Madison described as a den of "menacing preparations . . . under the influence and direction of a fanatic of the Shawanese tribe." After a standoff of nearly two months, Tenskwatawa's mixed forces of Shawnees, Kickapoos, Winnebagos, Potawatamis, and others (including some Creeks who had recently moved north to join the prophet) attacked Harrison's camp. Thus began the vastly overrated Bat-

tle of Tippecanoe, in which Harrison earned his nickname by holding the
field while losing roughly three times as many men as his Indian assail-
ants. Several days later the U.S. troops sealed their victory by burning
the prophet's already abandoned town, which, however, was soon re-
occupied.[79]

When Tecumseh—who until that time had seemed more concerned
with his accommodationist Indian enemies than with his expansionist
White ones—returned from his southern journey, he began actively seeking British military aid. News of this development allowed President
Madison, in his message to Congress seeking a declaration of war against
Great Britain in June 1812, to echo the words his fellow Virginian Jefferson
had inserted in the Declaration of 1776: "In reviewing the conduct of
Great Britain toward the United States our attention is necessarily drawn
to the warfare just renewed by the savages on one of our extensive frontiers—a warfare which is known to spare neither age nor sex and to be distinguished by features peculiarly shocking to humanity."[80]

Notwithstanding such overheated rhetoric, in the north the relationship between Indians and British during the War of 1812 was never more
than a marriage of convenience. After Tippecanoe, Tecumseh won some
brilliant triumphs against Harrison's forces on the battlefield, sometimes
despite rather than because of British aid. A pointless British and Indian
siege of Fort Miegs on the Maumee River, for instance, turned into a victory for Tecumseh's forces in April 1813 only because 800 Kentucky militiamen who had surprised a besieging cannon emplacement foolishly
pursued the small outparty that manned it toward the main British and
Indian encampment. Even then, Fort Miegs remained in U.S. hands, and
subsequent futile British-led attempts to assault it led many of
Tecumseh's Indian followers to abandon what they saw as a lost cause.
Defections continued, particularly after Oliver Hazard Perry's naval victory over the British fleet forced a complete British withdrawal from the
Lake Erie region. Harrison's forces pursued the British and Tecumseh's
remaining Indian forces up the Thames River of present-day Ontario. In
early October the British and Indians made their last stand. After a few
shots the Redcoats turned and ran. Between 700 and 800 Indians stood
their ground against well over 3,000 of Harrison's men until Tecumseh

fell dead of a gunshot wound to the chest. The fate of his body is uncertain, but it is likely that—like Metacom's long before—it was mutilated by the victors.[81]

As the Battle of the Thames sealed the defeat of Indian resistance in the north, conflict in the south was only beginning to reach its climax. The declaration of war by the United States allowed the British agents in Florida to recruit Indian and African-American allies openly; the Red Sticks, with their constituencies among Creeks and Seminoles, eagerly embraced the offers. In July 1813 a party of Red Sticks returning from Pensacola had traveled ninety miles toward home with arms and supplies when they were attacked at Burnt Corn Creek by Alabama militiamen. The Red Sticks won that minor skirmish, and sent Whites, métis, and accommodationist Creeks throughout the region into a panic. More than five hundred people—half militia, half civilians, many of them Muskogee Creeks and métis—gathered in a hastily fortified compound at the home of Samuel Mims on the Alabama River. Apparently, however, they did not take their fear of attack seriously enough. On one August day when the compound's gates were propped open with sandbags and many of the defenders were drunk, several hundred Red Sticks swooped down to kill at least half of those inside.[82]

This "Fort Mims Massacre" freed Whites to declare open season on the Red Sticks. From Georgia and the Mississippi Valley, various militias, accompanied by Choctaws, Chickasaws, and Creek accommodationists, descended into Creek country and on the Seminole towns of Florida. Most notably Jackson led some two thousand Tennessee and Kentucky militia and Cherokee, Choctaw, and Chickasaw forces on a scorched-earth campaign down the Coosa River. In a March 1814 assault on a fortified town at Horseshoe Bend, his combined forces slaughtered nearly eight hundred Red Stick men, women, and children. The man already known as "Old Hickory" for his steadfast leadership of Tennessee militiamen in defiance of professional federal soldiers subsequently marched his troops deliberately through the "Hickory Ground"—sacred Creek territory—to establish a post he called Fort Jackson. There, in August 1814, he imposed a peace treaty that forced the Creeks to yield 22 million acres to the United States. With one exception, the signers were not Red Sticks but accommodationist Creeks who had in fact fought alongside the U.S. militia-men.[83]

The legacy of 1763 hung heavily over these events and others during the War of 1812. The treaty of Fort Jackson demonstrates that for Old Hickory, as for the Paxton Boys before him, there was no real distinction between friendly and hostile Indians. Indeed, the entire Creek campaign stood firmly within a freelance frontier militia tradition that traced back through Gnadenhütten to Conestoga. Although Jackson held a legitimate commission as an officer of the Tennessee militia, he had no authority to negotiate a treaty. In taking charge of the proceedings at Fort Jackson, he took it upon himself to replace the U.S. commissioners originally appointed for the job, because he deemed their instructions too mild. Similar disregard for higher authority characterized Jackson's actions during the next several years. The Treaty of Ghent, which at the end of 1814 brought the conflict between the United States and Britain to an end, supposedly guaranteed to Britain's Indian allies the lands they had held before the war.[84] Emboldened by his famous victory over the British at New Orleans in January 1815, however, Jackson ignored both the treaty and the halfhearted instructions of the Madison administration to continue his conquest of Indian country. In 1818, during what became known as the First Seminole War, Old Hickory won the admiration of a huge sector of the U.S. population for his illegal invasion of Spanish territory, his even more illegal trial of two British subjects for the high crime of assisting the Indian enemies of the United States, and his still more illegal execution of both. Lost in all the hoopla over how Jackson gloriously "made law" rather than "quoted it" was the fact that at the same captured Florida fort where the two Britons at least were given the formality of a trial, Jackson had Hillis Hadjo and another Red Stick leader, Homathle Mico, summarily executed and dragged off to unmarked graves.[85]

By 1820, after the Adams-Onís Treaty between the United States and Spain had conveyed ownership of Florida to the republic, Jackson and his subordinates had imposed additional treaties on the Creeks, Cherokees, Choctaws, and Chickasaws. These documents transferred millions of acres in an arc stretching from Georgia through Alabama and Mississippi through western Tennessee—the "black belt" that would become the

Self-portrait of Hillis Hadjo, prophet of the Red Stick movement.
Watercolor, London, 1817. British Museum.

Cotton Kingdom—to White American hands. Jackson's attitude toward
the proceedings echoed that of Amherst in 1763. "I have long viewed treaties with the Indians [as] an absurdity not to be reconciled to the principles of our government," he explained to President James Monroe in 1817.
If "Indians are the subjects of the United States, inhabiting its territory
and acknowledging its sovereignty, then is it not absurd for the sovereign
to negotiate by treaty with the subject?" Therefore, "whenever the safety,

interest, or defense of the country should render it necessary for the government of the United States to occupy and possess any part of the territory, used by them for hunting," Congress had "the right to take it and dispose of it."[86]

In the Jacksonian era, it was no accident that two of the most successful political leaders in the United States were "Old Hickory" and "Old Tippecanoe," the men most responsible for the early nineteenth-century completion of the revolutionary work of ethnic cleansing begun in 1763. "The benevolent policy of the Government . . . in relation to the removal of the Indians beyond the white settlements is approaching to a happy consummation," now President Jackson announced to Congress in his annual message for 1830. "Toward the aborigines of the country no one can indulge a more friendly feeling than myself, or would go further in attempting to reclaim them from their wandering habits and make them a happy, prosperous people," he insisted. But there was little sense in continuing the doomed civilization policy and its fruitless efforts to allow at least some Native people to remain on eastern North American soil.

Humanity has often wept over the fate of the aborigines of this country, and Philanthropy has been long busily employed in devising means to avert it, but its progress has never for a moment been arrested, and one by one have many powerful tribes disappeared from the earth. To follow to the tomb the last of his race and to tread on the graves of extinct nations excite melancholy reflections. But true philanthropy reconciles the mind to these vicissitudes as it does to the extinction of one generation to make room for another . . . Nor is there anything in this which, upon a comprehensive view of the general interests of the human race, is to be regretted. Philanthropy could not wish to see this continent restored to the condition in which it was found by our forefathers. What good man would prefer a country covered with forests and ranged by a few thousand savages to our extensive Republic, studded with cities, towns, and prosperous farms, embellished with all the improvements which art can devise or industry execute, occupied by more than 12,000,000 happy people, and filled with all the blessings of liberty, civilization, and religion?

It was, Jackson concluded, "therefore, a duty which this Government owes to the new States to extinguish as soon as possible the Indian title to all lands which Congresses themselves have included within their limits."[87]

So, with the implementation of the policy known only slightly euphemistically as "Removal," the east at last ceased to be Indian country. Some Euro-American voices opposed the great Jacksonian national embrace of the Paxton Boys' principles, and White schoolchildren of the era even studied Logan's Lament as a model of sentimental elocution. Yet the same Jefferson who had made Logan famous had also advocated the manipulation of Indian debts to further a polite version of ethnic cleansing with relentless efficiency, even as he bemoaned the fate of a tragically vanishing race whose place would be taken by the White man's republic.[88] And in the Van Buren administration—the 1830s interval between "Old Hickory" and "Old Tippecanoe"—a second-tier Kentucky politician named Richard Mentor Johnson rose to become vice-president of the United States as the capstone to a political career based largely on the claim (which many others disputed) that he was the one who had shot Tenskwatawa's brother in the Battle of the Thames. With an Indian-hating frankness the Paxton Boys would have appreciated, his supporters rhymed their slogan: "Rumpsey dumpsey, Colonel Johnson killed Tecumseh."[89]

EPILOGUE:
EULOGY FROM
INDIAN COUNTRY

IN BOSTON in January 1836—the year Richard Mentor Johnson would be elected vice-president—a Native American who sometimes identified himself as "William Apess, a Pequot," twice delivered a historical lecture titled *Eulogy on King Philip.* "I do not arise," he told his audience,

> to spread before you the fame of a noted warrior, whose natural abilities shone like those of the great and mighty Philip of Greece, or of Alexander the Great, or like those of Washington—whose virtues and patriotism are engraven on the hearts of my audience . . . But it is to bring before you beings, made by the God of Nature, and in whose hearts and heads he has planted sympathies that shall live forever in the memory of the world . . .
>
> Yet those purer virtues remain untold . . . And who shall stand . . . but those few remaining descendants who now remain as the monument of the cruelty of those who came to improve our [Indian] race, and correct our errors? And as the immortal Washington lives endeared and engraven on the hearts of every white in America, never to be forgotten in time—even such is the immortal Philip honored, as held in memory by the degraded but yet grateful descendants who appreciate his character; so will every patriot, especially in this enlightened age, respect the rude yet all-accomplished son of

the forest, that died a martyr to his cause, though unsuccess-
ful, yet as glorious as the *American* Revolution.[1]

It is hard to tell which must have been most annoying to White Americans busily erasing Native people from both the landscape and their nation's past: the Indian orator's audacious comparison of Philip with the father of their country, his venomous attribution of "cruelty" to colonists
who supposedly "came to improve our race," or his assertion that the
Wampanoag's cause was "as glorious as the *American* Revolution." No
wonder the two self-published pamphlet editions of the speech that Apess
circulated in 1836 and 1837 sank into oblivion until literary scholars rediscovered them in our own day.[2] Demanding that familiar scenes be viewed
from an altered perspective, the *Eulogy* uncomfortably placed Native experiences at the heart of America's story.

William Apess (he also spelled his name "Apes") was an extraordinary figure, but his life nonetheless illustrates the grim circumstances of
the Native Americans who remained in the early nineteenth-century
east.[3] He was born in 1798, son of a Euro-Indian father and a mother who,
he claimed, was a Pequot but may have been an enslaved woman of African-American or mixed ancestry. When he was three or four years old, his
parents separated and left him with alcoholic and abusive grandparents in
Colchester, Connecticut. At age five, after his grandmother nearly beat
him to death, Colchester officials bound him out to servitude with a local
White family—the first of three with whom he would spend his childhood and glean six partial years of formal schooling. Over the objections
of his Baptist and Congregational masters, he began attending Methodist
meetings in about 1809 and experienced a religious conversion in 1813.
That year, after failing in several previous attempts to run away to freedom, he fled to Manhattan. There he enlisted as a drummer boy with a
New York militia troop that would see action in Canada while Tecumseh
was battling other U.S. forces during the War of 1812. Having never received the recruitment bonuses he had been promised, Apess left the
army without permission when the fighting ended in 1815. For over a year
he drifted around Native communities on the U.S.-Canadian border while

William Apess, Native American author of *Eulogy on King Philip.*
From the frontispiece of *A Son of the Forest: The Experience of William Apes, A Native of the Forest,* 2d ed. (New York, 1831). Rosenbach Museum and Library, Philadelphia.

fighting a serious drinking problem—a problem that continued after he returned to Connecticut to eke out a living at various jobs.[4]

By 1818 Apess had resumed attending Methodist meetings, temporarily abjured the bottle, been baptized, and felt the call to preach. As a licensed Methodist "exhorter" he traveled southern New England and the Hudson River Valley during the 1820s, speaking mostly to Indian and mixed-race audiences. Methodism had begun at the turn of the nineteenth century as a radically dissenting creed with much of its appeal among poor and marginalized people, including large numbers of African Americans and Indians; one-seventh of the Methodists in Providence, Rhode Island, in the late 1820s, for instance, were people of color. Yet in Apess' day the denomination's leaders were moving it away from its plebeian roots and retreating from their predecessors' commitment to racial equality. In this climate, the mainstream Methodist Episcopal Church denied Apess ministerial ordination, almost certainly because of his race. But in 1829 a

"Methodist Protestant" splinter group finally gave him a preaching license and authorized him to expand his peripatetic work.[5]

In 1833 the preacher visited the Wampanoag community of Mashpee and almost immediately became a central figure in a major local political controversy. Founded as a praying town by John Eliot's colleague Richard Bourne in 1660, Mashpee was now a community of some three hundred people with varying degrees of Indian ancestry. Legally wards of a board of White overseers, the Mashpees had long been struggling for the right to control their own affairs. Their appointed clergyman, a man named Phineas Fish, spent most of his time preaching to Anglo-Americans and actively opposed the Indians' calls for more autonomy. Soon after Apess arrived, the vast majority of Mashpees voted to adopt him into the community and announced that he was their choice to replace Fish and to act as their spokesman to the Massachusetts government. In July 1833 they issued an "Indian Declaration of Independence" announcing that "we, as a tribe, will rule ourselves, and have the right to do so; for all men are born free and equal, says the Constitution of the country."[6]

Thus began the "Mashpee Revolt." While petitioning the state legislature for their rights, the Indians ousted Fish and the overseers, convened an assembly, chose their own officials, and turned back Whites who tried to cut timber on their lands without permission. At an entirely peaceful meeting, a state official sent to investigate the situation arrested Apess on charges of assault and inciting a riot, which led to a thirty-day sentence in the county jail. Mashpee leaders retreated from open defiance but did not abandon their struggle, which Apess took to Boston newspapers and to supporters among abolitionists and other Euro-American reformers. In the "Marshpee Act" of 1834 the legislature gave the Indians a partial victory, granting them the right to elect their own selectmen and to control most local economic affairs, subject to the oversight of a White commissioner. For reasons that remain obscure, Apess' influence among the Mashpees declined rapidly soon thereafter, although he did organize a temperance society and form an independent church congregation in what was now known as the "Indian district." He fell into debt and by 1838 had retraced his boyhood route from New England to New York City. He died there a year later, probably of illnesses associated with the alcoholism he had battled off and on throughout his life.[7]

Apess' *Eulogy on King Philip*—composed as things began to fall apart for him at Mashpee—was the last, and perhaps greatest, in a series of publications that made him the most prolific Native American author of his generation. His literary career had begun in a way common in the evangelical Christian circles of his day. His first work was an autobiography, *A Son of the Forest,* published in 1829 and revised and republished in 1831. Like an expansive version of the Natick conversion narratives, the book conveys a standard Protestant tale of sin and rebirth and presents its message of salvation in rhetoric familiar to early nineteenth-century audiences; it shares much, for instance, with the genre of African-American slave narratives that had flourished since the appearance of *The Interesting Narrative of the Life of Olaudah Equiano* in 1789. Similarly orthodox religious themes shaped two other books published by Apess in 1831, *The Increase of the Kingdom of Christ: A Sermon* and *The Indians: The Ten Lost Tribes.*[8]

During the Mashpee Revolt, Apess stretched orthodox genres to more critical purposes in a book called *The Experiences of Five Christian Indians of the Pequot Tribe; or, An Indian's Looking-Glass for the White Man* (1833) and in a widely printed anonymous newspaper article titled "An Indian's Appeal to the White Men of Massachusetts." In 1835, after the revolt was over, he collected relevant documents and summarized the justice of the case in *Indian Nullification of the Unconstitutional Laws of Massachusetts Relative to the Marshpee Tribe; or the Pretended Riot Explained.* The titles of the latter two pieces evoked powerful messages about race in American life. David Walker's recently published *Appeal . . . to the Coloured Citizens of the World* (1829) had helped spark the Garrisonian abolitionist movement. The Nullification Crisis of 1832–33, in which South Carolinians defied the authority of President Jackson and the federal government, was explicitly about tariff policies, but everyone knew that the real issue was a state's right to keep African Americans in slavery. Similarly, of course, the "Indian Nullification" was about much more than who got to cut down trees in Mashpee.[9]

As these evocations of national affairs suggest, Apess' accounts of his own life and of the Mashpee Revolt engaged much bigger questions. Like 1763, 1836, when the *Eulogy* appeared, was not just any year in the tortured history of relations between Native and Euro-American people in the east and of race relations in North America more generally. Jackson was end-

ing his second term as president, and his policy of forced removal, enacted by Congress in 1830, was being relentlessly implemented. In Florida,
the president's old enemies the Seminoles were in the second year of a
new war with federal troops that would end in a draw in 1842. In Alabama, White squatters supported by the state government overran lands
guaranteed to the Creeks by an 1832 treaty and provoked them to take up
arms; that response provided an excuse for federal troops to force nearly
fifteen thousand people of the nation, many of them in shackles, to relocate in what would later become Oklahoma. The better-known Cherokee
turn on the "Trail of Tears" would not commence for two more years,
but a national debate raged in which those who defended the rights of the
"civilized tribes" of the southeast were severely outnumbered by the pro-
ponents of Jackson's policies.[10]

   With regard to broader questions of race and national identity as well,
1836 was an important year. The abolitionist movement was at its peak,
with the congressional "gag rule" on discussion of antislavery petitions,
state censorship of "incendiary literature" from the U.S. mails, and mob
attacks on speakers and newspaper editors showing how deeply the notion of racial equality threatened most White Americans, north and
south.[11] Also in 1836, slaveholders in Texas declared their independence
from Mexico, bringing into clearer focus issues of race, westward expansion, and the future of the eastern Indians being resettled in territories
just north of the "Lone Star Republic."[12] Against these backdrops,
Thomas Church's venomous century-old *Entertaining Passages Relating to
Philip's War* continued to be widely reprinted, and John Augustus Stone's
romanticized *Metamora* still played to packed audiences throughout the
United States, linking its fictionalized story of King Philip to powerful
messages about American history, race, and what would soon be known
as "Manifest Destiny."[13]

   And Apess composed his *Eulogy*. It is likely, but not certain, that he had
seen Stone perform, although it is difficult to trace any direct impact of
the play on the *Eulogy*. Far more important influences were Apess' personal experiences and his critical reading of some of the standard historical works of his day.[14] Two sources in particular shaped Apess' interpretation of Metacom, although, according to the lax citation standards of the
early nineteenth century, he did not feel compelled to acknowledge either

specifically in his text. First was Washington Irving's "Philip of Pokanoket," originally published in 1814 and reprinted as part of *The Sketch
Book of Geoffrey Crayon, Gent.*, in 1820. We know that Apess read this essay,
because an appendix to the 1831 edition of *A Son of the Forest* reprints
Irving's study "Traits of the Indian Character," which immediately pre-
cedes "Philip" in the *Sketch Book*.[15] Irving, scorning the one-sided portray-
als he read in the works of Thomas Church and Increase Mather ("a
worthy clergyman of the time, who dwells with horror and indignation
on every hostile act of the Indians, however justifiable, whilst he mentions with applause the most sanguinary atrocities of the whites"), used
"Philip of Pokanoket" to urge those who sought precedents for the American Revolution to identify with the Indians rather than with the Puritans.
The Indian leader whose forces fought "the whole British army," Irving
said, "was a patriot, attached to his native soil."[16]

Even more influential on Apess' *Eulogy*—but in a negative rather than
positive sense—were the speeches and writings of Daniel Webster, who
more than any other figure was responsible for creating the triumphantly
mythic story of the nation's history that sees its beginning at Plymouth
Rock. Particularly in an address commemorating the bicentennial of the
arrival of the *Mayflower* on 22 December 1620, Webster painted vivid verbal pictures of "Pilgrims" who planted seeds of liberty that would flower
in the American Revolution and bear glorious fruit in his own day:

> The peculiar original character of the New England Colonies, and
> certain causes coeval with their existence, have had a strong and de-
> cided influence on all their subsequent history, and especially the great
> event of the Revolution.
>
> Two thousand miles westward from the rock where their fathers
> landed, may now be found the sons of the Pilgrims, cultivating smil-
> ing fields, rearing towns and villages, and cherishing, we trust, the
> patrimonial blessings of wise institutions, of liberty, and religion.
> The world has seen nothing like this. Regions large enough to be em-
> pires, and which, half a century ago, were known only as remote and
> unexplored wildernesses, are now teeming with population, and pros-
> perous in all the great concerns of life; in good governments, the
> means of subsistence, and social happiness. It may be safely asserted,

that there are now more than a million of people, descendants of New England ancestors, living, free and happy, in regions which scarce sixty years ago were tracts of unpenetrated forests. Nor do rivers, or mountains, or seas resist the progress of industry and enterprise. Ere long, the sons of the Pilgrims will be on the shores of the Pacific.[17]

Pursuing Webster's themes, countless popular orators and writers in Apess' era compared the freedom-loving Pilgrims' struggle against King Philip to the Founding Fathers' struggle against King George, somehow managing to transform Metacom's War into a rehearsal for the American Revolution. As shown by those who still sing of "Pilgrim feet" that "a thoroughfare for freedom beat across the wilderness," Webster's vision of the American past penetrated deeply into the national consciousness.[18]

In the *Eulogy,* Apess' main purpose was to invert that vision, to compel his audience to see the Pilgrims as they might have looked to those who stood in Indian country:

Let the children of the pilgrims blush, while the son of the forest drops a tear, and groans over the fate of his murdered and departed fathers. He would say to the sons of the pilgrims, (as Job said about his birthday), let the day be dark, the 22d day of December, 1620; let it be forgotten in your celebration, in your speeches, and by the burying of the Rock that your fathers first put their foot upon. For be it remembered, although the gospel is said to be glad tidings to all people, yet we poor Indians never have found those who brought it as messengers of mercy, but contrawise. We say, therefore, let every man of color wrap himself in mourning, for the 22d of December and the 4th of July are days of mourning and not of joy.[19]

Sixteen years later, Frederick Douglass—who may or may not have read the *Eulogy*—similarly asked, "What to the American slave is your Fourth of July?" His answer, like Apess', was "that it reveals to him, more than all other days in the year, the gross injustice and cruelty to which he is the constant victim."[20]

Yet Webster had found a powerful antislavery message in the heritage of Plymouth Rock:

The African slave-trader is a pirate and a felon . . . If there be, within
the extent of our knowledge or influence, any participation in this
traffic, let us pledge ourselves here, upon the rock of Plymouth, to ex-
tirpate and destroy it. It is not fit that the land of the Pilgrims should
bear the shame longer.[21]

To the contrary, Apess vehemently insisted, the slave trade had been
rooted in New England's soil long before the Pilgrims had set foot upon
it.[22] "It appears from history," the *Eulogy* announced, that in the 1610s English explorers took "a native of the Island of Capawick [Chappaquiddick],
a place at the south of Cape Cod, whose name was Epenuel . . . by force,
with some twenty-nine others," who were "carried to London, and from
thence to be sold for slaves among the Spaniards."[23] And, as for the arrival
of freedom on the *Mayflower*, Apess noted that in

1620, the pilgrims landed at Plymouth, and without asking liberty
from any one they possessed themselves of a portion of the country,
and built themselves houses, and then made a treaty, and commanded them to accede to it. This, if now done, it would be called
an insult, and every white man would be called to go out and act the
part of a patriot, to defend their country's rights; and if every in-
truder were butchered, it would be sung upon every hilltop in the
Union, that victory and patriotism was the order of the day. And yet
the Indians, (though many were dissatisfied), without the shedding
of blood, or imprisoning any one, bore it. And yet for their kindness
and resignation toward the whites, they were called savages, and
made by God on purpose for them to destroy.[24]

And so on, for every cherished (if newly minted) New England historical image, Apess offered a chillingly reversed perspective. To a generation
that was inventing the modern myth of the First Thanksgiving, he
showed a Miles Standish who "goes forward with a black and hypocritical
heart, and pretends to prepare a feast for the Indians; and when they sit
down to eat, they seize the Indians' knives hanging about their necks, and
stab them to the heart. The white people call this stabbing, feasting the

savages." To New Englanders who thought themselves superior to Jacksonian southern advocates of removal, he gave a reminder that

> in 1647, the pilgrims speak of large and respectable tribes. But let us
> trace them for a few moments. How have they been destroyed, is it
> by fair means? No. How then? By hypocritical proceedings, by being
> duped and flattered; flattered by informing the Indians that their
> God was a going to speak to them, and then place them before the
> cannon's mouth in a line, and then putting the match to it and
> kill[ing] thousands of them. We might suppose that meek Christians
> had better gods and weapons than cannon; weapons that were not
> carnal, but mighty through God, to the pulling down of strong
> holds. These are the weapons that modern Christians profess to
> have; and if the pilgrims did not have them, they ought not to be
> honored as such. But let us again review their weapons, to civilize
> the nations of this soil. What were they: rum and powder, and ball,
> together with all the diseases, such as the small pox and every other
> disease imaginable; and in this way sweep off thousands and tens of
> thousands.[25]

Pressing his relentless alternative to Webster's angle of vision, Apess recounted in grim detail what he saw as the "daring robberies and barbarous deeds of death . . . committed by the American Pilgrims." At length,
"having laid a mass of history and exposition before you, the purpose of
which is to show that Philip and all the Indians generally, felt indignantly
toward whites," Apess turned to the events that transpired from the arrest
and death of Wamsutta, to the accession of Metacom, to the murder of
John Sassamon—a "traitor" who by "the laws of the Indians . . . had for-
feited his life" and was killed "doubtless by the order of Philip." Apess
took pains to point out that, despite repeated indignities, until Plymouth
authorities executed Sassamon's supposed executioners, "no hostility was
committed by Philip or his warriors."[26]

Finally, when Metacom "could no longer restrain his young men," and
the fighting began, Apess created a fictionalized scene of a great council,
at which

it appears that Philip made the following speech to his chiefs, counsellors and warriors:

"Brothers—you see this vast country before us, which the great Spirit gave to our fathers and us; you see the buffalo and deer that now are our support—Brothers, you see these little ones, our wives and children, who are looking to us for food and raiment; and you now see the foe before you, that they have grown insolent and bold; that all our ancient customs are disregarded; the treaties made by our fathers and us are broken, and all of us insulted; our council fires disregarded, and all the ancient customs of our fathers; our brothers murdered before our eyes, and their spirits cry to us for revenge. Brothers, these people from the unknown world will cut down our groves, spoil our hunting and planting grounds, and drive us and our children from the graves of our fathers, and our council fires, and enslave our women and children."[27]

In his struggle against enslavement, Philip became, in Apess' line of vision, a fighter for liberty fully comparable to Washington:

The blow had now been struck, the die was cast, and nothing but blood and carnage was before them. And we find Philip as active as the wind, as dexterous as a giant, firm as the pillows of heaven, and as fierce as a lion, a powerful foe to contend with indeed: and as swift as an eagle, gathering together his forces to prepare them for the battle . . .

At the great fight at Pocasset, Philip commanded in person, where he also was discovered with his host in a dismal swamp. He had retired here with his army to secure a safe retreat from the pilgrims, who were in close pursuit of him, and their numbers were so powerful they thought the fate of Philip was sealed . . . The situation of Philip was rather peculiar, as there was but one outlet to the swamp, and a river before him nearly seven miles to descend. The pilgrims placed a guard around the swamp for 13 days, which gave Philip and his men time to prepare canoes to make good his retreat; in which he did, to the Connecticut River, and in his retreat lost but fourteen

men. We may look upon this move of Philip's to be equal, if not superior, to that of Washington crossing the Delaware.[28]

However he may have compared to Washington in military genius, in
caring for his troops Apess' Philip was unquestionably superior. Despite
the sufferings of a wartime winter, for the Indians there was no Valley
Forge where some prospered while others starved:

> We would now notice an act in King Philip, that outweighs all the
> princes and emperors in the world. That is, when his men began to
> be in want of money, having a coat neatly wrought with
> wampampeag (i.e., Indian money), he cut it to pieces, and distrib-
> uted it among all his chiefs and warriors; it being better than the old
> continental money of the revolution, in Washington's day, as not
> one Indian soldier found fault with it, as we could ever learn; so that
> it cheered their hearts still to persevere to maintain their rights and
> expel their enemies.[29]

Apess remained silent on the racial beliefs and practices of the
slaveowning Washington, but nonetheless, as he brought his story of
Metacom to its climax, the nation's original sin took center stage:

> But we have another dark and corrupt deed for the sons of pilgrims
> to look at, and that is the fight and capture of Philip's son and wife,
> and many of his warriors, in which Philip lost about 130 men killed
> and wounded; this was in August 1676. But the most horrid act was
> in taking Philip's son, about ten years of age, and selling him to be a
> slave away from his father and mother. While I am writing, I can
> hardly restrain my feelings, to think a people calling themselves
> Christians should [engage in] conduct so scandalous, so outrageous
> . . . And surely none but such as believe they did right, will ever go
> and undertake to celebrate that day of their landing, the 22d of De-
> cember. Only look at it, then stop and pause. My fathers came here
> for liberty themselves, and then they must go and chain that mind,
> that image they professed to serve; not content to rob and cheat the
> poor ignorant Indians, but must take one of the King's sons, and

make a slave of him. Gentlemen and ladies, I blush at these tales, if you do not, especially when they professed to be a free and humane people. Yes, they did; [at the end of the Pequot War] they took a part of my tribe and sold them to the Spaniards in Bermuda, and many others; and then on the Sabbath day, these people would gather themselves together, and say that God is no respecter of persons; while the divines would pour forth, He says that he loves God and hates his brother, is a liar, and the truth is not in him. And at the same time they hating and selling their fellow men in bondage. And there is no manner of doubt but that all my countrymen would have been enslaved if they had tamely submitted.[30]

Apess' alternative view of the American past did not end with Philip's death, or with Metacom's body "quartered and hung up upon four trees; his head and one hand given to the Indian who shot him, to carry about to show. At which sight it so overjoyed the pilgrims that they would give him money for it." He had more to tell his audience, not just about their past but about a present when Creeks and Cherokees were leaving Georgia at the point of a gun and Seminoles—in the tradition of Metacom—were battling federal troops to a standoff in Florida. "How deep," he asked,

was the thought of Philip, when he could look from Maine to Georgia, and from the ocean to the lakes, and view with one look all his brethren withering before the more enlightened to come; and how true his prophesy, that the white people would not only cut down their groves, but would enslave them. Had the inspiration of Isaiah been there, he could not have been more correct. Our groves and hunting grounds are gone, our dead are dug up, our council-fires are put out, and a foundation was laid in the first Legislature to enslave our people, by taking from them all rights, which has been strictly adhered to ever since. Look at the disgraceful laws, disfranchising us as citizens. Look at the treaties made by Congress, all broken. Look at the deep-rooted plans laid, when a territory becomes a State, that after so many years the laws shall be extended over the Indians that live within their boundaries. Yea, every charter that has been given, was given with the view of driving the Indians out of the States, or dooming them to become chained under desperate laws, that would make them drag out a miserable life as one chained to the galley; and this is the course that has been pursued for nearly two hundred years. A fire, a canker, created by the pilgrims from across the Atlantic, to burn and destroy my poor unfortunate brethren, and it cannot be denied. What, then, shall we do, shall we cease crying, and say it is all wrong, or shall we bury the hatchet and those unjust laws, and Plymouth Rock together, and become friends[?] And will the sons of the pilgrims aid in putting out the fire and destroying the canker that will ruin all that their fathers left behind them to destroy? (by this we see how true Philip spoke.) If so, we hope we shall not hear it said from ministers and church members, that we are so good no other people can live with us, as you know it is a common thing for them to say, Indians cannot live among Christian people; no, even the President of the United States tells the Indians they cannot live among civilized people, and we want your lands and must have them and will have them. As if he had said to them, We want your land for our use to speculate upon, it aids us in paying off our national debt and supporting us in Congress to drive you off.

You see, my red children [President Jackson says], that our fathers carried on this scheme of getting your lands for our use, and we have now become rich and powerful; and we have a right to do with you just as we please; we claim to be your fathers. And we think we shall do you a great favor, my dear sons and daughters, to drive you out, to get you away out of the reach of our civilized people, who are cheating you, for we have no law to reach them, we cannot protect you although you be our children. So it is no use, you need not cry, you must go, even if the lions devour you, for we promised the land you have to somebody else long ago, perhaps twenty or thirty years; and we did it without your consent, it is true. But this has been the way our fathers first brought us up, and it is hard to depart from it; therefore, you shall have no protection from us.[31]

In light of all this, Apess continued, "you have been enabled to see that Philip's prophesy has come to pass; therefore, as a man of natural abilities, I shall pronounce him the greatest man that was ever in America; and so it will stand, until he is proved to the contrary, to the everlasting disgrace of the pilgrims' fathers."[32]

Exaggerated, one-sided, propagandistic? Certainly; but no more so than Webster's skewed view of the continent's past. And for Apess, the point was not so much to prove which angle of vision—facing east or facing west—was more accurate but to employ the comparison in the service of a larger truth. "Having now given historical facts, and an exposition in relation to ancient times," he concluded, "we have been enabled to discover the foundation which destroyed our common fathers, in their struggle together; it was indeed nothing more than the spirit of avarice and usurpation of power that has brought people in all ages to hate and devour each other." In the end, for Apess, the point of envisioning the past in this way was not to wallow in a sea of long-ago evils, but to confront them straight on, and so to find means to transcend them: "You and I have to rejoice that we have not to answer for our fathers' crimes, neither shall we do right to charge them one to another. We can only regret it, and flee from it, and from henceforth, let peace and righteousness be written upon our hearts and hands forever."[33]

"We have it in our power to begin the world over again," Thomas Paine had written in 1776, proposing a less painful way of breaking with the past. "A situation, similar to the present, hath not happened since the days of Noah until now. The birthday of a new world is at hand, and a race of men, perhaps as numerous as all Europe contains, are to receive their portion of freedom."[34] Receive it many of that race did. Yet, as Apess tried to get his readers to see, the new White Man's republic could not bloom in a pristine landscape already cleansed by a supernatural flood. North America was not a new world but an old one, the product of millennia of Native experience and centuries of interaction between colonizers and colonized. Unlike Noah and his family, the Revolutionaries and their successors had to unleash a very human deluge if they were to clear that old Indian world away and claim the continent as their own.

The waters they released from the fountains of the great deep could

displace Native Americans from the landscape but not from the continent's past. Try as orators like Webster might to imagine the "descendants of New England ancestors, living, free and happy, in regions which
scarce sixty years ago were tracts of unpenetrated forests," reminders that
the United States grew up in Indian country were everywhere those forests used to be. What citizens of the new nation could not obliterate, they
therefore appropriated to their own purposes, dressing as "Mohawks" to
throw tea into Boston Harbor, preserving Algonquian and Muskogean
place names on real estate maps, recasting Metacom as a White actor's
"Metamora," creating characters along the lines of *The Last of the
Mohicans* to die with obliging noble inevitability, modeling fraternal orga-
nizations and athletic mascots after what they wanted Indian people to
be.[35] In their darker moments, White Americans might even admit (and in
their worst moments celebrate) that their nation was born in a revolution
against Indians as well as against the crown, that its prosperity was based
on the expropriation of Native land, or that its participatory politics
rested on racial exclusion—for all these admissions still envisioned a continent on which, either gloriously or tragically, European "civilization"
and Indian "savagery" could never coexist. The flood was not the work of
human hands.

Thus conflict with stereotyped Indians could—indeed had to—become
central to the American story, but flesh-and-blood Indian people and the
histories they made for themselves could not. So, as White Americans
wrote their nation's past, their greatest erasure of all was of memories of
Indians who neither uncompromisingly resisted like the King Philip of
their imagination nor wholeheartedly assimilated like the Pocahontas of
their fantasies. Native people who instead struggled to find ways to incorporate European people, objects, and ideas into Indian country on Indian
terms—who adapted and changed in accordance with their own histories
and traditions rather than in accordance with Euro-American scripts—
could find no place in the mythology of a nation marching triumphantly
westward across the continent. When those who arrogated to themselves
the right to be called "Americans" seceded from the British Empire, they
also seceded from the past they shared with such living, breathing Indians
in eastern North America. Yet somehow the very violence with which
they revolted against an empire that suggested White and Indian people

might live beside each other, the very violence with which they rejected their own recent history, exposes the reality of the threat they faced: the racialized world the revolutionaries created was not the only one that might have been. As William Apess understood far too well, that was the real American tragedy.

A TECHNICAL NOTE

The spelling of Native American names varies enormously in original documents. For personal names, I have tried to use the most common spelling used in
English-language works today, even in cases in which, for instance, *Tekamthi*
might be closer to the original than Tecumseh. The words *Indians, Native Americans, Natives,* and *Native peoples* are used interchangeably, with the understanding
that these terms at first reflected generalizations imposed by Europeans on diverse North American peoples but later did approximate the always contested
view of nativists who articulated a sense of shared identity. I have avoided use of
the color terms *Red* and *White* for periods before the eighteenth century, and then
used them only when speaking of people on either side of the rigidifying cultural
divide who seemed to conceptualize the world in racial terms. At no point were
all Euro-Americans "White" or all Native Americans "Red." To emphasize that
the identities represented by these color terms were historically constructed
rather than the product of some natural or ancient inheritance, I have capitalized
the words throughout.

Designations and spellings for particular Indian nations follow the usages advocated in William C. Sturtevant's *Handbook of North American Indians*, volume
15: *Northeast,* edited by Bruce C. Trigger (Washington, D.C.: Smithsonian Institution, 1978), which contains useful synonymies of the variants and meanings of
terms appearing in historical documents. Remember that many such collective
terms were coined by outsiders (and thus sometimes convey less-than-flattering
images) and that almost all describe political configurations that did not coalesce
until long after European contact. The origins of both personal and group
names in diverse Native languages and the complicated, often erroneous, ways in
which those names have come down to us in English make it virtually impossible
to provide any consistent guide to their pronunciation.

To enhance readability, in all quotations from sources originating before 1830 I
have silently modernized spelling, capitalization, and punctuation and omitted
italics unless clearly intended for emphasis by the original author.

Notes

Prologue

1. David M. Potter, *The Impending Crisis, 1848–1861*, ed. Don E. Fehrenbacher (New York: Harper and Row, 1976), 267–280, quotation p. 275.

2. *The Papers of Thomas Jefferson*, ed. Julian P. Boyd et al., vol. 15 (Princeton: Princeton University Press, 1958), 392. As Herbert E. Sloan has shown, Jefferson's words—which referred to the national debt and resonated with his own financial crises—have often been taken out of context to support a more general desire to erase the cultural past; see Sloan, *Principle and Interest: Thomas Jefferson and the Problem of Debt* (New York: Oxford University Press, 1995), 50–85.

3. Melvin L. Fowler, "A Pre-Columbian Urban Center on the Mississippi," *Scientific American*, August 1975, 92–101.

4. Mark W. Mehrer, *Cahokia's Countryside: Household Archaeology, Settlement Patterns, and Social Power* (De Kalb: Northern Illinois University Press, 1995); Thomas E. Emerson, *Cahokia and the Archaeology of Power* (Tuscaloosa: University of Alabama Press, 1997).

5. R. Douglas Hurt, *Indian Agriculture in America: Prehistory to the Present* (Lawrence: University Press of Kansas, 1987), 7, 12–16, 40; Linda S. Cordell and Bruce D. Smith, "Indigenous Farmers," in *The Cambridge History of the Native Peoples of the Americas*, ed. Bruce G. Trigger and Wilcomb E. Washburn, vol. 1: *North America* (Cambridge: Cambridge University Press, 1996), pt. 1, pp. 247–248; Theda Perdue, *Cherokee Women: Gender and Culture Change, 1700–1835* (Lincoln: University of Nebraska Press, 1998), 13–59; Elisabeth Tooker, "Women in Iroquois Society," in *Extending the Rafters: Interdisciplinary Approaches to Iroquoian Studies*, ed. Michael K. Foster, Jack Campisi, and Marianne Mithun (Albany: State University of New York Press, 1984), 109–123.

6. Patricia Galloway, *Choctaw Genesis, 1500–1700* (Lincoln: University of Nebraska Press, 1995); Peter Navokov with Dean Snow, "Farmers of the Woodlands," in *America in 1492: The World of the Indian Peoples before the Arrival of Columbus*, ed. Alvin M. Josephy Jr. (New York: Vintage Books, 1992), 119–145.

7. William A. Turnbaugh, "Wide-Area Connections in Native North America," *American Indian Culture and Research Journal* 1, no. 4 (1976): 22–28; Bruce G. Trigger, *The Children of Aataentsic: A History of the Huron People to 1660*, vol. 1 (Montreal: McGill–Queens University Press, 1976), 62–66; Neal Salisbury, "The Indians' Old World: Native Americans and the Coming of Europeans," *William and Mary Quarterly*, 3d ser., 53 (1996): 435–458.

8. George R. Hamell, "Mythical Realities and European Contact in the Northeast during the Sixteenth and Seventeenth Centuries," *Man in the Northeast*, no. 33 (1987): 63–87; Helen C. Rountree, *The Powhatan Indians of Virginia: Their Traditional Culture* (Norman: University of Oklahoma Press, 1989), 100–113; Kathleen J. Bragdon, *Native People of Southern New England, 1500–1650* (Norman: University of Oklahoma Press, 1996), 140–155; Frederic W. Gleach, *Powhatan's World and Colonial Virginia: A Conflict of Cultures* (Lincoln: University of Nebraska Press, 1997), 28–34.

9. Population estimates—and all are only estimates, based on a variety of assumptions about when and to what extent the epidemics discussed in Chapter 2 decimated Native communities—tend to be for the United States or the North American continent as a whole or, somewhat more reliably, for relatively small regions. A recent conservative (and almost certainly too low) estimate reckons a total population of not quite 2.2 million north of Mexico, of which approximately 974,000 (roughly 44 percent) lived in eastern Canada and the north Atlantic, south Atlantic, Gulf, and central states. A widely cited figure near the higher end of the spectrum estimates a total of 7,898,000 north of Mexico, of which 44 percent for eastern North America would be 3,791,040; the midpoint between the two figures is 2,382,520. See Russell Thornton, *American Indian Holocaust and Survival: A Population History since 1492* (Norman: University of Oklahoma Press, 1987), 15–90, esp. 29, 31.

10. John J. McCusker and Russell R. Menard, *The Economy of British America, 1607–1789* (Chapel Hill: University of North Carolina Press, 1985), 54.

11. Frederick E. Hoxie, *The Indians versus the Textbooks: Is There Any Way Out?*, D'Arcy McNickle Center for the History of the American Indian Occasional Papers in Curriculum Series, no. 1 (Chicago, 1984); James H. Merrell, "Some Thoughts on Colonial Historians and American Indians," *William and Mary Quarterly*, 3d ser., 46 (1989): 94–119; Daniel K. Richter, "Whose Indian History?" ibid.,

50 (1993): 379–393; James A. Hijiya, "Why the West Is Lost," ibid., 51 (1992): 285–287. The term "master narrative" is borrowed from Nathan Irvin Huggins, "The Deforming Mirror of Truth," in *Black Odyssey: The African-American Ordeal in Slavery,* reissued ed. (New York: Vintage Books, 1990), xi–lvii, quotation p. xiii. For assertions of Iroquois influence on the Constitution, see Donald Grinde, *The Iroquois and the Founding of the American Nation* (San Francisco: Indian Historian Press, 1977); and Bruce E. Johansen, *Forgotten Founders: Benjamin Franklin, the Iroquois, and the Rationale for the American Revolution* (Ipswich, Mass.: Gambit, 1982). For refutations, see Elisabeth Tooker, "The United States Constitution and the Iroquois League," *Ethnohistory* 35 (1988): 305–336; and William A. Starna and George R. Hamell, "History and the Burden of Proof: The Case of the Iroquois Influence on the U.S. Constitution," *New York History* 77 (1996): 427–452. The highly politicized controversy has become increasingly bitter and *ad hominem.* See Johansen, "Native American Societies and the Evolution of Democracy in America, 1600–1800," *Ethnohistory* 37 (1990): 279–290; Tooker, "Reply to Johansen," ibid., 291–297; Johansen and Grinde, "The Debate Regarding American Precedents for Democracy: A Recent Historiography," *American Indian Culture and Research Journal* 14, no. 1 (1990): 61–88; and "Forum: The 'Iroquois Influence Thesis—Con and Pro,'" *William and Mary Quarterly,* 3d ser., 53 (1996): 587–636.

12. Charles A. Beard, "Written History as an Act of Faith," *American Historical Review* 39 (1934): 228.

1. Imagining a Distant New World

1. Carl Becker, "Every Man His Own Historian," *American Historical Review* 37 (1932): 228, 231. On the role of imagination in the writing of history, see R. G. Collingwood, *The Idea of History* (Oxford: Clarendon Press, 1946), 231–249; and James Axtell, *Beyond 1492: Encounters in Colonial North America* (New York: Oxford University Press, 1992), 3–74.

2. Julius E. Olson and Edward Gaylord Bourne, eds., *The Northmen, Columbus and Cabot, 985–1503* (New York: C. Scribner's Sons, 1906), 423–424; Samuel Eliot Morison, *The European Discovery of America: The Northern Voyages, A.D. 500–1600* (New York: Oxford University Press, 1971), 206–209; Peter E. Pope, *The Many Landfalls of John Cabot* (Toronto: University of Toronto Press, 1997), 11–42; [Richard Hakluyt the Younger], *Divers Voyages Touching the Discoverie of America, and the Ilands Adjacent unto the Same, Made First of All by Our Englishmen, and Afterward by the Frenchmen and Britons* (London: Thomas Woodcocke, 1582), fols. A1–B4 (2d

pagination); Reuben Gold Thwaites, ed., *The Jesuit Relations and Allied Documents: Travels and Explorations of the Jesuit Missionaries in New France, 1610–1791*, 73 vols. (Cleveland: Burrows Brothers, 1896–1901), 5: 119–121.

3. Olson and Bourne, *Northmen, Columbus and Cabot*, 423.

4. Hakluyt, *Divers Voyages*, fol. A3v.

5. James W. Bradley, "Iron Work in Onondaga, 1550–1650," in *Studies on Iroquoian Culture*, ed. Nancy Bonvillain (Rindge, N.H.: Department of Anthropology, Franklin Pierce College, 1980), 109–117.

6. E. B. O'Callaghan and B. Fernow, eds., *Documents Relative to the Colonial History of the State of New York*, 15 vols. (Albany, N.Y.: Weed, Parsons, 1853–1887), 9: 47–51.

7. Ruth M. Underhill, *Red Man's Religion: Beliefs and Practices of the Indians North of Mexico* (Chicago: University of Chicago Press, 1965), 20–29; Åke Hultkrantz, *The Religions of the American Indians*, trans. Monica Setterwall (Berkeley: University of California Press, 1979), 9–14; Mary A. Druke, "Linking Arms: The Structure of Iroquois Intertribal Diplomacy," in *Beyond the Covenant Chain: The Iroquois and Their Neighbors in Indian North America, 1600–1800*, ed. Daniel K. Richter and James H. Merrell (Syracuse: Syracuse University Press, 1987), 29–39.

8. [Cadwallader Colden], *The History of the Five Indian Nations Depending on the Province of New-York in America* (New York, 1727), 23–24; George Hamell, "Arent van Curler and the Underwater Grandfather," paper delivered at the Conference on Iroquois Research, Rensselaerville, N.Y., October 1988. Documents dating from the period of Van Curler's drowning do not mention this episode; see A. J. F. Van Laer, "Documents Relating to Arent van Curler's Death," *Dutch Settlers Society of Albany Yearbook* 3 (1927–28): 30–34. A Jesuit missionary journal of 1667 does, however, discuss both Van Curler's death and the custom of making offerings at the spot of his demise; Thwaites, *Jesuit Relations*, 61: 181–183.

9. Charles T. Gehring and William A. Starna, trans. and eds., *A Journey into Mohawk and Oneida Country, 1634–1635* (Syracuse: Syracuse University Press, 1988), 62; Johannes Megapolensis Jr., "A Short Account of the Mohawk Indians" (1644), in *In Mohawk Country: Early Narratives about a Native People*, ed. Dean R. Snow, Charles T. Gehring, and William A. Starna (Syracuse: Syracuse University Press, 1996), 45.

10. Barrie Reynolds, "Beothuk," in *Handbook of North American Indians*, ed. William C. Sturtevant, vol. 15: *Northeast*, ed. Bruce G. Trigger (Washington, D.C.: Smithsonian Institution, 1978), 103.

11. Hakluyt, *Divers Voyages*, fol. A5v.

12. David J. Weber, *The Spanish Frontier in North America* (New Haven: Yale University Press, 1992), 30–45, 49–59, 71–73; James W. Bradley, "Native Exchange

and European Trade: Cross Cultural Dynamics in the Sixteenth Century," *Man in the Northeast*, no. 33 (1987): 31–46. Skeletal remains of a "female [who] may have been a Negro (possibly a former slave)" and who had contracted the tropical disease yaws were interred in an Iroquois cemetery dated to the late 1590s; Charles F. Wray, Martha L. Sempowski, and Lorraine P. Saunders, *Tram and Cameron: Two Early Contact Era Seneca Sites* (Rochester, N.Y.: Research Division of the Rochester Museum and Science Center, 1991), 28–32.

13. The following is based on documents published in Lawrence A. Clayton, Vernon James Knight Jr., and Edward C. Moore, eds., *The De Soto Chronicles: The Expedition of Hernando De Soto to North America in 1539–1543*, 2 vols. (Tuscaloosa: University of Alabama Press, 1993), particularly the accounts generally attributed to "A Gentleman of Elvas" (1: 19–219) and Rogrigo Rangel as compiled by Gonzalo Fernández de Oviedo y Valdés (1: 247–305). The problematic nature of these texts is explored in Patricia Galloway, "The Incestuous Soto Narratives," in *The Hernando de Soto Expedition: History, Historiography, and "Discovery" in the Southeast*, ed. Galloway (Lincoln: University of Nebraska Press, 1997), 11–44; and Martin Malcom Elbl and Ivana Elbl, "The Gentleman of Elvas and His Publisher," ibid., 45–97. The most thorough analysis of the expedition is Charles Hudson, *Knights of Spain, Warriors of the Sun: Hernando de Soto and the South's Ancient Chiefdoms* (Athens: University of Georgia Press, 1997).

14. Clayton, Knight, and Moore, *De Soto Chronicles*, 1: 256.

15. Ibid., 257.

16. Ibid., 62.

17. Ibid.

18. Ibid., 288–289.

19. Ibid., 270–271. On the *Requirimiento* see Robert F. Berkhofer, *The White Man's Indian: Images of the American Indian from Columbus to the Present* (New York: Knopf, 1978), 123–124; and Patricia Seed, *Ceremonies of Possession in Europe's Conquest of the New World, 1492–1640* (New York: Cambridge University Press, 1995), 69–99. Patricia Galloway suggests that Oviedo may have inserted a paraphrase of the *Requirimiento* into Rangel's account for literary or legal effect ("The Incestuous Soto Narratives," 16), but, given the legal weight that the Spanish crown attached to the document, it seems likely that de Soto would have had its basic points repeatedly proclaimed, if only for the benefit of his own men.

20. Clayton, Knight, and Moore, *De Soto Chronicles*, 1: 83.

21. Carl Ortwin Sauer, *Sixteenth-Century North America: The Land and the People as Seen by the Europeans* (Berkeley: University of California Press, 1971), 158.

22. Clayton, Knight, and Moore, *De Soto Chronicles*, 1: 279.

23. Ibid., 98.

24. Henry S. Burrage, ed., *Early English and French Voyages, Chiefly from Hakluyt, 1534–1608* (New York: C. Scribner's Sons, 1906), 88.

25. Weber, *Spanish Frontier,* 3.

26. Bruce G. Trigger, *Natives and Newcomers: Canada's "Heroic Age" Reconsidered* (Kingston, Ont.: McGill–Queen's University Press, 1985), 129–135.

27. The published firsthand accounts of Cartier's three voyages to North America, on which the following section is based, are reprinted in Burrage, *Early English and French Voyages,* 1–102. See also the translations by H. P. Biggar, reprinted in Ramsay Cook, ed., *The Voyages of Jacques Cartier* (Toronto: University of Toronto Press, 1993).

28. Burrage, *Early English and French Voyages,* 19.

29. Ibid., 21.

30. Ibid., 25.

31. Ibid.

32. Percy J. Robinson, "The Origin of the Name Hochelaga," *Canadian Historical Review* 23 (1942): 295–296; idem, "Some of Cartier's Place-Names," ibid., 26 (1945): 401–405.

33. See Chapter 4.

34. Burrage, *Early English and French Voyages,* 65.

35. Ibid., 71.

36. Trigger, *Natives and Newcomers,* 131–132.

37. Burrage, *Early English and French Voyages,* 96.

38. Ibid.

39. Ibid., 102.

40. W. J. Eccles, *The Canadian Frontier, 1534–1760,* rev. ed. (Albuquerque: University of New Mexico Press, 1983), 12–18.

41. Marvin T. Smith, "Aboriginal Population Movements in the Early Historic Period Interior Southeast," in *Powhatan's Mantle: Indians in the Colonial Southeast,* ed. Peter H. Wood, Gregory A. Waselkov, and M. Thomas Hatley (Lincoln: University of Nebraska Press, 1991), 21–34; Vernon James Knight Jr., "The Formation of the Creeks," in *The Forgotten Centuries: Indians and Europeans in the American South, 1521–1704,* ed. Charles Hudson and Carmen Chaves Tesser (Athens: University of Georgia Press, 1994), 373–392; Patricia Galloway, *Choctaw Genesis, 1500–1700* (Lincoln: University of Nebraska Press, 1995).

42. William N. Fenton, "Problems Arising from the Historic Northeastern Position of the Iroquois," in *Essays on Historical Anthropology of North America Published in Honor of John R. Swanton* (Washington, D.C.: Smithsonian Institution, 1940), 159–251.

43. H. H. Lamb, *Climate: Present, Past and Future,* vol. 2 (London: Methuen,

1977), 463; Neal Salisbury, "The Indians' Old World: Native Americans and the Coming of Europeans," *William and Mary Quarterly*, 3d ser., 53 (1996): 444–449; Galloway, *Choctaw Genesis*, 67–74; Hudson, *Knights of Spain*, 417–440.

44. Henry F. Dobyns, "Estimating Aboriginal American Population: An Appraisal of Techniques with a New Hemispheric Estimate," *Current Anthropology* 7 (1966): 395–415; Sherburne F. Cook, "The Significance of Disease in the Extinction of the New England Indians," *Human Biology* 44 (1973): 485–508; Alfred W. Crosby, "Virgin Soil Epidemics as a Factor in the Aboriginal Depopulation in America," *William and Mary Quarterly*, 3d ser., 30 (1976): 176–207; Ann F. Ramenofsky, *Vectors of Death: The Archaeology of European Contact* (Albuquerque: University of New Mexico Press, 1987), 137–172.

45. Randolph J. Widmer, "The Structure of Southeastern Chiefdoms," in Hudson and Tesser, *Forgotten Centuries*, 137–139.

46. Kenneth L. Feder, "The Spanish *Entrada:* A Model for Assessing Claims of Pre-Columbian Contact between the Old and New Worlds," *North American Archaeologist* 15 (1994): 160; Hudson, *Knights of Spain*, 418–422; Ann F. Ramenofsky and Patricia Galloway, "Disease and the Soto Entrada," in Galloway, *Hernando de Soto Expedition*, 259–279.

47. Bruce G. Trigger, "Ontario Native People and the Epidemics of 1634–1640," in *Indians, Animals, and the Fur Trade: A Critique of "Keepers of the Game,"* ed. Shepard Krech III (Athens: University of Georgia Press, 1981), 22.

48. John Witthoft, "Ancestry of the Susquehannocks," in *Susquehannock Miscellany*, ed. John Witthoft and W. Fred Kinsey (Harrisburg: Pennsylvania Historical and Museum Commission, 1959), 19–59; Barry C. Kent, *Susquehanna's Indians* (Harrisburg: Pennsylvania Historical and Museum Commission, 1984), 15–21; Marvin T. Smith, "Aboriginal Depopulation in the Postcontact Southeast," in Hudson and Tesser, *Forgotten Centuries*, 257–275; James Axtell, *The Indians' New South: Cultural Change in the Colonial Southeast* (Baton Rouge: Louisiana State University Press, 1997), 23–24.

49. This language paraphrases the modern codification of the Great Law of the Iroquois League: "At the third council the War Chief of the Five Nations shall address the Chief of the foreign nation and request him three times to accept the Great Peace. If refusal steadfastly follows the war chief shall let the bunch of white lake shells drop from his outstretched hand to the ground and shall bound quickly forward and club the offending chief to death"; William N. Fenton, ed., *Parker on the Iroquois* (Syracuse: Syracuse University Press, 1968), book 3, p. 54.

50. As Robert L. Hall has noted, a remarkable Native American cultural amnesia surrounds Cahokia, which is named after an entirely unrelated Native group that lived nearby in the early eighteenth century. No one knows with certainty

which later Indian people of the region are descended from the residents of the Mississippian city, and, as far as we know, no people anywhere preserve even the faintest memory that the city existed; Hall, "Prehistoric Cahokia: A City without History?" paper presented at the Organization of American Historians' annual meeting, St. Louis, 31 March 2000.

2. Confronting a Material New World

1. James H. Merrell, "The Indians' New World: The Catawba Experience," *William and Mary Quarterly*, 3d ser., 41 (1984): 537–565, quotation p. 537.

2. David J. Weber, *The Spanish Frontier in North America* (New Haven: Yale University Press, 1992), 60–75; James Axtell, *After Columbus: Essays in the Ethnohistory of Colonial North America* (New York: Oxford University Press, 1988), 144–181; Laurier Turgeon, "French Fishers, Fur Traders, and Amerindians during the Sixteenth Century: History and Archaeology," *William and Mary Quarterly*, 3d ser., 55 (1998): 585–610; Oliver A. Rink, *Holland on the Hudson: An Economic and Social History of Dutch New York* (Ithaca: Cornell University Press, 1986), 50–116; W. J. Eccles, *France in America* (New York: Harper and Row, 1972), 27–59.

3. James W. Bradley, *Evolution of the Onondaga Iroquois: Accommodating Change, 1500–1655* (Syracuse: Syracuse University Press, 1987), 69–78; Laurier Turgeon, "The Tale of the Kettle: Odyssey of an Intercultural Object," *Ethnohistory* 44 (1997): 1–29.

4. Reuben Gold Thwaites, ed., *The Jesuit Relations and Allied Documents: Travels and Explorations of the Jesuit Missionaries in New France, 1610–1791*, 73 vols. (Cleveland: Burrows Brothers, 1896–1901), 4: 207.

5. George I. Quimby, *Indian Culture and European Trade Goods: The Archaeology of the Historic Period in the Western Great Lakes Region* (Madison: University of Wisconsin Press, 1966); James Axtell, *The European and the Indian: Essays in the Ethnohistory of Colonial North America* (New York: Oxford University Press, 1981), 245–271.

6. Daniel Gookin, *Historical Collections of the Indians of New England: Of Their Several Nations, Numbers, Customs, Manners, Religion and Government, before the English Planted There* [1674] (Boston: Belknap and Hall, 1792), 11.

7. Calvin Martin, "The Four Lives of a Micmac Copper Pot," *Ethnohistory* 20 (1975): 123–126.

8. Daniel K. Richter, *The Ordeal of the Longhouse: The Peoples of the Iroquois League in the Era of European Colonization* (Chapel Hill: University of North Carolina Press, 1992), 79–85.

9. Gookin, *Historical Collections*, 12.

10. Lynn Ceci, "The Value of Wampum among the New York Iroquois: A Case Study in Artifact Analysis," *Journal of Anthropological Research* 38 (1982): 97–107; idem, "Shell Bead Evidence from Archaeological Sites in the Seneca Region of New York State," paper presented at the Annual Conference on Iroquois Research, Rensselaerville, N.Y., October 1985, p. 10; E. S. Peña, "Wampum Production in New Netherland and Colonial New York: The Historical and Archaeological Context" (Ph.D. diss., Boston University, 1990).

11. Elisabeth Tooker, *An Ethnography of the Huron Indians, 1615–1649*, Bureau of American Ethnology Bulletin 190 (Washington, D.C.: U.S. Government Printing Office, 1964), 134–150; Richter, *Ordeal of the Longhouse*, 81–83; Elise M. Brenner, "Sociopolitical Implications of Mortuary Remains in 17th-Century Native Southern New England," in *The Recovery of Meaning: Historical Archaeology in the Eastern United States*, ed. Mark P. Leone and Parker B. Potter (Washington, D.C.: Smithsonian Institution Press, 1988), 154–174; Axtell, *European and Indian*, 110–128.

12. Patrick M. Malone, *The Skulking Way of War: Technology and Tactics among the New England Indians* (Baltimore: Johns Hopkins University Press, 1991), 37–42.

13. Thwaites, *Jesuit Relations*, 6: 297–305.

14. *The Works of Samuel de Champlain*, ed. H. P. Biggar, 6 vols. (Toronto: Champlain Society, 1922–1936), 2: 96, 129.

15. Malone, *Skulking Way of War*, 42–52.

16. Quoted in J. Frederick Fausz, "Fighting 'Fire' with Firearms: The Anglo-Powhatan Arms Race in Early Virginia," *American Indian Culture and Research Journal* 3, no. 4 (1979): 43.

17. Thwaites, *Jesuit Relations*, 24: 275–279, quotations p. 277.

18. Ibid., 6: 297.

19. Charles F. Wray and Harry L. Schoff, "A Preliminary Report on the Seneca Sequence in Western New York, 1550–1687," *Pennsylvania Archaeologist* 23, no. 2 (July 1953): 53–63; Peter P. Pratt, *Archaeology of the Oneida Iroquois*, vol. 1 (George's Mills, N.H.: Man in the Northeast, 1976), 143.

20. James Axtell, *Beyond 1492: Encounters in Colonial North America* (New York: Oxford University Press, 1992), 125–151.

21. Francis Jennings, *The Invasion of America: Indians, Colonialism, and the Cant of Conquest* (Chapel Hill: University of North Carolina Press, 1975), 85–104.

22. Mary W. Herman, "The Social Aspect of Huron Property," *American Anthropologist* 58 (1956): 1044–58; Conrad E. Heidenreich, *Huronia: A History and Geography of the Huron Indians, 1600–1650* (Toronto: McClelland and Stewart, 1971), 168–171, 223–227; William Cronon, *Changes in the Land: Indians, Colonists, and the Ecology of New England* (New York: Hill and Wang, 1983), 61–62.

23. David Peterson De Vries, "Voyages from Holland to America, A.D. 1632 to 1644," *Collections of the New-York Historical Society*, 2d ser., 3 (1857): 96–97.

24. Stephen R. Potter, *Commoners, Tribute, and Chiefs: The Development of Algonquian Culture in the Potomac Valley* (Charlottesville: University Press of Virginia, 1993), 17–18; Kathleen J. Bragdon, *Native People of Southern New England, 1500–1650* (Norman: University of Oklahoma Press, 1996), 146–148.

25. Brenner, "Sociopolitical Implications of Mortuary Remains," 150–151.

26. Charles T. Gehring and William A. Starna, trans. and eds., *A Journey into Mohawk and Oneida Country, 1634–1635: The Journal of Harmen Meyndertsz van den Bogaert* (Syracuse: Syracuse University Press, 1988), 5–6.

27. Cronon, *Changes in the Land*, 99, 105–107; Bruce G. Trigger, "Ontario Native People and the Epidemics of 1634–1640," in *Indians, Animals, and the Fur Trade: A Critique of "Keepers of the Game*," ed. Shepard Krech III (Athens: University of Georgia Press, 1981), 27–28.

28. Carolyn Merchant, *Ecological Revolutions: Nature, Gender, and Science in New England* (Chapel Hill: University of North Carolina Press, 1989), 36–38, 66, quotations p. 37.

29. David Thomas Konig, *Law and Society in Puritan Massachusetts: Essex County, 1629–1682* (Chapel Hill: University of North Carolina Press, 1979), 35–63; Patricia Seed, *Ceremonies of Possession in Europe's Conquest of the New World, 1492–1640* (Cambridge: Cambridge University Press, 1995), 16–40; Cronon, *Changes in the Land*, 53 (quotation).

30. Alfred W. Crosby Jr., *The Columbian Exchange: Biological and Cultural Consequences of 1492* (Westport, Conn.: Greenwood Press, 1972), 171; Peter A. Thomas, "Contrastive Subsistence Strategies and Land Use as Factors for Understanding Indian-White Relations in New England," *Ethnohistory* 23 (1976): 1–18; Denys Delâge, *Bitter Feast: Amerindians and Europeans in Northeastern North America, 1600–64*, trans. Jane Brierley (Vancouver: University of British Columbia Press, 1993; orig. publ. in French, 1985), 47; Sissel Schroeder, "Maize Productivity in the Eastern Woodlands and Great Plains of North America," *American Antiquity* 64 (1999): 499–516 (I am grateful to Verna L. Cowin for this last reference).

31. R. Douglas Hurt, *Indian Agriculture in America: Prehistory to the Present* (Lawrence: University Press of Kansas, 1987), 7, 12–16, 40.

32. Norman Clermont, "L'importance de la pêche en Iroquoisie," *Recherches Amérindiennes au Québec* 14 (1984): 17–24; Neal Salisbury, *Manitou and Providence: Indians, Europeans, and the Making of New England, 1500–1643* (New York: Oxford University Press, 1982), 22–39; Cronon, *Changes in the Land*, 49–51.

33. William A. Starna, George R. Hamell, and William L. Butts, "Northern

Iroquoian Horticulture and Insect Infestation: A Cause for Village Removal," *Ethnohistory* 31 (1984): 197–207; Matthew Dennis, *Cultivating a Landscape of Peace: Iroquois-European Encounters in Seventeenth-Century America* (Ithaca: Cornell University Press, 1993), 13–42.

34. Cronon, *Changes in the Land*, 143, 153–155.

35. Alfred W. Crosby, *Ecological Imperialism: The Biological Expansion of Europe, 900–1900* (Cambridge: Cambridge University Press, 1986), 171–194.

36. Quoted in Cronon, *Changes in the Land*, 136–137.

37. Quoted in Merchant, *Ecological Revolutions*, 89.

38. Thomas Hariot, *A Briefe and True Report of the New Found Land of Virginia* (Frankfurt-am-Main, 1590), 24–30.

39. *The Complete Works of Captain John Smith (1580–1631)*, ed. Philip L. Barbour, vol. 1 (Chapel Hill: University of North Carolina Press, 1986), 247.

40. Quoted in Helen C. Rountree, *Pocahontas's People: The Powhatan Indians of Virginia through Four Centuries* (Norman: University of Oklahoma Press, 1990), 64.

41. Quoted in Salisbury, *Manitou and Providence*, 103.

42. Crosby, *Ecological Imperialism*, 195–216; Adrian van der Donck, "Description of the New Netherlands" (2d ed., 1656), trans. Jeremiah Johnson, *Collections of the New-York Historical Society*, 2d ser., 1 (1841): 183 (quotation).

43. Macfarlane Burnet and David O. White, *Natural History of Infectious Disease*, 4th ed. (Cambridge: Cambridge University Press, 1972), 88–104; Kim Lanphear, "Biocultural Interactions: Smallpox and the Mohawk Iroquois" (Master's thesis, State University of New York at Albany, 1983), 15–17, 23–27, 35–54.

44. William Bradford, *Of Plymouth Plantation, 1620–1647*, ed. Samuel Eliot Morison (New York: Knopf, 1952), 270–271.

45. Crosby, *Columbian Exchange*, 44; Colin G. Calloway, *New Worlds for All: Indians, Europeans, and the Remaking of Early America* (Baltimore: Johns Hopkins University Press, 1997), 33–41, 178–187.

46. Richard White, *The Middle Ground: Indians, Empires, and Republics in the Great Lakes Region, 1650–1815* (Cambridge: Cambridge University Press, 1991), 1–23; José António Brandão, *"Your Fyre Shall Burn No More:" Iroquois Policy toward New France and Its Native Allies to 1701* (Lincoln: University of Nebraska Press, 1997), 72–81.

47. Nathaniel Knowles, "The Torture of Captives by the Indians of Eastern North America," *Proceedings of the American Philosophical Society* 82 (1940): 151–225; James Axtell and William C. Sturtevant, "The Unkindest Cut, or Who Invented Scalping?" *William and Mary Quarterly*, 3d ser., 36 (1980): 451–472.

48. Hariot, *Briefe and True Report*, 28.

49. Gehring and Starna, *Journey into Mohawk and Oneida Country*, 4, 32n.

50. John Phillip Reid, *A Better Kind of Hatchet: Law, Trade, and Diplomacy in the Cherokee Nation during the Early Years of European Contact* (University Park: Pennsylvania State University Press, 1976), 11–12; Richard White, "'Although I am Dead, I am Not Entirely Dead, I Have Left a Second of Myself': Constructing Self and Persons on the Middle Ground of Early America," in *Through a Glass Darkly: Reflections on Personal Identity in Early America,* ed. Ronald Hoffman, Mechal Sobel, and Fredrika J. Teute (Chapel Hill: University of North Carolina Press, 1997), 414–417; Claudio Saunt, *A New Order of Things: Property, Power, and the Transformation of the Creek Indians, 1733–1816* (Cambridge: Cambridge University Press, 1999), 101–102.

51. Hariot, *Briefe and True Report*, 29.

52. Marian W. Smith, "American Indian Warfare," *New York Academy of Sciences Transactions*, 2d ser., 13 (1951), 348–365; Daniel K. Richter, "War and Culture: The Iroquois Experience," *William and Mary Quarterly*, 3d ser., 40 (1983), 529–537.

53. Henry R. Schoolcraft, *Notes on the Iroquois; Or, Contributions to the Statistics, Aboriginal History, Antiquities, and General Ethnology of Western New York* (New York, 1846), 29.

54. Gookin, *Historical Collections*, 22.

55. Nathan Irvin Huggins, *Black Odyssey: The Afro-American Ordeal in Slavery*, reissued ed. (New York: Vintage Books, 1990), lxxv.

3. LIVING WITH EUROPEANS

1. On the 1995 film *Pocahontas*, see Gary Edgerton and Kathy Merlock Jackson, "Redesigning Pocahontas: Disney, the 'White Man's Indian,' and the Marketing of Dreams," *Journal of Popular Film and Television* 24, no. 2 (Summer 1996): 90–98; and Jill Lepore, Review of *The Scarlet Letter* and *Pocahontas*, *American Historical Review* 101 (1996): 1166–68. On the biblical resonance of the name Rebecca see Frances Mossiker, *Pocahontas: The Life and the Legend* (New York: Knopf, 1976), 169–170. The career of the Pocahontas myth in American culture is traced in Ann Uhry Abrams, *The Pilgrims and Pocahontas: Rival Myths of American Origin* (Boulder: Westview Press, 1999).

2. *The Letters of John Chamberlain*, ed. Norman Egbert McClure, 2 vols. (Philadelphia: American Philosophical Society, 1939); William Strachey, *The Historie of Travell into Virginia Britania* (1612), ed. Louis B. Wright and Virginia Freund, Publications of the Hakluyt Society, 2d ser., vol. 103 (London, 1953); Raphe Hamor, *A True Discourse of the Present State of Virginia, and the Successe of the Affaires There till the 18 of June, 1614* (London, 1615); *The Complete Works of Captain John Smith (1580–*

1631), ed. Philip L. Barbour, 3 vols. (Chapel Hill: University of North Carolina Press, 1986).

3. Helen Rountree, *The Powhatan Indians of Virginia: Their Traditional Culture* (Norman: University of Oklahoma Press, 1989), 80.

4. Barbour, *Complete Works of Smith*, 2: 274 (quotation); Helen C. Rountree, *Pocahontas's People: The Powhatan Indians of Virginia through Four Centuries* (Norman: University of Oklahoma Press, 1990), 8–10; Frederic W. Gleach, *Powhatan's World and Colonial Virginia: A Conflict of Cultures* (Lincoln: University of Nebraska Press, 1997), 22–35. Kathleen M. Brown notes that Powhatan—perhaps in violation of traditional patterns—arranged to have numerous male offspring of his wives and what may have been 100 or more shorter-term liaisons made subordinate chiefs in various villages that were part of his domain, but many of these may have also had some claim on office through their high-status mothers; Brown, *Good Wives, Nasty Wenches, and Anxious Patriarchs* (Chapel Hill: University of North Carolina Press, 1996), 51–53. It should also be noted that many of those described in English sources as Powhatan's "sons" may in fact have been his maternal nephews.

5. Strachey, *Historie of Travell*, 62.

6. Barbour, *Complete Works of Smith*, 2: 259. For an overview of the evidence, see J. A. Leo LeMay, *Did Pocahontas Save Captain John Smith?* (Athens: University of Georgia Press, 1992).

7. Frederic W. Gleach, "Controlled Speculation: Interpreting the Saga of Pocahontas and Captain John Smith," in *Reading beyond Words: Contexts for Native History*, ed. Jennifer S. H. Brown and Elizabeth Vibert (Peterborough, Ont.: Broadview Press, 1996), 34.

8. Barbour, *Complete Works of Smith*, 1: 274.

9. Strachey, *Historie of Travell*, 72.

10. McClure, *Letters of John Chamberlain*, 1: 470–471.

11. Quoted in Edmund S. Morgan, *American Slavery, American Freedom: The Ordeal of Colonial Virginia* (New York: W. W. Norton, 1975), 74.

12. Quoted in Grace Steele Woodward, *Pocahontas* (Norman: University of Oklahoma Press, 1969), 159.

13. Alden T. Vaughan, *American Genesis: Captain John Smith and the Founding of Virginia* (Boston: Little, Brown, 1975), 99.

14. Hamor, *True Discourse*, 63.

15. Ibid., 54, 6–11.

16. Barbour, *Complete Works of Smith*, 2: 258–262.

17. McClure, *Letters of Chamberlain*, 2: 12, 50 (first quotation), 56–57 (second quotation), 66.

18. J. Frederick Fausz, "Opechancanough: Indian Resistance Leader," in *Struggle and Survival in Colonial America*, ed. David G. Sweet and Gary B. Nash (Berkeley: University of California Press, 1981), 21–37.

19. Quoted in Vaughan, *American Genesis*, 163.

20. Quoted in Fausz, "Opechancanough," 34–35.

21. Woodward, *Pocahontas*, 6–7.

22. Robert S. Tilton, *Pocahontas: The Evolution of an American Narrative* (New York: Cambridge University Press, 1994), 186.

23. Barbour, ed., *Complete Works of Smith*, vol. 2, p. 261.

24. Bernd C. Peyer, *The Tutor'd Mind: Indian Missionary-Writers in Antebellum America* (Amherst: University of Massachusetts Press, 1997), 27–30.

25. Hamor, *True Discourse*, 40.

26. Barbour, *Complete Works of Smith*, 2: 261 (quotation); Brown, *Good Wives*, 42–45, 69–72.

27. K. I. Koppedrayer, "The Making of the First Iroquois Virgin: Early Jesuit Biographies of the Blessed Kateri Tekakwitha," *Ethnohistory* 40 (1993): 280. See also Nancy Shoemaker, "Kateri Tekakwitha's Tortuous Path to Sainthood," in *Negotiators of Change: Historical Perspectives on Native American Women*, ed. Shoemaker (New York: Routledge, 1995), 55–56.

28. James Oliver Robertson, *American Myth, American Reality* (New York: Hill and Wang, 1980), 6.

29. McClure, *Letters of John Chamberlain*, 2: 12.

30. William Ingraham Kip, comp. and trans., *The Early Jesuit Missions in North America* (New York: Wiley and Putnam, 1846), 105.

31. Koppedrayer, "The Making of the First Iroquois Virgin," 277–279.

32. J. N. B. Hewitt, "Orenda and a Definition of Religion," *American Anthropologist*, n.s., 4 (1902): 33–46; Kathleen J. Bragdon, *Native People of Southern New England, 1500–1650* (Norman: University of Oklahoma Press), 184 (quotation).

33. David Blanchard, ". . . To the Other Side of the Sky: Catholicism at Kahnawake, 1667–1701," *Anthropologica* 24 (1982): 79–84; Gregory Evans Dowd, *A Spirited Resistance: The North American Indian Struggle for Unity, 1745–1815* (Baltimore: Johns Hopkins University Press, 1992), 1–9.

34. Paul J. Lindholdt, ed., *John Josselyn, Colonial Traveler: A Critical Edition of Two Voyages to New-England* (Hanover, N.H.: University Press of New England, 1988), 95.

35. William S. Simmons, *Spirit of the New England Tribes: Indian History and Folklore, 1620–1984* (Hanover, N.H.: University Press of New England, 1986), 37–64; James Axtell, *The Invasion Within: The Contest of Cultures in Colonial North Amer-*

ica (New York: Oxford University Press, 1985), 12–19; Gleach, *Powhatan's World*, 35–43.

36. Reuben Gold Thwaites, ed., *The Jesuit Relations and Allied Documents: Travels and Explorations of the Jesuit Missionaries in New France, 1610–1791* (Cleveland: Burrows Brothers, 1896–1901), 10: 119–121 (emphasis added); 52: 153.

37. James Axtell, *The European and the Indian: Essays in the Ethnohistory of Colonial North America* (New York: Oxford University Press, 1981), 68–76.

38. Johannes Megapolensis Jr., "A Short Account of the Mohawk Indians" (1644), in *In Mohawk Country: Early Narratives about a Native People*, ed. Dean R. Snow, Charles T. Gehring, and William A. Starna (Syracuse: Syracuse University Press, 1996), 45.

39. Thomas Lechford, *Plain Dealing; Or, News from New-England* (1642), *Collections of the Massachusetts Historical Society*, 3d ser., 3 (1833): 124.

40. John W. O'Malley, *The First Jesuits* (Cambridge, Mass.: Harvard University Press, 1993), 18.

41. Thwaites, *Jesuit Relations*, 56: 59; 51: 81.

42. Daniel K. Richter, *The Ordeal of the Longhouse: The Peoples of the Iroquois League in the Era of European Colonization* (Chapel Hill: University of North Carolina Press, 1992), 98–104.

43. Thwaites, *Jesuit Relations*, 43: 265; 45: 207; 51: 123, 187.

44. Richter, *Ordeal of the Longhouse*, 126–128.

45. James P. Ronda, "Generations of Faith: The Christian Indians of Martha's Vineyard," *William and Mary Quarterly*, 3d ser., 38 (1981): 392–393. For a sensitive discussion of the motives and meanings of Christianity in Native communities see John Webster Grant, *Moon of Wintertime: Missionaries and the Indians of Canada in Encounter since 1534* (Toronto: University of Toronto Press, 1984), esp. 38–70, 239–263.

46. James Axtell, *After Columbus: Essays in the Ethnohistory of Colonial North America* (New York: Oxford University Press, 1988), 120; Shoemaker, "Kateri Tekakwitha's Path," 66.

47. Blanchard, ". . . To the Other Side of the Sky," 90.

48. T[homas] C[hurch], *Entertaining Passages Relating to Philip's War* (1716), in *So Dreadfull a Judgment: Puritan Responses to King Philip's War, 1676–1677*, ed. Richard Slotkin and James K. Folsom (Middletown, Conn.: Wesleyan University Press, 1978), 397, 398–399, 401.

49. Ibid., 451–452.

50. Roy Harvey Pearce, *Savagism and Civilization: A Study of the Indian and the American Mind* (1953; reprint, Berkeley: University of California Press, 1988), 176–

178; Jill Lepore, *The Name of War: King Philip's War and the Origins of American Identity* (New York: Knopf, 1998), 191–226; Scott C. Martin, "Interpreting Metamora: Nationalism, Theater, and Jacksonian Indian Policy," *Journal of the Early Republic* 19 (1999): 73–101.

51. Quoted in Eugene R. Page, ed., *Metamora and Other Plays by John Augustus Stone, Silas S. Steele, Charles Powell Clinch, Joseph M. Field, H. J. Conway(?), John H. Wilkins, Joseph Stevens Jones, John Brogham* (Princeton: Princeton University Press, 1941), 4.

52. John Augustus Stone, *Metamora; Or, The Last of the Wampanoags* (1829), in Page, *Metamora and Other Plays*, 17, 12, 25.

53. Church captured Metacom's real-life wife, whose name was Wootonekanuske, along with their nine-year-old son a few days before his forces caught up with the Wampanoag leader in 1676. We know that they languished for several months in a Plymouth jail, but their ultimate fate is unclear (Lepore, *Name of War*, 150). The early nineteenth-century Pequot preacher and author William Apess asserted that the boy was sold into slavery; see William Apes[s], *Eulogy on King Philip, as Pronounced at the Odeon, in Federal Street, Boston* (Boston: published by the author, 1836), 45; and the Epilogue to this volume.

54. Stone, *Metamora*, 39–40.

55. Jean M. O'Brien, *Dispossession by Degrees: Indian Land and Identity in Natick, Massachusetts, 1650–1790* (Cambridge: Cambridge University Press, 1997), 3–4; see also David Murray, *Forked Tongues: Speech, Writing, and Representation in North American Indian Texts* (Bloomington: Indiana University Press, 1991), 37–38. A further link between the two images of King Philip is provided by the fact that actor Forrest owned an 1827 edition of Church's *Entertaining Passages* and appears to have modeled his stage costume on its reprint of Paul Revere's 1772 fanciful engraving of Metacom; Lepore, *Name of War*, 197–198.

56. *John Eliot's Indian Dialogues: A Study in Cultural Interaction*, ed. Henry W. Bowden and James P. Ronda (Westport, Conn.: Greenwood Press, 1981), 47–49.

57. Ibid., 121, 123–124, 145.

58. Alden T. Vaughan, *New England Frontier: Puritans and Indians, 1620–1675*, 3d ed. (Norman: University of Oklahoma Press, 1995), 235–263.

59. Henry Whitfield, *Strength Out of Weaknesse: Or a Glorious Manifestation of the Further Progresse of the Gospel among the Indians of New-England* (1652), *Collections of the Massachusetts Historical Society*, 3d ser., 4 (1834): 165.

60. Daniel Gookin, *Historical Collections of the Indians of New England: Of Their Several Nations, Numbers, Customs, Manners, Religion and Government, before the English Planted There* (1674) (Boston: Belknap and Hall, 1792), 40–67 (quotation p. 42); Alden T. Vaughan and Daniel K. Richter, "Crossing the Cultural Divide: Indians

and New Englanders, 1605–1763," *Proceedings of the American Antiquarian Society* 90 (1980): 33–35; Francis Jennings, *The Invasion of America: Indians, Colonialism, and the Cant of Conquest* (Chapel Hill: University of North Carolina Press, 1975), 250–251; Axtell, *Invasion Within*, 240; Harold W. Van Lonkhuyzen, "A Reappraisal of the Praying Indians: Acculturation, Conversion, and Identity in Natick, Massachusetts, 1646–1730," *New England Quarterly* 63 (1990): 396.

61. "A Relacion of the Indyan Warre, by Mr. [John] Easton, of Roade Isld., 1675," in *Narratives of the Indian Wars, 1675–1699*, ed. Charles H. Lincoln (New York: C. Scribner's Sons, 1913), 7.

62. Neal Salisbury, "Introduction: Mary Rowlandson and Her Removes," in Mary Rowlandson, *The Sovereignty and Goodness of God, Together with the Faithfulness of His Promises Displayed*, ed. Salisbury (Boston: Bedford Books, 1997), 2 (quotation); James D. Drake, *King Philip's War: Civil War in New England, 1675–1676* (Amherst: University of Massachusetts Press, 1999), 35–56.

63. Virginia DeJohn Anderson, "King Philip's Herds: Indians, Colonists, and the Problem of Livestock in Early New England," *William and Mary Quarterly*, 3d ser., 51 (1994): 602.

64. Ibid., 601.

65. Gookin, *Historical Collections*, 7–9; Neal Salisbury, *Manitou and Providence: Indians, Europeans, and the Making of New England, 1500–1643* (New York: Oxford University Press, 1982), 101–109.

66. William Bradford, *Of Plymouth Plantation, 1620–1647*, ed. Samuel Eliot Morison (New York: Knopf, 1952), 80–81.

67. Salisbury, *Manitou and Providence*, 115–116.

68. Neal Salisbury, "Indians and Colonists in Southern New England after the Pequot War: An Uneasy Balance," in *The Pequots in Southern New England: The Fall and Rise of an American Indian Nation*, ed. Laurence M. Hauptman and James D. Wherry (Norman: University of Oklahoma Press, 1990), 83–84; Jack Campisi, *The Mashpee Indians: Tribe on Trial* (Syracuse: Syracuse University Press, 1991), 67–74.

69. Betty Groff Schroeder, "The True Lineage of King Philip (Sachem Metacom)," *New England Historical and Genealogical Register* 144 (1990): 211–214; Russell Bourne, *The Red King's Rebellion: Racial Politics in New England, 1675–1678* (New York: Oxford University Press, 1991), 26–27 (quotations). The evidence on southern New England Algonquian kinship is contradictory, and both patrilineal and matrilineal principles apparently applied in an "ambilineal" system, but offices seem most often to have descended from father to son. See Bragdon, *Native People of Southern New England*, 156–168.

70. Lindholdt, *John Josselyn*, 103, 101. On the function of conspicuous display for "entrepreneurial" leaders, see Elise M. Brenner, "Sociopolitical Implications

of Mortuary Remains in 17th-Century Native Southern New England," in *The Recovery of Meaning: Historical Archaeology in the Eastern United States,* ed. Mark P. Leone and Parker B. Potter (Washington, D.C.: Smithsonian Institution Press, 1988), 147–181.

71. David Pulsifer, ed., *Records of the Colony of New Plymouth in New England,* 12 vols. in 10 (Boston: Press of W. White, 1855–1861), 3: 192.

72. Lepore, *Name of War,* xvi.

73. Jennings, *Invasion of America,* 290n.

74. Lynn Ceci, "The First Fiscal Crisis in New York," *Economic Development and Cultural Change* 28 (1980): 839–847; John J. McCusker, *Money and Exchange in Europe and America, 1600–1775* (Chapel Hill: University of North Carolina Press, 1978), 157n.; William Cronon, *Changes in the Land: Indians, Colonists, and the Ecology of New England* (New York: Hill and Wang, 1983), 102–103.

75. Vaughan, *New England Frontier,* 161–173.

76. Bourne, *Red King's Rebellion,* 89.

77. Ibid., 86–95.

78. Douglas Edward Leach, *Flintlock and Tomahawk: New England in King Philip's War* (New York: Macmillan, 1958), 28–29.

79. Lepore, *Name of War,* 21–26, quotation p. 21.

80. James Drake, "Symbol of a Failed Strategy: The Sassamon Trial, Political Culture, and the Outbreak of King Philip's War," *American Indian Culture and Research Journal* 19, no. 2 (1995): 111–141.

81. Easton, "Relacion of the Indyan Warre," 10–11; Axtell, *Invasion Within,* 147–148.

82. Though limited in its understanding of Algonquian culture, the most detailed and well-balanced account of the military events of Metacom's War remains Leach, *Flintlock and Tomahawk,* which should be read in conjunction with Drake, *King Philip's War,* esp. pp. 109–167.

83. Easton, "Relacion of the Indyan Warre," 10.

84. Rountree, *Pocahontas's People,* 86–127.

85. Quoted in T. H. Breen, "A Changing Labor Force and Race Relations in Virginia, 1660–1710," *Journal of Social History* 7 (1973–1974): 4.

86. "A True Narrative of the Late Rebellion in Virginia, by the Royal Commissioners, 1677," in *Narratives of the Insurrections, 1675–1690,* ed. Charles M. Andrews (New York: C. Scribner's Sons, 1915), 111.

87. Wilcomb E. Washburn, *The Governor and the Rebel: A History of Bacon's Rebellion in Virginia* (Chapel Hill: University of North Carolina Press, 1957).

88. Quoted in ibid., 135.

89. Rountree, *Pocahontas's People,* 97–105; Francis Jennings, "Glory, Death, and

Transfiguration: The Susquehannock Indians in the Seventeenth Century," *Proceedings of the American Philosophical Society* 112 (1968): 15–53.

90. Alexander Spotswood to Peter Schuyler, 25 January 1720, Pennsylvania Provincial Council Records, vol. F, pp. 13–21, Pennsylvania State Archives, Harrisburg.

4. NATIVE VOICES IN A COLONIAL WORLD

1. For a collection of some of the surviving documents written by New England Indians, see Ives Goddard and Kathleen J. Bragdon, *Native Writings in Massachusett*, 2 vols. (Philadelphia: American Philosophical Society, 1988). The literature on the ways in which Europeans and Euro-Americans have used imagined images of Indians to make both positive and negative statements about their own societies is vast. See in particular Robert F. Berkhofer Jr., *The White Man's Indian: Images of the American Indian from Columbus to the Present* (New York: Knopf, 1978); Olive Patricia Dickason, *The Myth of the Savage and the Beginnings of French Colonialism in the Americas* (Edmonton: University of Alberta Press, 1984); and Philip J. Deloria, *Playing Indian* (New Haven: Yale University Press, 1998).

2. John Eliot and Thomas Mayhew, *Tears of Repentance: Or, A Further Narrative of the Progress of the Gospel Amongst the Indians in New-England* (1653), *Collections of the Massachusetts Historical Society*, 3d ser., 4 (1834): 244.

3. Ibid., 197–260. The five men who testified at the October 1652 assembly were Totherswamp, Waban, Nataôus (William of Sudbury), Monequassun, and Ponampam. In addition to the narratives they delivered on that occasion, *Tears of Repentance* includes other confessions of faith previously recorded for Totherswamp, William of Sudbury, and Monequassun; two earlier statements by Ponampam; and narratives of ten others who were not able to speak in October: Peter, John Speen (two narratives), Robin Speen (three), Nishohkou (two), Magus, Poquanum (two), Nookau (two), Antony, Owussumag, and Ephraim.

4. Ibid., 237–240, paragraphing added. An undated earlier narrative by Monequassun appears on pp. 234–237.

5. (Cambridge, Mass., 1663).

6. Charles L. Cohen, "Conversion among Puritans and Amerindians: A Theological and Cultural Perspective," in *Puritanism: Transatlantic Perspectives on a Seventeenth-Century Anglo-American Faith*, ed. Francis J. Bremer (Boston: Massachusetts Historical Society, 1993), 235–236. For a more critical view of Eliot's motives and writings, see Francis Jennings, *The Invasion of America: Indians, Colonialism, and the Cant of Conquest* (Chapel Hill: University of North Carolina Press, 1975), 228–253.

7. Jill Lepore, *The Name of War: King Philip's War and the Origins of American Identity* (New York: Knopf, 1998), 28–33; Alden T. Vaughan, *New England Frontier: Puritans and Indians, 1620–1675*, 3d ed. (Norman: University of Oklahoma Press, 1995), 245.

8. Eliot and Mayhew, *Tears of Repentance*, 243, 245.

9. David Murray, *Forked Tongues: Speech, Writing, and Representation in North American Indian Texts* (Bloomington: Indiana University Press, 1991), 5–33.

10. Eliot and Mayhew, *Tears of Repentance*, 232. On Waban, see Anon., *The Day-Breaking, If Not the Sun-Rising of the Gospell with the Indians in New-England* (1647), *Collections of the Massachusetts Historical Society*, 3d ser., 4 (1834): 1–8; Thomas Shepard, *The Clear Sun-Shine of the Gospel Breaking Forth upon the Indians in New England* (1648), ibid., 62–63; Jennings, *Invasion of America*, 239–241; Harold W. Van Lonkhuyzen, "A Reappraisal of the Praying Indians: Acculturation, Conversion, and Identity in Natick, Massachusetts, 1646–1730," *New England Quarterly* 63 (1990): 399–402; and Bernd C. Peyer, *The Tutor'd Mind: Indian Missionary-Writers in Antebellum America* (Amherst: University of Massachusetts Press, 1997), 35–44.

11. Cohen, "Conversion among Puritans and Amerindians," 237; J. William T. Youngs, "The Indian Saints of Early New England," *Early American Literature* 16 (1981–1982): 241; Patricia Caldwell, *The Puritan Conversion Narrative: The Beginnings of American Expression* (Cambridge: Cambridge University Press, 1983), 1–2; Robert James Naeher, "Dialogue in the Wilderness: John Eliot and the Indian Exploration of Puritanism as a Source of Meaning, Comfort, and Ethnic Survival," *New England Quarterly* 62 (1989): 355 (quotation).

12. Edmund S. Morgan, *Visible Saints: The History of a Puritan Idea* (1963; reprint, Ithaca: Cornell University Press, 1965), 66–69.

13. Thomas Goodwin, quoted in Francis J. Bremer, *The Puritan Experiment: New England Society from Bradford to Edwards* (New York: St Martin's Press, 1976), 22.

14. Henry Whitfield, *Strength Out of Weaknesse: Or a Glorious Manifestation of the Further Progresse of the Gospel among the Indians of New-England* (1652), *Collections of the Massachusetts Historical Society*, 3d ser., 4 (1834): 172.

15. Morgan, *Visible Saints*, 90–91; Charles Lloyd Cohen, *God's Caress: The Psychology of Puritan Religious Experience* (New York: Oxford University Press, 1986), 201–202.

16. Caldwell, *Puritan Conversion Narrative*, 163–198.

17. For a somewhat different reading of these issues than that presented here, see Cohen, "Conversion among Puritans and Amerindians," 233–256.

18. Eliot and Mayhew, *Tears of Repentance*, 255–256. The others who associated their attention to the Word with either their own or their relatives' illnesses were

Totherswamp (p. 230), Waban (p. 231), John Speen (p. 247), Robin Speen (p. 248), and Nookau (p. 254).

19. Ibid., 259.

20. Morgan, *Visible Saints*, 68–69.

21. Language referring to the gift of faith can be found in the narratives of Monequassun (see "at last God showed me mercy, and showed me what I should do," above, and his earlier confession in Eliot and Mayhew, *Tears of Repentance*, 236–237), William of Sudbury (ibid., 233–234), Ponampam (pp. 240–241), Robin Speen (p. 249), and Nishohkou (p. 251). The combat between faith and despair is vividly described by all these narrators as well as by Totherswamp (p. 230), Waban (p. 232), and Magus (p. 253).

22. Cohen, *God's Caress*, 203.

23. Only Totherswamp spoke unambiguously of assurance ("This is the love of God to me, that he giveth me all mercy in this world," Eliot and Mayhew, *Tears of Repentance*, 231); Monequassun was more ambiguous in linking statements such as "Christ hath provided the new covenant to save believers" with expressions of his "desire to believe." Statements that seem to reflect "evangelical sorrow"—none of them unambiguous—are found only in the narratives of Totherswamp ("he giveth me all mercy in this world, and for them I am thankful; but I confess I deserve Hell," p. 231), William of Sudbury ("But still [I] do foolishly and not according to my prayer," p. 234), and Monequassun ("I thank God for all his mercies every day: and now I confess before God that I loath myself for my sins").

24. "The relation of Mr[. John] Collins" [c. 1650], in *The Diary of Michael Wigglesworth, 1653–1657: The Conscience of a Puritan*, ed. Edmund S. Morgan (1946; reprint, New York: Harper and Row, 1965), 113 (quotation); Cohen, *God's Caress*, 213–214n.

25. Eliot and Mayhew, *Tears of Repentance*, 246–247.

26. Puritans, as Calvinist Protestants, counted the Ten Commandments differently from Jews, Roman Catholics, and Lutherans, reckoning four as involving sins against God ("Thou shalt have no other gods before me"; "Thou shalt not make unto thee any graven image"; "Thou shalt not take the name of the Lord thy God in vain"; "Remember the Sabbath Day, to keep it holy") and six as involving sins against people ("Honor thy father and thy mother"; "Thou shalt not kill"; "Thou shalt not commit adultery"; "Thou shalt not steal"; "Thou shalt not bear false witness"; "Thou shalt not covet"), which, of course, also were sins against the heavenly Father. The discussion following in the text relies on the correlation of specific sins with particular commandments outlined in *The Whole Duty of Man, Containing a Practical Table of the Ten Commandments: Wherein the Sins Forbid-*

den, and the Duties Commanded, or Implied Are Clearly Discovered by Famous Mr. William Perkins (London, 1674)—an extraordinary seventeenth-century model of brevity that manages to sum everything up in two columns of a single broadside page.

27. Ponampam and Ephraim confessed their general sinfulness but made no reference to specific commandments they had broken; Eliot and Mayhew, *Tears of Repentance*, 240–242, 258–259.

28. Nishohkou (ibid., 250), Poquanum (p. 254), Nookau (p. 255), and Owussumag (p. 258) charged themselves with adultery. These three, as well as Totherswamp (p. 229), William of Sudbury (p. 232), Monequassun ("I thought I had done all manner of sins in the sight of God, because he seeth lust in the heart"), Ponampam (p. 242), Peter (p. 246), John Speen (p. 247), Robin Speen (p. 248), Magus (p. 253), and Antony (p. 256), accused themselves of lust or lusts. None of the narrators provided any details. On the Puritans' expansive definition of lust, see Cohen, *God's Caress*, 220. On the significance of the control of sensuality in Puritan definitions of civility, see Michael Zuckerman, "Pilgrims in the Wilderness: Community, Modernity, and the Maypole at Merry Mount," *New England Quarterly* 50 (1977): 255–277.

29. Theft was mentioned with no elaboration by Monequassun ("lusts, thefts, and many other sins"), Nishohkou (Eliot and Mayhew, *Tears of Repentance*, 250), Magus (p. 253), and Poquanum (p. 254). Similarly vague references to gambling were made by Totherswamp (p. 229) and Robin Speen (p. 248). Lying was confessed by William of Sudbury (p. 233), Ponampam (p. 242), Poquanum (p. 254), and Nookau (p. 255); covetousness by Waban (p. 231) and Poquanum (p. 254); killing by Ponampam (p. 242); and hatred or anger toward others by Waban (p. 231), William of Sudbury (p. 9), Peter (p. 246), and Poquanum (p. 254).

30. Ibid., 282. Ponampam (p. 242), Robin Speen (p. 248), Nishohkou (p. 250), and Poquanum (p. 254) also refer to the First Commandment.

31. Ibid., 247, 252. Nishohkou confessed that he "heard of that good way, the keep the Sabbath . . . but yet again I sinned in it, because I did not reverence the Word of God (pp. 250–251). In addition, Peter said, "Now I believe that it is God's command that we should labor six days and keep the Sabbath on the seventh day" (p. 246), but he did not specifically charge himself with violating the Fourth Commandment.

32. Morgan, *Diary of Wigglesworth*, 104. All those who referred to violations of either the First or Fourth Commandments (William of Sudbury, John Speen, Robin Speen, Nishohkou, Magus, and Poquanum) were joined by Monequassun in his preliminary narrative (Eliot and Mayhew, *Tears of Repentance*, 236) and Nookau (p. 255) in accusing themselves of the sin of pride.

33. Cohen, *God's Caress*, 218–220.

34. Caldwell, *Puritan Conversion Narrative*, 28.

35. Eliot and Mayhew, *Tears of Repentance*, 243.

36. Anon., *Day-Breaking, If Not the Sun-Rising*, 4.

37. Eliot and Mayhew, *Tears of Repentance*, 227.

38. Cotton Mather, *The Triumphs of the Reformed Religion in America: The Life of the Renowned John Eliot* . . . (Boston, 1691), 83 (quotation); James Axtell, *The Invasion Within: The Contest of Cultures in Colonial North America* (New York: Oxford University Press, 1985), 232.

39. Eliot and Mayhew, *Tears of Repentance*, 258, 232, 250, 254, 248; emphases added.

40. Ibid., 252–253, 229.

41. Quoted in Neal Salisbury, "Red Puritans: The 'Praying Indians' of Massachusetts Bay and John Eliot," *William and Mary Quarterly*, 3d ser., 31 (1974): 50. The closest any of the narrators came to laying the blame on his parents was Ponampam, who said (with the same emphasis on the personal pronoun found in other confessions) that "when I heard the Catechism, 'that God made me,' I did not believe it, because I knew I sprang from my father and mother, and therefore I despised the Word"; Eliot and Mayhew, *Tears of Repentance*, 242; see also p. 241.

42. I am grateful to Rachel Wheeler for helping me to think through these issues.

43. Eliot and Mayhew, *Tears of Repentance*, 258, 246, 252, 256, 258.

44. Ibid., 235, 246. On Cohannet and the founding of Natick, see Jean M. O'Brien, *Dispossession by Degrees: Indian Land and Identity in Natick, Massachusetts, 1650–1790* (Cambridge: Cambridge University Press, 1997), 31–64.

45. Jennings, *Invasion of America*, 241–243; Elise Brenner, "To Pray or to Be Prey: That Is the Question: Strategies for Cultural Autonomy of Massachusetts Praying Town Indians," *Ethnohistory* 27 (1980): 135–152.

46. Henry Whitfield, *The Light Appearing More and More towards the Perfect Day; Or, a Farther Discovery of the Present State of the Indians in New-England* (1651), *Collections of the Massachusetts Historical Society*, 3d ser., 4 (1834): 139–140; Van Lonkhuyzen, "A Reappraisal of the Praying Indians," 402–405.

47. On the significance of migration in New English narratives (most saints found in the move confirmation that human effort did not lead to spiritual rebirth), see Caldwell, *Puritan Conversion Narrative*, 119–134.

48. Eliot and Mayhew, *Tears of Repentance*, 233.

49. Shepard, *Clear Sun-Shine of the Gospel*, 42.

50. James P. Ronda, "Generations of Faith: The Christian Indians of Martha's Vineyard," *William and Mary Quarterly*, 3d ser., 48 (1991): 394; Peyer, *Tutor'd Mind*,

39–40; Neal Salisbury, "'I Loved the Place of My Dwelling': Puritan Missionaries and Native Americans in Seventeenth-Century Southern New England," in *Inequality in Early America*, ed. Carla Gardina Pestana and Sharon V. Salinger (Hanover, N.H.: University Press of New England, 1999), 111–133.

51. Allen W. Trelease, *Indian Affairs in Colonial New York: The Seventeenth Century* (Ithaca: Cornell University Press, 1960), 239–241.

52. Lawrence H. Leder, ed., *The Livingston Indian Records, 1666–1723* (Gettysburg: Pennsylvania Historical Association, 1956), 48–51; reprinted with permission.

53. Nancy L. Hagedorn, "'A Friend to Go between Them': Interpreters among the Iroquois, 1664–1775" (Ph.D. diss., College of William and Mary, 1995), 18–19, 238; Trelease, *Indian Affairs in Colonial New York*, 204–214; Lawrence H. Leder, "Robert Livingston (1664–1728), Secretary for Indian Affairs, and His Papers," in Leder, *Livingston Indian Records*, 9–10 (quotation).

54. Jennings, *Invasion of America*, 131–132.

55. *Oxford English Dictionary*, 2d ed. (Oxford: Oxford University Press, 1989), s.v. "treaty," def. 2; Gregory E. Dowd, "Domestic Dependency: The Colonial Idea of National Dependency in Pontiac's War," paper delivered at the Omohundro Institute of Early American History and Culture Sixth Annual Conference, Toronto, 10 June 2000.

56. William N. Fenton, "Structure, Continuity, and Change in the Process of Iroquois Treaty Making," in *The History and Culture of Iroquois Diplomacy: An Interdisciplinary Guide to the Treaties of the Six Nations and Their League*, ed. Francis Jennings, William N. Fenton, and Mary A. Druke (Syracuse: Syracuse University Press, 1985), 27–30; Richard White, "'Although I Am Dead, I Am Not Entirely Dead, I Have Left a Second of Myself': Constructing Self and Persons on the Middle Ground of Early America," in *Through a Glass Darkly: Reflections on Personal Identity in Early America*, ed. Ronald Hoffman, Mechal Sobel, and Fredrika J. Teute (Chapel Hill: University of North Carolina Press, 1997), 410–413.

57. Reuben Gold Thwaites, ed., *The Jesuit Relations and Allied Documents: Travels and Explorations of the Jesuit Missionaries in New France, 1610–1791*, 73 vols. (Cleveland: Burrows Brothers, 1896–1901), 22: 291–293.

58. Michael K. Foster, "Another Look at the Function of Wampum in Iroquois-White Councils," in Jennings, Fenton, and Druke, *History and Culture of Iroquois Diplomacy*, 99–114; Daniel K. Richter, *The Ordeal of the Longhouse: The Peoples of the Iroquois League in the Era of European Colonization* (Chapel Hill: University of North Carolina Press, 1992), 41–49.

59. Fenton, "Structure, Continuity, and Change," 29–30.

60. Daniel K. Richter, "Onas, the Long Knife: Pennsylvanians and Indians,

1783–1794," in *Native Americans and the Early Republic*, ed. Frederick Hoxie, Ronald Hoffman, and Peter Albert (Charlottesville: University Press of Virginia, 1999), 128–130.

61. Determining historical values for commodities is an inexact science, but one florin in New York wampum value was worth approximately six pence in Massachusetts currency in the 1670s. The Massachusetts pence was in turn worth 4.8 pence sterling. Thus 150 florins in wampum would equal 720d sterling, or £3 (calculated from exchange rates discussed in John J. McCusker, *Money and Exchange in Europe and America, 1600–1775: A Handbook* [Chapel Hill: University of North Carolina Press, 1978], 157n.). Kendall gave the same gifts (sometimes supplemented by an additional ten loaves of bread) to each of the five Iroquois nations as their spokesmen separately arrived in Albany during September and October; Leder, *Livingston Indian Records*, 54.

62. Mary A. Druke, "Linking Arms: The Structure of Iroquois Intertribal Diplomacy," in *Beyond the Covenant Chain: The Iroquois and Their Neighbors in Indian North America, 1600–1800*, ed. Daniel K. Richter and James H. Merrell (Syracuse: Syracuse University Press, 1987), 33.

63. Trelease, *Indian Affairs in Colonial New York*, 228–239; E. B. O'Callaghan and B. Fernow, eds., *Documents Relative to the Colonial History of the State of New York*, 15 vols. (Albany, N.Y.: Weed, Parsons, 1853–1887), 15: 513–514 (quotation).

64. O'Callaghan and Fernow, *Documents Relative to Colonial New York*, 15: 520–521.

65. Ibid., 521–522.

66. Ibid., 528–529.

67. Leder, *Livingston Indian Records*, 47.

68. Richter, *Ordeal of the Longhouse*, 134–135.

69. Trelease, *Indian Affairs in Colonial New York*, 60–84, 138–168.

70. Charles T. Gehring, ed. and trans., *Fort Orange Court Minutes, 1652–1660* (Syracuse: Syracuse University Press, 1990), 453.

71. Arthur C. Parker, *The Constitution of the Five Nations: Or, The Iroquois Book of the Great Law*, New York State Museum Bulletin 184 (Albany: University of the State of New York, 1916); Thwaites, *Jesuit Relations*, 63: 185–187; William N. Fenton, *The Great Law and the Longhouse: A Political History of the Iroquois Confederacy* (Norman: University of Oklahoma Press, 1998), 199.

72. O'Callaghan and Fernow, *Documents Relative to Colonial New York*, 3: 271.

73. Anthony McFarlane, *The British in the Americas, 1480–1815* (London: Longman, 1994), 188–198; Stephen Saunders Webb, *1676: The End of American Independence* (Cambridge, Mass.: Harvard University Press, 1984), 169–244, 303–404.

74. Francis Jennings, *The Ambiguous Iroquois Empire: The Covenant Chain Confed-*

eration of Indian Tribes with English Colonies from Its Beginnings to the Lancaster Treaty of 1744 (New York: W. W. Norton, 1984), 141–185.

75. Daniel K. Richter, "Iroquois versus Iroquois: Jesuit Missions and Christianity in Village Politics, 1642–1686," Ethnohistory 22 (1985): 1–16.

76. Richter, Ordeal of the Longhouse, 141–161.

77. [Cadwallader Colden,] The History of the Five Indian Nations Depending on the Province of New-York In America (New York, 1727), xv; Treaty minutes, 12 July 1697, New York Colonial Manuscripts, vol. XLI, fol. 93, New York State Archives, Albany.

78. O'Callaghan and Fernow, Documents Relative to Colonial New York, 3: 557–558 (quotation); Jennings, Ambiguous Iroquois Empire, 191–194.

79. Leder, Livingston Indian Records, 45–46.

80. On accommodation see Gregory Evans Dowd, A Spirited Resistance: The North American Indian Struggle for Unity, 1745–1815 (Baltimore: Johns Hopkins University Press, 1992), xxi, 20–21.

5. Native Peoples in an Imperial World

1. Portions of this chapter appeared in different form in "Native Peoples of North America and the Eighteenth-Century British Empire," in The Oxford History of the British Empire, ed. W. Roger Louis, vol. 2: The Eighteenth Century, ed. P. J. Marshall (Oxford: Oxford University Press, 1998), 347–364.

2. W. J. Eccles, France in America (New York: Harper and Row, 1972), 118–147.

3. Jack P. Greene, "An Uneasy Connection: An Analysis of the Preconditions of the American Revolution," in Essays on the American Revolution, ed. Stephen G. Kurtz and James H. Hutson (Chapel Hill: University of North Carolina Press, 1973), 32–80; John M. Murrin, "Political Development," in Colonial British America: Essays in the New History of the Early Modern Era, ed. Jack P. Greene and J. R. Pole (Baltimore: Johns Hopkins University Press, 1984), 408–456.

4. T. H. Breen, "An Empire of Goods: The Anglicization of Colonial America, 1690–1776," Journal of British Studies 25 (1986): 467–199; John J. McCusker and Russell R. Menard, The Economy of British America, 1607–1789 (Chapel Hill: University of North Carolina Press, 1985), 277–294; Jack P. Greene, Pursuits of Happiness: The Social Development of Early Modern British Colonies and the Formation of American Culture (Chapel Hill: University of North Carolina Press, 1988), 170–206; Carole Shammas, The Pre-Industrial Consumer in England and America (Oxford: Oxford University Press, 1990); Cary Carson, Ronald Hoffman, and Peter J. Albert, eds., Of Consuming Interests: The Style of Life in the Eighteenth Century (Charlottesville: University Press of Virginia, 1994).

5. David Hackett Fischer, *Albion's Seed: Four British Folkways in America* (New York: Oxford University Press, 1989), 605–632; A. G. Roeber, "'The Origin of Whatever Is Not English among Us': The Dutch-Speaking and the German-Speaking Peoples of Colonial British America," in *Strangers within the Realm: Cultural Margins of the First British Empire,* ed. Bernard Bailyn and Philip D. Morgan (Chapel Hill: University of North Carolina Press, 1991), 220–283; Maldwyn A. Jones, "The Scotch-Irish in British America," ibid., 284–313.

6. Patricia U. Bonomi, *Under the Cope of Heaven: Religion, Society, and Politics in Colonial America* (New York: Oxford University Press, 1986), 131–216. The transatlantic dimensions of what was once seen as the quintessentially American phenomenon have recently become increasingly clear. See Susan Dureden, "A Transatlantic Community of Saints: The Great Awakening and the First Evangelical Network, 1735–1755," *American Historical Review* 91 (1986): 811–832; and Frank Lambert, *Inventing the "Great Awakening"* (Princeton: Princeton University Press, 1999).

7. In 1660 African Americans accounted for a mere 3.6 percent of the population of the English Chesapeake colonies, and by 1700 for only 13.1 percent. By 1740 that percentage had risen to 28.3, and in the newer colonies of South Carolina and Georgia to 46.5; McCusker and Menard, *Economy of British America,* 222. Virginia's landmark Black Code dates only to 1705; Betty Wood, *The Origins of American Slavery: Freedom and Bondage in the English Colonies* (New York: Hill and Wang, 1997), 92.

8. By far the best account of the British victory and its consequences is Fred Anderson, *Crucible of War: The Seven Years' War and the Fate of Empire in British North America, 1754–1766* (New York: Knopf, 2000).

9. Rhys Isaac, *The Transformation of Virginia, 1740–1790* (Chapel Hill: University of North Carolina Press, 1982), 36–37. Even serious popular treatments of the colonial period tend to give the early eighteenth century short shrift. From opposite ends of the political spectrum, Ronald Takaki's *A Different Mirror: A History of Multicultural America* (Boston: Little, Brown, 1993) has almost nothing to say about the century between Bacon's Rebellion and the Declaration of Independence, while Paul Johnson's *A History of the American People* (New York: HarperCollins, 1997) hastily dismisses the era merely as when "the final pieces of the jigsaw of early America are beginning to fit in place" (85).

10. James Axtell, *After Columbus: Essays in the Ethnohistory of Colonial North America* (New York: Oxford University Press, 1988), 43.

11. Howard H. Peckham, *The Colonial Wars, 1689–1762* (Chicago: University of Chicago Press, 1964); W. A. Speck, "The International and Imperial Context," in Greene and Pole, *Colonial British America,* 399–401; Bruce P. Lenman, "Colonial

Wars and Imperial Instability, 1688–1793," in Louis, *Oxford History of British Empire*, 2: 151–163.

12. Treaty minutes, 17–18 June 1689, Notebook, Indians of North America, Miscellaneous Papers, American Antiquarian Society, Worcester, Mass. (quotation); Daniel K. Richter, "Cultural Brokers and Intercultural Politics: New York-Iroquois Relations, 1664–1701," *Journal of American History* 75 (1988): 48–55. On the American implications of the Glorious Revolution see Richard S. Dunn, "The Glorious Revolution and America," in Louis, *Oxford History of British Empire*, vol. 1: *The Origins of Empire*, ed. Nicholas Canny (Oxford: Oxford University Press, 1998), 445–466.

13. Allen W. Trelease, *Indian Affairs in Colonial New York: The Seventeenth Century* (Ithaca: Cornell University Press, 1960), 254–363; Daniel K. Richter, *The Ordeal of the Longhouse: The Peoples of the Iroquois League in the Era of European Colonization* (Chapel Hill: University of North Carolina Press, 1992), 162–213.

14. Bacqueville de La Potherie, *Histoire de l'Amérique Septentrionale*, vol. 4 (Paris, 1722), 190–266; E. B. O'Callaghan and B. Fernow, eds., *Documents Relative to the Colonial History of the State of New York*, 15 vols. (Albany, N.Y.: Weed, Parsons, 1853–1887), 4: 904–910, quotation p. 905; Anthony F. C. Wallace, "Origins of Iroquois Neutrality: The Grand Settlement of 1701," *Pennsylvania History* 24 (1957): 223–235.

15. John Stoddard et al., Journal of Negotiations at Albany, 26 August–28 September 1724, Massachusetts Archives Series, vol. 29, fol. 181, Massachusetts State Archives, Boston (quotation); Richter, *Ordeal of the Longhouse*, 214–235.

16. James Axtell, *The Invasion Within: The Contest of Cultures in Colonial North America* (New York: Oxford University Press, 1985), 61–64.

17. The community that Native people now call Kanesatake is usually referred to in French source documents by one of three geographic locations—all within a few miles of Montreal—that it occupied in the late seventeenth and early eighteenth centuries: La Montagne (1676), Rivière des Prairies (1696), and Lac des Deux Montagnes (1721). See William N. Fenton and Elisabeth Tooker, "Mohawk," in *Handbook of North American Indians*, ed. William C. Sturtevant, vol. 15: *Northeast*, ed. Bruce G. Trigger (Washington, D.C.: Smithsonian Institution, 1978), 472–473.

18. Richter, *Ordeal of the Longhouse*, 167–169, 196–197; O'Callaghan and Fernow, *Documents Relative to Colonial New York*, 9: 685–687, quotation p. 687.

19. Evan Haefeli and Kevin Sweeney, "Revisiting *The Redeemed Captive*: New Perspectives on the 1704 Attack on Deerfield," *William and Mary Quarterly*, 3d. ser., 52 (1995): 3–46.

20. Gordon M. Day, *The Identity of the St. Francis Indians*, Canadian Ethnology Service Paper no. 71 (Ottawa: National Museums of Canada, 1981).

21. Peter H. Wood, "The Changing Population of the Colonial South: An Overview by Race and Region, 1685–1790," in *Powhatan's Mantle: Indians in the Colonial Southeast*, ed. Peter H. Wood, Gregory A. Waselkov, and M. Thomas Hatley (Lincoln: University of Nebraska Press, 1989), 52–53; David J. Weber, *The Spanish Frontier in North America* (New Haven: Yale University Press, 1992), 100–145.

22. Amy Turner Bushnell, "Ruling 'the Republic of Indians' in Seventeenth-Century Florida," in Wood, Waselkov, and Hatley, *Powhatan's Mantle*, 134–150; James Axtell, *The Indians' New South: Cultural Change in the Colonial Southeast* (Baton Rouge: Louisiana State University Press, 1997), 25–44.

23. Quoted in Weber, *Spanish Frontier in North America*, 144.

24. Peter H. Wood, *Black Majority: Negroes in Colonial South Carolina from 1670 through the Stono Rebellion* (New York: Knopf, 1974), 13–40.

25. Theda Perdue, *Slavery and the Evolution of Cherokee Society, 1540–1866* (Knoxville: University of Tennessee Press, 1979), 3–35.

26. Gary B. Nash, *Red, White, and Black: The Peoples of Early North America*, 3d ed. (Englewood Cliffs, N.J.: Prentice Hall, 1992), 131 (quotation); Weber, *Spanish Frontier in North America*, 141–145.

27. Nash, *Red, White, and Black*, 128–143.

28. Charles Hudson, *The Southeastern Indians* (Knoxville: University of Tennessee Press, 1976), 434–440.

29. Verner W. Crane, *The Southern Frontier, 1670–1732* (1928; reprint, New York: W. W. Norton, 1981), 108–186, quotation p. 182; Tom Hatley, *The Dividing Paths: Cherokees and South Carolinians through the Era of Revolution* (New York: Oxford University Press, 1993), 23–28.

30. Peter Wraxall, *An Abridgment of the Indian Affairs Contained in Four Folio Volumes, Transacted in the Colony of New York, from the Year 1678 to the Year 1751*, ed. Charles Howard McIlwain (Cambridge, Mass.: Harvard University Press, 1915), 219n.

31. Eccles, *France in America*, 146–147; Winstanley Briggs, "Le Pays des Illinois," *William and Mary Quarterly*, 3d. ser., 47 (1990): 30–56; Weber, *Spanish Frontier in North America*, 172–186.

32. Treaty of Utrecht, in Joel H. Wiener, ed., *Great Britain: A Documentary History*, vol. 1: *Foreign Policy and the Span of Empire, 1689–1971* (New York: Chelsea House, 1972), 39.

33. Richmond P. Bond, *Queen Anne's American Kings* (Oxford: Clarendon Press, 1952); Eric Hinderaker, "The 'Four Indian Kings' and the Imaginative Construc-

tion of the First British Empire," *William and Mary Quarterly*, 3d ser., 53 (1996): 487–526.

34. Dorothy V. Jones, *License for Empire: Colonialism by Treaty in Early America* (Chicago: University of Chicago Press, 1982), 21–35.

35. William Andrews to Secretary of Society for the Propagation of the Gospel, 20 April 1716, Records of the Society for the Propagation of the Gospel, Letter Books, series A (microfilm, London: MicroMethods, 1964), vol. 11, pp. 319–320 (quotation); Richter, *Ordeal of the Longhouse*, 214–235.

36. Richard White, *The Middle Ground: Indians, Empires, and Republics in the Great Lakes Region, 1650–1815* (Cambridge: Cambridge University Press, 1991), 1–185.

37. Michael N. McConnell, *A Country Between: The Upper Ohio Valley and Its Peoples, 1724–1774* (Lincoln: University of Nebraska Press, 1992), 6–60.

38. Marvin T. Smith, "Aboriginal Population Movements in the Early Historic Period Interior Southeast," in Wood, Waselkov, and Hatley, *Powhatan's Mantle*, 21–34; Vernon James Knight Jr., "The Formation of the Creeks," in *The Forgotten Centuries: Indians and Europeans in the American South, 1521–1704*, ed. Charles Hudson and Carmen Chaves Tesser (Athens: University of Georgia Press, 1994), 373–392; Crane, *Southern Frontier*, 276–302.

39. J. Leitch Wright Jr., *Creeks and Seminoles: The Destruction and Regeneration of the Muscogulge People* (Lincoln: University of Nebraska Press, 1986), 1–20; Kathryn E. Holland Braund, *Deerskins and Duffels: Creek Indian Trade with Anglo-America, 1685–1815* (Lincoln: University of Nebraska Press, 1993), 6–10, 26–80.

40. Daniel H. Usner Jr., *Indians, Settlers, and Slaves in a Frontier Exchange Economy: The Lower Mississippi Valley before 1783* (Chapel Hill: University of North Carolina Press, 1992), 77–104; Patricia Galloway, *Choctaw Genesis, 1500–1700* (Lincoln: University of Nebraska Press, 1995); idem, "'The Chief Who Is Your Father': Choctaw and French Views of the Diplomatic Relation," in Wood, Waselkov, and Hatley, *Powhatan's Mantle*, 254–255 (quotation).

41. Richard L. Haan, "Covenant and Consensus: Iroquois and English, 1676–1760," in *Beyond the Covenant Chain: The Iroquois and Their Neighbors in Indian North America, 1600–1800*, ed. Daniel K. Richter and James H. Merrell (Syracuse: Syracuse University Press, 1987), 41–57.

42. *The Official Papers of Francis Fauquier Lieutenant Governor of Virginia, 1758–1768*, ed. George Reese, vol. 1 (Charlottesville: University Press of Virginia, 1981), 120. I am indebted to Brendan McConville for this reference.

43. Mary A. Druke, "Iroquois Treaties: Common Forms, Varying Interpretations," in *The History and Culture of Iroquois Diplomacy: An Interdisciplinary Guide to*

the Treaties of the Six Nations and Their League, ed. Francis Jennings, William N. Fenton, and Mary A. Druke (Syracuse: Syracuse University Press, 1985), 85–98; Robert A. Williams Jr., *Linking Arms Together: American Indian Treaty Visions of Law and Peace, 1600–1800* (New York: Oxford University Press, 1997); Timothy J. Shannon, *Indians and Colonists at the Crossroads of Empire: The Albany Congress of 1754* (Ithaca: Cornell University Press, 2000), 117–140; James H. Merrell, *Into the American Woods: Negotiators on the Pennsylvania Frontier* (New York: W. W. Norton, 1999), 253–276. On the spread of northern diplomatic customs to southern peoples by the 1740s, see Theda Perdue, "Cherokee Relations with the Iroquois in the Eighteenth Century," in Richter and Merrell, *Beyond the Covenant Chain*, 135–149.

44. James H. Merrell, *The Indians' New World: Catawbas and Their Neighbors from European Contact through the Era of Removal* (Chapel Hill: University of North Carolina Press, 1989), 244.

45. Laurence M. Hauptman, "Refugee Havens: The Iroquois Villages of the Eighteenth Century," in *American Indian Environments: Ecological Issues in Native American History*, ed. Christopher Vecsey and Robert W. Venables (Syracuse: Syracuse University Press, 1980), 128–139; Peter C. Mancall, *Valley of Opportunity: Economic Culture along the Upper Susquehanna, 1700–1800* (Ithaca: Cornell University Press, 1991), 27–70.

46. Patrick Frazier, *The Mohicans of Stockbridge* (Lincoln: University of Nebraska Press, 1992); Thomas F. McHugh, "The Moravian Mission to the American Indian: Early American Peace Corps," *Pennsylvania History* 33 (1966): 412–431.

47. Jean Lunn, "The Illegal Fur Trade Out of New France, 1713–1760," *Canadian Historical Association Annual Report* (Ottawa, 1939), 61–76.

48. Colin G. Calloway, *The Western Abenakis of Vermont, 1600–1800: War, Migration, and the Survival of an Indian People* (Norman: University of Oklahoma Press, 1990); Kenneth M. Morrison, *The Embattled Northeast: The Elusive Ideal of Alliance in Abenaki-Euramerican Relations* (Berkeley: University of California Press, 1984).

49. Laura E. Conkey, Ethel Boissevain, and Ives Goddard, "Indians of Southern New England and Long Island: Late Period," in Sturtevant, *Handbook*, 15: 177–185; Christian F. Feest, "Virginia Algonquians," ibid., 262–263; Daniel Vickers, "The First Whalemen of Nantucket," *William and Mary Quarterly*, 3d ser., 40 (1983): 560–583; James H. Merrell, "Cultural Continuity among the Piscataway Indians of Colonial Maryland," ibid., 36 (1979): 548–570.

50. Daniel R. Mandell, *Behind the Frontier: Indians in Eighteenth-Century Eastern Massachusetts* (Lincoln: University of Nebraska Press, 1996).

51. James Axtell, *Beyond 1492: Encounters in Colonial North America* (New York: Oxford University Press, 1992), 125–151.

52. Quoted in Braund, *Deerskins and Duffels*, 30.

53. Adolph G. Benson, ed., *The America of 1750: Peter Kalm's Travels in North America*, vol. 2 (New York: Wilson-Erickson, 1937), 518–521.

54. George I. Quimby, *Indian Culture and European Trade Goods: The Archaeology of the Historic Period in the Western Great Lakes Region* (Madison: University of Wisconsin Press, 1966), 63–80; Francis Jennings, *The Invasion of America: Indians, Colonialism, and the Cant of Conquest* (Chapel Hill: University of North Carolina Press, 1975), 97–104; Arthur J. Ray, "Indians as Consumers in the Eighteenth Century," in *Old Trails and New Directions: Papers of the Third North American Fur Trade Conference*, ed. Carol Judd and Arthur J. Ray (Toronto: University of Toronto Press, 1980), 255–271.

55. James H. Merrell, "'Our Bond of Peace': Patterns of Intercultural Exchange in the Carolina Piedmont," in Wood, Waselkov, and Hatley, *Powhatan's Mantle*, 196–222.

56. Conrad Weiser to James Logan, 16 September 1736, Logan Papers, vol. 10, fol. 62, Historical Society of Pennsylvania, Philadelphia.

57. *A Treaty of Friendship Held with the Chiefs of the Six Nations, at Philadelphia in September and October, 1736* (Philadelphia, 1737), 13.

58. J. Leitch Wright, *The Only Land They Knew: The Tragic Story of the American Indians in the Old South* (New York: Free Press, 1981), 172–173, 234–237; David B. Guldenzopf, "The Colonial Transformation of Mohawk Iroquois Society" (Ph.D. diss., State University of New York at Albany, 1986).

59. Axtell, *Beyond 1492*, 150–151; T. H. Breen, "Narratives of Commercial Life: Consumption, Ideology, and Community on the Eve of the American Revolution," *William and Mary Quarterly*, 3d ser., 50 (1993): 471–501.

60. Braund, *Deerskins and Duffels*, 26–80, quotation p. 43.

61. O'Callaghan and Fernow, *Documents Relative to Colonial New York*, 6: 177.

62. Albright G. Zimmerman, "The Indian Trade of Colonial Pennsylvania" (Ph.D. diss., University of Delaware, 1966), 463–464; Thomas Elliot Norton, *The Fur Trade in Colonial New York, 1686–1776* (Madison: University of Wisconsin Press, 1974), 92–94, 101–102, 148–149, 221–223; Stephen H. Cutcliffe, "Colonial Indian Policy as a Measure of Rising Imperialism: New York and Pennsylvania, 1700–1755," *Western Pennsylvania Historical Magazine* 64 (1981): 240–244; Richter, *Ordeal of the Longhouse*, 268–270, 384–385.

63. J. Russell Snapp, *John Stuart and the Struggle for Empire on the Southern Frontier* (Baton Rouge: Louisiana State University Press, 1996), 21–45.

64. W. J. Eccles, "The Fur Trade and Eighteenth-Century Imperialism," *William and Mary Quarterly*, 3d ser., 40 (1983): 341–362.

65. Colin G. Calloway, *The American Revolution in Indian Country: Crisis and Di-*

versity in Native American Communities (Cambridge: Cambridge University Press, 1995), xvi.

66. Gregory Evans Dowd, *A Spirited Resistance: The North American Indian Struggle for Unity, 1745–1815* (Baltimore: Johns Hopkins University Press, 1992), 23–46.

67. Ibid., xvii–xxii, quotation p. xxii.

68. Alden T. Vaughan, "From White Man to Redskin: Changing Anglo-American Perceptions of the American Indian," *American Historical Review* 86 (1982): 917–953; Nancy Shoemaker, "How Indians Got to Be Red," ibid., 102 (1997), 624–644.

69. Thomas Brainerd, *The Life of John Brainerd, The Brother of David Brainerd, and His Successor as Missionary to the Indians of New Jersey* (Philadelphia: Presbyterian Publication Committee, 1865), 233–235 (I am grateful to Gregory Dowd for this reference). The idea of separate creations was not new in the eighteenth century. "When we relate the creation of Adam, in broken language and to the best of our ability, they cannot or will not understand it in regard to their own nation or the Negroes, on account of the difference in skin color," a seventeenth-century Dutch colonist reported. It is unclear whether the Indians he spoke to were Mohawks, Mahicans, or Munsees, but they insisted that "the world was not created the way we believe it was and as told in Genesis 1 and 2" (Adriaen Cornelissen van der Donck, "Description of New Netherland, 1653," trans. Diederik Goedhuys, in *In Mohawk Country: Early Narratives about a Native People,* ed. Dean R. Snow, Charles T. Gehring, and William A. Starna [Syracuse: Syracuse University Press, 1996], 129–130). What appears to be new in the mid-eighteenth century was the linkage of the idea of separate creations to a militant call for action against European intruders on lands the Master of Life intended for Indians.

70. Colin G. Calloway, *Crown and Calumet: British-Indian Relations, 1783–1815* (Norman: University of Oklahoma Press, 1987), 51–97; Merrell, *Into the American Woods,* 276–301.

71. Jacqueline Peterson, "Many Roads to Red River: Métis Genesis in the Great Lakes Region, 1680–1815," in *The New Peoples: Being and Becoming Métis in North America,* ed. Jacqueline Peterson and Jennifer S. H. Brown (Lincoln: University of Nebraska Press, 1985), 185–193; James H. Merrell, "'The Cast of His Countenance': Reading Andrew Montour," in *Through a Glass Darkly: Reflections on Personal Identity in Early America,* ed. Ronald Hoffman, Michel Sobel, and Fredrika J. Teute (Chapel Hill: University of North Carolina Press, 1997), 13–39.

72. Denys Delâge, *Le pays renversé: Amérindiens et européens en Amérique du nord-est, 1600–1664* (Montreal: Boréal Express, 1985), 246–267; Michael D. Green, *The*

Politics of Indian Removal: Creek Government and Society in Crisis (Lincoln: University of Nebraska Press, 1982), 17–29, quotation p. 26.

73. Francis Jennings, *The Ambiguous Iroquois Empire: The Covenant Chain Confederation of Indian Tribes with English Colonies from Its Beginnings to the Lancaster Treaty of 1744* (New York: W. W. Norton, 1984), 301–346; W. J. Eccles, *The Canadian Frontier, 1534–1760,* rev. ed. (Albuquerque: University of New Mexico Press, 1983), 157–185.

74. James Axtell, *The European and the Indian: Essays in the Ethnohistory of Colonial North America* (New York: Oxford University Press, 1981), 225–227; Anderson, *Crucible of War,* 160–165; Merrell, *Into the American Woods,* 37 (quotation).

75. Francis Jennings, *Empire of Fortune: Crowns, Colonies and Tribes in the Seven Years' War in America* (New York: W. W. Norton, 1988), 396–404.

76. David Corkran, *The Cherokee Frontier: Conflict and Survival, 1740–1762* (Norman: University of Oklahoma Press, 1966), 142–272; Hatley, *Dividing Paths,* 92–140.

77. Alexander Spotswood to Peter Schuyler, 25 January 1720, Pennsylvania Provincial Council Records, vol. F, pp. 13–21, Pennsylvania State Archives, Harrisburg. See Chapter 3, above.

78. Jones, *License for Empire,* 44; Wilbur R. Jacobs, *Wilderness Politics and Indian Gifts: The Northern Colonial Frontier, 1748–1763* (1950; reprint, Lincoln: University of Nebraska Press, 1966), 66–67, 184–185; White, *Middle Ground,* 256–268.

79. Quoted in Kenneth M. Morrison, "Native Americans and the American Revolution: Historic Stories and Shifting Frontier Conflict," in *Indians in American History: An Introduction,* ed. Frederick E. Hoxie (Arlington Heights, Ill.: Harlan Davidson, 1988), 98.

80. *The Annual Register, or a View of the History, Politics, and Literature, for the Year 1763,* 2d ed. (London, 1765), 22.

6. Separate Creations

1. For introductions to the vast historical literature on these aspects of the Revolutionary experience, see Gordon S. Wood, *The Radicalism of the American Revolution* (New York: Knopf, 1991); Eric Foner, *Tom Paine and Revolutionary America* (New York: Oxford University Press, 1976); Mary Beth Norton, *Liberty's Daughters: The Revolutionary Experience of American Women, 1750–1800* (New York: Little, Brown, 1980); and Gary B. Nash, *Race and Revolution* (Madison, Wis.: Madison House, 1990), 57 (quotation).

2. J. Hector St. John de Crèvecoeur, *Letters from an American Farmer* (1782; reprint, New York: E. P. Dutton, 1957), 39.

3. Theodore Roosevelt, *The Winning of the West*, 4 vols. (1889–1896; reprint, Lincoln: University of Nebraska Press, 1995), 2: 373–375; 3: 44–46.

4. W. J. Eccles, *France in America* (New York: Harper and Row, 1972), 207–212; James Sullivan et al., eds., *The Papers of Sir William Johnson*, 14 vols. (Albany: University of the State of New York, 1921–1965), 10: 659–660 (quotation).

5. Gregory E. Dowd, "The French King Wakes Up at Detroit: 'Pontiac's War' in Rumor and History," *Ethnohistory* 34 (1990): 254–278.

6. Michael N. McConnell, *A Country Between: The Upper Ohio Valley and Its Peoples, 1724–1774* (Lincoln: University of Nebraska Press, 1992), 159–181; Sullivan et al., *Papers of Johnson*, 10: 648–649 (quotation).

7. Samuel Hazard, ed., *Minutes of the Provincial Council of Pennsylvania, from the Organization to the Termination of the Proprietary Government*, vol. 8 (Harrisburg: Theo. Fenn, 1852), 269 (quotation), 766–767; John W. Jordan, ed., "Journal of James Kenny, 1761–1763," *Pennsylvania Magazine of History and Biography* 37 (1913): 12–13; C. Hale Sipe, *The Indian Wars of Pennsylvania* (Harrisburg: Telegraph Press, 1929), 407–412.

8. Sullivan et al., *Papers of Johnson*, 10: 680.

9. [Robert Navarre?,] *Journal of Pontiac's Conspiracy*, ed. M. Agnes Burton, trans. R. C. Ford (Detroit: Clarence Monroe Burton, [1912]), 22–32.

10. John Heckewelder, *History, Manners, and Customs of the Indian Nations Who Once Inhabited Pennsylvania and the Neighbouring States*, ed. William C. Reichel (1819; reprint, Philadelphia: Historical Society of Pennsylvania, 1876), 291.

11. Jordan, "Journal of Kenny," 171–173. See also "A Narrative of the Captivity of John M'Cullough, Esq.," in Archibald Loudon, *A Selection of Some of the Most Interesting Narratives, of Outrages, Committed by the Indians, in Their Wars with the White People*, vol. 1 (Carlisle, Pa.: A. Loudon, Whitehall, 1808), 321–325.

12. Alfred A. Cave, "The Delaware Prophet Neolin: A Reappraisal," *Ethnohistory* 46 (1999): 265–290.

13. Sullivan et al., *Papers of Johnson*, 10: 690–691, 694–695.

14. Anthony F. C. Wallace, *King of the Delawares: Teedyuscung, 1700–1763* (Philadelphia: University of Pennsylvania Press, 1949), 258–266.

15. Ian K. Steele, *Warpaths: Invasions of North America* (New York: Oxford University Press, 1994), 234–242; Woody Holton, *Forced Founders: Indians, Debtors, Slaves, and the Making of the American Revolution in Virginia* (Chapel Hill: University of North Carolina Press, 1999), 138–139; Howard H. Peckham, *Pontiac and the Indian Uprising* (Princeton: Princeton University Press, 1947), 130–220, quotation pp. 218–219.

16. Sullivan et al., *Papers of Johnson*, 10: 728.

17. McConnell, *A Country Between*, 159–196, quotation p. 192.

18. Peckham, *Pontiac and the Indian Uprising*, 236–238; Fred Anderson, *Crucible of War: The Seven Years' War and the Fate of Empire in British North America, 1754–1766* (New York: Knopf, 2000), 529–550.

19. John Shy, *Toward Lexington: The Role of the British Army in the Coming of the American Revolution* (Princeton: Princeton University Press, 1965), 135–139. On the smallpox episode, see Bernhard Knollenberg, "General Amherst and Germ Warfare," *Mississippi Valley Historical Review* 41 (1954–55): 489–494; Knollenberg and Donald H. Kent, "Communications," ibid., 762–763; and Elizabeth A. Fenn, "Biological Warfare in Eighteenth-Century North America: Beyond Jeffery Amherst," *Journal of American History* 86 (2000): 1552–80.

20. Paul A. W. Wallace, ed., *The Travels of John Heckewelder in Frontier America* (1958; reprint, Pittsburgh: University of Pittsburgh Press, 1985), 71–84, quotation p. 72.

21. John R. Dunbar, ed., *The Paxton Papers* (The Hague: M. Nijhoff, 1957), 193–194.

22. Ibid., 57–58. What exactly the Paxton Boys hoped to do when they went to Wyoming in 1763 is unclear; they may even have been intent on driving out the Susquehanna Company settlers. Nonetheless, they were deeply enraged by the gory scene they came upon after the Indian raid. On the later relationship of several of the Paxton leaders to the Susquehanna Company, for which they would put their bloody skills to work to drive rival White settlers out of the Wyoming Valley, see James Kirby Martin, "The Return of the Paxton Boys and the Historical State of the Pennsylvania Frontier, 1764–1774," *Pennsylvania History* 38 (1971): 117–133.

23. James H. Merrell, *Into the American Woods: Negotiators on the Pennsylvania Frontier* (New York: W. W. Norton, 1999), 282–288.

24. Brooke Hindle, "The March of the Paxton Boys," *William and Mary Quarterly*, 3d ser., 3 (1946): 461–486; James E. Crowley, "The Paxton Disturbance and Ideas of Order in Pennsylvania Politics," *Pennsylvania History* 37 (1970): 317–339.

25. Dunbar, *Paxton Papers*, 101–104.

26. Ibid., 104.

27. Peter A. Butzin, "Politics, Presbyterians, and the Paxton Riots, 1763–64," *Journal of Presbyterian History* 51 (1973): 70–84.

28. As Elizabeth Perkins has pointed out, concepts of race remained ill formed throughout the late eighteenth century, and much of the violence between Whites and Indians in this period "seems too personal, too immediate, too *intimate* to represent the categorical racialism that would gain respectability by the 1840s"; *Border Life: Experience and Memory in the Revolutionary Ohio Valley* (Chapel Hill: University of North Carolina Press, 1998), 136–137. Nonetheless, it seems

clear that on both sides, in periods of peak violence among members of communities of Whites and Indians who in fact did know each other quite well on personal terms, militants defined the other in categorical terms best described as "racial."

29. Shy, *Toward Lexington*, 122–135, 192–204, quotation p. 122.

30. Sullivan et al., *Papers of Johnson*, 10: 977–985, quotation p. 982.

31. Peter Marshall, "Colonial Protest and Imperial Retrenchment: Indian Policy, 1764–1768," *Journal of American Studies* 5 (1971): 1–17; John R. Alden, "The Albany Congress and the Creation of the Indian Superintendencies," *Mississippi Valley Historical Review* 27 (1940): 193–210; J. Russell Snapp, *John Stuart and the Struggle for Empire on the Southern Frontier* (Baton Rouge: Louisiana State University Press, 1996), 54–78.

32. McConnell, *A Country Between*, 196–206; Francis Jennings, *Empire of Fortune: Crowns, Colonies, and Tribes in the Seven Years' War in America* (New York: W. W. Norton, 1988), 438–453; Anderson, *Crucible of War*, 617–637.

33. Peckham, *Pontiac and the Indian Uprising*, 301–311.

34. Richard White, *The Middle Ground: Indians, Empires, and Republics in the Great Lakes Region, 1650–1815* (Cambridge: Cambridge University Press, 1991), 269–314; Eccles, *France in America*, 212–220; Jennifer S. H. Brown, *Strangers in Blood: Fur Trade Company Families in Indian Country* (Vancouver: University of British Columbia Press, 1980), 1–50; Colin G. Calloway, *Crown and Calumet: British-Indian Relations, 1783–1815* (Norman: University of Oklahoma Press, 1987), 51–76.

35. John Richard Alden, *John Stuart and the Southern Colonial Frontier: A Study of Indian Relations, War, Trade, and Land Problems in the Southern Wilderness, 1754–1775* (1944; reprint, New York: Gordian Press, 1966), 215–239, 262–281; Dorothy V. Jones, *License for Empire: Colonialism by Treaty in Early America* (Chicago: University of Chicago Press, 1982), 36–92.

36. Jones, *License for Empire*, 93–119.

37. Wallace, *Travels of Heckewelder*, 71; G. S. Rowe, "The Frederick Stump Affair, 1768, and Its Challenge to Legal Historians of Early Pennsylvania," *Pennsylvania History* 49 (1982): 259–288; Alden T. Vaughan, "Frontier Banditti and the Indians: The Paxton Boys' Legacy, 1763–1775," ibid., 51 (1984): 19–22; Linda A. Ries, "'The Rage of Opposing Government': The Stump Affair of 1768," *Cumberland County History* 1, no. 1 (Summer 1984): 21–45.

38. Tom Hatley, *The Dividing Paths: Cherokees and South Carolinians through the Era of Revolution* (New York: Oxford University Press, 1993), 183–186; Sullivan et al., *Papers of Johnson*, 5: 737 (quotation).

39. Thomas Jefferson, *Notes on the State of Virginia* (1785; reprint, New York: Harper and Row, 1964), 60–61.

40. On Jefferson's complicated dual fascination with Logan's Lament and the expropriation of Indian lands, see Anthony F. C. Wallace, *Jefferson and the Indians: The Tragic Fate of the First Americans* (Cambridge, Mass.: Harvard University Press, 1999).

41. Randolph C. Downes, *Council Fires on the Upper Ohio: A Narrative of Indian Affairs in the Upper Ohio Valley until 1795* (Pittsburgh: University of Pittsburgh Press, 1940), 152–178; McConnell, *A Country Between*, 255–282.

42. Dunbar, *Paxton Papers*, 101.

43. E. B. O'Callaghan and B. Fernow, eds., *Documents Relative to the Colonial History of the State of New York*, 15 vols. (Albany, N.Y.: Weed, Parsons, 1853–1887), 8: 111–137, quotation p. 112; Alden, *John Stuart and Southern Colonial Frontier*, 272; Snapp, *John Stuart and Struggle for Empire*, 74–75; Holton, *Forced Founders*, 3–38.

44. Anderson, *Crucible of War*, 741–746.

45. O'Callaghan and Fernow, *Documents Relative to Colonial New York*, 8: 475–477.

46. Holton, *Forced Founders*, 3, 38.

47. Pauline Maier, *American Scripture: Making the Declaration of Independence* (New York: Knopf, 1997), 154–170, 239.

48. Worthington Chauncey Ford, ed., *Journals of the Continental Congress, 1774–1789*, vol. 2 (Washington, D.C.: U.S. Government Printing Office, 1905), 152–153.

49. Moncure Daniel Conway, ed., *The Writings of Thomas Paine*, vol. 1 (New York, 1894), 100.

50. Harley L. Gibb, "Colonel Guy Johnson, Superintendent General of Indian Affairs, 1774–82," *Papers of the Michigan Academy of Science, Arts and Letters* 27 (1941): 596–600.

51. Philip M. Hamer, "John Stuart's Indian Policy during the Early Months of the American Revolution," *Mississippi Valley Historical Review* 17 (1930): 351–366; Hatley, *Dividing Paths*, 191–203; Wallace, *Jefferson and the Indians*, 50–60; Maier, *American Scripture*, 26, 79–80, 250.

52. Quoted in David Waldstreicher, *In the Midst of Perpetual Fetes: The Making of American Nationalism, 1776–1820* (Chapel Hill: University of North Carolina Press, 1997), 31.

53. Alfred F. Young, *The Shoemaker and the Tea Party: Memory and the American Revolution* (Boston: Beacon Press, 1999), 103–104.

54. Bernard Bailyn, ed., *Pamphlets of the American Revolution, 1750–1776*, vol. 1 (Cambridge, Mass.: Harvard University Press, 1965), 447, 455.

55. Ford, *Journals of Continental Congress*, 2: 142.

56. Quoted in Snapp, *John Stuart and Struggle for Empire*, 178.

57. Barbara Graymont, *The Iroquois in the American Revolution* (Syracuse: Syra-

cuse University Press, 1972), 48–222; Colin G. Calloway, *The American Revolution in Indian Country: Crisis and Diversity in Native American Communities* (Cambridge: Cambridge University Press, 1995), 46–64.

58. Louise Phelps Kellogg, ed., *Frontier Advance on the Upper Ohio, 1778–1779* (Madison: State Historical Society of Wisconsin, 1916), 138–145, 157, 168–169, 202–205; C. Hale Sipe, *The Indian Chiefs of Pennsylvania* (Butler, Pa.: Ziegler Printing, 1927), 410–418; White, *Middle Ground*, 315–468.

59. Wallace, *Travels of Heckewelder*, 93–114, 156–193; Thomas P. Slaughter, *The Whiskey Rebellion: Frontier Epilogue to the American Revolution* (New York: Oxford University Press, 1986), 75–78.

60. Wallace, *Travels of Heckewelder*, 193–200, quotation p. 193.

61. Quoted in Sipe, *Indian Wars of Pennsylvania*, 650.

62. Quoted in ibid., 651.

63. Francis Jennings, "The Indians' Revolution," in *The American Revolution: Explorations in the History of American Radicalism*, ed. Alfred F. Young (De Kalb: Northern Illinois University Press, 1976), 319–348; James H. Merrell, "Declarations of Independence: Indian-White Relations in the New Nation," in *The American Revolution: Its Character and Limits*, ed. Jack P. Greene (New York: New York University Press, 1987), 197–223.

64. Quoted in Calloway, *American Revolution in Indian Country*, 276.

65. Calloway, *Crown and Calumet*, 3–18; Isabel Thompson Kelsay, *Joseph Brant, 1743–1807: Man of Two Worlds* (Syracuse: Syracuse University Press, 1984), 320–552.

66. *Pennsylvania Archives*, 1st ser., vol. 10 (Philadelphia: Joseph Severns, 1854), 45 (quotation); Reginald Horsman, "American Indian Policy in the Old Northwest, 1783–1812," *William and Mary Quarterly*, 3d ser., 18 (1961): 35–40; Jones, *License for Empire*, 139–156.

67. Hazard et al., *Pennsylvania Archives*, 1st ser., 10: 54.

68. The best summary of these events is Wiley Sword, *President Washington's Indian War: The Struggle for the Old Northwest, 1790–1795* (Norman: University of Oklahoma Press, 1985).

69. Andrew R. L. Cayton, "'Noble Actors' upon 'the Theatre of Honour': Power and Civility in the Treaty of Greenville," in *Contact Points: American Frontiers from the Mohawk Valley to the Mississippi, 1750–1830*, ed. Cayton and Fredrika J. Teute (Chapel Hill: University of North Carolina Press, 1998), 252–267; Richard White, "The Fictions of Patriarchy: Indians and Whites in the Early Republic," in *Native Americans and the Early Republic*, ed. Frederick E. Hoxie, Ronald Hoffman, and Peter J. Albert (Charlottesville: University Press of Virginia, 1999), 62–84.

70. Robert F. Berkhofer Jr., *The White Man's Indian: Images of the American Indian from Columbus to the Present* (New York: Knopf, 1978), 134–153; Bernard W.

Sheehan, *Seeds of Extinction: Jeffersonian Philanthropy and the American Indian* (Chapel Hill: University of North Carolina Press, 1973), 119–181; Reginald Horsman, "The Indian Policy of an 'Empire for Liberty,'" in Hoxie, Hoffman, and Albert, *Native Americans and the Early Republic*, 37–61; Daniel K. Richter, "'Believing That Many of the Red People Suffer Much for the Want of Food': Hunting, Agriculture, and a Quaker Construction of Indianness in the Early Republic," *Journal of the Early Republic* 19 (1999): 601–628.

71. Quoted in Sheehan, *Seeds of Extinction*, 171.

72. Paul A. Hutton, "William Wells: Frontier Scout and Indian Agent," *Indiana Magazine of History* 74 (1978): 183–222; Andrew R. L. Cayton, *Frontier Indiana* (Bloomington: Indiana University Press, 1996), 199–204.

73. J. Leitch Wright Jr., *Creeks and Seminoles: The Destruction and Regeneration of the Muscogulge People* (Lincoln: University of Nebraska Press, 1986), 129–153.

74. J. Leitch Wright Jr., *Anglo-Spanish Rivalry in North America* (Athens: University of Georgia Press, 1971), 135–172.

75. Harold D. Moser and Sharon Macpherson, eds., *The Papers of Andrew Jackson*, vol. 2 (Knoxville: University of Tennessee Press, 1984), 91–192.

76. Emma Helen Blair, trans. and ed., *The Indian Tribes of the Upper Mississippi Valley and Region of the Great Lakes*, vol. 2 (Cleveland, 1911), 273–279 (quotations); R. David Edmunds, *Tecumseh and the Quest for American Indian Leadership* (Boston: Little, Brown, 1984), 73–98; Gregory Evans Dowd, *A Spirited Resistance: The North American Indian Struggle for Unity, 1745–1815* (Baltimore: Johns Hopkins University Press, 1992), 169–173; Kathryn E. Holland Braund, *Deerskins and Duffels: Creek Indian Trade with Anglo-America, 1685–1815* (Lincoln: University of Nebraska Press, 1993), 185–188; Joel W. Martin, *Sacred Revolt: The Muskogees' Struggle for a New World* (Boston: Beacon Press, 1991), 133–168; Claudio Saunt, *A New Order of Things: Property, Power, and the Transformation of the Creek Indians, 1733–1816* (Cambridge: Cambridge University Press, 1999), 233–272.

77. Blair, *Indian Tribes*, 2: 277; Braund, *Deerskins and Duffels*, 187.

78. Alfred A. Cave, "The Failure of the Shawnee Prophet's Witch-Hunt," *Ethnohistory* 42 (1995): 445–475; Wright, *Creeks and Seminoles*, 156–171.

79. John Sugden, *Tecumseh: A Life* (New York: Henry Holt, 1997), 226–236; Cayton, *Frontier Indiana*, 209–225.

80. James D. Richardson, *A Compilation of the Messages and Papers of the Presidents, 1789–1897*, 10 vols. (New York, 1896–1899), 1: 493, 503–504 (quotations).

81. Edmunds, *Tecumseh*, 153–216.

82. H. S. Halbert and T. H. Ball, *The Creek War of 1813 and 1814* (1895; reprint, Montgomery: University of Alabama Press, 1969), 125–176.

83. Wright, *Creeks and Seminoles*, 172–180.

84. Ibid., 206–207.

85. Charles Sellers, *The Market Revolution: Jacksonian America, 1815–1846* (New York: Oxford University Press, 1991), 90–102; John William Ward, *Andrew Jackson: Symbol for an Age* (1953; reprint, New York: Oxford University Press, 1962), 57–63, quotation p. 63.

86. Harold D. Moser, David R. Hoth, and George H. Hoemann, eds., *The Papers of Andrew Jackson,* vol. 4 (Knoxville, Tenn., 1994), 95.

87. Richardson, *Compilation of Papers of Presidents,* 3: 519–522 (quotations); Reginald Horsman, *Race and Manifest Destiny: The Origins of American Racial Anglo-Saxonism* (Cambridge, Mass.: Harvard University Press, 1981), 202.

88. On Logan's Lament and elocutionary education in the nineteenth century, see Carolyn Eastman, "The Indian Censures the White Man: 'Indian Eloquence' and American Reading Audiences in the Early Republic," paper presented at the McNeil Center for Early American Studies, Philadelphia, 30 April 1999.

89. Sugden, *Tecumseh's Last Stand,* 136–181, 252n. (quotation).

EPILOGUE

1. William Apes[s], *Eulogy on King Philip, as Pronounced at the Odeon, in Federal Street, Boston* (Boston: published by the author, 1836), 1–2. All quotations of the *Eulogy* are from this edition. Employing idiosyncratic punctuation perhaps better suited for oral delivery than for the printed page, the first part of the second paragraph appears in the original as follows: "Yet those purer virtues remain untold. Those noble traits that marked the wild man's course lie buried in the shades of night; and who shall stand? I appeal to the lovers of liberty. But those few remaining descendants who now remain as the monument of the cruelty of those who came to improve our race, and correct our errors; and as the immortal Washington lives endeared and engraven on the hearts of every white in America, never to be forgotten in time—even such is the immortal Philip honored . . . " The punctuation changes silently made in the text seem to me to be the only way to make sense of the words.

2. Primary credit for spreading the word about Apess belongs to Barry O'Connell, editor of *On Our Own Ground: The Complete Writings of William Apess, a Pequot* (Amherst: University of Massachusetts Press, 1992) and of the abridged paperback edition, *A Son of the Forest and Other Writings by William Apess, a Pequot* (Amherst: University of Massachusetts Press, 1997). See also Kim McQuaid, "William Apes, Pequot: An Indian Reformer in the Jackson Era," *New England Quarterly* 50 (1977): 605–625; Arnold Krupat, *The Voice in the Margins: Native American Literature and the Canon* (Berkeley: University of California Press, 1989), 143–149;

idem, *Ethnocriticism: Ethnography, History, Literature* (Berkeley: University of California Press, 1992), 227–229; David Murray, *Forked Tongues: Speech, Writing, and Representation in North American Indian Texts* (Bloomington: Indiana University Press, 1991), 57–64; Karim M. Tiro, "Denominated 'SAVAGE': Methodism, Writing, and Identity in the Works of William Apess, a Pequot," *American Quarterly* 48 (1996): 653–679; and Bernd C. Peyer, *The Tutor'd Mind: Indian Missionary-Writers in Antebellum America* (Amherst: University of Massachusetts Press, 1997), 117–165.

3. The title page of the 1836 edition of the *Eulogy* gives the author's name as "the Rev. William Apes, an Indian"; the abridged second edition uses "the Rev. William Apess, An Indian" (Boston: published by the author, 1837).

4. O'Connell, *On Our Own Ground*, xxvii–xxxviii, lxxix–lxxxi.

5. Nathan O. Hatch, *The Democratization of American Christianity* (New Haven: Yale University Press, 1989), 81–93, 201–206; Tiro, "Denominated 'SAVAGE,'" 661; Peyer, *Tutor'd Mind*, 137–139.

6. McQuaid, "William Apes," 614–622; Peyer, *Tutor'd Mind*, 139–147, quotation p. 143.

7. Jack Campisi, *The Mashpee Indians: Tribe on Trial* (Syracuse: Syracuse University Press, 1991), 99–108; Barry O'Connell, "Apess, William," in *Encyclopedia of North American Indians*, ed. Frederick E. Hoxie (Boston: Houghton Mifflin, 1996), 30–31.

8. Krupat, *Voice in the Margins*, 143–149; Peyer, *Tutor'd Mind*, 148–153. On the slave narrative genre, see Robert J. Allison, "Introduction: Equiano's Worlds," in *The Interesting Narrative of the Life of Olaudah Equiano, Written by Himself*, ed. Allison (Boston: Bedford Books, 1995), 1–26.

9. O'Connell, *On Our Own Ground*, xxxix–lxxvii. With the exception of "An Appeal," all these works are reprinted in that volume.

10. John K. Mahon, *History of the Second Seminole War, 1835–1842* (Gainesville: University of Florida Press, 1967); Michael Green, *The Politics of Indian Removal: Creek Government and Society in Crisis* (Lincoln: University of Nebraska Press, 1982); Thurman Wilkins, *Cherokee Tragedy*, 2d ed. (Norman: University of Oklahoma Press, 1986).

11. James Brewer Stewart, *Holy Warriors: The Abolitionists and American Slavery* (New York: Hill and Wang, 1976), 50–89.

12. Reginald Horsman, *Race and Manifest Destiny: The Origins of American Racial Anglo-Saxonism* (Cambridge, Mass.: Harvard University Press, 1981), 208–228.

13. Jill Lepore, *The Name of War: King Philip's War and the Origins of American Identity* (New York: Knopf, 1998), 191–226. See also Chapter 3, above.

14. Apess specifically cites, for instance, Samuel G. Drake's 1832 *Biography and History of the Indians of North America* (*Eulogy*, 8).

15. O'Connell, *On Our Own Ground*, 60–69; Peyer, *Tutor'd Mind*, 159–165.

16. Washington Irving, *The Sketch Book* (New York: T. Y. Crowell, 1891), 219–233, quotations pp. 225, 229, 232.

17. *The Works of Daniel Webster*, vol. 1 (Boston: Charles C. Little and James Brown, 1851), 14, 30–31, 45.

18. O'Connell, *On Our Own Ground*, xx; Ann Uhry Abrams, *The Pilgrims and Pocahontas: Rival Myths of American Origin* (Boulder: Westview Press, 1999), 73–107.

19. Apess, *Eulogy*, 20.

20. Frederick Douglass, "What to the Slave Is the Fourth of July" (1852), in *The Frederick Douglass Papers*, ed. John W. Blassingame, 1st ser., vol. 2 (New Haven: Yale University Press, 1982), 388. On the use of the Fourth of July by Apess, Douglass, and other people of color in the nineteenth century, see David Waldstreicher, *In the Midst of Perpetual Fetes: The Making of American Nationalism, 1776–1820* (Chapel Hill: University of North Carolina Press, 1997), 349–352.

21. *Works of Webster*, 1: 45.

22. On early nineteenth-century New Englanders' tendency to deny the history of racial slavery in their region and to replace it with "a triumphant narrative of a historically free, white New England in which a few people of color were unaccountably marooned," see Joanne Pope Melish, *Disowning Slavery: Gradual Emancipation and "Race" in New England, 1780–1860* (Ithaca: Cornell University Press, 1988), quotation p. 3.

23. Apess, *Eulogy*, 8. Apess conflated two distinct events here. Epenow and two others were captured by Edward Harlow in 1611, and some twenty others (including the famous Squanto) by Thomas Hunt in 1614; this latter group was taken to Malaga, Spain, where Hunt attempted to sell them into slavery. See O'Connell, *On Our Own Ground*, 279n.; and Neal Salisbury, "Squanto: Last of the Patuxets," in *Struggle and Survival in Colonial America*, ed. David G. Sweet and Gary B. Nash (Berkeley: University of California Press, 1981), 233–235.

24. Apess, *Eulogy*, 10–11.

25. Ibid., 12, 19.

26. Ibid., 7, 25, 32–34.

27. Ibid., 35–36. Readers of early nineteenth-century patriotic histories expected great commanders to stir their men with oratory on the eve of battle, and historians obliged them with appropriate harangues, even if they had to make them up, as Apess apparently did here (Lepore, *Name of War*, 215–220). But even as he worked within standard literary conventions, Apess showed his audience an alternative perspective on their cherished past. The words he put in Metacom's mouth confirmed White stereotypes of Indian eloquence, with their evocations

of a Great Spirit no seventeenth-century Algonquian would have acknowledged and their descriptions of buffalo never seen anywhere near New England. Yet, in powerful refutation of Webster, the same words charged the Pilgrim Fathers with the crime of slavery.

28. Apess, *Eulogy*, 36–38.

29. Ibid., 39.

30. Ibid., 45–46.

31. Ibid., 48, 53–54. Intentionally or not, Apess' reference to Andrew Jackson took on added significance on the date of his original speech, 8 January 1836, which was the anniversary of Jackson's victory at the Battle of New Orleans in 1815, and the occasion of public celebrations in much of the nation; Waldstreicher, *Perpetual Fetes*, 349.

32. Apess, *Eulogy*, 55–56.

33. Ibid., 56, 60.

34. *The Writings of Thomas Paine*, ed. Moncure Daniel Conway, vol. 1 (New York: G. P. Putnam's Sons, 1894), 118–119.

35. Philip J. Deloria, *Playing Indian* (New Haven: Yale University Press, 1998).

ACKNOWLEDGMENTS

No one knew it at the time, but this book had its origins at a conference for high school teachers, held in honor of Alden T. Vaughan at the American Antiquarian Society in 1994. There, almost by accident, the phrase "facing east" was born; in subsequent years it took on a life of its own. Frank Bremer was largely responsible for organizing that conference, and so, as always, Alden and Frank became great silent influences on my work, although I never much discussed the book's grand scheme with either of them. Other subliminal contributors include Michael McConnell, who once wrote about "standing in Indian country," and Peter Wood, who, I discovered at a late stage of this project, was also playing with variations on the title "Facing East." I thank Peter for yielding the title to me. I also owe a debt to Barry O'Connell for his rediscovery of William Apess and to Charles Cohen for his work on Natick conversion narratives, although neither may entirely approve of the direction in which I have taken the issues they brought forward. Because one of the main purposes of *Facing East* is to encourage different ways of telling old stories, it often uses examples and episodes familiar to professional historians and so relies heavily on the research of previous scholars—none of whom should be held accountable for my use or abuse of their studies.

Several venues provided opportunities to try out ideas that found their way into this book: a session of the Columbia University Seminar on Early American History and Culture in 2001, the Sixth Annual Omohundro Institute of Early American History and Culture Conference in 2000, the Midwest American Association for Eighteenth-Century Studies annual meeting in the same year, a University of Pennsylvania History Department talk in 1998, a session of Michael Zuckerman's evening "salon" in 1996, a conference at the Lawrence Henry Gipson Institute at Lehigh University in 1994, and two of Warren Hofstra's periodic "backcountry" conferences at Shenandoah University during the 1990s. Valuable comments on drafts of chapters or of material related to the book came from Frank Bremer, Jennifer S. H. Brown, Colin Calloway, Krista Camenzind, Greg Dowd, Patricia Galloway, Christopher Grasso, Evan Haefeli, the late Francis Jennings, Roger Louis, Peter Marshall, Brendan McConville, William Shade, John Smolenski, Laurier Turgeon, and Rachel Wheeler. James Merrell, Neal Salisbury, and several anonymous reviewers read the entire manuscript—some of it multiple times— and greatly improved it. My editor, Joyce Seltzer, relentlessly pushed me to bring my fragmentary visions into coherent focus.

Conversations and correspondence with countless colleagues have also helped to hone my ideas and strengthen my spirits at low points in the creative process. For intellectual and personal support, I thank in particular Amy Baxter-Bellamy, David Commins, Richard Dunn, Ronald Hoffman, Bruce Kuklick (who, not entirely helpfully, suggested that instead of facing east, a historian ought to face downward from the perspective of an omniscient god), Lynn Hollen Lees, Lonna Malmsheimer, Elaine Mellen, Philip Morgan, Peter Onuf, Bill Pencak, Kim Rogers, Fredrika Teute, Neil Weissman, and Todd and Karen Wronksi. James W. Farrell prepared the maps. W. Scott Roberts dealt heroically with computer problems. Cheryl Parsons and my fellow singers in Cantate Carlisle kept me sane.

This project was begun at one great institution and completed at another. Dickinson College provided intellectual nurture, a sympathetic community of colleagues and students, and vital financial support through its Faculty Committee on Research and Development. The University of Pennsylvania provided the impetus to get it done, brilliant colleagues to help hone ideas, graduate students to further sharpen the argument, and the McNeil Center for Early American Studies to provide one of the most stimulating scholarly environments anywhere. But the most supportive environment has been my family: Sharon as editor, critic, and guide; and Tom and Mary, who kept me facing home.

INDEX

ourselves; that great mass of our life spread over work and leisure, our treatment of people, our use of money, our Saturday nights as well as our Sunday mornings, our habits as well as our hymns.

I beseech you therefore, brethren, by the mercies of God, that you present your bodies a living sacrifice, holy, acceptable unto God, which is your reasonable service.

*
**

Reasonable service: I consulted seven other translations of these words and they agree that the words mean more than just the proper thing to do. "Service" here really means worship. "Reasonable" would be better translated, "of the reason, of the mind" or even "spiritual." In other words, "Present your bodies a living sacrifice which is the worship of your minds."

There is no more spiritual act than to offer God the living sacrifice of our bodies as the direct outcome of our worshiping mind grasping His love and mercy. Our reason expresses its devotion by surrendering the body to God. Thus the reality of our worship is put to the test in everyday life, wherever our body is.

This is why Jesus' picture of judgment is focused on the body and the mind behind it: on the hand that provided food for the hungry, the voice that welcomed the stranger, the gift that clothed the naked, the feet that visited the sick and imprisoned; and the thought behind them all that made these deeds of the body worship pleasing to God.

For he whom Jesus loved hath truly spoken:
The holier worship which Christ deigns to bless,

Restores the lost and binds the spirit broken
And feeds the widow and the fatherless.

I beseech you therefore by the mercies of God, that
you present your bodies a living sacrifice, holy, acceptable unto God, which is your *spiritual worship*.

For this is the dedication God wants.

———————————

MOST GRACIOUS GOD, lift up our hearts as we behold
your mercies. May we be kindled in a way we have failed to
be kindled before. By your Spirit enlighten and warm us,
that from our fire others may be lighted and warmed too.
Through Christ we ask it. AMEN.

21

Lifelong Lent

The Practice of Religion

The semantic origin of the word "Lent" is the Middle English *Lencten* meaning spring. *Lencten* and length could well have the same root, as spring is the time when the days lengthen.

The spiritual origin of Lent is something else. Around the year A.D. 200 the *Apostolic Tradition* of Hippolytus tells us that the pre-Easter period was used to prepare candidates for baptism. This culminated in a strict fast on the Friday and Saturday before Easter. The first Council of Nicea in A.D. 325 mentions a six-week period. Because Sunday was never a fast day, piety sought to conform the time to exactly forty days, after the example of Moses, Elijah, and Christ's temptation in the wilderness. In late fifth-century Rome, the fast began on the Wednesday before the first Sunday in Lent. Public penance in sackcloth and ashes by grievous sinners, desiring restoration, also took place at that time. As this tradition died out in the ninth century, it became customary for the faithful to be reminded of their need for penitence—hence the ash mark.

So the interwoven strands of Lent are instruction, self-denial, and penitence, and each strand includes the positive side of reconciliation between God and mankind. With it all comes a preparedness for the divine action of Holy Week. Who could quarrel with this?

My only plea is for the enlargement of Lent. Its emphasis on gospel instruction, self-denial, penitence, and reconciliation is the essence of living the Christian life throughout the whole year, not just during a special six weeks. Obviously there is a psychological contrast which heightens the joy of Easter by that which goes before it. But if the gospel means anything, it means that every Sunday is Easter. Every Sunday is the Lord's Day, for that is the day on which He rose. His risen Power and Presence should be evident in every gathering for worship. The joy of the Lord should be perceived in people who constantly come and go in daily self-denial, in regular reconciliation, and in practical penitence.

*
**

With that in mind, let us look at our text in the New English Bible translation of 1 Timothy 4:7:

Keep yourself in training for the practice of religion.

Training for the practice of religion is a constant business—three hundred and sixty-five days a year—a lifelong Lent.

Paul is writing to his young friend and helper, Timothy. In this chapter, he gets across the idea:

To train and exercise your body is a good enough thing, for it brings with it the limited benefit of physical fitness. But remember that everyone's body, no matter how fit, dies sooner or later. So you see, it is even better to exercise your spiritual nature; to train it for the practice of religion. This will bring you unlimited benefit, not only for this life but for the life to come. That is why it is vitally important to keep yourself in training for the practice of religion.

Now training of any sort involves one necessary element—discipline. A person can have access to a splendid library of volumes on every conceivable subject and still be abysmally ignorant of the wealth of knowledge they contain. It takes a certain discipline to sit down, shut out all distractions, open a book, and concentrate on what is written so as to transfer knowledge from print to the head. We need a similar discipline to bring knowledge of God from the pages of His Word to our own inmost being.

Many resist the idea of discipline of any kind, especially self-discipline. A great deal of power in the world, including human power, is wasted if it is neither controlled nor directed. It is undisciplined. The river which meanders widely down to the sea, though it carries a large volume of water, cannot be used easily as a source of power. Yet quite a small stream, disciplined by steep banks and a narrow channel, can turn a mill wheel or drive a turbine. The control, the hemming in, and the direction produce the usable power.

Today, people are apt to reject discipline because they think they are more free without it. In actual fact, they are not. The pianist who avoids the discipline of practicing is not free to place her fingers unerringly on the keys. The football player who dodges the discipline of training is not free to play with the same stamina or exhibit the same skill as the man who has been at all the practices. The student who skips the discipline of studying is not free to find the right answers during the exams.

In every sphere in which people avoid the necessary discipline, they are free only to make mistakes, go wrong, and fail. And if that is true of music, football, and studies, it applies equally well to our religious experience. There is a discipline required for training ourselves. If we neglect it, we needn't wonder why our faith is feeble or scarcely alive.

Among the troops in both World Wars it was especially noticeable that the ones who held on to a vital faith were those who maintained some kind of strict, regular practice. Whether orthodox Jews who on Friday nights began their observance of the Sabbath, or Christians who read their pocket New Testaments daily, they practiced their religion. In whatever form, they practiced it with regularity, independent of passing circumstance or personal whim. Thus a certain toughness was built into their lives, and their faith, far from deteriorating, was strengthened.

If we have any ideas of being a disciple of Christ, let us remember that a disciple is a person who follows a discipline—one who is taught, guided, and controlled by another. Nobody who wants to be "free" in the foolish, untrained way can ever be a disciple following Christ's discipline. At a class for new church members, I once asked what they found most difficult about living the Christian life. One person said, "The hardest part is not to want to direct yourself, but to let Christ direct you."

***

In Christ's discipline, which will keep us in training for the practice of religion, what is involved? We find the answer in Jesus' own life. He followed a certain pattern of habit and discipline. We all know how powerful a force custom or habit is—just ask the person who is trying to stop smoking or keep dieting! But if the power of a bad habit can carry us in a way we should not go, the power of a good habit can take us in the right direction.

On two occasions Luke tells us specifically about Christ's regular routine. The first is in Luke 4 in which Jesus has

come back to His hometown, Nazareth, after the temptation in the wilderness—the most exacting experience of His
life, so far. No mention is made of how He is feeling. It
simply says:

> He went into the synagogue on the Sabbath Day, as
> His custom was. . . .

You will notice that Jesus didn't take the day off to get
over this exhausting experience. No, He was at worship "as
His custom was." It is unlikely there would be anything
special about the Nazareth synagogue; the services would
be no more perfect than those you and I know. Ordinary
townspeople would make up the congregation, many of
them materialistic in outlook. No doubt some of the old
Rabbis would be a bit pompous and boring, and the seats
pretty hard. Yet Jesus was there, for worship was His regular
custom. God had priority.

Christ's discipline means that we must first of all choose
our priorities. We cannot have everything in life; it is a
matter of selection. We must put some things first, and leave
out others. Whatever we rate top priority is what we really
worship. Judging by the large amount of time we devote to
it, we obviously consider it worthy of our main attention.

Some men worship their automobiles, spending long
hours lovingly tinkering, cleaning, polishing, and restoring
them. Some women worship their houses and decor. Many
worship at the shrine of the television set, and its programs
rule their lives. I once knew a man who told me quite
seriously that he could never come to church on a Sunday
morning because that was when he played golf. Golf or
God? No need to ask his priority!

Over the years, I've noticed that one way people try to
get off the issue as to why they should come to worship is
by criticizing the relevance of its various forms to their

personal tastes. Such a discussion will produce as many different ideas as there are participants, all based on the *subjective:* "How do I feel about this?" The whole purpose of worship is to focus on God—the *object* of our love and praise, thanksgiving and confession, intercession and supplication. Dr. William Temple, one-time Archbishop of Canterbury, gave this outstanding definition of worship:

> Worship is to quicken the conscience by the Holiness
>   of God;
>   to feed the mind with the Truth of God;
>   to purge the imagination by the Beauty of God;
>   to open the heart to the Love of God;
>   to devote the will to the Purpose of God.

Worship is a turning away from self to God. So what will our custom be, week by week and year by year? The worship of God or that other priority in our lives?

"Keep yourself in training for the practice of religion." We cannot do it without the discipline of making, like Jesus, a deliberate choice: choosing our priority.

*
**

The second discipline—the discipline of using our time—goes hand in hand with the first. We all have an equal amount of time—twenty-four hours a day—but we are extremely unequal in our use of it. Some people accomplish ten times as much as others, not necessarily because they have conspicuous talents others are denied, but simply because they use each day well.

When it comes to giving God priority, there is no use thinking that someday we will find the time. No one has ever "found" time, although it has often been "lost." We delude ourselves if we think that one day we will accidentally stumble on a big chunk of time we can make available for the hard discipline of something we are now carefully avoiding. If we are to use each day well, God must be in it. We will never find time for God. We must make time.

Does this mean we should be constantly thinking about religion to the exclusion of all else? No way! We live in a world which makes demands of us; we have obligations to fulfill and a great deal to do. Christianity is not a matter of constantly thinking about religion, but rather daily living out, in love, the essence of the faith which teaches that we are God's children; Jesus is with us and working through us to the extent we let Him; we are all kin. This means that God is involved in each day and the most mundane jobs, the most commonplace happenings and the most ordinary people are in some way linked to the Eternal.

Before the Battle of Edgehill in 1642, General Sir Jacob Astley led his army in the following prayer:

> O Lord, Thou knowest how busy we must be this day. If we forget Thee, do not Thou forget us. For Christ's sake, Amen.

Even if we only say a simple prayer at the beginning (or at some time) of each new day, we are on the way to realizing it is God's day—a new chance at another twenty-four hours of fresh opportunity; another fragment of time in which acts of eternal worth may be done. Whether it is one day with many more to follow or it proves to be our last day on earth, it will contain a dimension, a depth, a reality, a purpose, and a use that nothing can destroy—for God is present in it.

*
**

Jesus lived a busy life among ordinary men and women. He shared in their activities, their joys, and sorrows. He was guest in many homes, meeting all kinds of people. He was the breadwinner for a family. He worked at a bench. He taught by the roadside. He healed the sick. No one ever used the day so well. But He had a secret, a further discipline and custom which kept His public worship of God, His outgoing works for others, and His own spiritual life in balance—regular prayer; a private fellowship with the Eternal. Luke tells us in Luke 22 that just before His betrayal:

> He came out . . . to the Mount of Olives, as was His custom . . . and prayed.

We will never learn to use time well, until we are prepared to refuse the company of others in order to be alone with God. Jesus was able to bring God's power to people publicly because, beforehand, He Himself had gone away privately to receive that same power from God through prayer. Worship in the synagogue was not dull or unreal to Jesus because it was not the only time in the week He came in contact with His Father. He was constantly in touch. Public worship was simply the time when all the family could gather around.

If ever you find Sunday morning worship of your Heavenly Father dull, boring, unreal, or irrelevant, ask yourself when you last spoke with God trustingly in private. Ask yourself if your Saturday night is the best preparation for your Sunday morning. For if God had no part in yesterday, He will not suddenly become real today.

"Keep yourself in training for the practice of religion," says Paul. What does this involve but these three disciplines: the discipline of choosing God first; the discipline of using time well; and the discipline of refusing the constant company of others that, being alone with God, we may receive power to do His will when we return among men and women.

These disciplines were Christ's custom. We, too, must bear the same kindly yoke if we will be His disciples all year through. In the words of Richard Chevenix Trench:

> Lord, what a change within us one short hour
>   Spent in Thy presence will avail to make!
>   What heavy burdens from our bosoms take;
> What parched grounds refresh, as with a shower.
> We kneel, and all around us seems to lower;
>   We rise, and all, the distant and the near,
>   Stands forth in sunny outline, brave and clear.
> We kneel, how weak! We rise, how full of power!
>
> Why, therefore, should we do ourselves this wrong
> Or others, that we are not always strong;
> That we are ever overborne with care;
>   That we should ever weak or heartless be,
> Anxious or troubled, when with us is prayer,
>   And joy and strength and courage are with Thee?

"Keep yourself in training for the practice of religion." Lifelong Lent.

———————————

HEAVENLY FATHER, as we approach Holy Week, may we prepare ourselves to hear your voice speaking to us personally. Thus may we find the strength we need day to day, all year through, to live victoriously as you would have us do. Bless us now through Christ. AMEN.

22

Palm Sunday

A Hand in It

How should we approach Holy Week and its events?
John Ruskin, the famous writer and art critic of
the last century, once said, "You ought to imagine yourself
present, as in the body, at each recorded act in the life of
the Redeemer." His idea was that as you read the various
happenings in the gospels you should imagine yourself
actually there as each scene unfolds; watching, listening,
and aware of the whole drama.

This helpful advice does not go quite far enough. For the
true seeker will discover that, when it comes to the gospel,
none of us can really sustain the role of detached observer.
The incidents draw us in to become participants rather than
spectators. We find ourselves identifying first with one
character and then with another, or perhaps recognizing a
bit of ourselves in each until we discover we can no longer
keep the events at arm's length. This is the wonder of the
effect of the Holy Spirit on the Bible: we become involved.
Although we might prefer a seat in the stalls or a place in
the balcony, the Word reaches out to us: "Come on up.
This is your life. Here is your place in the drama. On stage!"

Although Sir Alfred Munnings, the well-known British

painter of horses, often spent time admiring beautiful churches, he was not a churchman. Knowing this, an elderly lady once asked him why he never went to worship. He replied (no doubt partly in jest), "I'm sorry, but I wouldn't know what to do with my hands!" This excuse may receive top marks for novelty, but it simply does not make the grade.

If any active, practical person ever feels that sitting in church with empty hands is not his or her scene, it is only because they have not realized that meaningful worship depends on our participation in the gospels and seeing something of ourselves in the men and women who leap from the pages—so much so, that our hands are full, especially during Holy Week. We have a hand in it.

*
**

One thing our hands hold is a coat—our own equivalent of the cloak or robe in the East. People used to reach out and touch Christ's hem for healing. Around the Cross, the greedy soldiers gambled for the one good piece of clothing Jesus possessed—His seamless robe. But today, it is not His coat reached for in need or in greed, but yours and mine, which we grasp—just as the crowd that first Palm Sunday spread their garments in His path. And coats cost a lot more than palm branches.

We know the story of Sir Walter Raleigh who, seeing Queen Elizabeth I hesitate over a muddy patch directly in her path, instantly whipped the cloak from his shoulders and placed it on the ground to save the royal foot from the mire. We moderns may consider it nothing more than a gallant gesture from a certain period. Yet way back in 2 Kings 9:13, after Jehu was anointed king, his former fellow officers spread their cloaks on the stairway he was ascending. You can see what it signifies—disregard of self.

Most people take good care of their coats, their cloaks, their robes. It is like their outermost shell—the outward, protective covering of their bodies. To lay it on the ground for another (under the head of an accident victim for example) is to give something of yourself. Jehu's fellow officers were not only making a gesture of submission before their new king, they were expressing wholehearted allegiance in action: "I'm your man. There, under your feet, is the symbol of me. I am yours to command."

All these aspects are behind the deeds of those in the crowd that first Palm Sunday who spread their coats in Jesus' way and hailed His arrival with exuberance. Preachers sometimes use this entry into Jerusalem to illustrate human fickleness: "On Sunday they cry, 'Hosanna!'; on Friday, 'Crucify!' " That may have been true of some, but if there was one group within that shouting throng which does not deserve such blanket condemnation, it was the people who threw down their garments in His way. Behind the act, is not only the hint of humility and the gesture of allegiance but also a great lack of calculation.

The picture that comes to my mind is of a soccer match in Scotland, held in a crowded stadium. The weather (not always as supportive as the eager fans) is such that most people wear some sort of headgear, known colloquially as "bunnets" (bonnets). When their team scores, you can see nothing above the supporters but an absolute shower of "bunnets" thrown high in the air by exuberant fans. No one is in the least concerned about losing a hat. The sheer joy of the team's victory overrides all careful calculation.

Does your joy over the victory of Christ ever startle anyone by its uncalculating exuberance? Or are we so cautiously hanging on to our hats and fiercely clutching our coats that we would not cause a single eyebrow to be raised in questioning wonder? If we never let go of ourselves, never rashly spread out our coats to smooth His path, then chances are that we will never reach out to touch the hem of His garment for our cleansing. What are you doing with your coat this Palm Sunday?

*
**

The second thing in which we have a hand this Holy Week is a crown of thorns. When you prune roses you tackle them cautiously. Such is the nature of thorns that you handle them with great care. You won't die if someone pushes a bundle of them down upon your head, but you'll suffer considerable pain and humiliation. This is what those who insult Christ hold in their gloved hands: a crown of thorns—part of the original ignominy and ridiculing of Jesus.

No doubt the humorist of the Jerusalem garrison had thought up the best one yet for the delectation of his coarse comrades. "They say he's a king. Let's dress him up like one! Your old red robe, Gaius, it's so faded it almost looks like royal purple. Drape it around him. He needs a scepter— here's a reed. A crown? Wait a minute, I've an idea!" And away the humorist goes, eventually bringing back a roughly plaited mass of thorns. "Hail, King of the Jews!" he cries, forcing it down on Christ's brow. "Come on, men, kneel. Kneel! Don't you recognize a king when you see one?" They all laugh and spit in Christ's face. All the trimmings of royalty—without power; all the gestures of homage— without sincerity.

This is the contrast to the cloaks spread before Jesus' coming. This is the parody of allegiance. And if we think we would never indulge in such an insult, just reflect on the tie-in with Christ's words, "Why do you call Me Lord and not do what I tell you?" Is it not a greater mockery if we ostensibly make Christ our King and then pointedly ignore His royal decrees? Listen to His commands: "Take up your cross and follow Me. Love those who hate you. Pray for those who despitefully use you and persecute you. Forgive unto seventy times seven."

There are crowns which are mock crowns. If our lives are given to self-seeking—profit before people; pride before humility; the opinion of others before the judgment of God—then we are only giving Him the name "King" and not the true status. We place no real crown upon His head, merely a hurtful mockery. "Crown Him with many crowns," we sing. Yes, but how many are sharp, painful, and humiliating?—much more so than the plaited thorns fashioned by His enemies. Imagine being thus crowned by friends! Have we never shown a hand in this by pointedly ignoring His way? Calling Him "Lord" with our lips, but not with our lives?

*
**

The last thing in which we have a hand this Holy Week is a fearsome thing: I have here a genuine handmade Roman nail of a type suitable for crucifixion, eleven and a half inches long and heavy. It was found in Scotland at Inchtuthil in Perthshire, and carbon-dated to around A.D. 100. When I feel the weight, touch the sharp point of this piece of iron, and place it on my wrist (the body could not be supported by only a hand, the flesh would tear) where it would shatter both bone and nerve, I realize with wonder how reticent, how restrained, and how brief is the gospel account: "There, they crucified Him." There is no attempt to shock: no mention of the excruciating pain of crucifixion. We are told nothing of being laid on the wood and the nails being driven in; the intolerable jolt as cross and victim are lifted up and then thrust down into the socket; the long crawling hours of agony and public shame; the unnatural position of the body; the draining down of the blood; the gasping for breath; the awful thirst.

On occasion, a public figure cries, "I'm being crucified," which simply makes a mockery of the word. Yet for the One to whom it really happened, all the physical horror represented by this nail was the least part of it. Something much more horrendous than pain had to be faced. Something that Paul attempts to depict in the mind-stretching phrase, "Christ was made sin for us; He, who knew no sin." Something we hear in the heart-rending cry, "My God, why hast Thou forsaken Me?" The nail speaks to us of physical suffering, yet it was far more than that.

The nail also speaks to us in a metaphorical way. We sometimes talk of "nailing a lie"—pinning down and killing it for what it is. We are all bidden to take up our crosses—that which is borne and carried for Christ's sake. Though we are saved by the one Cross of Christ, on our own crosses we must proceed ruthlessly to nail down our old selfish nature to the hard wood with resolute, unrelenting blows. Like the crucifixion squad, we have to watch with hard eyes as our lower self, writhing and pleading, dies. This is what it means to be crucified with Christ: to die to self, and with Him rise to a new life here and now. Until we "nail" the self, this simply cannot be.

The nail speaks to us of one last matter. It reminds us of the mark it leaves—a nailprint. Thomas, when the others told him they had seen the Lord, said, "Unless I see in His hands the print of the nails, and put my finger into the print of the nails—I will not believe." But when Jesus actually stood before them and stretched out His hands to Thomas, it was enough.

Sad to say, the only print with which most people today are concerned is newsprint. Yet through it, they can be conned, misled, and fed propaganda. The only print worth believing in wholeheartedly is the nailprint. Why? Newsprint concentrates on the material. Despite this particular nail being preserved almost nineteen hundred years, its very appearance—fragile point, rusting, brittle—represents only too clearly the end of all material things in the grip of time.

Another Roman nail once left its mark on outstretched hands. That nail is long gone, but the print it left has continued for twenty centuries to speak to people in their inmost being, convincing them that this is their Lord and their God.

> See, from His head, His hands, His feet,
>   Sorrow and love flow mingled down;
> Did e'er such love and sorrow meet,
>   Or thorns compose so rich a crown?

Aye, we shake our heads in sorrowful wonder over the thorns and the nails. But Isaac Watts in his hymn goes on to spread the coat of His allegiance before the Living Lord:

> Were the whole realm of nature mine,
>   That were an offering far too small;
> Love so amazing, so divine,
>   Demands my soul, my life, my all.

Are you still holding onto your coat this Palm Sunday?

O GRACIOUS LORD, as we look on the events of Holy Week, we are filled with mixed emotions—our hearts are uplifted, joyful, and exuberant on Palm Sunday and at Easter; we look on the Last Supper with dread and trepidation. Ever remind us that all this hangs together like your seamless robe—your life is all of one piece from the cradle of Bethlehem through the Cross of Calvary and the empty tomb to your Presence now at God's right hand interceding for us through your Spirit. May we be aware of you now amongst us; that we may not need to imagine ourselves there, as you are here. AMEN.

23

Easter

Red-Letter Certainties

Biblical scholarship rarely makes front-page headlines. A former professor, now founder of a publishing company, decided to rectify this lack and a few years ago set up a group called "The Jesus Seminar." His selected scholars vote on what, in their estimation, are the geniune words of Jesus. They cast their votes into a box by a system of different-colored beads. Red signifies "authentic"; pink, "maybe"; gray, "probably not"; and black, "not at all." Eventually they hope to publish a "Jesus Bible" printed in the appropriate colors. According to them, if you want to be dead certain what Jesus said, then you must find it "red certain!"

As an example of their notoriety-seeking style, look at the group's vote on the Lord's Prayer. They came up with quite a lot of pink but only one red-letter word. For them, the genuine word was the original Aramaic *Abba* which Jesus used for "Father."

While I have considerable reservations about The Jesus Seminar, it set me thinking about the original Hebrew words set amid the New Testament Greek. There are not many but surely if red-letter certainties exist, they are to be found in these words which cover the teaching, death, resurrection, and consummation of the One we hail today— indeed the whole spectrum of this unique Being who is Jesus, the Christ.

*
**

Let us look more closely at this first Aramaic word: *Abba*—Father—used by Jesus in the testing time of Gethsemane. It speaks volumes more than a formal "Father" or "Dear Father," and certainly much more than "Dear parent," for being a parent (one who begets or gives birth) by no means guarantees a deep, lasting relationship with the offspring. This shining fragment, "Father," conveyed by the word *Abba* goes far beyond the formal courtesy which acknowledges paternity. It speaks of intimacy, love, and trust. All the translations do well to leave this Christ-used word untouched.

Perhaps you can remember an occasion in your life when you were young and had some big problem on your mind weighing you down. You went to your father and began quite well, "Father, there's something I want to t–tell you." And then as it really got to you, you burst out, "Oh Daddy, help me!" That is the way Jesus uses the word *Abba* in Gethsemane.

Before Christ, no Jew would have dared apply such a term of endearment to the Most High. But such is His relationship with the Holy One that we are allowed to glimpse a completely new vision of God. This is the significance of Jesus' words: "I am the Way, the Truth, and the Life. No one comes to the Father but by Me." Other religions may approach a Divine Being, but only Christ brings us to One in such a personal, intimate, family relationship. God is no impersonal fate; no president of the immortals who, with capricious hand, in the words of Omar Khayyam:

> . . . [the] helpless Pieces of the game he plays
> Upon this Chequer-board of Nights and Days,
>   Hither and thither moves, and checks, and slays,
> And one by one back in the Closet lays.

Not the God Jesus reveals. Not the God to whom Jesus submits.

We must all learn to say "Thy will be done" if we would drink of His cup. But first—and this makes a world of difference—we must in our heart of hearts cry: "Father! Oh Daddy, help me!" *Abba*—a red-letter certainty.

*
**

Here is another—*Gabbatha*. Jesus is arrested. Because the country is under Roman occupation, the Jewish authorities have no right to sentence Him to death, though they have already decided that nothing less will satisfy them. So they take Him to the Roman governor. Pilate cannot find Jesus guilty, and tries to get Him released under the old custom of freeing a condemned prisoner at Passover. "Let Him be scourged," he says, knowing that some action is expected. And this is done.

With a body lacerated from the iron-tipped lash, Jesus becomes the focus of the soldiers' horseplay. They have their fun with an old robe, a reed, and a crown of thorns. It is in this condition that Pilate parades Jesus before the chief priests: "Ecce Homo"—Behold the Man. "Crucify Him!" they cry. Pilate, who can find no fault in Him, is still unwilling. Then the Jewish authorities play their trump card. Knowing Pilate's past record, they say craftily, "If you let this man go, you are not Caesar's friend." It was, of course, treason for a Roman governor to countenance any possible rival to Caesar. Thus we read in John 19:13:

> When Pilate heard these words, he brought Jesus out and sat down on the judgment seat in a place called The Pavement [in Hebrew, *Gabbatha*].

And so it was on this pavement that Jesus was judged and condemned by sinners. His crime? Showing the world righteousness, justice, and mercy—God's Love in action. Yet we would not have it. We still won't. "The teaching of mercy is foreign to the German race and is, according to the Nordic sentiment, an ethic for cowards and idiots." This is an excerpt from the school textbooks German children were reading in the early 1940s. We know well the cost of such philosophy in terms of death and destruction.

At Dachau, amid the remnants of gas chambers and mounds of mankind, a bronze is inscribed:

> May the power of force be overcome
> And Fate yield to the law of Justice and Mercy.

To make this prayer a reality is both our personal and worldwide need. We neglect such truth at our peril. It is so easy for individuals and nations to strut their hour upon the pavement of history—beguiled by pride, power, and the latest cleverness; to sit in judgment of Christ, mocking His Way, scorning His law of Love, and effectively condemning Him by their sheer indifference. Easy perhaps—but so dangerous! For He is not on trial—we are. His righteous love and merciful justice stand as God's law forever. We do not break it. We break ourselves denying it. And that's a red-letter certainty!

Gabbatha—the judgment pavement—but who is judging whom?

*
**

By the side of a road in Fife, there is a monument to Alexander III of Scotland, the last of the Celtic kings. It tells the passerby that on March 19, 1286, "he was accidentally killed near this spot." Yes, accidentally killed—and we know precisely where. *Golgotha* is where Jesus died—the exact spot is still unknown. But one thing is sure. He was not accidentally killed. He was not a pawn of fate, the hapless victim of circumstance. Jesus Himself says: "I lay down My life. No one takes it from Me. I lay it down of Myself." The death of Christ is His voluntary sacrifice for us.

Golgotha, a skull—in Latin *Calvaria* (from which we get Calvary) and in Greek *Kranion*—was the place where it happened. But as we try to face what exactly happened there, we have to stand silent in awe and humility. Yet many will not. They can see nothing here beyond a gross end to an otherwise admirable life filled with noble, though often impractical, moral teaching. They cannot believe that they need saving and cleansing by this strange figure on the Cross. They never asked Him to do anything for them. They will save themselves, if necessary, with self-help remedies of new knowledge and skill. Yet this is not possible, for our remedies are as contaminated as we are. We need to be helped out of mankind's morass. It's not a matter of stronger backs and better bootstraps. The Cross on Golgotha is the only way out and up. Are we too proud in mind and heart to take it?

"Is it nothing to you all ye who pass by? Is there any sorrow like unto My sorrow?" This is God in Christ suffering willingly for us. Once for all, the Sinless One, bearing the fatal load of the sinful, dies at the hands of those He came to save. Only when the Spirit's light shines upon Golgotha do we glimpse a mystery beyond explaining, but not beyond experiencing; beyond formula, but not faith. As J. R. Moreland says:

> The hands of Christ seem very frail
> For they were broken by a nail.
> But only they reach Heaven at last
> Whom these frail, broken hands hold fast.

That is a red-letter certainty!

*
**

Abba—the Love of the Father. *Gabbatha*—the Judgment of sinners. *Golgotha*—the Sacrifice that saves. And now, *Rabboni* (Rabbuni)—the Aramaic version of Rabbi.

This word comes as a startled exclamation from the lips of one who made the greatest discovery anyone can make— Jesus Christ is risen. He is alive! It is not something Mary Magdalene was argued into. Indeed, recognition of the truth was really an amazed response to the Stranger who in the garden calls her by name: "Mary!" Then, we are told, she turned and said to Him in Hebrew, "Rabboni!" which means "Master." "Teacher."

Note that Mary did not find Christ. He found her— heartbroken, blinded by tears, and searching for a corpse. Outside the tomb she spoke to Someone who she thought must have been the gardener for she could barely see through blurred eyes. As had been discovered earlier that day, the sepulcher was still empty, and it drew her like a magnet. "Where have you laid Him?" she asked. Clearly she turned her back on Him before waiting for an answer. We know she was still focusing on the tomb, because when Jesus uttered the one word "Mary!" we read, "she *turned* and said, 'Rabboni!' "

Our recognition of the Risen Christ is the direct outcome

of Jesus finding and calling each one of us personally by name. If we don't recognize Him until then, it is because our eyes are still fixed on the tomb. But that is not where He is. We've turned our backs on Him. We're looking in the wrong direction. We realize this, the moment we hear Him call our names. Suddenly everything is different. We turn! Our lives no longer face toward a tomb, but toward a triumph. "Master!" we cry with amazed joy as we recognize the Risen Christ. "Rabboni!"—red-letter certainty!

*
**

One final word—*Maranatha*. We find this Aramaic phrase in the closing verses of 1 Corinthians. Depending how the word is subdivided, it can mean the Lord has come, the Lord is at hand—*Maran Atha*. To this statement of fact, even nominal Christians can say, "Amen! He has come. So be it!"

But the most probable meaning lies in a slightly different division of the phrase, not *Maran Atha*, but *Marana Tha*, which is the imperative watchword of the faith: "Our Lord, come!" It is echoed in the Greek by the writer of Revelation at the end of the Bible: "Even so, come, Lord Jesus!" These words not only express the Christian's ultimate conviction about the Christ who will come again in glory as the consummation of all things, but also of the living Lord sought now in the midst of things, so that we cry, "Come, Lord Jesus—Resurrection and Life! Come—Companion of the way, Revealer of the Father, Savior of our souls!" Then:

Lo! Jesus meets us. Risen from the tomb,
Lovingly He greets us, Scatters fear and gloom;
Let His Church with gladness Hymns of triumph
    sing,
For her Lord now liveth; Death hath lost its sting.

Thine is the glory, Risen, conquering Son;
Endless is the victory Thou o'er death hast won.

Out of the ancient words of dusty fragments steps the
Master of life made new. This is *the* red-letter certainty—
He is Risen! And faith cries in glad response, "Even so,
come, Lord Jesus—here and now—to us!"

ALMIGHTY GOD, may we know that every Sunday is
Easter; indeed, every day. For you, O Risen Christ, are
with us through all life's changing scenes. Walking with you
day by day, our joys are doubled and our sorrows halved.
We are given the strength as we need it to meet life's
demands. May this no longer be theory for us, but joyful
reality. Even so, come to us now, Lord Jesus. AMEN.

About the Author

In April 1991 the Reverend Campbell Gillon marked his eleventh year as Senior Minister of Georgetown Presbyterian Church, Washington, D.C. Called from the Church of Scotland in 1980, he is widely recognized for his illuminating and powerful affirmation of the message of biblical faith in a way relevant to the experience of the modern generation.

A leading force in inter-church cooperation and Chaplain of the St. Andrews Society of Washington, D.C., Campbell Gillon stands in the tradition of the great Scottish preachers. Week after week, his sermons demonstrate that proclamation of the Christian faith, far from being an anachronism as some would charge, can be a living, challenging, transforming art.

Campbell Gillon was born in Edinburgh in 1927. His father and three uncles preceded him as ministers of the Church of Scotland. After three years of Army service at the end of World War II, he graduated with a Master of Arts from the University of Glasgow, and completed Divinity training at Trinity College, Glasgow, studying under Professor William Barclay, the noted Scottish New Testament scholar.

The initial Gillon pastorate was the historic rural parish of Buittle, following which he occupied the pulpit of Milton-St. Stephens, a heavily populated inner-city church in

Glasgow. In 1964, with the union of Milton-St. Stephens and Glasgow's noted Renfield Street Church, he became minister of the united charge—the new Renfield Church. Under his leadership, the Renfield Church Center was built, the first of its kind in Scotland, to include a sanctuary, chapel, restaurant, concert hall, gymnasium, Presbytery offices, and other community-oriented facilities.

In 1973, Campbell Gillon was invited to Cathcart Old Parish Church, also in Glasgow, with its foundation of eight hundred years of Christian worship. He served there until called in 1980 to Georgetown Presbyterian Church— a landmark congregation with the longest unbroken Christian ministry of worship and active service in the nation's capital.

Campbell and Audrey Gillon, married in 1949, have three daughters, two of whom are ministers in the Church of Scotland: Wendy Drake, in sole charge of St. Martins, Edinburgh; and Sheila Blount, Chaplain of Cornton Vale Women's Prison and co-pastor with her husband of the historic Falkirk Old Parish Church. Their third daughter, Carol Colling, an executive officer with the Department of Social Security (U.K.), is an ordained elder. The Gillons have seven grandchildren.

For relaxation, Campbell Gillon plays the piano and organ and writes songs and hymns. The Gillons live in Alexandria, Virginia.